Day by Day

Day by Day

the bible reading fellowship
OPENING THE BIBLE

Text copyright © BRF 1993

Published by
The Bible Reading Fellowship
Peter's Way
Sandy Lane West
Oxford
OX4 5HG
ISBN 0 7459 2598 7
Albatross Books Pty Ltd
PO Box 320, Sutherland
NSW 2232, Australia
ISBN 0 7324 0820 4

First edition 1993
All rights reserved

Acknowledgments

Good News Bible copyright © American Bible Society 1966, 1971 and 1976, published by the Bible Societies and Collins.

The Alternative Service Book 1980 copyright © The Central Board of Finance of the Church of England.

The Jerusalem Bible copyright © 1966, 1967 and 1968 by Darton, Longman & Todd Ltd and Doubleday & Company, Inc.

The New Jerusalem Bible copyright © 1985 by Darton, Longman & Todd Ltd and Doubleday & Company, Inc.

The *Revised Standard Version* of the Bible, copyright © 1946, 1952, 1971 by the Division of Christian Education of the National Council of the Churches of Christ in the USA.

The *New Revised Standard Version* of the Bible, copyright © 1989 by the Division of Christian Education of the National Council of the Churches of Christ in the USA.

The Holy Bible, *New International Version*, copyright © 1973, 1978, 1984 by International Bible Society. Used by permission of Hodder and Stoughton Limited.

Extracts from the Book of Common Prayer of 1662, the rights in which are invested in the Crown in perpetuity within the United Kingdom, are reproduced by permission of the Crown's patentee, Cambridge University Press.

The Holy Bible, *Living Bible Edition*, copyright © Tyndale House Publishers 1971, published by Kingsway.

Extracts from the *Authorized Version* of the Bible (The King James Bible), the rights of which are vested in the Crown, are reproduced by permission of the Crown's Patentee, Cambridge University Press.

New English Bible, © 1970 by permission of Oxford and Cambridge University Presses.

Revised English Bible © 1989 by permission of Oxford and Cambridge University Presses.

A catalogue record for this book is available from the British Library

Printed and bound in Slovenia

Contents

SECTION 7

Four weeks on God's Work of Art, a letter to the young church at Ephesus, and some New Testament prayers.

Shelagh Brown and Marcus Maxwell

SECTION 8

Five weeks on Jonah (the prophet who didn't want to prophesy); on the priesthood of Jesus (in a letter to Jewish Christians); and the visions of glory (and horror) seen by Ezekiel.

Adrian Plass and Shelagh Brown

SECTION 9

Six weeks on Harvest; on present suffering, future glory and the love of God in Romans 8; and on ways to listen to God and ways to speak to God.

Joyce Huggett and Shelagh Brown

SECTION 10

Six weeks on praying the Scriptures, on the Messiah (in Isaiah 52 and 53) and on Christmas.

Henry Wansbrough, Shelagh Brown and Rosemary Green

Introduction

Here is a book of Bible readings and prayers—to take you day by day through the whole year. For every day there is a Bible passage, a comment, and then either a prayer or a way to pray in and reflect on what you have read.

The point of our Bible reading is to encounter the living God—who loves each one of us with a very great and passionate love—and to let him enter deeper into us day by day to make us aware of his love for us and for his world. As our awareness of being loved increases so will our love for God and for other people, and we shall find ourselves changing. The Apostle Paul knew all about the process, and described how it happens:

> **Now the Lord is the Spirit, and where the Spirit of the Lord is, there is freedom. And we, who with unveiled faces all reflect the Lord's glory, are being transformed into his likeness with ever-increasing glory, which comes from the Lord, who is the Spirit.**

> 2 Corinthians 3:17–18 (NIV)

One of the ways for us to see the glory of the Lord is to read the Bible and to reflect on it, and then a bit of the glory sticks to us and we start to shine as well. That is what Jesus told us to do in the Sermon on the Mount:

> **You are the light of the world. A city on a hill cannot be hidden. Neither do people light a lamp and put it under a bowl. Instead they put it on its stand, and it gives light to everyone in the house. In the same way, let your light shine before men, that they may see your good deeds and praise your Father in heaven.**

> Matthew 5:14–16 (NIV)

There is a section on the Sermon on the Mount starting in week 27 and running on for four weeks. All the *Day by Day* readings are arranged in sections, and you will find the contents of them on page 5. They begin at the beginning with the creative word that God spoke in the darkness, when he set the galaxies spinning in space, and they finish with Christmas—simply because Christmas always comes at the end of the year.

Easter is always changing its date, so I have put it in April. If you want to read the right readings on the right days you can either move on a few pages or jump some and move back at the start of Holy Week or on Good Friday.

There are plenty of readings about Pentecost and the Holy Spirit, because we live in the age of the Spirit. Pentecost, or Whit Sunday, itself comes just seven weeks after Easter Sunday, so if you read Easter on the right day then Pentcost will fall into its proper place. The days from Christmas Eve to the end of the year are labelled with their own date.

You will find that Sundays are different in *Day by Day*, just as they are different in *New Daylight*, from which all these readings are taken. On Sundays we nearly always look either at the Eucharist or at prayer, and starting in week 27 you will find a series of six Sundays on how to pray in different ways: with St Francis of Assisi, St Ignatius, St Augustine of Hippo, St Theresa of Lisieux, Corrie ten Boom, and in a dialogue between God and the one who prays.

I hope that run-down of how this book is arranged will be useful to you—and I hope and pray that you will enjoy it, and meet with God-in-Christ as you read and pray.

Shelagh Brown
Commissioning Editor

Words

For four weeks we are going to look at words. At the word which God speaks, the words which we speak, and the words which the prophet Jonah didn't want to speak, because he didn't want God to be kind and merciful to a nation of foreigners. But God loved the foreigners just as much as he loved Jonah and the rest of his own people—and we are going to see what sort of 'person' this God is. The Bible says that he loves us, that he is the source and giver of life, and that he shines into our darkness like light.

Jesus told his disciples, 'I am the light of the world.' After the resurrection he spoke to St John in a vision and said, 'I am the root and offspring of David, the bright morning star.' He speaks to us in many ways to lead us to himself. The wise men were led to Jesus by the light of a star and the stars can light the way for us to a greater and deeper faith. The gospel of Christ is still good news for the space age, and in *The Gospel of Outer Space*, Robert Short puts the gospel and the stars together.

In the book of the film *E. T.*, the boy Elliott is lying on the floor of a forest looking up at the night sky, while he watches over E. T.'s transmitter to the stars. A soft voice starts to speak to him, 'opening up his youthful mind, wider, wider. "Still bound to their planet, Earthlings cannot deal with the ache of universal love", said the golden whisper echoing through the endless corridors . . . The message shot through his whole being—a message meant to be carried by a creature much more evolved than himself, a creature whose inner nature was such that it could love a star and be loved in return by the overwhelming solar force . . .'

Short believes 'the love that speaks to us through E. T., a love eternal, universal, and finally victoriously overwhelming all enemies is also a fair description of the message of God's love for all humankind as 'carried' to us by Christ. The New Testament says that Christ is the 'Word of God'—the One through whom God tells us how much he loves us.

But the prophet Jonah didn't want to tell the people of Nineveh what God was like, and he wouldn't speak the word of life to them.

Go and find them

Now the tax collectors and 'sinners' were all gathering around to hear him. But the Pharisees and the teachers of the law muttered, 'This man welcomes sinners, and eats with them.' Then Jesus told them this parable: 'Suppose one of you has a hundred sheep and loses one of them. Does he not leave the ninety-nine in the open country and go after the lost sheep until he finds it? And when he finds it, he joyfully puts it on his shoulders and goes home. Then he calls his friends and neighbours together and says, "Rejoice with me; I have found my lost sheep."'

If a sheep is lost then the shepherd who wants to find it will have to go to the place where it is—not the place where it isn't. Today's reading is about lost people whom Jesus went and found by being friends with them and having meals with them. Some of them were prostitutes and some were tax collectors. Zacchaeus was a tax collector—and in Luke's Gospel it says that he climbed up a tree so that he could see Jesus passing by.

But Jesus didn't pass by. He told Zacchaeus to come down from the tree and get a meal ready—because Jesus wanted to come to dinner. Zacchaeus invited all his friends to the party (people like him they would have been—worthy and respectable people wouldn't have been friends with him). And that day yet another lost sheep was found—because the shepherd went to the place where he was to find him, and ate a meal there. A meal that was paid for with illegally collected taxes. Zacchaeus would have paid his own salary, like all the other tax collectors, by making the Jews pay more than the Romans demanded. It was no wonder the Jews hated him. But Jesus loved him.

A thought

Who will you eat with at the Lord's table today? And who do you think Jesus would be eating with today in our society?

SB

Creative words

In the beginning God created the heavens and the earth. The earth was without form and void, and darkness was upon the face of the deep; and the Spirit of God was moving over the face of the waters. And God said, 'Let there be light'; and there was light.

In *The Magician's Nephew* by C.S. Lewis, there is a marvellous account of how Aslan creates Narnia:

'The Lion was pacing to and from about that empty land and singing his new song. It was softer and more lilting than the song by which he had called up the stars and the sun; a gentle, rippling music. And as he walked and sang the valley grew green with grass. It spread out from the Lion like a pool. It ran up the sides of the little hill like a wave. In a few minutes it was creeping up the lower slopes of the distant mountains, making that young world every moment softer...'

The only way we can ever talk about anything is to use words. But the words are only descriptions of reality—and what the Bible writers (and modern physicists) are doing when they speak about the creation of the world is struggling to describe a mystery in words that we can understand.

'God said, "Let there be light."' A creative energy went forth from God and everything began. Many scientists now believe in the 'big bang' theory—that at a moment at the beginning of time (because before that moment there was no time) something mysterious and mighty exploded into existence from which everything that is developed.

God spoke his creative word in the darkness, and the heavens (the galaxies spinning round in space) came into existence—and then, perhaps after thousands of millions of years of creation, men and women like you and me, being created by the God of love to have a relationship with him for ever.

A meditation

Think of C.S. Lewis' Lion pacing round and singing the song that brings the grass into existence. Then think of the unfathomable mystery of the Creator God speaking the word that brought all things into existence ... including you and me.

SB

11

Strong words

In the musical *My Fair Lady* Freddie sings a song to Eliza Dolittle about how marvellous it is to be walking up and down on the street where she lives. But that demonstration of how he feels isn't enough for Eliza and she explodes into a protest song: 'Words, words, words, I'm so sick of words. I get words all day through, first from him, and now from you. Is that all you blighters can do? Don't talk of stars, burning above. If you're in love—Show me!'

Words are powerful. When any of us said something she didn't like, my grandmother used to quote Will Carleton at us: 'Boys flying kites haul in their white-winged birds; You can't do that way when you're flying words... Thoughts unexpressed may sometimes fall back dead. But God Himself can't kill them when they're said.'

For the ancient Jews a word had its own existence and went off and did things. When Isaac had given Jacob his blessing he couldn't take it back—even when he discovered that Jacob had tricked him into giving it. Once he had spoken the words they had started to act. But it wasn't only human beings who spoke. God spoke a word that brought the whole universe into existence.

Now faith is the assurance of things hoped for, the conviction of things not seen. For by it the men of old received divine approval. By faith we understand that the world was created by the word of God, so that what is seen was made of things which do not appear.

The words 'that what is seen was made out of things which do not appear' were written two thousand years ago. But they could have been written today by a physicist about the mystery of matter—the stuff that you and I and rocks and all living things are made of. We can see it, and it seems to be solid, but in fact it consists of particles so small that they cannot be seen even under the most powerful microscope.

A thought

Think about the words you will say today. How will they affect people? Kind words. Critical words. Swear words. Words that will make people sad. Words that will make people smile. Creative words, that will make things happen. Then, in the stillness, wonder about the mystery of creation—and understand by faith that the world was created by the word of God.

SB

Word of light

For . . . we preach . . . not ourselves, but Jesus Christ as Lord, with ourselves as your servants for Jesus' sake. For it is the God who said, 'Let light shine out of darkness,' who has shone in our hearts to give the light of the knowledge of the glory of God in the face of Christ.

Yesterday we thought about the Word which God spoke in the darkness to bring the whole of creation into existence. Today we think about the Word which God speaks into our darkness to bring the new creation into existence. Just as God said 'let light shine out of darkness' at the creation of the word, so he shines into the darkness of human hearts.

The Bible says that Christians are 'a new creation', who have seen the light of the knowledge of the glory of God (which is his nature and character) shining out of the face of Christ. That shining is a creative word from God, and more often than not we hear it through the preaching of the word, which is the gospel or the good news.

Paul says what that good news is, and what the Christian message is—that 'Jesus is Lord'. That is a tremendous claim to make—and the people who made it, right back at the beginning of Christianity, were Jews. They knew that there was only one God, Jehovah, and that he alone was to be worshipped. Yet the word 'Lord' in the New Testament is the same word that the Old Testament uses for God.

The beginning of Mark's Gospel says that John the Baptist called people to 'Prepare the way of the Lord', and those words come from Isaiah, whose next sentence is 'make straight the desert a highway for our God' (Isaiah 40:3). So Mark is saying that if they will prepare the way then their God will come to them. And he does. Yet the one who comes is a man—'Jesus Christ, the Son of God' (Mark 1:1).

A prayer

Lord God, I have seen something of the light of the knowledge of your glory in the face of Jesus Christ. Let me see it shining more brightly day by day. May I walk in the light of it all the days of my life—until the dawning of that perfect day when I see him face to face and am like him.

SB

Abiding word

You have been born anew, not of perishable seed but of imperishable, through the living and abiding word of God; for 'All flesh is like grass and all its glory like the flower of the grass. The grass withers, and the flower falls, but the word of the Lord abides for ever.' That word is the good news which was preached to you.

The 'word' that God speaks—the word of good news—will never die like the grass. Therefore neither will we—because we are born of a seed that is eternal seed.

A human baby is born when a woman's tiny egg is fertilized by a man's even tinier seed—and then grows within her womb, nourished and protected, until it's ready to be born. The mother will labour, and then a baby girl or a baby boy will come into the world and utter its first cry. But one day, whether as a child or an adult, that baby will die. Its flesh is perishable—like goods on supermarket shelves marked with a 'sell-by' date. Soon after it the milk will go sour and the chicken will go off... They don't keep forever—and neither do we. We might die at seven months, seven years, or seventy years or more. But die we shall.

We're like grass that withers and dies—and like daisies and dandelions: beautiful for a few days but then the flowers fall. They aren't everlasting—and even so-called everlasting flowers are really dead and dried flowers.

But there can be that in us which is everlasting. We can be born of an imperishable seed, 'the living and abiding word of God.'

***

A way to pray

Think of fresh food on the shelves of a supermarket—eatable, but perishable. Think of yourself, and all the people that you love—just as perishable as food and flowers. But then think of Jesus Christ, who is the word of God—alive, and (if we believe) dwelling in our hearts by faith.

'I am the resurrection and the life; he who believes in me, though he die, yet shall he live, and whoever lives and believes in me shall never die.'

John 11:25–26

SB

14

Creation tells

The heavens are telling the glory of God; and the firmament proclaims his handiwork. Day to day pours forth speech, and night to night declares knowledge. There is no speech, nor are there words; their voice is not heard; yet their voice goes out through all the earth, and their words to the end of the world.

This Psalm says that the universe itself is the way that God speaks to us. We don't hear any speech or any words—yet by its very existence it has a voice that we can hear.

In Romans 1:19–20 Paul says that the world itself reveals to people that there is a God, and shows us something of what he is like. Paul is writing about wicked men who have been suppressing the truth which in their heart of hearts they know: 'For what can be known about God is plain to them, because God has shown it to them. Ever since the creation of the world his invisible nature, namely, his eternal power and deity, has been clearly perceived in the things that have been made. So they are without excuse ...'

Perhaps we find it hard to believe in God, now that we know something of the vastness of the universe. But the sheer size of it need not make any difference. Scientists tell us that our human bodies are mid-way between the immense largeness of the starry heavens and the immeasurable smallness of the particles that our bodies and all matter are composed of. I find that fact curiously comforting, when I occasionally get afflicted with what Teilhard de Chardin called 'the malady of space-time'. It can also make me stunned and awed at the glory of God—as modern science spells out to me the amazing, wonderful speech of the stars and the universe.

A meditation

Sit in silence for a few moments and let the heavens speak to you of the glory of God. Think of the vastness of the astronomical distances of space, and the sheer size of it all. It may stun you and frighten you—but let it also comfort you, that our God can make such a universe.

SB

Just like him

In many and various ways God spoke of old to our fathers by the prophets; but in these last days he has spoke to us by a Son, whom he appointed the heir of all things, through whom also he created the world. He reflects the glory of God and bears the very stamp of his nature, upholding the universe by his word of power.

When we want to communicate with each other we use words. We speak them to each other and we write them, telling each other what we think, what we are like, and what we want of each other. In an especially important relationship, if we love someone, then we tell them we love them, and let them know we want them to return our love. Words are about communicating what's inside us to another person, so that they know and understand.

But there are other sorts of words as well. There's our 'body language'—about the way we look at each other and the way we sit and move. There are the presents we might give each other.

The more we love someone the more we shall take the trouble to get our communication just right—so that we speak the clearest and most loving words we can (whether in actual words or in actions).

The passage that we have read today, written to Jewish Christians, is saying that God spoke to their ancestors in many and various ways—but that now, in these last days, he has spoken by a Son.

The writer is making an amazing statement about Jesus. He is saying that he bears the very stamp of God's nature. He is like a seal that people stamp in wax and then seal on a document—and what is then seen is the exact impression of the original seal. He is also the shining out of the glory, or the character, of God. God is just like Jesus. Jesus is the Word of God and has the very nature of God.

A way to pray

Sit in silence for a few moments—and tell God any difficulties you have in believing in him. Then think about what you know of Jesus. Pray that the Holy Spirit will reveal Jesus to you more and more clearly—so that you might see and know the glory of God in the Son who is the Word of God.

SB

Just touch him . . .

As Jesus was on his way, the crowds almost crushed him. And a woman was there who had been subject to bleeding for twelve years, but no-one could heal her. She came up behind him and touched the edge of his cloak, and immediately her bleeding stopped. 'Who touched me?' Jesus asked. When they all denied it, Peter said, 'Master, the people are crowding and pressing against you.' But Jesus said, 'Someone touched me; I know that power has gone out from me.' Then the woman, seeing that she could not go unnoticed, came trembling and fell at his feet. In the presence of all the people, she told why she had touched him and how she had been instantly healed. Then he said to her, 'Daughter, your faith has healed you. Go in peace.'

Today many of us will be going to Holy Communion. We shall touch bread and wine and know that as we eat and drink we are feeding on the body and blood of Christ. We cannot see him, but by faith we know he comes to us afresh in love and in power. He is the Saviour of the world, and salvation has to do with spiritual health and wholeness. It is a process that lasts a lifetime (though sometimes some parts of it happen dramatically and very quickly, and sometimes it includes physical healing), and we have to know that we need it, and want it.

This woman wanted it. She had had an issue of blood for twelve years—and as well as the weariness and tiredness and lack of energy which that would have brought about, she would have ranked as unclean. And when she touched Jesus she would have made him unclean, according to Jewish Law.

She desperately wanted to be whole—and she knew that Jesus could make her whole. So in faith she put out her hand to touch him, and knew immediately that she had been healed. Something had happened. She had drawn power from him (just as we can—through Holy Communion as well as other ways). But salvation cannot stay a secret. Jesus brought it, and her, out into the open—and then spoke words she would remember all her life: 'Daughter, your faith has healed you. Go in peace.'

SB

17

Just as we are

For the word of God is living and active, sharper than any two-edged sword, piercing to the division of soul and spirit, of joints and marrow, and discerning the thoughts and intentions of the heart. And before him no creature is hidden, but all are open and laid bare to the eyes of him with whom we have to do.

In these weeks we are trying to understand what 'the word of God' is and what it does. We have thought about what a 'word' can do—that even the words we speak can have a profound effect, and that the word which God speaks makes the most marvellous and mighty things happen: the whole universe, and our earth—with its wonderful creatures, and human creatures as the most wonderful of all, created for a relationship with God.

God does not only speak a creative word that brings things into existence. He speaks a personal word to you and to me and to everyone; and that word penetrates our spirit.

It makes a demand and an offer which each one of us has to face and then accept or reject. William Barclay says when we take God's word seriously we immediately realize that it isn't something to be studied or read or written about, 'it is something to be done', and it is 'one of the facts of history that wherever men have taken God's word seriously things have begun to happen'.

We can refuse to listen to the word of God and we can refuse to do what we ought to do—but one day we shall have to face the consequences. God sees us just as we are, and because he loves us he wants us to see ourselves as we are.

A way to pray

Shut your eyes and imagine Jesus speaking to you. He loves you. Yet his words are like a sword, that cut deep into your heart. Or like a surgeon's knife.

*The wounded surgeon plies the steel!
That questions the distempered part;
Beneath the bleeding hands we feel
The sharp compassion of the healer's art.*
T.S. Eliot, *Little Gidding*

SB

Called to speak

Now the word of the Lord came to me saying, 'Before I formed you in the womb I knew you, and before you were born I consecrated you; I appointed you a prophet to the nations.' Then I said, 'Ah, Lord God! Behold, I do not know how to speak, for I am only a youth.' But the Lord said to me, 'Do not say, "I am only a youth"; for to all to whom I send you you shall go, and whatever I command you you shall speak. Be not afraid of them, for I am with you to deliver you, says the Lord.' Then the Lord put forth his hand and touched my mouth; and the Lord said to me, 'Behold, I have put my words in your mouth.'

When God has a special task for someone to do he speaks to them to tell them what it is, and there always seems to be some sort of inner turmoil in that person. 'What, me Lord? Surely not—You must be mistaken... I'm hopeless at public speaking, and I'm not mature enough.' That was Jeremiah's reaction, and it was very like Moses' reaction when God called him to lead the Israelites out of Egypt into the promised land: 'O my Lord, I am not eloquent... I am slow of speech and of tongue... Lord, send, I pray, some other person' (Exodus 4:10–13).

Jeremiah and Moses were prophets, who were called to speak the word of God in a special way. Sometimes they experienced it as something burning with them, so that they had to speak. 'If I say, "I will not mention him, or speak any more in his name," there is in my heart as it were a burning fire shut up in my bones, and I am weary with holding it in, and I cannot', Jeremiah complained (20:9).

It isn't comfortable to be a prophet. People don't like what prophets say, so they persecute them. A prophet speaks about the things in society that are wrong and that God requires to be put right—and society answers back by telling them to mind their own business or by putting them in prison. Unjust governments hate prophets. They hated them in Jeremiah's day and they hate them in ours.

A question

What am I to say, Lord?

SB

Guiding word

How sweet are thy words to my taste, sweeter than honey to my mouth! Through thy precepts I get understanding; therefore I hate every false way. Thy word is a lamp to my feet and a light to my path.

Psalm 119 is the longest Psalm there is, and all 176 verses contain the word 'word' in one form or another (precept; testimony; promise; law; statute; ordinance; commandment). A Jew's heart lifted up with delight when he thought about the word of God, and the whole Psalm is a hymn of praise at the wonder of the words that God has given.

When the psalmist tastes them they are sweeter than honey, and they give him understanding. The Psalm says a hundred things that they do—but today's section particularly says that 'Thy word is a lamp to my feet and a light to my path'. It shows us the right way to go.

Yesterday we were thinking about the way that God's word came to the prophets to call them to a special task. But we also believe that it comes to us, to show us what to do. We seem to hear it in our hearts, and then the dark path ahead, that we couldn't see, lights up for us—at least for the next stretch of it. The Holy Spirit who dwells in our heart is showing us the way.

A promise and a prayer

Your ears shall hear a word behind you saying, 'This is the way, walk in it', when you turn to the right or when you turn to the left.

Isaiah 30:21

Lord God, you have promised to show me the right way to go. I bring to you now all the things I am not sure about in my future . . . The things that lie ahead today . . . tomorrow . . . and in the years to come. Thank you that I shall hear your voice telling me the right way to go.

'This God is our God for ever and ever; he will be our guide even unto death.'

Psalm 48:14

SB

His delight

The Lord created at the beginning of his work, the first of his acts of old. Ages ago I was set up, at the first, before the beginning of the earth. When there were no depths I was brought forth, when there were no springs abounding with water. Before the mountains had been shaped, before the hills, I was brought forth; before he had made the earth with its fields, or the first of the dust of the world. When he established the heavens, I was there . . . when he marked out the foundations of the earth, then I was beside him, like a master workman; and I was daily his delight, rejoicing . . . in the sons of men.

This passage is about wisdom, whom the Jews wrote about as a person. They said (not in the Scriptures, but in other writings) that before the foundations of the world God dandled two children on his knees—his wisdom and his word. The revelation of God that was given to the Jews was incomplete, but it was very deep. They knew that God was personal, and that he loved the human race. Their understanding of God was that a mighty energy went out from him like a word, to create all that is—and that all that is was created with wisdom.

Just as God was a person, so wisdom and the word were also personal, rejoicing over the world and delighting in the people who lived in it. Do you realize that the God who created you actually delights in you?

A meditation

Think of the galaxies spinning round on their orbits in space . . . Think of this earth—and the sun and the moon. Think of a blackbird . . . a dolphin . . . a seal . . . and other living creatures. Think about a person whom you love . . . and then think about yourself, and be aware of yourself—sitting on your chair, or perhaps sitting up in your bed. Think of the wisdom that made all these things . . . of the energy of the word that made them . . . and of the personal, loving God, who made you and me and all that is, delighting in his world and his creatures.

SB

Mind pictures

God speaks to us in dreams and in visions. When St John was in exile on the Isle of Patmos, God gave him a vision which was a revelation of Jesus Christ and of the things that were to come. It is a book filled with strange and wonderful symbols, and we don't always know what they mean. But if we see the pictures in our mind's eye—and really look at them—they will speak the truth of God deep into our hearts. They aren't meant for us to analyse with our intellects. Symbolism is about a far deeper level of communication than that. In chapter 19 John describes his vision of heaven:

And the twenty-four elders and the four living creatures fell down and worshipped God who is seated on the throne, saying, 'Amen. Hallelujah!' And from the throne came a voice crying, 'Praise our God, all you his servants, you who fear him, small and great.' Then I heard what seemed to be the voice of a great multitude, like the sound of many waters and like the sound of mighty thunderpeals, crying, 'Hallelujah! For the Lord our God the Almighty reigns. Let us rejoice and exult and give him the glory, for the marriage of the Lamb has come, and his Bride has made herself ready; it was granted her to be clothed with fine linen, bright and pure'—for the fine linen is the righteous deeds of the saints. And the angel said to me, 'Write this: Blessed are those who are invited to the marriage supper of the Lamb.'

Christ is the Lamb whose marriage is about to happen, and his Bride is 'the holy city, new Jerusalem' (21:2), which is filled with 'the saints'—the holy ones, who belong to God, and who do holy things. They have 'washed their robes and made them white in the blood of the Lamb' (7:14), so they have 'the right to the tree of life and that they may enter the city by the gates' (22:14). But outside the city are 'the dogs and sorcerers and fornicators and murderers and idolaters, and every one who loves and practises falsehood' (22:15). Inside there will be those who did those unholy things in the past. But they won't have gone on doing them.

A meditation

Shut your eyes and think about John's vision of heaven. See it in your mind's eye, and let God speak to you through it.

SB

Fierce Love

Then I saw heaven opened, and behold a white horse! He who sat upon it is called Faithful and True, and in righteousness he judges and makes war. His eyes are like a flame of fire, and on his head are many diadems; and he has a name inscribed which no one knows but himself. He is clad in a robe dipped in blood, and the name by which he is called is The Word of God.

Our reading for today tells us the next thing that John saw in his vision—and underlying the vision is the truth that God communicates with us in many ways—to tell us about the wonder of his love for us, and also the fierceness of it.

'When Christianity says that God loves man, it means that God *loves* man: not that He has some 'disinterested', because really indifferent, concern for our welfare, but that in awful and surprising truth, we are the objects of His love. You asked for a loving God: you have one. The great spirit you so lightly invoked, the 'lord of terrible aspect', is present: not a senile benevolence that drowsily wishes you to be happy in your own way ... but the consuming fire Himself, the Love that made the worlds ...' (C.S. Lewis, *The Problem of Pain*).

We give our greatest energy to the things and the people that we love best, and we want them to be the best they can be. We'll give more attention and time to making a meal for someone special than to making our morning tea and toast (which isn't to say that we are not special or that we aren't important). If a person we love very much has gone on drugs or started to drink too much we shall mind about it very deeply, and work out ways of fighting against what has happened—just as a mother and father will use every resource they can to fight a cancer that is destroying their beloved child.

Just so does the One in John's vision fight against evil, because it destroys the people whom he created and loves.

A meditation

Think about the things in ordinary life that are destructive and hurtful—the things that distress you most. How can you fight against them, in the power of God?

SB

Tell by doing

For I received from the Lord what I also delivered to you, that the Lord Jesus on the night when he was betrayed took bread, and when he had given thanks, he broke it, and said, 'This is my body which is [broken] for you. Do this in remembrance of me.' In the same way also the cup, after supper, saying, 'This cup is the new covenant in my blood. Do this, as often as you drink it, in remembrance of me.' For as often as you eat this bread and drink the cup, you proclaim the Lord's death until he comes.

When we eat the bread and drink the cup of Holy Communion we are preaching or proclaiming the death of Jesus. This word 'proclaim' is sometimes translated 'preach', and the original Greek is a word that means to 'tell thoroughly'.

Sometimes we miss the importance and the point of the eating and drinking. Sometimes in churches the minister holds up the bread and the wine after blessing them, and some people see this as the high point of the service. A bell rings, to signify their belief that the Spirit has descended to make the body of Christ in the bread and wine.

But the high point of the service, and the glory of Christ, is that in order to give himself to us he died on a cross—for us. That is what is at the heart of Christianity.

Christmas and Easter and Good Friday and Pentecost are all aspects of one event, which is the self-giving of the Creator to his creatures. One of the ways he gives himself is through the created things of bread and wine, and as we eat them, in believing faith, his life is renewed in us: 'Feed on him in your hearts by faith, with thanksgiving.'

But the Christ on whom we feed is the Christ who died for us. When you next eat the bread and drink the wine of Holy Communion, in the company of your fellow Christians who are the body of Christ, think of the fact that what you are all doing is to proclaim and to preach the death of Christ.

Consider

St Paul's words: 'I decided to know nothing among you except Jesus Christ and him crucified.'

1 Corinthians 2:2

SB

But we're Christians!

The tax collectors and sinners, however, were all crowding round to listen to him, and the Pharisees and scribes complained saying, 'This man welcomes sinners and eats with them.'

When I do an evening of 'funny stuff' for a church or group of churches, the event is usually well attended, I'm pleased to say. People love to laugh, and if there's a serious thought or two thrown in as well, they seem to accept that quite happily. When, however, I have been involved in concerns to raise money or consciousness for Aids sufferers, or Prison Fellowship, or Third World poverty, the attendance has been considerably lower.

The material I use is exactly the same, but there seems to be a reluctance to come close to these sorts of issues, even in such an indirect way. Some folk have quite openly expressed their distaste for any Christian activity connected with Aids, and Prison Fellowship is consistently under-funded and poorly supported, despite the fact that they do some marvellous work.

Not many Christians want to get their hands dirty, but those who do see miracles sometimes. Jesus didn't stay at the Jewish Hilton and make evangelistic visits to sinners. He was *with* them— eating with them, making real friends with them, telling stories, answering questions, untainted but fully involved. The Scribes and Pharisees couldn't stand it, just as some people still can't stand it nowadays.

Recently, a friend of mind came out of prison and was looking for lodgings in a nearby town. We found an establishment listed in the local directory as a 'Christian Hotel'. When I phoned the number and explained what was needed the lady on the other end of the line said, 'Well, I'm not sure. We do have to be very careful who we take, because we are a *Christian* hotel, you see . . .'

God help us as a church, if we're saying, 'We do have to be very careful who we take, because we are a *Christian* church, you see . . .'

Think

Do we make real friends with those we don't approve of? Are we ready to get our hands dirty in God's service? (Read Matthew 25:31–46.)

AP

Tuesday Week 3
LUKE 15:4 (NJB)

Shepherds or policemen?

'Which one of you with a hundred sheep, if he lost one, would fail to leave the ninety-nine in the desert and go after the missing one till he found it?'

Here, Jesus is asking the Scribes and Pharisees to take a 180 degree turn in their attitude to sinners. From scolding to caring; from abandoning to searching out; from indifference to love.

Some years ago one of our major universities undertook studies into the nature and components of successful counselling. After much research, observation and discussion, three major factors were identified as essential characteristics of an effective counsellor. They were as follows:

(1) The effective counsellor must be willing to enter the world of his client.

(2) He must not be condemnatory of the person he is counselling.

(3) He must value that person demonstrably.

A little reflection might have saved that university an awful lot of time and trouble. Two thousand years ago Jesus (who is sometimes called the Mighty Counsellor) entered our world, not to condemn us, but to show how much he valued us by dying on that horrible cross.

I wonder how the Scribes and Pharisees coped with a suggestion that they should be shepherds rather than policemen; that it was worth an enormous expenditure of time and effort to seek out just one of those grubby little sinners and save him from the consequences of his separation from God.

Seven years ago I was a lost sheep myself, despite the fact that I had been a Christian for more than twenty years. Emotionally distraught, out of work, and no longer attending a church, I said to my wife one day that if there was a God who loved me he could come and help, and if there wasn't, it didn't matter anyway. The good shepherd heard my bleat and came, particularly through certain friends who worked for the shepherd, rather than the religious police force.

A prayer

Thank you for coming into our world, Jesus. I'd like to help you in your search. Show me something specific that I can do.

AP

Searching with tears

And when he found it, would he not joyfully take it on his shoulders and then, when he got home, call together his friends and neighbours saying to them, 'Rejoice with me, I have found my sheep that was lost.' In the same way, I tell you, there will be more rejoicing in heaven over one sinner repenting than over ninety-nine upright people who have no need of repentance.

When my youngest son, David, was a little boy, we went to Cornwall for a family holiday. One afternoon we decided to spend some time on the beach at Newquay. After an hour or so of sandcastle building, paddling and ice-cream consumption, we realized that David was missing. An hour later, after searching every square yard of the beach, we could still find no trace of him. Bridget, my wife, was pacing aimlessly up and down the beach, tears in her eyes, desperately hoping that the small figure would appear.

Meanwhile, I made my way to the lifeguard point and asked the young man on duty to call David over the public address system. That didn't work either. A great darkness began to settle over my heart. My mouth had dried up and I was unable to keep my eyes from the thin white line where the sea met the shore. I was terrified. It must have been half an hour later when the friend who was with us on the beach found David playing quietly on the sand two hundred yards or so from where we had last seen him. The relief and joy in our little party was palpable. I hoisted David up onto my shoulders and carried him back to the car.

Jesus wanted his listeners to understand that his search for the lost—the shepherd's search for his sheep—is conducted with even more passion and urgency than our desperate hunt for David on that summer day. No wonder they rejoice in heaven when one sinner repents. God is crackers about us.

Reflect

Jesus searches for us with tears in his eyes. When he finds us the whole of heaven goes bonkers with happiness.

AP

Sharing sorrow and joy

Or again, what woman with ten drachmas would not, if she lost one, light a lamp and sweep out the house and search thoroughly till she found it? And then, when she had found it, call together her friends and neighbours, saying to them, 'Rejoice with me, I have found the drachma I lost.' In the same way, I tell you, there is rejoicing among the angels of God over one repentant sinner.

This story (presumably told so that the ladies could get the point of the sheep story) reminds me of the occasion when Bridget lost all our holiday money when she was pushing one of the children round the shops at Hailsham. She rang me at work to pass on the bad news and was clearly astonished by the calm and muted manner with which I responded.

'Okay, Bridget,' I purred soothingly, 'not to worry—I'll sort it out somehow. It's only money...' Little did Bridget know that this warm act of forgiveness and understanding was solely attributable to the fact that I was surrounded by a little circle of child-care trainees who had been enduring my views on the need for warmth and forgiveness in dealing with kids in care. When I arrived home later I discovered that the money had been found and returned to Bridget, so I was able to perpetuate the myth of my tolerance and generosity of spirit.

We certainly rejoiced together over the return of that cash, but we didn't invite any neighbours in to share our joy. Perhaps that is one of the lessons of this little parable. We are not very good at inviting others into the centre of our joys and our tragedies. Births, weddings, housewarmings and deaths tend to be the only occasions when this happens in grey old England. But we are the body of Christ, and we belong to each other. Some of the warmest and most memorable moments in the history of the little house-group that Bridget and I lead have been the times when individuals have made a gift to the rest of us of quite small joys and sorrows. This kind of sharing often requires an act of the will.

A prayer

Father, I'm not really very good at giving my life to other people. Please help me to be more generous and courageous.

AP

28

A story of God

Then he said, 'There was a man who had two sons. The younger one said to his father, "Father, let me have the share of the estate that will come to me." So the father divided the property between them. A few days later, the younger son got together everything he had and left for a distant country where he squandered his money on a life of debauchery.'

The Bible tells us that Jesus used stories all the time in his contacts with the crowds who flocked to hear him. Now I happen to know, as a feeble but committed story-teller myself, that the best stories are the ones that are based on fact—things that have really happened to me or to people I know. This famous story has the same ring of truth about it. During that invaluable period of sixteen years or so, when he was (presumably) a working carpenter, Jesus must have put together a sizeable mental portfolio of memories and anecdotes. This is probably one of them. I wish there was more story-telling and less preaching in the Church these days.

I have often wondered why the prodigal left home so deliberately. Unlike sheep and drachmas, he didn't get lost—he went. Perhaps he looked at his elder brother, po-faced, aridly virtuous and miserable, and decided anything was better than ending up like that. It seems more likely, though, that he made the common mistake of separating the gifts from the giver. It can take a long time to realize that we have lost touch with the springs of our own joy and pleasure, and

the process can be a subtle one. Some Christians, convinced that they are working for God, arrange religious activities that seem quite laudable, but if those activities don't have their roots in the will of God they are going to bloom once, then die.

The prodigal is incapable, at this stage, of realizing that as the good things flow away from him, nothing else will flow in to replace them—not as long as he is away from home, that is. The principle holds good for all of us.

Reflect

Jesus took his life, rolled it up in a ball and gave it to us. He lost the life he loved, so that we would never be hungry. Maybe it's best to work from home . . .

AP

Stuck in a pigsty

'When he had spent it all, that country experienced a severe famine, and now he began to feel the pinch; so he hired himself out to one of the local inhabitants who put him on his farm to feed the pigs. And he would willingly have filled himself with the husks the pigs were eating but no one would let him have them.'

Most of my working life has been spent caring for children in trouble. Some of them came from appalling backgrounds, and, inevitably, I came into contact with many of the parents of these confused teenagers. I met wives who had endured continual battering from their husbands, and men who had served frequent sentences in prison as a result of their consistently inexpert criminal activities. The children themselves were often locked into patterns of behaviour that had never brought them anything but negative responses.

Again and again I was struck by the apparent inability of unhappy people to explore alternatives in lifestyle or behaviour that would immediately make a difference. Why stay with a man who beats you up every other day? Why persist in acts of petty crime when the police catch you every time? It was only when I reached a point of intolerable pain and had to make an involuntary withdrawal from work and church that I realized that I was exactly the same. I had completely ignored the need to tackle some very obvious problems in my own life.

The prodigal son in this story is exactly the same. His descent from riches and riotous living to the ignominy of the pigs must have been a relatively gradual one. He could have made the decision to go home at any stage, but he seems to have been unaware of this option until he reached a point where his need was so great that he had to consider any alternative.

Lots of us are blinkered to obvious needs in our lives, and others usually see where we are heading long before we come to our senses. Prayer, sensitivity and practical help could prevent a few of us from hitting rock-bottom.

A prayer

Father, take the blinkers away so that we can see the changes that need to be made in our lives. If there are people known to us who are heading for disaster, give us the sensitivity and wisdom to help them.

AP

Reconciliation of God

And he is the head of the body, the church; he is the beginning and the firstborn from among the dead, so that in everything he might have the supremacy. For God was pleased to have all his fulness dwell in him, and through him to reconcile to himself all things, whether things on earth or things in heaven, by making peace through his blood, shed on the cross. Once you were alienated from God and were enemies in your minds because of your evil behaviour. But now he has reconciled you by Christ's physical body through death to present you holy in his sight, without blemish and free from accusation—if you continue in your faith, established and firm, not moved from the hope held out in the gospel.

If you go to Holy Communion today, will you remember how it is that you can have communion with God, and eat and drink at his table? This passage spells it out and so do the words of invitation: 'Draw near with faith. Receive the body of our Lord Jesus Christ which he gave for you, and his blood which he shed for you. Eat and drink in remembrance that he died for you, and feed on him in your hearts by faith with thanksgiving,' (*Alternative Service Book*).

A recent television programme showed an ex-IRA bomber in training for the Roman Catholic priesthood. He knew that he had been forgiven and that he had been reconciled to God. Before that, he had been an enemy of God, but now he was a friend. Then I began to wonder how well his reconciliation with his previous human enemies was progressing.

A prayer

Lord Jesus Christ, thank you for dying so that I could be reconciled to God. I am your friend, and you are my friend. You are the friend of sinners, and you love your enemies and transform them into friends. Send me into the world to do the same thing. Amen

SB

At least I'll eat

'Then he came to his senses and said, "How many of my father's hired men have all the food they want and more, and here am I dying of hunger! I will leave this place and go to my father and say: Father, I have sinned against heaven and against you; I no longer deserve to be called your son; treat me as one of your hired men." So he left the place and went back to his father.'

Let's not get too sentimental about this lad. No doubt he has some very warm and nostalgic memories of home. But his primary motivation for returning is an eminently sane and practical one. He wants some food. He is hungry. He is lacking the fuel that sustains life at its most basic level. Sin isn't much fun when you're dying of starvation.

Coming to our senses in a spiritual sense is a very similar experience. When worldly distractions lose their potency and props are snapped or fatally weakened, men and women know suddenly that their spirits are thin and emaciated. Only the bread of life can make any difference to this sort of terminal malnutrition.

It is worth mentioning, though, to those who are dithering about whether to leave the pigs or not, that this God who is offering sustenance is the one who created kites, and sex, and good wine, and spring flowers, and children's eyes. Coming home to him will not just be survival—it could turn out to be an awful lot of fun.

I can easily picture this 'oik' of a prodigal—a sort of New Testament Baldrick—crawling up the road towards home, rehearsing his little set speech over and over again, boldly perhaps, and then with cringing humility, hoping to strike a note that will be effective with a potentially furious parent. Most of us expect very little from God, especially if, like myself, we have been encouraged at an early stage to look at ourselves as miserable, crawling, verminous little creatures, tolerated by God, but only when he holds his nose and averts his eyes. The prodigal wasn't expecting much, but he was in for a shock.

A prayer

For those who are thinking of starting the journey back to the Father, we pray for courage. If there's anything we can do to help, please show us clearly so that we don't mess things up.

AP

A hurricane of love

While he was still a long way off, his father saw him and was moved with pity. He ran to the boy, clasped him in his arms and kissed him. Then his son said, 'Father, I have sinned against heaven and against you. I no longer deserve to be called your son.'

I have annoyed some of my evangelical friends occasionally by telling them of an acquaintance who came to his Christian faith as a result of attending classes in Buddhism. After obediently emptying his mind of almost everything that normally occupied it, he found that Jesus filled the mental vacuum that remained. Eventually he cancelled the Buddhist classes, joined a local church and made a commitment to Christ.

The same thing happens to the prodigal son in this story. He is a 'long way off' when his father spots him (probably from an upstairs window) and can hardly have expected such an early response. Too often the attitude of Christians to their non-believing acquaintances reminds me of the old joke about a country yokel who is asked for directions by a traveller:

'Well,' says the yokel, 'Oi wouldn't start from 'ere if I was you ...'

God knows where people are and when he should meet them. Sometimes they come along very strange roads indeed.

Here we see the dear old prodigal hit by a hurricane as he lopes along, learning his little speech by heart as he goes.

The hurricane is his father, of course, overjoyed to see the son he has always loved so much, and not ashamed to sprint down the road, holding his robes up with one hand. What an extraordinarily vulnerable picture of God that is.

With his father's arms wrapped round his head, the surprised prodigal manages to bleat out a muffled version of the set speech he's been rehearsing. His repentance is embraced with joy. Repentance and forgiveness are not opposite ends of the spectrum. They are parts of the same joyful experience.

Reflect

We know nothing about how and when God will call and meet people. Our job is to be obedient and carry out orders, however strange they may seem sometimes.

AP

So happy you're home!

But the father said to his servants, 'Quick! Bring out the best robe and put it on him; put a ring on his finger and sandals on his feet. Bring the calf we have been fattening, and kill it; we will celebrate by having a feast, because this son of mine was dead and has come back to life; he was lost and is found.' And they began to celebrate.

Having children of my own has taught me more about the fatherhood of God than anything else. When one of my children is naughty I feel an intensity of love towards him or her that yearns for a resolution of the problem. I don't mean that I never lose my temper or act irrationally (such a claim would qualify me for a degree in hypocrisy). But I do greet them, when they stumble through the apology barrier, as if they had never done anything wrong. It's so nice to have them back!

What a surprise for the prodigal. He would have settled for three meals a day and a bed in the barn. Instead he's covered with gifts and told that there's going to be a party to celebrate his return. The fragile little pose that he'd prepared for this first big encounter would hardly have been proof against such extravagant, limitless generosity. The face would have crumpled, a tear or two would have appeared—Daddy really wanted him back.

I met a prodigal the other day, a man who ran away from home when he was fourteen, and didn't return until he was nearly twenty. He planned to drive home in style to surprise Dad. But on the way his car broke down. He had to ring his parents for help. The stylish return lost some of its dignity as the young man was towed home in a lifeless vehicle by his beaming father. Lots of people break down on their way back to God. Don't worry if it happens to you—he'll come and get you.

A prayer

Thank you for loving us so much when we are naughty. I wish I really knew how much you like to be with me. I still break down from time to time. Please rescue me when it happens.

AP

Furious!

Now the elder son was out in the fields, and on his way back, as he drew near the house, he could hear music and dancing. Calling one of the servants he asked what it was all about. The servant told him, 'Your brother has come, and your father has killed the calf we had been fattening because he has got him back safe and sound.' He was angry then and refused to go in . . .

People often ask me if the characters in my books are based on real individuals. They are particularly interested in a couple called Stenneth and Victoria Flushpool, self-appointed moral watchdogs in the imaginary church community that we encounter in *The Sacred Diary of Adrian Plass*. Do they really exist? I refuse to answer that question on the grounds that it may incriminate me, but I can tell you that people from different places all over the country claim that I must have visited *their* church before writing the book, because the Flushpools (under another name) are definitely members of their congregation.

One thing is sure; no one has ever openly identified himself or herself with any negative character of the Flushpool variety. Perhaps some defensive mechanism prevents such recognition. I wonder if the Pharisees and Scribes recognized themselves in the elder brother of the prodigal story? These ancient Jewish Flushpools hated to see sinners relaxing with Jesus. Like the prodigal's miserable sibling, they had never taken the trouble to discover the true nature of the God whom they claimed to serve. They could have had a party if they'd wanted—they never asked.

Watch out for Flushpools in the church. They coax people into conversion, then tell them off afterwards because they're not perfect immediately; they elevate man-made activities onto a sacred level; they mistrust laughter and relaxation; they are stern and unhappy. We must pray for them especially if we *are* them . . .

A prayer

We pray for relaxation and joy throughout your Church, Father. Forgive us for allowing religious activities to atrophy and become meaningless. Help us to be shepherds rather than policemen.

AP

Come to the party!

And his father came out and began to urge him to come in; but he retorted to his father, 'All these years I have slaved for you and never once disobeyed any orders of yours, yet you never offered me so much as a kid for me to celebrate with my friends. But, for this son of yours, when he comes back after swallowing up your property—he and his loose women—you kill the calf we had been fattening.'

Do you sulk? I do. It is recorded elsewhere that I am a master of the shuddering sigh, the kind that indicates profound suffering, bravely borne. The whole point of a sulk is that you advertise your misery, and then refuse comfort or help when it's offered. My wife ruins my best sulks by tickling me.

Here we see the elder brother locked into a monster sulk. Hanging about outside the life and light of his brother's party he is clearly hoping that his father will come and plead with him to come in. That will give him the opportunity to refuse. Sure enough, out comes Dad, anxious that his other son should share the fun, the joy, and the fatted calf. The resentful lad pours out his anger and hurt at this point, unable to contain himself any longer.

Many Christians would be able to identify with this deep, stress-filled anger towards God. I met a bank manager once who, years ago, prayed for his younger brother to be healed from a terminal illness. The brother died, and the resulting disappointment and fury remained unexpressed for decades.

Strange as it may sound, many of us need to forgive God for what he has done to us, or failed to do for us. Of course, we know that he can't really have got it wrong, but that doesn't take the hurt away. Let's climb up on his lap and cry out our frustration and pain. Let's beat our fists against his chest like small children and let him see our confused passion.

He can handle it. He will put his arms round us until our anger dissolves in tears, and we realize that he loves us after all, and always did.

A prayer

Father, if there are unresolved issues between us, I'd like to face them and sort them out. It's very hard to argue with someone who's perfect, but I do feel angry with you sometimes. Help me to express my feelings to you and trust your response.

AP

Getting it right

The father said, 'My son, you are with me always and all I have is yours. But it was only right we should celebrate and rejoice, because your brother here was dead and has come to life; he was lost and is found.'

The elder brother has the same problem as many Christians in this age. He simply cannot understand that families at their best operate on the same principle as the three musketeers—'all for one and one for all.' When one is happy everyone rejoices, and when one mourns, the rest mourn with him or her.

The apostle Paul (who never read Dumas, but must have met him by now) put it rather differently. He said that each of us is part of Christ's body on earth, and that all parts, including the unusual ones, are vital to the function of the whole.

I used to belong to a Bible-study group which included a lady who made superb cakes, and a man who had a deep understanding and appreciation of God's forgiveness. We shared the cake and the forgiveness with equal enthusiasm, and we did not insist that the cake-maker should have hands laid on her to increase her sense of forgiveness. Nor did we send the man off for an intensive course in cake-making. Over the past couple of decades there has been an lot of emphasis on individual spiritual success. Articles entitled 'Washing up the Christian Way' and 'Carpet-laying in the Spirit' have implied that every aspect of

life must be victoriously and overtly claimed for God. Perhaps there is some truth in that, but how much more important it is that we share, value and appropriate each other's talents and blessings, and that we add our strength to the carrying of each other's burdens.

The elder brother got it wrong. The Scribes and Pharisees got it wrong. Perhaps we could have a shot at getting it right.

Reflect

Perhaps we have undervalued some people because their gifts or perceptions do not come high on our list of priorities. Perhaps we hug what we have and are to ourselves, instead of letting it belong to the body. Let's take a fresh look at the people around us.

AP

Love

Right at the centre of the Bible there is a love story. That is true in two senses. If we actually open the book in the middle we are likely to see the Song of Songs and find ourselves reading some of the most beautiful love poetry ever written. But to know the whole story is to know that the relationship between God and his people is likened to that of a bridegroom and bride or a husband and wife.

The Lord God is the husband of Israel, and the heartache of the prophet Hosea shows us the heartache of God over his unfaithful wife. Jesus said that heaven would be a wedding feast, and in Revelation John sees 'the holy city . . . prepared as a bride adorned for her husband' (21:2). God is the divine lover, and he loves each one of us. As we read the songs of human love in the Song of Songs they show us the love of God, and Jews and Christians have always seen in it an allegory of the relationship between God and his beloved people. The Jewish *Mishnah* says that 'all the Writings are holy, but the Song of Songs is the Holy of Holies' (the innermost place in the Jewish temple where the presence of God dwelt).

Jesus gave his followers a new commandment: 'That you love one another as I have loved you.' And he followed that with a promise. 'By this shall all men know that you are my disciples, if you have love one for another' (John 13:34–35). After the death and the resurrection of Jesus the disciples realized with astonished delight just how much he did love them—with a love that was stronger than death. The New Testament is full of it, and the good news of resurrection, eternal life and the forgiveness of our sins.

John's first letter is about all those things, and that is where we start our next section. Then we move on to the love song that is called the Song of Songs.

Holy Communion

In a church I used to belong to, the Rector would stop on after the evening service and invite us to send up written questions. It was very popular, and he was very competent, and usually I found his answers very helpful. But once I didn't.

My question was: 'I don't find the service of Holy Communion at all helpful. What can I do about it?' I was hoping for useful advice, but instead, when he got to my bit of paper he looked very severely at the congregation—and I hoped he hadn't recognized my writing. He read it out, and then said scornfully: 'So you don't find it helpful to see your Lord's death set out in front of you...' I cannot now remember the rest of his answer, but it was useless. It wasn't until years later, through reading St John's Gospel and Frank Lake's *Clinical Theology*, that I began to understand.

When a meal is eaten it becomes part of the eater. So when Jesus gives us bread and wine, saying this is my body, this is my blood, he is saying that just as physical food has to be eaten for physical life, so spiritual food has to be eaten for spiritual life. But whereas food is physical and impersonal, the food and drink of the Eucharist are spiritual and personal.

The bread and wine which we eat and drink are a sacrament, an outward sign of an inner eating and drinking of the being of Christ, in which God gives himself to us. A transformation takes place: not the transformation of earthly food into our human bodies, but a transformation made by God in which spiritual food transforms human beings into the body of the Christ who died for us. He was also the Christ who was raised to life. So at Communion we share in the life of the one who died and yet is 'alive for ever more'. We are (already) the body of Christ, but we still need the new life to flow into us. Sharing and communion take place all the time in the Christian life, because they are what the Christian life is. The drama of the Communion service is its outward and visible sign.

I am the living bread that came down from heaven. If anyone eats this bread, he will live for ever. The bread that I will give him is my flesh, which I give so that the world may live ... Whoever eats my flesh and drinks my blood has eternal life, and I will raise him to life on the last day.

SB

The overture

That which was from the beginning, which we have heard, which we have seen with our eyes, which we have looked upon and touched with our hands, concerning the word of life—the life was made manifest, and we saw it, and testify to it, and proclaim to you the eternal life which was with the Father and was made manifest to us—that which we have seen and heard we proclaim also to you, so that you may have fellowship with us; and our fellowship is with the Father and with his Son Jesus Christ. And we are writing this that our joy may be complete.

These four verses are like the overture of a musical, in which we are given snatches of the tunes to come. John wants his readers to have fellowship with him and his church—that is, he wants them to be united. That unity comes about when they share in God's eternal life, and John can't imagine any greater joy than knowing that the people he loves also know God.

So here, in a nutshell, is the message which brings eternal life. That life, which is God's own life, broke into our world in the form of Jesus—the real man (we could touch him with our hands) who was still so much more than an ordinary man. Jesus is the one who made manifest (made visible to us) the eternal God.

We often wonder what God is really like. It's one of the questions asked by adults and children alike. And no picture we can draw, no description we can write, can do justice to God. Yet God has given us the best description possible. What is God like? Like Jesus.

So, says John, come with me and let me show you Jesus, and the love of God and the life of God which Jesus reveals. And let me show you what it means to belong to him: what we get out of it, and what he asks from us.

Meditate

'That which was from the beginning'—God—has come to us in Jesus. Think of all the things that make us feel distant from God. God has stepped over them all to come to us.

MM

Holiness and sin

This is the message we have heard from him and proclaim to you, that God is light and in him is no darkness at all. If we say we have fellowship with him while we walk in darkness, we lie and do not live according to the truth; but if we walk in the light, as he is in the light, we have fellowship with one another, and the blood of Jesus his Son cleanses us from all sin. If we say we have no sin, we deceive ourselves, and the truth is not in us. If we confess our sins, he is faithful and just, and will forgive our sins and cleanse us from all unrighteousness. If we say we have not sinned, we make him a liar, and his word is not in us.

Holiness and sin are words which have nearly lost their meaning in the modern world. Holiness has come almost to mean mealy-mouthed hypocrisy, sin a pleasurable naughtiness, like eating cream cakes when we're on a diet. Yet they sum up the nature of the gap between human beings and God—a difference like light and darkness. If there is one thing the whole Bible agrees on about God it is that he is holy—that he is totally pure, totally moral, totally without evil. And sin is the opposite of that; it is turning away from the light of God and going our own way. When that happens (and when doesn't it?) there is a distance between us and God that seems unbridgeable.

The essence of the gospel is that God, in his immense love, has found a way to bridge the gap, by sending Jesus to die for us, to 'become sin for us' as Paul put it in 2 Corinthians 5:21. It is through Jesus that God has brought us back to himself. This, says John, is something we can never afford to forget, for it is not enough simply to believe it. We have to live it as well. But more about that tomorrow.

Prayer

Almighty God, you have taught us to call you Father. But don't let us forget your purity, your light, your holiness. Give us a vision of your distance from all that is evil, because only then can we begin to understand the greatness of your love which has reached across that distance to bring us back to you.

MM

Jesus for the defence

My little children, I am writing this to you so that you may not sin; but if any one does sin, we have an advocate with the Father, Jesus Christ the righteous; and he is the expiation for our sins, and not for ours only but also for the sins of the whole world. And by this we may be sure that we know him, if we keep his commandments . . . he who says he abides in him ought to walk in the same way in which he walked.

'The worst advertisements for Christ are Christians.' I don't know who said that, but it's often true. The opposite is equally true, of course; it is how Christians behave which attracts people to Jesus. In fact, the plain and simple test of our relationship with Jesus is the one John sets out here. Do we live like Jesus?

It's easy to say no. Of course we don't. But that doesn't let us off the hook. We may say that we can't ever be like Jesus (this side of heaven, anyway), but we are still called to walk in his footsteps, and we have to take that call seriously. In today's reading, John sets out the two sides of following Jesus. On the one hand, we are to be like him, and to obey his commands (especially the one to love). That is how we can test our Christianity. When we are in doubt, we have to ask, 'What would Jesus do?' and then try to do it.

On the other hand, we know that we will often fail, and when that happens, we can count on his forgiveness. John uses the image of a law-court. Jesus is like the defending lawyer, always ready to stick up for us. It's worth noting that it is the promise of 'Jesus for the defence' which comes first. Because we know that Jesus is on our side we can set out to following him and to be like him, knowing that when we fail he will still be with us. If it weren't for that, we wouldn't dare to try.

Think

How seriously do we take our call to be like Jesus? Are we tempted not to bother because it's too hard? Or do we really believe Jesus is on our side?

MM

42

The old and the new

Beloved, I am writing you no new commandment, but an old command-ment which you had from the beginning; the old commandment is the word which you have heard. Yet I am writing you a new commandment, which is true in him and in you, because the darkness is passing away and the true light is already shining. He who say he is in the light and hates his brother is in the darkness still. He who loves his brother abides in the light, and in it there is no cause for stumbling. But he who hates his brother is in the darkness and walks in the darkness, and does not know where he is going, because the darkness has blinded his eyes.

The commandment which John refers to here must surely be the commandment to love one another (John 13:34), which he has written about in his Gospel.

It may seem to be an old command-ment because his readers have known it all their Christian lives. But in another sense it is new. First, it is new because it is the sign of the new relationship which Jesus has opened up with God. The command to love is the sign of the new life which comes from God and which makes Christians children of God. This is God's love, which is experienced in a new way by his people, and which they must share with each other.

Secondly, it's new because it has to be renewed each day. We can't obey it in a once-for-all way. Every time we meet someone, every time we come into a new situation the commandment of Jesus is there, staring us in the face: 'here and now you must love'.

The newness comes in putting the old commandment into practice. It is as we ask, 'What is the loving thing to do or say here?' that we find new ways of showing love, new ways of helping, tolerating or caring for each other.

Prayer for a new day

Father, as I begin the same old routine, let me see your command to love in a fresh light. Help me to see those who need my love, and as I look at them, speak again the command: 'Love one another, as I have loved you.'

MM

43

World, flesh and devil

Do not love the world or the things in the world. If any one loves the world, love for the Father is not in him. For all that is in the world, the lust of the flesh and the lust of the eyes and the pride of life, is not of the Father but is of the world. And the world passes away, and the lust of it; but he who does the will of God abides for ever.

The devil isn't actually mentioned in this passage (he comes later) but two out of three isn't bad! It will be obvious by now that John likes opposites: light and dark, truth and lies, love and hate, and now God and the world. At first, it may seem strange to set God and the world as opposites. After all, didn't God create the world? Yes. John makes that plain in his Gospel; Jesus came into a world which was his—but it did not recognize him (John 1:10). And that is why the world is the opposite of God.

In John's Gospel and letters, 'the world' doesn't just mean all the stuff God made. It means the human world which has turned its back on God. As Christians, we are used to thinking of God's love for the world ('God loved the world so much that he sent his Son'—John 3:16). And that makes us think that somehow the world must be lovable. But just turn on the TV, and we see how little the world recognizes God.

That shows us something of the greatness of God's love (and more about that later). It also tells us that Christians live in a hostile environment. We have to be on our guard. For instance, we live in a society which stresses the need for individual enterprise, for wealth and for success. How well does that fit with Jesus stress on caring for the weak, for giving to the poor and for being a servant to others?

The way of the world is not often the way of God, and so we have to ask, 'Am I putting God first, or am I being pressurized into the world's way of thinking?'

Think

What things do we put first in our lives? Where do they fit with God's values?

MM

World, flesh and devil (2)

Children, it is the last hour; and as you have heard that antichrist is coming so now many antichrists have come; therefore we know that it is the last hour. They went out from us but they were not of us; for if they had been of us, they would have continued with us; but they went out, that it might be plain that they all are not of us. But you have been anointed by the Holy One, and you all know . . . this is the antichrist, he who denies the Father and the Son.

In yesterday's reading, John warned his readers against the 'lust of the flesh'. When we hear that phrase, we almost always think about sex. But it's not what John means, and it's not what preachers used to mean when our title trio were a popular subject.

Today's reading is much nearer to what it means. The people John is opposing in his letter started out as members of his church, but have gone their own way. More importantly, they have altered the teaching of the gospel into something more pleasing to them. Probably, they didn't like the idea that Jesus was a real human person. It seemed offensive to them that the spiritual God should get involved with material things; they preferred their religion to be an other-worldly thing, something which belonged purely to the spirit and was not involved with the things of the world.

Their view had only one thing wrong with it: it wasn't true. Instead of listening to God they had followed their own desires (spiritual though they may have seemed) and ended up doing their own thing instead of God's. And that's what 'the flesh' is. It's giving way to our desires and not God's. Sometimes we can kid ourselves that we're being spiritual, but in fact we are giving way to our human weakness as much as we would with more physical desires. And when we do that, we end up denying God.

Think

What do we like least about our faith? The demands it makes? The pleasures it sometimes seems to deny? The challenge it makes to our own way of thinking?

Pray

Bring our doubts and dislikes to God. Ask for guidance and help at the points of weakness.

MM

45

How can he and how can we?

Then the Jews started arguing among themselves, 'How can this man give us his flesh to eat?' Jesus replied to them: 'In all truth I tell you, if you do not eat the flesh of the Son of man and drink his blood, you have no life in you.'

It was no wonder they found it difficult. We have heard the words so often that we are used to them. But for them it was outrageous. They never drank the blood of any creature anyway, because their Law told them not to. And what Jesus was saying sounded like cannibalism—which the early Christians were accused of because of the words said at Communion: 'Take, eat, this is my body.'

We describe what Jesus is talking about as 'the benefits of his death and passion'. By faith we trust in them, and by faith they enter into us—which means that Christ enters into us and grows within us. As the bread of Communion is put into our empty hand, and we take it and eat it, and as the cup is given to us and we take it and drink it, just so do we accept Christ into our heart. 'He came to his own and his own people did not accept him. But to those who did accept him he gave power to become children of God, to those who believed in his name who were born not from human stock or human desire or human will but from God himself (John 1:11–13 NJB).

The new life within us is the life of Christ and we share in the divine nature. Christ showed us that in all its glory when he died for us and rose again for us. And now he calls us to live out that life in the world.

Almighty God, we thank you for feeding us with the body and blood of your Son Jesus Christ. Through him we offer you our souls and bodies to be a living sacrifice. Send us out in the power of your Spirit to live and work to your praise and glory. Amen.

Alternative Service Book

SB

Victory song

See what love the Father has given us, that we should be called children of God; and so we are. The reason why the world does not know us is that it did not know him. Beloved, we are God's children now; it does not yet appear what we shall be, but we know that when he appears we shall be like him, for we shall see him as he is. And every one who thus hopes in him purifies himself as he is pure.

While we look at the dangers John warns us of, things might seem a bit dismal, with sin, doom and gloom all around. But now we jump back a few verses to put things in perspective. Jesus *has* won the victory, and those who belong to him are truly God's children. Of course, it would be conceited (and untrue) to suppose that God loves Christians more than he loves anyone else. But it is only when we accept that love and respond to it that we can enter into a proper relationship with him. After all, you can't have much of a family when children don't ever speak to their parents, no matter how much they are loved.

In the family of God, the children are given a promise: that they will share in all the joy and wonder of knowing God face to face. We can't really imagine what that means, but John tells us that we will be like Jesus. In the end, we will share fully in that close parent and child love which led Jesus to call God his Father. That relationship won't be spoilt by our disobedience or weakness, or by our failure to love each other.

It lies in the future, in the life of heaven which is being truly like Christ. Yet already we are allowed to call God our Father, and already we have the certainty of his love for us—a love which sent Jesus to bring us home, and to win the victory over death, the world, the flesh and the devil. Until then, we are on our way, travelling in hope, but already singing the victory song. All that we do in our life here is part of the preparation for that final victory, when we shall see him as he is.

Meditate

Therefore . . . let us run with perseverance the race that is set before us, looking to Jesus the pioneer and perfecter of our faith.

Hebrews 12:1–2

MM

47

World, flesh and devil (3)

Every one who commits sin is guilty of lawlessness; sin is lawlessness. You know that [Jesus] appeared to take away sins, and in him there is no sin. No one who abides in him sins; no one who sins has either seen him or known him. Little children, let no one deceive you. He who does right is righteous, as he is righteous. He who commits sin is of the devil; for the devil has sinned from the beginning. The reason the Son of God appeared was to destroy the works of the devil.

'Surely you don't expect people to believe in the devil nowadays?' We hear that question often enough. And in a sense it doesn't matter too much whether or not we believe in the devil. But there are certainly times when evil seems much bigger than the sins of individuals. There are times when it simply gets out of hand. Wars which leaders on both sides would stop, if only they knew how. Great industries which crush the rights of weak and poor people, with no one really being responsible—the system itself does the harm. And when we look at some of the horrors of recent times, such as the Nazis, Stalin and the Pol Pot regime in Cambodia, we see an evil which seems much greater than the sins of any single person.

If there is no devil, it seems likely that there's something very similar, whatever we may call it.

In today's reading John again presents the great choice. We can be lined up with God, or with evil. We can choose God and good, or the devil. But there is no middle ground.

When we belong to God, though, we are on the winning side, for Jesus appeared to destroy the works of the devil. In the cross and resurrection, we see God's victory.

Meditate

Think of the signs of evil we see in the world around us. They seem overwhelming at times. Great crimes and petty ones flood the news. Picture Jesus on the cross. There he bears the sins of the world. There he takes all that evil can throw at him. There he dies. Imagine the first Easter morning. Jesus is risen. Evil has failed, and the victory is God's.

MM

Love and death

For this is the message which you have heard from the beginning, that we should love one another, and not be like Cain who was of the evil one and murdered his brother. And why did he murder him? Because his own deeds were evil and his brother's righteous. Do not wonder, brethren, that the world hates you. We know that we have passed out of death into life, because we love the brethren. He who does not love abides in death. Any one who hates his brother is a murderer, and you know that no murderer has eternal life abiding in him.

Here John takes up a theme from Jesus' teaching—the idea that hatred is much the same as murder (see Matthew 5:21–22). It seems harsh, and even silly. After all, hatred and anger can be put right, but murder is much more final. And that is true. But of course, the point is that our actions come from our attitudes and feelings. Few murderers kill in cold blood. Usually, it's out of anger. And while very few of us are likely ever to come near to killing someone, still the way we think about them is important.

Our attitude to people shows what value we put on them. Those we hate are people we are saying (secretly, to ourselves) are worth nothing. They could be wiped out and never missed. But God has put a value on them—Jesus has died for them. And if we belong to Jesus, then we have to value them too. We have to love them.

There's more to it than that, though. Our attitude to others affects us. Hatred and bitterness destroy us. I know people who have been very badly done to. As a result, they have become bitter and hateful; their own lives have become warped and twisted. No doubt they were once in the right, but that has passed away. Because they failed to find love (yes, even for their enemies) they have committed a sort of spiritual suicide. John knew what he was writing about: 'He who does not love abides in death.'

Think

What secret resentments do we hold on to? Do we cling to them in our deepest hearts? If we do, then it is time to get them into the open. Show them to God, and ask him to teach us to love.

MM

Truly human

Beloved, do not believe every spirit, but test the spirits to see whether they are of God; for many false prophets have gone out into the world. By this you know the Spirit of God: every spirit which confesses that Jesus Christ has come in the flesh is of God, and every spirit which does not confess Jesus is not of God. This is the spirit of antichrist, of which you heard that it was coming, and now it is in the world already.

Here we come to one of the major differences between John and his opponents. In some way, they denied that Jesus was fully human. Probably they thought that the 'Christ' was separate from Jesus the man—a sort of Christ-spirit that came to Jesus but was not Jesus. (Notice that for John, he is 'Jesus Christ' but the opponents deny 'Jesus'—not Christ.) But we need to realize that Jesus was truly human.

In fact, Jesus defines what it means to be human. We all admit that there is something more, something better, than what we actually are and do. We fall short of even our own ideals. So we say, 'I'm only human.' But we're wrong. We're less than human. Or at least, less than truly human. It's when we look at Jesus that we see what it means to be truly human. In Jesus we see someone who is totally at peace with God, someone who is totally true to his faith, totally true to himself. We see someone who is strong, yet compassionate, loving but honest with those he loves. In fact, we see a person as God intends people to be.

In Jesus, God has given us a pattern for our lives, and even better, a promise of what we will be like. Jesus is the blueprint for what God wants to do in our lives. So when we look at our own shortcomings, we can say, 'Yes, there is something better, and I see it in Jesus. But God has promised that I will be like him.'

Meditate

God has promised that we will be like Jesus. Think of what we find most attractive in Jesus. Think of what we find least attractive in ourselves. Offer our worst parts to God and thank him that he is already at work in us 'conforming us to the image of Christ' (Romans 8:29).

MM

Experiencing the Spirit

By this we know that we abide in him and he in us, because he has given us of his own Spirit. And we have seen and testify that the Father has sent his Son as the Saviour of the world. Whoever confesses that Jesus is the Son of God, God abides in him, and he in God. So we know and believe the love God has for us. God is love, and he who abides in love abides in God, and God abides in him. In this is love perfected with us, that we may have confidence for the day of judgment, because as he is so are we in this world.

When I had been a Christian for only a short time, I began to worry about the Holy Spirit. Did I really have the Holy Spirit? How could I tell? The answer I was given was that I knew because Jesus promised the Spirit to all who have faith in him. Since I had faith, I had the Spirit.

That argument is sound enough. But there's more to it than that. Here the argument is the other way round. We know we belong to Jesus, because we have the Spirit. In other words, John expects his readers to *experience* the Spirit. For some people, this causes no problem. The Spirit gives the gift of speaking in tongues, prophecy or whatever. He makes his presence felt. Others worry about this. Isn't it too emotional, too 'spectacular'? And anyway, such obvious gifts are not for everyone (see 1 Corinthians 12:30).

There are at least two answers. Today we'll look at the first. The most important sign of the Spirit's presence is a growing love for others. Time and again, John stresses the need for Christians to love.

But we can get the impression that this is something we do by sheer will-power. It isn't. It is something the Spirit of the God who is himself love does in us. We learn to love under the guidance and with the help of God's Spirit. Our part is to be *prepared* to love. The rest will follow.

Think

Ask, 'Am I prepared to love? Am I prepared to be a channel through which the Spirit of love will flow? When we have the (honest) answer, tell it to God. Ask for his help to open ourselves to his Spirit.

MM

Afraid of love

There is no fear in love, but perfect love casts out fear. For fear has to do with punishment, and he who fears is not perfected in love. We love, because he first loved us. If any one says, 'I love God,' and hates his brother, he is a liar; for he who does not love his brother whom he has seen, cannot love God whom he has not seen. And this commandment we have from him, that he who loves God should love his brother also.

Yesterday we thought about how the presence of the Holy Spirit shows itself in love. Today's reading points towards a second way of looking at it. Very often, we hold back from the Spirit, the presence of God in our lives, simply out of fear. We are scared of letting go of our lives and handing them over to God. So we hold back. We hold back on our prayers, we hold back in our worship, and we mutter darkly about the dangers of religious enthusiasm.

We see the same sort of thing in human lovers. We want to give ourselves in some way to the one we love, but we are scared. We fear that he/she will take advantage of us, or refuse us, or (worst of all) not return our love with the same strength.

With human lovers, those are real dangers. But not with God. God has already given his all, in Jesus. We are to love him because he has loved us, and given himself first. Because of that we know that God will not reject us, that he will not take advantage of us, and that he has already poured out his love for us on the cross. Once we abandon ourselves to God, we will truly see the Spirit at work in us. We will begin to love others. Sometimes they *will* abuse and reject our love. But when that happens we will be able to find shelter in the one who has already loved us totally.

Meditate

Imagine Jesus on the cross. Arms spread wide, helpless. Arms spread in welcome. Here is no one who will abuse our self-giving. Here is someone who gives himself. Arms spread wide in offering.

Relax. Open your own arms. Here I am, Lord. Take me. Do what you will with me, for you do it in love.

MM

Christ living in me

Anyone who does eat my flesh and drink my blood has eternal life, and I shall raise that person up on the last day. For my flesh is real food and my blood is real drink. Whoever eats my flesh and drinks my blood lives in me and I live in that person.

The more we meditate about eating the flesh and drinking the blood of Christ the more profound we shall find it. We know what happens when we eat and drink ordinary food and drink. They nourish us and become part of us. But when we eat the wheat that bread is made of, and drink the grapes that wine is made from, we don't become a stalk of wheat or turn into a vine. The radical difference when we eat and drink Christ is that we become more and more like Christ. Whoever accepts the benefits of Christ's death and passion has within herself or himself all that Christ is and has done and will do.

'I have been crucified with Christ, and yet I am alive; yet it is no longer I, but Christ living in me. The life that I am now living, subject to the limitations of human nature, I am living in faith, faith in the Son of God, who loved me and gave himself for me' (Galatians 2:19–20 NJB). It was St Paul who wrote that, but it is just as true of everyone who eats and drinks the body and blood of Christ in faith.

All that Christ has we have, because he is in us and we are in him. He lives in the presence of God. So do we. He was raised up from the dead in the glory of the Father. On the last day he will raise us up from the dead. He was sent into the world to redeem it because God loves it. Now, as he was sent, so he sends us—not to give our flesh and blood for the life of the world, because he has done that once for all and for ever. But we have to tell the world that he has done it, and that 'God so loved the world that he gave his only Son, that whoever believes in him should not perish but have eternal life' (John 3:16). 'May we who share Christ's body live his risen life; we who drink his cup bring life to others; we whom the Spirit lights give light to the world' (ASB).

SB

53

Fragrant

The Song of Songs, which is Solomon's. O that you would kiss me with the kisses of your mouth! For your love is better than wine, your anointing oils are fragrant, your name is oil poured out; therefore the maidens love you. Draw me after you, let us make haste. The king has brought me into his chambers. We will exult and rejoice in you; we will extol your love more than wine; rightly do they love you.

A French commentator called this book *Le plus beau chant de le creation*, 'the most beautiful song in creation'—and the Hebrew title means it is the greatest song there has ever been. This is a book about God, but we learn about the love of God as we read about the love of a man and woman for each other. The original Hebrew has masculine and feminine verb forms, so I have taken a leaf out of George Knight's commentary and written HE or SHE in these notes. We don't know who they were anyway, and using these capital-lettered pronouns seems to make them symbolize Man and Woman.

SHE is in love—and she wants HIM to kiss her. There is a beautiful equality about woman and man in the Song. Her desires are as strong as his, and this is as it should be. SHE finds his love is more exhilarating than drinking wine, and his personality (a person's 'name' stands for his nature) is so wonderful that it is like a beautiful smell ... It's as if the essential nature is giving itself away in its fragrance—and I find myself remembering the times when I come home on a summer evening and just breathe in the smell of the honeysuckle that's filling my front garden, or when I bury my nose in the sweetness of clean washing that I have just taken off the line.

A prayer

But thanks be to God, who in Christ always leads us in triumph, and through us spreads the fragrance of the knowledge of him everywhere.

2 Corinthians 2:14

SB

54

Comely

I am very dark, but comely, O daughters of Jerusalem, like the tents of Kedar, like the curtains of Solomon. Do not gaze at me because I am swarthy, because the sun has scorched me. My mother's sons were angry with me, they made me keeper of the vineyards; but, my own vineyard I have not kept!

SHE is feeling uncomfortable, and perhaps trying to boost up her own self-confidence. The daughters of Jerusalem are staring at her because she is sunburnt, a peasant girl out of the fields. They are probably members of Solomon's harem, and she thinks they are looking down on her.

When we are feeling low it can help to say to ourself: 'I am very dark, but comely'. We may be feeling fed up with ourself, or we may know that other people are fed up with us and looking down on us. *The Shorter Oxford Dictionary* says that 'comely' means 'fair, pretty, beautiful, nice...', but it can also imply 'a homelier style of beauty, which pleases without exciting admiration'. We may just be very ordinary people, but each one of us can say to ourself: 'I am unique in the universe ... there is no one else in the whole world like me ... and God created me and God loves me'. I love the 'Butterfly Song', which is about all sorts of creatures thanking God for being themselves—a butterfly, an elephant, a worm, a robin—and every chorus finishes with the human creature saying: 'And I just thank you Father for making me Me'. We may have made a mess of our life (SHE confesses that 'my own vineyard I have not kept'), but God can remake us and somehow take the broken pieces and make them into something better.

A meditation

Sit still on your chair, and be quiet. What is your own opinion of yourself? Have you any idea of how other people regard you? Think of the good things about yourself and think of the places where you often fail and make mistakes. Then say to yourself 'I am very dark, but comely...' and dare to believe it.

SB

My beloved

I compare you, my love, to a mare of Pharaoh's chariots. Your cheeks are comely with ornaments, your neck with strings of jewels . . .

While the king was on his couch, my nard gave forth its fragrance . . . My beloved is to me a cluster of henna blossoms in the vineyards of Engedi.

Behold, you are beautiful, my love; behold, you are beautiful; your eyes are doves. Behold, you are beautiful, my beloved, truly lovely. Our couch is green; the beams of our house are cedar, our rafters are pine.

HE and SHE have fallen in love, and they are taking great delight in each other—body as well as personality. For the Hebrew a person was 'body, soul and spirit', and if Christianity had stuck with its Jewishness we would never have torn apart those things which God has joined together. The Church has been affected by Greek thought, which 'separates the ideal from the actual, heaven from earth, time from eternity, body from soul, male from female, love from sex', and this separation has brought about in the West 'the promiscuous and permissive society that the rest of the world despises' (Knight).

The lovers are lying on the floor of a forest, with cedar trees and pine trees sheltering them like a house. We don't know what they are doing (apart from adoring each other) because it doesn't say. Perhaps they are betrothed by now—and remember how serious betrothal was: Joseph considered divorcing Mary, 'his betrothed wife', when he found out she was pregnant. Or perhaps they are married. The Jews said that the *shekinah*, the glory of God, shone over the husband and wife when they were in their marriage bed.

A thought

He who loves his wife loves himself. For no man ever hates his own flesh, but nourishes and cherishes it, as Christ does the church.

Ephesians 5:28–29

SB

Loved and lovely

I am a rose of Sharon, a lily of the valleys.

As a lily among brambles, so is my love among maidens.

As an apple tree among the trees of the wood, so is my beloved among young men. With great delight I sat in his shadow, and his fruit was sweet to my taste. He brought me to the banqueting house, and his banner over me was love. Sustain me with raisins, refresh me with apples; for I am sick with love. O that his left hand were under my head, and that his right hand embraced me!

SHE is becoming more aware of her preciousness to HIM, and of how special she is. Love has an incredible effect on us, and it transforms us. When we are loved by our beloved everything about us becomes more beautiful.

In HIS eyes SHE stands out like a lily growing in the middle of a bramble thicket full of prickles. But HE is also special to HER. 'As an apple tree among the trees of the wood, so is my beloved among young men.' HE isn't like the other, ordinary trees. HE is different—with sweet apples for her to eat.

'O taste and see that the Lord is good!', the Psalmist urges us (34:8), and SHE has tasted HER beloved. But it isn't only apples that HE feeds her with. There is a whole banquet to be eaten, with a banner held up over them proclaiming the name of the feast to be love.

To think about

How do we 'taste and see that the Lord is good'? Think of the good things in your life, that you enjoy. Think of the bad things, that disappoint you and that you would like to go away. To taste, and then to eat, is to allow God to enter in to all those things—good and bad alike. Then the happiness will be deeper and the heartache and sorrow shared.

SB

My beloved

My beloved spake, and said unto me, Rise up, my love, my fair one, and come away. For, lo, the winter is past, the rain is over and gone; The flowers appear on the earth; the time of the singing of birds is come, and the voice of the turtle is heard in our land; The fig tree putteth forth her green figs, and the vines with the tender grape give a good smell. Arise, my love, my fair one, and come away . . . My beloved is mine, and I am his: he feedeth among the lilies. Until the day break, and the shadows flee away, turn, my beloved, and be thou like a roe or a young hart upon the mountains . . .

These are some of the loveliest and best loved lines in the whole of English literature, which is why I have suddenly switched to the Authorized Version. They seem best in the language of Shakespeare, and the language seems to convey the meaning even better.

In HER passionate statements about HIM we shall notice a change of emphasis as we read our way through the book. There are three declarations which are similar, but different. The first one begins with 'My beloved is *mine*', and then says, 'and I am his'. SHE is telling the world that HE belongs to HER, and the emphasis is on HER. The second statement says 'I am my beloved's and my beloved is mine' (6:3)—so there is an almost equal statement, but with HIS possession of HER coming first. Then in the final statement, SHE is totally taken up with HIM. 'I am my beloved's, and his desire is for me . . .' (7:10)

It seems to be true of lovers the world over that we can never keep quiet about it. We have to tell other people about our beloved—and it's the second greatest wonder in the world to know that our beloved loves us. The greatest wonder of all, to be gloried in and delighted in, is that God loves us.

A meditation

Sit still for a few minutes, and consider the fact that God loves you. 'I am my beloved's, and his desire is for me . . .'

SB

58

All fair

Behold, you are beautiful, my love, behold, you are beautiful! Your eyes are doves behind your veil. Your hair is like a flock of goats, moving down the slopes of Gilead. Your teeth are like a flock of shorn ewes that have come up from the washing, all of which bear twins, and not one among them is bereaved ... Your two breasts are like two fawns, twins of a gazelle, that feed among the lilies. Until the day breathes and the shadows flee, I will hie me to the mountain of myrrh and the hill of frankincense. You are all fair, my love; there is no flaw in you.

Another love poem—in which HE admires HER. It was written in the Middle East, in an ancient nation whose economy was based on sheep. So HE uses things out of that culture to describe various things about HER: hair like flock of goats; teeth like a flock of shorn ewes all of them with twins— which means there are no toothless gaps in the beloved's smile. They aren't at all the pictures that we would use to describe our twentieth-century beloved. But the love is the same—and we in our technological age know most of what those Old Testament lovers were singing about.

We always think our beloved is perfect—at least at the beginning! And when later on in the relationship we discover the blemishes in the beloved we want them to go away—not because we love any less, but precisely because we love.

To consider

...Christ loved the church and gave himself up for her, that he might sanctify her, having cleansed her by the washing of water with the word, that he might present the church to himself in splendour, without spot or wrinkle or any such thing, that she might be holy and without blemish.

Ephesians 5:25–27

SB

59

Life and living

As the living Father sent me and I draw life from the Father, so whoever eats me will also draw life from me. This is the bread which has come down from heaven; it is not like the bread our ancestors ate: they are dead, but anyone who eats this bread will live for ever.

The Christian life is a life lived in union with Christ. Frank Lake, in *Clinical Theology*, wrote of the symbiotic union of a baby with its mother. The baby has a life that it only experiences as life with its mother, in union with its mother. Not a separate life. A shared life. A life that draws its being and its well-being from its mother's milk and its mother's love. Frank Lake knew that was an inadequate image for our life in God-in-Christ. But it can show us something of the truth, and perhaps as we meditate on the imagery it will show us more. Lake even used the outrageous imagery of the parasite, which cannot live at all unless it lives on its host—and he made even that speak of the life that we draw from God.

C.S. Lewis said something like it but more acceptably: 'God wills our good, and our good is to love him . . . That is, whether we like it or not, God intends to give us what we need, not what we think we want. Once more, we are embarrassed by the intolerable compliment, by too much love, not too little . . . If we will not learn to eat the only food that the universe grows—the only food that any possible universe ever can grow—then we must starve eternally' (*The Problem of Pain*).

The opposite of starving eternally is eternal life. 'Anyone who does eat my flesh and drink my blood has eternal life . . . anyone who eats this bread will for ever.'

Then he took bread, and when he had given thanks, he broke it and gave it to them, saying, 'This is my body given for you; do this in remembrance of me.' He did the same with the cup after supper, and said, 'This cup is the new covenant in my blood poured out for you.'

Luke 22:19—20 NJB

SB

60

Between persons

A garden locked is my sister, my bride, a garden locked, a fountain sealed. Your shoots are an orchard of pomegranates with all choicest fruits, henna with nard, nard and saffron, calamus and cinnamon, with all trees of frankincense, myrrh and aloes, with all chief spices—a garden fountain, a well of living water, and flowing streams from Lebanon.

HE likens HER virginity to a locked garden and a sealed fountain. Inside the garden, after it has been unlocked, there is a great richness of growing things: an orchard (or, rather, a paradise) of pomegranates, and the choicest of fruits and sweet-smelling trees. Also within the garden there is a fountain, 'a well of living water'. The garden isn't for any Tom, Dick or Harry to come and enjoy for just 'one night of love'—and when that happens the ravaged garden and the one who ravages it are equally damaged—even if they are consenting adults. The garden in all its beauty and potential creativity is for one man alone.

SHE and HE together have become a revelation of the glory of God, whose name and nature is Love. Love doesn't float around in the sky like a pink cloud, because it happens between persons. George Knight, in his lovely commentary on this book, says that for all their deep probing into human nature the Greeks could never have written the Song of Songs: 'They loved love and worshipped beauty—both of which are mere abstractions. The covenant people knew the joy of loving a *person*.' And in that joy-giving love between a man and a woman (both of them equally loving and passionate) which the Song describes so beautifully, Jews and Christians have always seen a reflection of the love between God and us.

To think about

Then he showed me the river of the water of life, bright as crystal, flowing from the throne of God and of the lamb . . .

Revelation 22:1

SB

Different

Awake, O north wind, and come, O south wind! Blow upon my garden, let its fragrance be wafted abroad. Let my beloved come to his garden, and eat its choicest fruits.

I come to my garden, my sister, my bride, I gather my myrrh with my spice, I eat my honeycomb with my honey, I drink my wine with my milk.

Eat, O friends, and drink: drink deeply, O lovers!

SHE is inviting HIM to know HER, in the way that Genesis 4:1 speaks of Adam knowing his wife Eve. This invitation is as far as the east is from the west as a merely sexual offer of a female body to a male.

It is about the deep, mysterious knowing that a man and a woman can have of each other—and the awfulness, holy dread fascination (and fun and delight) of encountering the 'other' 'flesh of my flesh and bone of my bone'—but different, just as God and human beings are different. And the difference and the otherness offers the greatest possibility for creative union.

Spirit can totally indwell and infuse matter, just as fire can totally inter-penetrate iron. The fire is still fire and the iron is still iron, but it is aglow with the fire, in what Charles Williams called the doctrine of co-inherence.

God does desire to penetrate us, and to enter us, and in *That Hideous Strength* C.S. Lewis said that in relation to God we are all female. But the God who desires to enter and penetrate us, made his image and likeness known by creating us male and female. The creativity between the sexes shows us just a faint glimpse of the love of God and the vast creativity which flows out of that love. As well as that, a woman always has some of the so-called masculine qualities within her (what Jung called her *animus*), and a man some feminine qualities (his *anima*) and we do our own individual acts of creation in a union of both: the drive and initiative of 'fathering', plus the wisdom and receptiveness of 'mothering'.

SB

My friend

I adjure you, O daughters of Jerusalem, if you find my beloved, that you tell him I am sick with love.

What is your beloved more than another beloved, O fairest among women? What is your beloved more than another beloved, that you thus adjure us?

My beloved is all radiant and ruddy, distinguished among ten thousand. His head is the finest gold . . . His body is ivory work, encrusted with sapphires. His legs are alabaster columns, set upon bases of gold. His appearance is like Lebanon, choice as the cedars. His speech is most sweet, and he is altogether desirable. This is my beloved and this is my friend . . .

If the person we love goes away, and we don't know why, we are desperate to find them again. And sometimes we involve our mutual friends. 'If you see him, tell him about me . . .' SHE wants them to tell HIM that she is sick with love. They want to know what's so special about HIM, and then SHE launches out on another ecstatic description of what HE is like and how marvellous HE is.

Perhaps, when SHE tells them 'My beloved is all radiant' SHE is saying that HIS love for HER is shining out of HIS face—and probably SHE is radiant with love when SHE looks at HIM. When Moses came down from his encounter with God on Mount Sinai it says that his face shone—so brightly that the Israelites couldn't bear to look at it.

SHE finishes HER description by telling them two beautiful things about HIM which have not always gone together in the relationship between the sexes: 'This is my beloved and this is my friend'.

A thought

It is the God who said 'Let light shine out of darkness,' who has shone in our hearts to give the light of knowledge of the glory of God in the face of Christ.

2 Corinthians 4:6

SB

Married love

I am my beloved's, and his desire is for me. Come, my beloved, let us go forth into the fields, and lodge in the villages; let us go out early to the vineyards, and see whether the vines have budded, whether the grape blossoms have opened and the pomegranates are in bloom. There I will give you my love.

SHE is looking forward to the consummation of the love between HERSELF and HER beloved, and we need to hold on to the fact that in Jewish thought there is no separation between body, soul and spirit. I know Christian men who despise their own physical desires for their wives, and think those desires are defiling and debasing—and they are ashamed when because of the strength of their sexual hunger they have to satisfy them. I know Christian women who have little or no physical desire for their husbands and simply 'put up with it'.

God created us male and female, in the image of and likeness of God, and the earthy and beautiful sex act connects us to both earth and heaven. God intended it that way. He could have made a universe that reproduced itself like amoebae—simply by splitting. But a person (body/soul/spirit) who just 'has sex' with the body does great damage to the rest of the person— because body, soul and spirit are one. It is fascinating that the Puritans were very enthusiastic about married love, and they took their attitude from the Bible.

A prayer

Lord God, you who created us in your image and likeness, male and female, help us to see the likeness between a man and his wife, and Christ and his Church . . . and help us to dare to contemplate the consummation that awaits us.
And I saw the holy city, new Jerusalem, coming down out of heaven from God, prepared as a bride adorned for her husband.

Revelation 21:2

SB

Commitment

Set me as a seal upon your heart, as a seal upon your arm; for love is strong as death, jealousy is cruel as the grave. Its flashes are flashes of fire, a most vehement flame. Many waters cannot quench love, neither can floods drown it. If a man offered for love all the wealth of his house, it would be utterly scorned.

This is perhaps the greatest hymn to love that has ever been written, and it is uttered by a woman. SHE asks HIM to 'take her herself into his very heart and make *her* the seal of their love' (Knight).

The greatest commandment of all is this: '...you shall love the Lord your God with all your heart and all your soul and all your strength and all your mind'— and the Jew was told to bind the words of that on his hand (or arm), rather like a seal.

Real love is a total commitment for ever. It never ends. 'Love is strong as death...'—and even death by crucifixion can't kill it. On the other side of the tomb it meets its disciples, on the resurrection morning and for forty days afterwards. It goes away again, but then, in 'a rush of wind and a dazzle of tongued flames' our Lord the Spirit 'expressed himself toward the flesh and spirit of the disciples' (Charles Williams, *The Descent of the Dove*).

O perfect Love, all human thought transcending.
lowly we kneel in prayer before thy throne,
that theirs may be the love which knows no ending,
whom thou for evermore dost join in one.

O perfect Life, be thou their full assurance
of tender charity and steadfast faith,
of patient hope, and quiet brave endurance,
with childlike trust that fears nor pain nor death.

Grant them the joy which brightens earthly sorrow,
grant them the peace which calms all earthly strife;
and to life's day the glorious unknown morrow
that dawns upon eternal love and life.

Mrs D.F. Gurny

SB

The Song of Songs

This morning when I was having my time of quiet, one of the things on my heart was the final section of notes on the Song, which I planned to write today. When I opened my *Daily Light* I found such a marvellous set of parallel verses from the Song and the rest of the Bible that I thought they would make an absolutely fitting end to these last two weeks, when we have been looking at the love of God for men and women by looking at the love between a man and a woman.

Daily Light was put together and prayed over by the Bagster family nearly a hundred years ago, and ever since Christians have found that their daily reading spoke just the word that they need to hear. So here are the morning readings for 22 September, which sets verses about God and Christ alongside verses about HIM in the Song of Songs

My meditation of him shall be sweet: I will be glad in the Lord.

As the apple tree among the trees of the wood, so is my beloved among the sons. I sat down under his shadow with great delight, and his fruit was sweet to my taste.
For who in the heaven can be compared unto the Lord? who among the sons of the mighty can be likened unto the Lord?

My beloved is white and ruddy, the chiefest among ten thousand.
One pearl of great price.
The Prince of the kings of the earth.

His head is as the most fine gold; his locks are bushy, and black as a raven.
The head over all things.
He is the head of the body, the church.

His cheeks are as a bed of spices, as sweet flowers.
He could not be hid.

His lips like lilies, dropping sweet smelling myrrh.
Never man spake like this man.

His countenance is as Lebanon, excellent as the cedars.
Make thy face to shine upon thy servant.
Lord, lift thou up the light of thy countenance upon us.

References: Psalm 104:34; Song of Songs 2:3; Psalm 89:6; Song of Songs 5:10; Matthew 13:46; Revelation 1:5; Song of Songs 5:11; Ephesians 1:22; Colossians 1:18; Song of Songs 5:13; Mark 7:24; Song of Songs 5:13; John 7:46; Song of Songs 5:15; Psalm 31:16; Psalm 4:6

SB

The God connection

When I want to drill a hole in the outside wall of my house (for a bracket for a hanging basket), or do my ironing in the garden out in the sunshine, the cables on the power drill and the iron are too short. So I use an extension lead—to connect up with the power source. That is what Jesus is for us. The one who makes the God connection for us. And for the next five weeks we are looking at how it happens.

First in a School of Prayer—and prayer is like a telephone line to God. A line that runs through Jesus and is Jesus. 'I am the true and living way to God', he said. He is the way through, and the connection, and he is also God. When we have looked at prayer we look at Jesus' life here on earth as John tells some of it to us in his Gospel. People who met Jesus: Mary and Martha and Lazarus (whom he raised from the dead); and Simon Peter; and Judas (who betrayed him); and the Pharisees. All of them had personal encounters with the living Jesus—and all of them had the choice of letting Jesus be the one who connected them to God (although some rejected him).

Surely it was better for them—to have Jesus there in the middle of them? But according to him it wasn't. 'It is better for you that I go away,' he said to his disciples, 'because if I do not go, the Helper will not come to you. But if I do go away, then I will send him to you' (John 16:7 GNB).

The Helper, who is the Holy Spirit, makes the God connection for us. Not with a long lead that reaches down from heaven into our hearts, so that we connect with a God who is a long way away. The Holy Spirit of Jesus comes to live in our hearts—and that means in the hearts of all of us who say 'Yes' to his love for us and accept the forgiveness he offers us. It is 'better' that Jesus went away, because now he is here for all of us through all the ages.

> **God's plan is to make known his secret to his people, this rich and glorious secret which he has for all peoples. And the secret is that Christ is in you, which means that you will share in the glory of God. So we preach Christ to everyone. With all possible wisdom we warn and teach them in order to bring each one into God's presence as a mature individual in union with Christ.**

Colossians 1:27–28 (GNB)

Only by prayer

'Teacher, I brought you my son, who is possessed by a spirit that has robbed him of speech . . . I asked your disciples to drive out the spirit, but they could not.' 'O unbelieving generation,' Jesus replied, 'how long shall I stay with you? How long shall I put up with you? Bring the boy to me' . . . [He] rebuked the evil spirit, 'You deaf and dumb spirit,' he said, 'I command you, come out of him and never enter him again.' The spirit shrieked, convulsed him violently and came out. The boy looked so much like a corpse that many said, 'He's dead.' But Jesus took him by the hand and lifted him to his feet, and he stood up.

Now heading up 'Springboard', the Archbishops' initiative for the Decade of Evangelism, Canon Michael Green was for many years in parish ministry—and as part of that ministry, involved in the deliverance from the occult. He possesses the gift of 'discernment of spirits' (1 Corinthians 12:10) and it is accompanied by a certain physical sensation. 'I felt it first in Ghana,' he writes, 'when somebody fainted across me at the moment of commitment to Christ: a feeling of intolerable evil led me simply to call on the name of Jesus again and again. The person revived and is a bold and dynamic Christian worker today . . . The most sensational and one of the earliest experiences I had was when entering a room where a possessed person was standing (and raving). The person screeched aloud and shrank to the wall . . . I felt an immediate, almost palpable sense of evil, went up to the person and commanded the evil thing that was causing the trouble to name itself. This it did, to my great surprise. Then, having nothing but the Gospels to go on, I commanded it by name to come out. It did—and the person crashed to the ground!' (*I Believe in Satan's Downfall*, Hodder & Stoughton, 1981, page 133).

The disciples hadn't managed to drive out the spirit and they asked Jesus why. The answer was that 'This kind can come out only by prayer.' But it doesn't say that Jesus took time out to pray. He cast out the demon at once. The prayer would have been the ongoing, intimate spiritual relationship which he had with his Father. The prayer of relationship enables us to get the prayer of intercession right—in accordance with the will of God.

SB

Prayer is relating

Most people who are fortunate enough to make a trip to Israel find themselves enrolling for a school of prayer in that the teaching of Jesus, indeed, of the entire Bible, seems to come to life in a new way. That has certainly been my experience. I think, for example, of the afternoon when my husband and I were travelling on an over-crowded bus near the Sea of Galilee. On the seat near where I stood, a little Jewish boy was sitting on his father's knee. I watched while he looked up into his father's face stroked his cheek, whispered, 'Abba', and then snuggled into his father's arms where he fell asleep.

As I gazed at the touching scene, my mind went to that occasion I described in my introduction—when Jesus' disciples begged him, 'Lord, teach us to pray'— and to Jesus' reply: 'When you pray say, Father...' In Aramaic, as in modern Hebrew, the word for 'father' is that word I had heard the small boy use: 'Abba', 'daddy'.

There on the bus, the proverbial penny dropped as I realized that, in inviting the disciples to address God as Father, Jesus was implying that true prayer begins with the kind of closeness to God this small boy was enjoying with his father. The disciples had seen for themselves that Jesus enjoyed this one-ness with God, but it would not have occurred to them that they could also approach their Creator in this way. Although the prophets had spoken of the father-hood and motherhood of God, nowhere in Jewish literature did anyone address God as Father or Mother. On the contrary, God was addressed as a remote figure, awesome in holiness, unapproachable in splendour and majesty, a wrathful Judge whose name was so sacred it could not be written, let alone spoken.

Homework

Although many of us were taught the Lord's Prayer when we were children, and although we know in our heads that we can call God 'Father' deep down many of us fear that God is a stand-offish, distant being. Think about your own prayers. How do you address God? As 'Father'? In some similar way? Or with words which reflect fear of him rather than adoration?

A prayer

Father, teach me to relate to you as Jesus did—as one who knows they can enjoy closeness to you.

JH

69

Prayer is trusting

A Chinese boy once told me how he felt when he first believed that God is a God of love. 'It was such a relief,' he said. 'I had been brought up to believe in many gods—all hostile. They needed to be placated with food and money otherwise they would be angry. But now I know that God loves me. It's marvellous.'

That young man, although he had only been a Christian for a few months, had learned a lesson all pupils in the school of prayer must grasp—the reason why Jesus instructed his disciples 'When you pray... pray along these lines: "Our Father in heaven..."' (Matthew 6:8–9). Jesus wanted to assure his disciples that the one to whom they prayed was not the distant, unapproachable being they feared him to be. He is the heavenly Father the psalmist and the prophets so frequently referred to—the trustworthy, caring one:

'As a father has compassion on his children, so the Lord has compassion on those who fear him' (Psalm 103:13).

'When Israel was a child, I loved him, and I called my son out of Egypt... I myself taught Ephraim to walk, I myself took them by the arm, but they did not know that I was the one caring for them, that I was leading them with human ties, with leading strings of love, that, with them, I was like someone lifting an infant to his cheek, and that I bent down to feed them' (Hosea 11:1).

'As a mother comforts her child, so will I comfort you...' (Isaiah 66:13).

Homework

Re-read the verses I have quoted. Then take a piece of paper and divide the page into two. On one side write the heading 'Earthly father and mother'. In this column list words which describe your mother and father. Head the other column 'Heavenly Father'. Write down words which you would use to describe the God of the verses we have read.

A prayer

Father in heaven, when the thought of you wakes in our hearts, let it not wake like a frightened bird that flies about in dismay, but like a child waking from its sleep with a heavenly smile.

Søren Kierkegaard

JH

Prayer is being loved

True prayer begins with intimacy with God. That is the first lesson we learn in the school of prayer. The second is that this God is utterly trustworthy. When, like the Chinese boy I mentioned yesterday, we find ourselves trusting in the innate goodness of God and when the bottom line of our faith assures us that he is love, then prayer becomes the place where we rest and luxuriate in the love of our heavenly Father. The psalmist seems to have discovered this. He could testify: 'I have held my soul in peace and in silence as a child in its mother's arms' (Psalm 131:2).

For Jesus, too, prayer was the place where he experienced his Father's never-failing love. At the beginning of his public ministry this became evident when, having descended into the waters of baptism, he emerged to hear his Father announce: 'This is my Son, whom I love; with him I am well pleased' (Matthew 3:17). Again, towards the end of his public ministry, we see him in the Garden of Gethsemane being crushed almost to death by sorrow and we hear him screaming out: 'Abba, Father ...' In response: 'An angel from heaven appeared to him and strengthened him' (Luke 22:43).

Jesus clearly longs that we should similarly experience the joy of being loved by God. So he offers us an invitation: 'Come to me, all you who labour and are overburdened, and I will give you rest' (Matthew 11:28).

'Come with me by yourselves to a quiet place and get some rest' (Matthew 6:31).

So the third lesson to learn is that prayer means being loved by God and resting in that love.

Homework

Think of an occasion when you have seen or felt a child kicking and screaming in the arms of a parent who was trying to cuddle it. Aware that even the most loving father and mother cannot hold and caress such a child, ask God to show you whether you are behaving similarly towards him—whether you have fallen into the trap many people fall into: because they do not love God very much, they believe that he does not love them very much.

A prayer

Father, may I rest in you alone. May If ind in you my source of hope, my safety and my glory.

My adaptation of Psalm 62:5–6

JH

Praying is worshipping

I once watched an elderly lady completely caught up in the worship of God as she sang the chorus: 'Then sings my soul, my Saviour God to Thee, How great Thou art, how great Thou art.' As the hymn continued, my eyes travelled from the wrinkle faced woman to a little girl who was sitting in front of her. She, too, seemed lost in wonder, love and praise. As I watched, some words of the prayer Jesus taught us came rushing into my mind: 'This, then, is how you should pray: "Our Father in heaven, hallowed be your name" ' (Matthew 6:9).

The word 'hallowed' is usually translated 'holy'. It really means different or separate. So Jesus seems to be suggesting that, when we pray, we should treat God's name differently from other names, giving it a unique place in our thinking. But the word 'name' which he uses means far more than our normal usage of that word—actual names like Jane or John. It means the personality or character. If we put these two sets of instructions together, we are faced with the challenge to give to God the unique place in our thinking and affections which his personality and nature deserve. In other words, Jesus seems to be spelling out the fact that to pray is to worship.

Such worship is only possible for those in whom the Holy Spirit is at work. It is he who lights within our hearts the flame of love which results in us reverencing, admiring and adoring God and abandoning ourselves to him. It is he who ignites our spirit with the divine fire which gives rise to the desire to proclaim the splendour and wonder and beauty of the Living God—to declare his worth-ship.

Homework

Paul claims: 'The Holy Spirit helps us . . . in our praying. For we don't even know . . . how to pray as we should; but the Holy Spirit prays for us with such feeling that it cannot be expressed in words' (Romans 8:26–27). Since the Holy Spirit's role is so important, ask God to in-breathe you afresh with that prayer-giving Spirit.

A prayer

Breathe on me, Spirit of Jesus
Fill me again, Holy Spirit of God.

JH

72

Prayer is surrendering to God

Evelyn Underhill once claimed that worship involves both coming to adore God's splendour and flinging ourselves and all we have at his feet. In other words, worship begins with delighting in God and being assured that he delights in us even more than a good mother delights in her baby or than a lover delights in the beloved. It goes on to abandon oneself to God. Jesus sums up this dimension of prayer this way:

'This, then, is how you should pray: hallowed be your name, your kingdom come—your will be done on earth as it is in heaven' (Matthew 6:9).

Some Bible commentators suggest that here we see Jesus using a very familiar Hebrew teaching technique—saying everything twice. First expressing a concept one way, then, by way of explanation, repeating it using different words. If this is what Jesus is doing, it would appear that he is exhorting us, not only to worship his heavenly Father with our lips but to worship him with our lives by handing over to him our will, heart, life—everything we have and are. He goes further, claiming that wherever and whenever his will is done, his kingdom is furthered.

Through John, Jesus puts it this way: 'Look, I am standing at the door, knocking. If one of you hears me calling and opens the door, I will come in to share a meal at that person's side' (Revelation 3:2). Although, for much of the time, we remain lukewarm and inattentive to his love, God continues to woo us and to invite us to an intimacy symbolized by a meal-for-two where we and he will not be separated by a table but will sit 'side by side' just as John and Jesus did at the Last Supper.

Homework

True prayer is not about us bending God's will but about us bringing our will in line with his. Ask yourself whether you can pray the most important prayer a Christian can ever pray—'Your will be done.'

A prayer

Take me and all I have, do with me whatever you will. Send me where you will. Use me as you will. I surrender myself and all I possess, absolutely and entirely, unconditionally and forever, to your control.

Jim Borst, *Coming to God*

JH

Prayer is asking

'This, then, is how you should pray... Give us today our daily bread...
Ask, and you will be given what you ask for... For everyone who asks,
receives... If a child asks his father for a loaf of bread, will he be given a
stone instead? If he asks for fish, will he be given a poisonous snake? Of
course not! And if you hardhearted, sinful men know how to give good
gifts to your children, won't your Father in heaven even more certainly
give good gifts to those who ask him for them?'

I was in the middle of typing those promises when a friend telephoned. 'It's such a mystery,' she said when she told me how ill she has been. 'I've prayed and friends have prayed and nothing seems to happen. What's gone wrong?' Many people would sympathize with my friend's frustration. They read Jesus' promises and James' rebuke, 'the reason you don't have what you want is that you don't ask God for it,' (James 4:2) and they protest: 'But we have asked.'

The secret lies in Hebrews 7:25. There we are told that Jesus 'always lives to intercede' for us. Since Jesus is praying for us day and night, whenever we pray for anyone or anything we need to make sure that our prayer is brought in line with the prayer Jesus is praying in the same situation. Listening and asking go together. For example, before we beg God to heal someone, we need to discover whether that is what Jesus is praying for.

Take my friend, for example. Although she has received only a fraction of the healing she would like, she freely testifies that through her illness God has enriched her life through the generosity of friends and by showing her a dimension of his love she had never encountered before. She has also discovered, for the first time in her life, how to be still, not simply to know about God but to meet him. Pain, for her, has been the avenue along which God has walked to greet and touch her and bring about a greater wholeness.

A way to pray

*Think of someone for whom you have
been praying. Ask God to show you what
he is praying for in this situation.*

JH

74

I want to see

Then they came to Jericho. As Jesus and his disciples, together with a large crowd, were leaving the city, a blind man, Bartimaeus . . . was sitting by the roadside begging. When he heard that it was Jesus of Nazareth, he began to shout, 'Jesus, Son of David, have mercy on me!' Many rebuked hm and told him to be quiet, but he shouted all the more, 'Son of David, have mercy on me!' Jesus stopped and said, 'Call him.' So they called to the blind man, 'Cheer up! On your feet! He's calling you.' Throwing his cloak aside, he jumped to his feet and came to Jesus. 'What do you want me to do for you?' Jesus asked him. The blind man said, 'Rabbi, I want to see.' 'Go,' said Jesus, 'your faith has healed you.' Immediately he received his sight and followed Jesus along the road.

In my church there is a man of 85 years old who was a distinguished surgeon at a famous London hospital. A lifetime of healing—superb diagnosis, accurate incisions, delicate stitching—and to do that he had to see clearly. Now he can hardly see at all. Not even to read his beloved Bible, that he has studied and delighted in for the whole of his life. He has prayed just as Bartimaeus prayed: 'Lord, I want to see.' But he can't. Neither can thousands of other blind people—men and women. Victims of bilharzia and other water-related diseases (80 per cent of all blindness in Africa comes from water-related diseases). The many Christians among the blind may have prayed Bartimaeus' prayer: 'Lord, I want to see . . .' and Jesus said to Bartimaeus, 'Your faith has healed you.'

So is their trouble their lack of faith? Some would say 'yes'. But that is a hopeless answer which gives the sufferer a deep sense of guilt. When the answer to our prayers is 'No', then the way to pray is to tell God of our pain, our desolation and our deep disappointment. Then God in Christ who knew the deepest dereliction of the human spirit in the agony of the cross, will be there for us, and with us. He knows what it is not to know the answers: 'My God, my God, why . . .?'

SB

Prayer is listening

Listening prayer and asking prayer form two sides of the same coin. Those who are developing the kind of intimate, trusting, loving relationship with God we have been thinking about over the past few days find themselves close enough and attentive enough to him to hear his still, small, voice. That is important because God begs us to tune into his voice. Through Moses he says: 'You have today made this declaration about the Lord; that he will be your God, but only if you follow his ways... and listen to his voice' (Deuteronomy 26:16). Through the psalmist he urges: 'Be still, and know that I am God' (Psalm 46:10).

At Jesus' transfiguration he again reminds us of the importance of listening to his Son: 'Jesus took Peter, James and John with him and led them up a high mountain, where they were all alone. There he was transfigured before them. His clothes became dazzling white, whiter than anyone in the world could bleach them. And there appeared before them Elijah and Moses, who were talking with Jesus... Then a cloud appeared and enveloped them, and a voice came from the cloud: "This is my Son, whom I love. Listen to him!"' (Mark 9:2–4, 7).

God speaks in a whole variety of ways. Through the Bible, through notes like these, through creation, through other people. The psalmist became skilled in learning the vocabulary of creation: 'The heavens are telling the glory of God; they are a marvellous display of his craftsmanship. Day and night they keep on telling about God. Without a sound or word, silent in the skies, their message reaches out to all the world' (Psalm 19:1–4).

Jesus could insist on the importance of listening to God because he, himself, knew how to listen to his Father. So much so that he could claim: 'The words I say are not my own but are from my Father who lives in me. And he does his work through me' (John 14:10).

Homework

Think of a time when you sense you have heard God speak to you—through the Bible, through nature, through a sermon or a friend or in some other way. Thank him.

A prayer of Samuel

'Speak, Lord, for your servant is listening.'

Samuel 3:10

JH

Prayer is helplessness

Last week we examined a little of Jesus' teaching on prayer. This week, we continue to learn from his teaching, look at the way he responded to people's prayers and watch him at prayer. For Jesus and others in New Testament times, prayer was often an admission of helplessness laced with the belief that God can and will do something about it. This was the way Mary prayed at the wedding in Cana. When the caterers ran out of wine, Mary came to Jesus and simply whispered a statement of fact: 'They have no more wine' (John 2:3). This five-word prayer could have been condensed into the one word 'Help!' It triggered off the first public miracle performed by Jesus.

Luke shows that the prayer of helplessness can sometimes be completely wordless. He tells of an occasion when an elderly woman who had been haemorrhaging for years crept up behind Jesus and stealthily touched the edge of his robe. 'Immediately her bleeding stopped' and Jesus admitted: 'I know that power has gone out from me' (Luke 8:44, 46). 'Then the woman, seeing that she could not go unnoticed, came trembling and fell at his feet. In the presence of all the people, she told why she had touched him and how she had been instantly healed. Then he said to her, 'Daughter, your faith has healed you. Go in peace' (Luke 8:47–48).

The prayer of helplessness was a method of prayer Jesus himself used. We hear him resorting to this kind of prayer at the grave of his friend Lazarus. He knew that he was about to perform the most astonishing miracle of his life— bringing someone back from the dead. Before he spoke to Lazarus, he just cried out to his Father: 'Jesus looked up and said, "Father..."' (John 11:41). Perhaps he was also saying 'Help!'

Homework

Think of occasions when you have simply said the equivalent of 'Help' to God. Recall the way in which he came to your rescue.

A way to pray

Think of personal, international or local matters about which you feel helpless at the moment. Then practise the prayer of helplessness by simply holding the situation in the presence of God, believing that he knows how best to act in the circumstances and that he will make himself; his power and his love known.

JH

Prayer is loving

Henri Nouwen once wrote to those who keep a prayer journal: 'Our journal must reflect a "global consciousness", ears that hear the sobbing moan of the world's hungry, that reflect that pigs in Indiana have superior housing to a billion humans on this planet.'

Jesus' teaching and prayer practice persuade us of the truth of this claim. 'This, then, is how you should pray: "*Our* Father in heaven... Give *us* today *our* daily bread"' (Matthew 6:9, 11 italics mine). In other words, although we respond to Jesus' invitation to go into our room, shut the door and pray in private, we do not beguile ourselves into believing that we can ever pray alone. We are always one tiny part of the great communion of saints who, down the ages and throughout the world, have joined in creating an unending wave of prayer. So we pray, not, my Father but *our* Father, recognizing that we are one small droplet in that great ocean of prayer and praise.

We also pray, not, give me today my daily bread but give us today our daily bread. In other words, prayer broadens our horizons to include the needs of others, gives birth to compassion for their plight and prompts us, where possible, to be the answer to our own prayers by sharing our resources with them. This means that prayer is often costly as it demands of us that we give time, energy, money or resources to those for whom we pray. In the Gospels we see how Jesus prayed his life:

'Jesus called his disciples to him and said, "I have compassion for these people; they have already been with me three days and have nothing to eat. I do not want to send them away hungry, or they may collapse on the way."' The disciples protested that they had only seven loaves and a few small fish between them whereupon Jesus told the crowd to sit on the ground. 'Then he took the seven loaves and the fish... broke them and gave them to the disciples, and they in turn to the people. They all ate and were satisfied' (Matthew 15:32, 36–37).

Homework

Ask God to show you how you can be the answer to the prayers you are praying for others.

A prayer

Keep me, O Lord, from praying selfishly.

JH

Prayer is forgiving

Yesterday we observed that, in the teaching and example of Jesus, true prayer is always translated into action. Nowhere is this brought out more clearly or forcibly than in the prayer we have been studying: the Lord's Prayer. Here Jesus says: 'Pray along these lines... forgive us our sins, just as we have forgiven those who have sinned against us' (Matthew 6:9, 12). The literal translation of this injunction is: 'Forgive us our sins in proportion as we forgive those who have sinned against us.' Jesus goes on to explain precisely what this means in practice: 'Your heavenly Father will forgive you if you forgive those who sin against you; but if you refuse to forgive them, he will not forgive you' (Matthew 7:15). In other words, our forgiveness of others and God's forgiveness of us overlap and intertwine. The one is dependent on the other. If we ask God for forgiveness while we are bearing a grudge or harbouring resentment against someone, we are wasting our time and our breath. To quote from Jesus' words again: 'If you are standing before the altar in the Temple... and suddenly remember that a friend has something against you, leave your sacrifice there beside the altar and go and apologize and be reconciled to him, and then come and offer your sacrifice to God' (Matthew 5:23–26).

To forgive means, among other things, to set free, to let go of resentment or bitterness or hatred. When someone has hurt us or let us down, not once, but over a period of time, it is not always easy to forgive. It may have to happen in stages. The first stage is to remember the hurt as vividly and accurately as possible. And the second stage is to recollect that there is a sense in which we have every right to punish the person for the injury they have inflicted. Then comes the third stage: to step out of the realm of rights and into the realm of grace; to let go of the resolve to punish as well as any negative feelings we may have been harbouring. The final stage, if the person is still alive, is to act out the forgiveness in some way which seems appropriate.

Homework

Read Luke 23:32–43, noticing how Jesus puts into practice what he preached.

A prayer

Give me a forgiving heart, O God

JH

Jesus at prayer

For yesterday's project we read Luke's account of that moving moment when Jesus, having been scourged and insulted, condemned to death and led out to Golgotha with two criminals, hung from the cross, gazed at the friends who had turned deserters, his captors and his enemies and cried: 'Father, forgive these people . . . for they don't know what they are doing' (Luke 23:34). In Lent, it seems appropriate to meditate on the way Jesus practised what he preached when he urged his disciples to forgive. But the cross was not the only place from which Jesus forgave people. When he rose from the dead, he appeared to those who must have been smarting under the memory of the way they had failed him. So we find Jesus and Peter together on the sea shore one week after the resurrection. When Jesus most needed Peter's support on the night before his crucifixion, Peter, instead, denied three times that he even knew him. Now, Jesus gives Peter three opportunities to affirm his love for Jesus: ' "Simon, son of John, do you really love me?" "Yes, Lord," Peter said . . . "Then take care of my sheep . . . Follow me" ' (John 21:14–19).

The value of standing on this holy ground where we watch Jesus put his own teaching into practice is that it reminds us that, just as he forgave these people mentioned in the Gospel narrative, so he has forgiven us for the failures of the past and continues to set us free from the sin which would spoil our present relationship with him. This draws from us the longing and the courage to imitate him.

Homework

Think of someone—past or present— who has hurt or offended you in some way. With the memory of the hurt alive on the surface of your memory come, as it were, to the foot of Christ's cross. It might help to kneel in front of a cross or to hold a small cross in your hand. Let surface any bitterness or hatred or resentment have been harbouring against this person. Recognize that, as Jesus hung from the cross, he forgave you. In turn, ask for the grace similarly to forgive.

A prayer

Father, give me the grace to let go of the bitterness and resentment I have been harbouring and so to set . . . free.

JH

80

Praying is being forgiven

If you did yesterday's homework, you may have been brought face to face with your own failure. This might have felt uncomfortable but it will have been important. Because sin is talked about so little today, it is easy for Christians to fall into the trap of believing that they have nothing to confess. Then Jesus' instructions: 'Pray along these lines: "forgive us our sins, just as we have forgiven those who have sinned against us"' (Matthew 6:12) make little sense. When we are aware of our own need for forgiveness, then these words make perfect sense.

The word for 'sin' which Jesus uses here literally means 'debt'—the failure to pay that which is due... And yesterday's homework possibly highlighted the fact that we owe others understanding or love. Maybe we have failed to understand how much they are hurting, how insecure, unloved, lonely or frustrated they feel. Although is does not excuse the behaviour which caused us to be crushed, it does explain it and could help us to be more gracious. The word 'forgive' which Jesus uses means to set free, to let go. The opposite means to cling to, to tie up, to restrict. It is easy so to cling to feelings of bitterness, rage, hatred, resentment, that we restrict communication between ourselves and the person who has hurt us. Church fellowships can be split down the middle in this way—people being polite to each other but refusing to co-operate with each other and therefore restricting the usefulness of others.

Homework

When we become aware that we have failed God we need to come to the cross afresh, confess the failure and go on to receive the cleansing and forgiveness God loves to give. God does not want us to grovel. Neither is there a need to analyse the nature of our failure. It is enough, as someone has put it, to cry, 'Sin! Sin! Sin! Help! Help! Help!' and to enter the welcoming arms of the God who 'is merciful and pardons even those who have rebelled against him' (Daniel 9:9).

A prayer

Heavenly Father... Forgive us all that is past; and grant that we may serve you in newness of life to the glory of your name.

The Order of Holy Communion, ASB

JH

The promise of God

When the people heard this, they were cut to the heart and said to Peter and the other apostles, 'Brothers, what shall we do?' Peter replied, 'Repent and be baptised, every one of you, in the name of Jesus Christ so that your sins may be forgiven. And you will receive the gift of the Holy Spirit. The promise is for you and your children and for all who are far off— for all whom the Lord our God will call.' With many other words he warned them; and he pleaded with them, 'Save yourselves from this corrupt generation.' Those who accepted his message were baptised, and about three thousand were added to their number that day.

Today's passage is a marvellous summary of how to begin the Christian life, and how to go on with it and to live it. We start by repenting—by admitting our sins and by turning our back on them—or at least being willing to; sometimes our sins seem to draw us as powerfully as drugs draw an addict. The power of God, however, is greater than the power of sin, and there is a promise of a powerful helper—God the Holy Spirit—to live in us. But first comes forgiveness, and then baptism, to signify the washing away of sin and the drowning and death of the old life. Perhaps it isn't pushing symbolism too far to think of the water of a new womb for a new birth.

Then comes the gift of the Holy Spirit, which is the gift of God—and the promise running right down the years to us and to our children. We are living in a corrupt generation just as those early disciples were, and equally need to be saved and delivered from it.

Three thousand were saved and delivered on the Day of Pentecost—and then they started to live out the new life within them. The Bible says how they sustained it. 'They devoted themselves to the apostles' teaching and to the fellowship, to the breaking of bread and to prayer . . .' Four things for the Christian to do which are like the four legs of a table—if one goes missing or is shorter than the others, then the table either falls over or has to be propped up. So ask yourself, is the table of your Christian life steady?

SB

The unfeeling Lord

A man named Lazarus, who lived in Bethany, was ill. Bethany was the town where Mary and her sister Martha lived. (This Mary was the one who poured the perfume on the Lord's feet and wiped them with her hair; it was her brother Lazarus who was ill.) The sisters sent Jesus a message: 'Lord, your dear friend is ill.' When Jesus heard it, he said, 'The final result of this illness will not be the death of Lazarus; this has happened in order to bring glory to God, and it will be the means by which the Son of God will receive glory.' Jesus loved Martha and her sister and Lazarus. Yet when he received the news that Lazarus was ill, he stayed where he was for two more days. Then he said to the disciples, 'Let us go back to Judaea.'

When he arrived at Bethany, Jesus was greeted with the news that Lazarus was dead. His deliberate delay must have seemed cruel and heartless. Even we, knowing that he was about to restore his friend to life, may well ask whether the grief caused by that delay was really justified.

Similar things happen everyday. Despite the messages poured out in prayer, people die, disasters occur, and with no miraculous happy ending to sweeten the bitter pill. The doubts Martha and Mary must have felt (does Jesus really love us?) are echoed daily in our own lives. So perhaps Jesus' delay was worth the pain it caused. For in this story he has given us a message about the apparently fatal delays that God still seems to make.

From the sisters' viewpoint, and from ours, all was tragedy. But for Jesus, sharing the eternal view of God, death was only sleep—a rest on the way into eternal life. Lazarus was the friend of Jesus, who is the giver of eternal life. Jesus' friends cannot truly die and, to prove that, he brought Lazarus back to life again—for a while. But physical death, and true life, would still come to him eventually.

Meditate

I am the resurrection and the life. Whoever believes in me will live, even though he dies; and whoever lives and believes in me will never die. Do you believe this?

John 11:25–26

MM

God's last word

Many of the people who had come to visit Mary saw what Jesus did [raise Lazarus from death], and they believed in him. But some of them returned to the Pharisees and told them what Jesus had done ... One of them, named Caiaphas, who was High Priest that year, said, 'What fools you are! Don't you realize that it is better for you to let one man die for the people, instead of having the whole nation destroyed?' Actually, he did not say this of his own accord; rather, as he was High Priest that year, he was prophesying that Jesus was going to die for the Jewish people, and not only for them, but also to bring together into one body all the scattered people of God. From that day on the Jewish authorities made plans to kill Jesus.

Jesus had demonstrated power which could only have come from God. So the rulers decided to kill him. Strange? Not really. They knew where they were as things stood. But with Jesus around, things were bound to change. Perhaps the Romans would see this as the beginning of rebellion. Perhaps the people would reject the rulers they had and follow Jesus. Faced with worries like that, the power of God was a threat to be got rid of.

Many people still see Jesus as a threat. I remember a young couple who were very impressed with our church, and came regularly. But then they stopped. 'This type of religion asks for too much,' they said. 'We don't want to change.' Jesus offers more than we can imagine, but he also threatens us with change. For some, that is too much.

So the high priest decided to kill Jesus 'for the sake of the nation' (and where have we heard that one before?). But God would have the last word. Jesus was indeed going to die for the nation, but not as a convenient political sacrifice. He was going to die as the Lamb of God who takes away the sins of the world.

A prayer

God, make me unafraid of change. Give me the grace to welcome all that you have to offer, and do with me as you will.

MM

Dangerous company

A large number of people heard that Jesus was in Bethany, so they went there, not only because of Jesus but also to see Lazarus, whom Jesus had raised from death. So the chief priests make plans to kill Lazarus too, because on his account many Jews were rejecting them and believing in Jesus.

Earlier in the Gospel (chapter 9) Jesus healed a blind man. The blind man was thrown out of the synagogue for refusing to deny Jesus. Now Lazarus is in danger because he has received help from Jesus. Jesus, it seems, is dangerous company. Certainly that is what John wants us to realize. Following Jesus can mean getting into trouble.

Through history, and today in many parts of the world, being a Christian can be dangerous. Persecution can be religious, when members of other faiths feel threatened; or political, when Christians feel called to oppose what they see as injustice; or personal, when people react against someone who is 'different'.

In Britain, following Jesus rarely brings physical threats, but it can still feel uncomfortable. We are used, on the whole, to a safe and secure life, so it can come as a shock to find that if we are willing to stand up and let our faith be known, we are liable to be mocked or avoided. There is always the temptation to be quiet about it and not to let ourselves be seen as different. Perhaps Lazarus wished it was possible for him to be quiet about what had happened to him, but I doubt it. Jesus had done something truly marvellous, and my own suspicion is that Lazarus was quite happy to let it be known—even if it was dangerous.

The point is that as we become more aware of what Jesus has done for us, we care less and less about what other people think about us. So when we get worried about the cost of following Jesus, the answer is to meditate more on what he has done.

Think

What problems has your faith caused for you? How did you respond? Pray for all those who find Jesus' company dangerous.

MM

The way of life

'Do not be worried and upset,' Jesus told them. 'Believe in God and believe also in me. There are many rooms in my Father's house, and I am going to prepare a place for you. I would not tell you this if it were not so. And after I go and prepare a place for you, I will come back and take you to myself, so that you will be where I am. You know the way that leads to the place where I am going.' Thomas said to him, 'Lord, we do not know where you are going; so how can we know the way to get there?' Jesus answered him, 'I am the way, the truth, and the life; no one comes to the Father except by me.'

Thomas was right, of course. Jesus was speaking about his death, and no one knows where that path leads. For us in this life, death is the final barrier along our way. It stands like a great wall in front of us. We do our best to ignore it, and forget it as quickly as we can once we have seen it—because it is a terrible mystery.

When I am called on to talk to people who have been bereaved, that mystery is one of the things which makes their feeling of loss so terrible. There is the sense of grief, of course, but underneath it is the realization that here is something we just cannot deal with ourselves. In the face of death, everyone's self-sufficiency fails.

Jesus had the answer. In effect, he said, 'You can't see the way through that final barrier, but I can. Follow me, and I'll see you through.' Jesus was about to die in order to open up a way through death into eternal life. Without him, death is the final end, the total separation from the life of God. With him, it is the gateway into the glory of God himself.

A prayer

Lo, Jesus meets us,
Risen from the tomb,
Lovingly he greets us,
Scatters fear and gloom
Let the church with gladness
hymns of triumph sing
For her Lord now liveth;
death hath lost its sting.

Edmond Budry

MM

Spiritual hygiene

Simon Peter answered, 'Lord, do not wash only my feet then! Wash my hands and head, too!' Jesus said, 'Anyone who has had a bath is completely clean and does not have to wash himself, except for his feet. All of you are clean—all except one' (Jesus already knew who was going to betray him; that is why he said, 'All of you, except one, are clean.')

Where I live, dogs are very popular pets. That's fine, unless you go for a walk at night. In that case, you're more than likely to step in something unpleasant, and then there's a lot of messy foot-scraping to do. It's very like the image Jesus uses here of the Christian life.

When we turn to Jesus, we are set free from our sins. We no longer live a life that is apart from God. We are clean. But all too often, we give in to temptation, and sin in some way or other. It doesn't mean that we no longer belong to God, or that he has turned his back on us, or that we have totally failed him. We are still on his path, but we need to get cleaned up again. Like us, Peter and the other disciples had made a new start in life with Jesus. But they still let him down (Peter was about to deny he even knew Jesus). It wasn't the end, though, because Jesus would forgive them and start again.

It is when we confess our sins and start again that Jesus cleans us up. But it is vital that we do get clean. When we fail to confess our sins, our sense of guilt festers, and it interferes with our prayer and worship. Our Bible reading tails off, and soon God begins to seem distant. We have built a barrier between us and him.

So when you let him down, by doing wrong or failing to do what is right, don't despair but don't ignore it either. Put it right again, and let Jesus wash your feet.

Think

Have you anything hidden away that needs to be brought to God to be put right? If you have, do it now!

MM

Darkness

As soon as Judas took the bread, Satan entered him. Jesus said to him, 'Be quick about what you are doing!' None of the others at the table understood why Jesus said this to him. Since Judas was in charge of the money bag, some of the disciples thought that Jesus had told him to go and buy what they needed for the festival, or to give something to the poor. Judas accepted the bread and went out at once. It was night.

'It was night.' This simple sentence rings full of doom. The powers of darkness are closing in on Jesus, attempting to blot him out. But the doom is not for Jesus, who goes willingly to death in order to defeat evil, but for Judas. He has turned his back on the light and deliberately gone out into the darkness. The picture is a terrible one, as the night engulfs him, and he is lost.

When Jesus was asked who would betray him, he said it would be the one he gave the bread to, and then he offered it to Judas. I can't help seeing one last chance being offered. Judas did not have to take the bread. He did not have to betray Jesus, even at this late stage. But I think it was already too late for him. He had developed the habit of evil.

Every time we choose to do wrong (no doubt saying, 'Just this once!') we turn our backs on the light. It becomes easier and easier to sin. The first theft, lie or deception brings guilt, but the second or third or fourth is done without thinking. So at last, Judas, who has already got into the habit of taking the disciples' money, is prepared to take Jesus' life and 'Satan entered him.' He went out into the darkness. Damnation is not handed out by God so much as bought by us in instalments.

Meditate

There is much evil in the world, and the habit of evil is hard to break. But Jesus has broken the power of evil on the cross. So pray for those who embrace evil, that the grace of God will still embrace them.

MM

Put on love . . .

Put on then, as God's chosen ones, holy and beloved, compassion, kindness, lowliness, meekness, and patience, forbearing one another and, if one has a complaint against another, forgiving each other; as the Lord has forgiven you, so you also must forgive. And above all these put on love, which binds everything together in perfect harmony.

Today is a spelling out of the Christian way of love—the way we live out the love of Christ. We clothe ourselves in love as the outer garment—and underneath we wear the qualities that Christ lived out in his flesh. There is the compassion that has a heart of pity. Christianity brought that quality into the world, and 'it is not too much to say that everything that has been done for the aged, the sick, the weak in body, and in mind, the animal, the child, the woman, has been done under the inspiration of Christianity' (Barclay). The word that Paul uses for kindness can also be used 'of wine which has grown mellow with age, and which has lost its harshness' (Barclay). We love it when someone is kind to us—and a line in a Faber hymn says: 'And the heart of the Eternal is most wonderfully kind'.

Humility is an awareness of our creatureliness—and once we realize it our pride fades away like the morning mist when the bright light of the sun shines on it. If God has made us, and holds us in being, what have we got to be proud of? We can be entranced and delighted and adoring—but not proud. Gentleness is a mixture of strength and sweetness—like a strong, sweet-tempered horse. Patience goes on bearing with people in their prickliness and awkwardness and nastiness—just as the divine patience goes on bearing with them (and us).

Love holds all the qualities together and binds them and us together. Perhaps at the dismissal after the Communion we can remember the qualities of love . . . 'Go in peace, to love and serve the Lord.' When we respond 'In the name of Christ, Amen', we shall be saying 'Yes' to living out the love of Christ in the world . . .

SB

The light of God

For God so loved the world that he gave his only Son, that whoever believes in him should not perish but have eternal life. For God sent the Son into the world, not to condemn the world, but that the world might be saved through him. He who believes in him is not condemned; he who does not believe is condemned already, because he has not believed in the name of the only Son of God. And this is the judgment, that the light has come into the world, and men loved darkness rather than light, because their deeds were evil. For every one who does evil hates the light, and does not come to the light, lest his deeds should be exposed. But he who does what is true comes to the light, that it may be clearly seen that his deeds have been wrought in God.

When my friends come to supper I light my room with the soft glow of candle-light, backed up by the low light of 25 watt bulbs in table lamps. Everything looks beautiful (even us!) because candlelight is a gentle light.

But when I want to clean my house I draw my curtains right back and let the light of day shine into all the hidden places: the corners where the spiders have made their webs and the places under furniture where I discover peanuts and paper-clips.

We see how things really are in a clear, bright light—not in a dim light or in the darkness. So what happens when we come into the light of God? Well, we see ourselves as we really are. We see that we're not very good at loving, even the people we love most, and that we are not what we should be. But we also begin to see God as he really is. It starts to dawn on us, like the warmth of the sun's rising,

that the light shining into our hearts is the light of love. And just as I let the light of day shine into my room when I want to clean it, so does God shine his light into our hearts. He cleans them by forgiving our sins, and then comes and lives in them. So long as we'll come to the light and let him do it.

A prayer

Eternal Light, shine into my heart and let me see myself. Then let me see your glory shining in the face of Jesus Christ.

SB

90

I am the light

Again Jesus spoke to them, saying, 'I am the light of the world; he who follows me will not walk in darkness, but will have the light of life.'

Jesus is speaking to the Pharisees. They were like the people in our reading yesterday, who loved darkness rather than light, because their deeds were evil. They hated the light—and in the darkness of a Friday they put it out. But in the glory of Easter morning the light shone out again—and the risen Christ appeared to his astonished, terrified and delighted followers.

He doesn't appear to us in the same way. But he still calls us to follow him, and he still makes the same promises.

You probably know Holman Hunt's painting 'The Light of the World'. Christ is standing outside a house and knocking on the door. There is no handle on the outside, because if Christ is to go inside the owner of the house will have to open the door and invite him in.

Years ago, when my life was in a dreadful mess and I was deeply unhappy, a curate called John Collins told me about that picture. He said that if I would ask Christ into my heart he would change my life and forgive my sins. So I went home, knelt by my bed, and read out the verse John had given me: 'Behold, I stand at the door and knock; if any one hears my voice and opens the door, I will come in to him and eat with him, and he with me' (Revelation 3:20). Then I prayed, 'Lord, I open the door of my heart now. Please come in.'

I know that he did, because I knew then (with a deep certainty that nothing has ever been able to shake) that God is my Father, that he loves me, and that my sins are forgiven. I have sometimes prayed other prayers since asking Christ to enter rooms in the house of my life that I had kept locked. But that first prayer totally changed my life.

A way to pray

Sit in silence and let the light of Christ shine into your heart—and into every room in the house of your life. Then, if you are willing, invite him to come in—perhaps for the first time, or perhaps into places where you have never allowed him before.

SB

A place for me

'Do not let your hearts be troubled. Trust in God; trust also in me. In my Father's house are many rooms; if it were not so, I would have told you. I am going there to prepare a place for you. And if I go and prepare a place for you, I will come back and take you to be with me that you also may be where I am.'

The disciples know now that Jesus is going away—and he knows that they are troubled. So he speaks to them to comfort them—and what he said to them still comforts people and is often read out at funerals. A Christian man who hadn't very long to live told me once how much he loved this passage

'I look on it rather like this. When I was a boy we came back from New Zealand. I was aged about twelve and my father was looking for a parish. I went straight to a preparatory school and during my first term there he was appointed to a parish in Buckinghamshire. At the end of the term I travelled by train to his new parish—and when I got out at the station there he was to meet me ... and to drive me home. And the home he took me to I had never seen before, but when I got there I was shown up to a room and there were some of my familiar things around me. My father and my mother were there—and that was home. There wasn't a great problem about adjusting at all—and I rather feel that heaven is going to be like that. First of all we shall have our Father and the Lord Jesus Christ there, and that in some

way it will probably be not as unfamiliar as we think. But he will have prepared a place for us and we will know it—as our place' (*Drawing Near to the City: Christians speak about dying*, Shelagh Brown).

A prayer

Lord Jesus, thank you that you have gone to prepare a place for us—and that means a place for me. Thank you that one day you will come and take me there—and that I'll be with you for ever. I shall like that—and I'm looking forward to it. But I'm still frightened of dying. Help me not to be—whenever it happens. Amen.

SB

How can we know?

[Jesus said] 'You know the way to the place where I am going.' Thomas said to him, 'Lord, we don't know where you are going, so how can we know the way?' Jesus answered, 'I am the way and the truth and the life. No one comes to the Father except through me.'

I love the way that Thomas is brave enough to contradict Jesus. 'You know the way to the place where I am going,' says Jesus, and Thomas immediately says, 'How can we? We don't know *where* you are going!' It's a valid point. But if Thomas had really been listening to what Jesus had just been saying, then he would have known. Jesus is going to his Father's house. There are many rooms there (and one of them would be Thomas' room—a place for Thomas). The way into the Father's house is through the Son—and earlier on in John's Gospel Jesus has used the picture of a sheep-fold and a shepherd: 'I tell you the truth, I am the gate for the sheep ... whoever enters through me will be saved. He will come in and go out, and find pasture ... I have come that they may have life, and have it to the full. I am the good shepherd. The good shepherd lays down his life for the sheep' (John 10:7, 9, 11).

The Son who is the good shepherd will give his life for the sheep. But he isn't a dead shepherd or a dead son. He's alive! (They don't know that yet, but they will.) God the Son is the true (not false) and living (not dead) way to God

the Father. Perhaps we don't have to 'be a Christian' to come to God. But whoever comes must know something of the true nature of God—that she or he comes to a God who is loving, merciful and forgiving. No one can thrust into the holy presence of God holding out the entry ticket of their own good life. Merit won't get anyone in. But I believe that the mercy of God will let anyone in who asks for that mercy.

A prayer

Lord Jesus, help me to listen to you—and to ask you questions (like Thomas) when I don't understand (and when perhaps I haven't listened). Thank you that you are the way, the truth and the life—and that you are merciful. Amen.

SB

93

Seeing God

Now it is Philip who isn't understanding Jesus. Philip has been listening, but what Jesus has said is mind-blowing:

'If you really knew me, you would know my Father as well. From now on, you do know him and have seen him.'

What a thing for a Jew to say! That really to know him is also to know God the Father. And not just to know God the Father but to have seen him as well. How can they have seen him? But they want to.

Philip said, 'Lord, show us the Father and that will be enough for us.' Jesus answered: 'Don't you know me, Philip, even after I have been among you such a long time? Anyone who has seen me has seen the Father. How can you say, "Show us the Father"?'

Some rather silly Christians say that we cannot say anything about God, since God is beyond all our understanding and imagining and words cannot describe him. But the Son whom John says is the Word of God had no such hang-ups.

Anyone who has seen me has seen the Father.

Bishop John Robinson once wrote

that in Jesus we can see 'the human face of God'. To know what Jesus is like is to know what God is like. So God sits down at a table and has a party with sinners—and he invites them to a party that is also a wedding. The wedding of his Son to his bride the Church, and the Church is made up of beloved and forgiven sinners. The Son who is also the Shepherd gave his life for them—and the Shepherd is also 'The Lamb of God, who takes away the sin of the world' (John 1:29). One image isn't enough to tell us what God is like. But the one and only Son can tell us—and show us. 'No one has ever seen God; the only Son, who is in the bosom of the Father, he has made him known' (John 1:18 RSV).

A prayer

Father God, I am so glad that you are like Jesus. Jesus, thank you so much for showing us what your Father is like. Amen.

SB

Believe me!

'Don't you believe that I am in the Father, and that the Father is in me? The words I say to you are not just my own. Rather, it is the Father, living in me, who is doing his work. Believe me when I say that I am in the Father and the Father is in me; or at least believe on the evidence of the miracles themselves.'

Jesus is saying a terrible thing. Terrible if it isn't true and terrible if it is. Terrible meaning 'extremely bad' if he is making a false claim about himself. Terrible with the meaning 'awesome' if what he claims is true. But I have never heard anyone say that Jesus was 'bad'. Muslims, who believe that 'there is one God, Allah', put Jesus among their prophets (though less important than Muhammad). They say we have got our belief about Jesus wrong because our Scriptures are corrupted. But those who know about these things say that they are probably the best attested documents in history. It is unreasonable to say that Jesus was a good man who gave us the greatest moral teaching the world has ever known. The Gospel writers don't leave us that option.

We don't have to be able to explain it. We just have to put our trust in Jesus and follow him. We can study his life in the Gospels and reflect on it in the rest of the New Testament. And we shall understand the New even better if we study the Old. It was Jesus' 'Bible', and Luke says that at the start of his ministry he read it out in the synagogue: 'The Spirit of the Lord is on me, because he has anointed me to preach good news to the poor ...' (Luke 4:18).

A reflection

Read again the words from John and from Luke. In silence, let them sink into you. Let them stay inside you—and deepen your faith in Jesus, the Christ (or anointed one) of God and the Son of God.

SB

The wisdom of God

My son, if you accept my words and store up my commands within you, turning your ear to wisdom and applying your heart to understanding, and if you call out for insight and cry aloud for understanding, and if you look for it as for silver and search for it as for hidden treasure, then you will understand the fear of the Lord and find the knowledge of God. For the Lord gives wisdom, and from his mouth come knowledge and understanding.

If we pray for wisdom, God will give it to us. 'If any of you lacks wisdom, let him ask of God, who gives to all men generously and without reproaching, and it will be given him. But let him ask in faith, with no doubting...' (James 1:5–6). Wisdom isn't cleverness. It isn't about being intellectual and passing examinations. It is something far greater and deeper than that. It was through wisdom that God created the world, and later on, in Proverbs, Wisdom says that 'when he marked out the foundations of the earth, then I was beside him, like a master workman; and I was daily his delight, rejoicing before him always, rejoicing in his inhabited world and delighting in the sons of men' (Proverbs 8:29b–31). In the New Testament Christ is 'the power of God and the wisdom of God'—and we too can be given power and wisdom if we pray for it.

A way to pray

Think now of a situation in your life where you really need wisdom. Tell God about it (it can help to write things down) and ask him to give you wisdom. Don't doubt that he will... trust him. Spend a few moments just reflecting about the situation... and when you have an idea or thought, now or later write that down and consider it. The wisdom that made the galaxies and field mice and poplar trees and people will be given to you for your need.

SB

Have faith in me

'I tell you the truth, anyone who has faith in me will do what I have been doing. He will do even greater things than these, because I am going to the Father. And I will do whatever you ask in my name, so that the Son may bring glory to the Father. You may ask me for anything in my name, and I will do it.'

Some people find these words very hard to believe—and they think wistfully, 'If only I had more faith then I would be able to heal the sick and feed the hungry and perform miracles. Whatever I prayed for would happen—if only I had more faith...' And the person feels depressed and a bit feeble. Yet if we add up how many hospitals have been founded and run in the name of Christ, and how many hungry have been fed by Christian organizations, then Christians have done 'more' healings, and fed 'more' people than Jesus did on earth.

We tend to hanker after miracles. And sometimes they happen. But it doesn't seem to be the norm. In yesterday's passage Jesus asks his disciples to believe what he says about his relationship with the Father. But if they can't manage to believe just because of his words then perhaps they can believe on the evidence of the miracles. It's rather like Thomas' encounter with the risen Christ: 'Unless I see the nail marks in his hands and put my finger where the nails were, and put my hand into his side, I will not believe,' he says to the other disciples. A week later Jesus comes and stands among the disciples and invites Thomas to do what he wanted. It doesn't say whether Thomas does it or not. Simply that 'Thomas said to him, "My Lord and my God!" Then Jesus told him, "Because you have seen me you have believed; blessed are those who have not seen and yet have believed"' (John 20:24–29).

A reflection

Jesus says he will do anything that we ask in his name. The key to unlocking that is always to pray 'Your will be done' then it will be—though you pray it for someone else they can resist and refuse both the love and the will of God. 'Do you want to get well?' Jesus asks (John 5:6). What if the answer is 'No'?

SB

Obey me and love me

'If you love me, you will obey what I command. And I will ask the Father, and he will give you another Counsellor to be with you for ever—the Spirit of truth. The world cannot accept him, because it neither sees him nor knows him. But you know him, for he lives with you and will be in you.'

It seems strange to link love with obedience. But in our own culture it happens all the time—though not in the way that Jesus meant it. For us love is about lovely feelings and freedom—and love can be a total dictator. If two people fall in love then love says to them 'You must follow your hearts—and do just what you desire. Don't worry! It doesn't matter that one or both of you are married to someone else. You must obey your instincts and this delicious feeling of falling in love that's washing over you!' And when the feeling stops and they fall out of love (or one of them does) then they obey that feeling as well. Their feelings are in charge of what they do—and they obey the voice of love. But it isn't true love who is speaking to them.

When we love Christ that brings another power and another presence into our lives. The power of the love of God, who knows always what true love has to do in any situation. Instead of Ten Commandments carved on stone they are written on hearts of flesh. Written by the Spirit of God on our hearts, and he can do it because he lives in our hearts. John Powell SJ wrote a lovely book entitled *Happiness is an Inside Job*. So is love—and it is the job of the Holy Spirit of God living within us, Counsellor and Comforter and the Spirit of truth. For those disciples that beautiful indwelling by the God of love lay in the future—but not very far in the future. First, the death and resurrection of Christ, then the pouring out of the Spirit of Christ.

A prayer

Lord, teach me how to pray and how to love. Give me the gift of true love—and give me yourself. I know you love me. And I love you—although my love isn't as passionate as I desire it to be. Show me the way to love.

SB

I will come to you

'I will not leave you as orphans; I will come to you. Before long, the world will not see me any more, but you will see me. Because I live, you also will live. On that day you will realise that I am in my Father, and you are in me, and I am in you.'

As I write these notes the sad little faces of orphaned children look out of our television screens in Britain. There are hundreds of them, in what was once Yugoslavia. The parents who loved them and looked after them are dead—and the people who care for them can never replace their own mothers and fathers.

In the Bible God has a deep compassion for orphans and for widows—and the letter of James says, 'Religion that God our Father accepts as pure and faultless is this: to look after orphans and widows in their distress...' (1:27).

The affliction is that they are not loved and cared for as once they were. The beloved presence has gone away, and the orphans are on their own. But it isn't going to be like that for the followers of Jesus. Neither for the disciples (who had known his physical presence with them) nor for us. 'I will come to you,' Jesus says—and the witness of Christians ever since the beginning has been that he does. An astonishing union and communion takes place. Christ is in the Father, and we are in Christ, and Christ is in us.

A way to pray

O let the Son of God enfold you
With His Spirit and His love,
Let Him fill your heart and satisfy your
soul.
O let Him have the things that hold you,
And his Spirit like a dove
Will descend upon your life and make
you whole.

John Wimber (© Mercy Publishing)

SB

We will come to you

'Whoever has my commands and obeys them, he is the one who loves me. He who loves me will be loved by my Father, and I too will love him and show myself to him.' Then Judas (not Judas Iscariot) said, 'But, Lord, why do you intend to show yourself to us and not to the world?' Jesus replied, 'If anyone loves me, he will obey my teaching. My Father will love him, and we will come to him and make our home with him. He who does not love me will not obey my teaching. These words you hear are not my own; they belong to the Father who sent me.'

Was Jesus saying that before either he or his Father will love us we have to do just what he tells us and also to love him? If he was then the gospel isn't good news. It's bad. Because we'll never manage either the living or the loving on our own. In his brilliant commentary on John's Gospel, William Temple helps us to understand what this difficult passage really means:

'The Father loves all his children with an infinite love, such love as could be expressed only by giving His only-begotten Son. Yet there is a special love also in His heart for those who love that Son. The universal love of God is not a featureless uniformity of good-will. Good-will to all there is; but also for each whatever special quality of love is appropriate to him; and there must be a special quality of love for those who love the Son whom the Father loved before the foundation of the world. The Son Himself, who is the 'express image' of the Father's universal love, has a special quality of love (how could it be other-wise?) for those who love Him in return; and to them He will manifest Himself (*Readings in St John's Gospel*, Macmillan, 1959).

A prayer

Lord God, I thank you for this amazing truth—that you will make your home in my heart. You who created the galaxies, and our world, and me . . . you who are Father, Son and Holy Spirit, Creator and Lover.

SB

The peace of Jesus

'All this I have spoken while still with you. But the Counsellor, the Holy Spirit, whom the Father will send in my name, will teach you all things and will remind you of everything I have said to you. Peace I leave with you; my peace I give you. I do not give to you as the word gives. Do not let your hearts be troubled and do not be afraid.'

The hearts of the disciples *were* troubled—and in view of all the things Jesus had been saying to them it wasn't surprising. He was going away—and they didn't really understand where, even though he told them. And he had spoken of a grain of wheat falling into the ground and dying. It would glorify God in the process and produce many more grains of wheat. But the original grain of wheat wouldn't be there any longer, and neither would Jesus. Not in the same form and not in the same way. No wonder they were troubled. But he knew what was going on in their hearts (he always does) and told them not to be afraid and not to be troubled. They would have a going away present from him. His own special peace. The peace of God which passes all understanding. A peace in which everything is in tune and nothing is out of tune, because all things are in a right relationship with all other things and creatures—and with the Creator God himself That peace wasn't just for those first followers of Jesus. It was for all of us. Paul discovered it—and knew it even in the midst of his suffering:
'Therefore, since we have been justi-

fied through faith, we have peace with God through our Lord Jesus Christ… And we rejoice in the hope of the glory of God. Not only so, but we also rejoice in our sufferings, because we know that suffering produces perseverance; perseverance character; and character, hope. And hope does not disappoint us, because God has poured out his love into our hearts by the Holy Spirit, whom he has given us' (Romans 5:1–5).

A way to pray

Read those verse from Romans slowly—and reflect how one thing leads to another. Is what Paul says true for you?

SB

The way to God

'You heard me say, "I am going away and I am coming back to you." If you loved me, you would be glad that I am going to the Father, for the Father is greater than I. I have told you now before it happens, so that when it does happen you will believe. I will not speak with you much longer, for the prince of this world is coming. He has no hold on me, but the world must learn that I love the Father and that I do exactly what my Father has commanded me. Come now; let us leave.'

Jesus is on his way to the Father. But it will be a terrible journey. The way of sorrows or the *via dolorosa*. What lies ahead is a hideously unjust trial and a hideously unjust death. The evil prince of this world will attack the prince of peace. The one whose name and nature is Abaddon, the destroyer, will try to destroy the Son of God and put out the light of the world.

He won't succeed—but the disciples don't know that yet. They go with him on his way—and as they go he will go on teaching them. Three more chapters that are among the greatest in the whole Bible come between leaving the upper room and the betrayal in the Garden of Gethsemane. But before the resurrection and the pouring out of the Spirit there has to be a death.

A way to pray

Think about Jesus doing exactly what the Father commanded him—and what it cost him. Think about the agony, the death—and then the disciples' desolation. But then think about the wonder of that first Easter morning—and the wonder of Pentecost, when they knew the Christ who died and rose again within their hearts, in the Spirit. Do you know the glory of all those things? If you do, then be thankful...

SB

Death and Resurrection

Six days before the Jewish Passover—and before his own crucifixion—Jesus went up to Jerusalem with his disciples. Some Greeks came up to the disciples with a request, 'Sir,' they said, 'We would like to see Jesus.' Then Jesus spoke about his death.'The hour has come for the Son of Man to be glorified. I tell you the truth, unless an ear of wheat falls to the ground and dies, it remains only a single seed. But if it dies, it produces many seeds . . . Now is my heart troubled, and what shall I say? Father, save me from this hour?' No, it was for this very reason I came to this hour. Father, glorify your name!' Then a voice came from heaven. 'I have glorified it, and will glorify it again.'

The glory of anything is its essential nature shining out of it, and the nature of the God who is love would shine out brighter than the sun through the death of Jesus on the cross. In the next three weeks we shall see the glory of the love of God in the suffering of God-in-Christ. We shall read about those things which are at the heart of the Christian faith. The death on Good Friday—and the resurrection on Easter morning. The words that Jesus had spoken before his death began to make sense. 'I am the resurrection and the life; he who believes in me, though he were dead, yet shall he live, and whoever lives and believes in me shall never die' (John 11:25 RSV).

Those words are often said at a funeral as the minister walks into the chapel in front of the coffin. I have heard them ringing out many times, and sometimes had the privilege of saying them myself when I take the service. For me there is a thrill of glory even in the midst of the sorrow, and a deep awareness of the difference that the death and resurrection of Christ makes to our death. But the desolation of Good Friday comes before the glory of Easter morning, and we shall get to the glory by remembering the agony.

My body and my blood

I have just come back from Holy Communion and am deeply aware, for the thousandth time, of the wonder and superb symbolism of the sacrament that Jesus gave to us. I held out my hands to receive the bread and put it in my mouth. I chewed it, then I swallowed it. After that I drank the red wine from the silver cup. And both the body and blood of Christ became part of my body and blood.

Ever since I set out to follow Christ and invited him to enter my heart, I have believed that he is with me. But this reminder and remembrance is a powerful sacrament of the glory of the Christian life. Paul wrote to the Colossians about the riches of the glory of the mystery which God had made known, 'which is Christ in you, the hope of glory' (1:27). To touch the bread, and to be aware of it becoming part of me as I eat it, and to feel the wine in my mouth, entering me and becoming my being, is a unique strengthening and empowering. The Christ who gave us that sacrament '…opened wide his arms for us on the cross; he put an end to death by dying for us and revealed the resurrection by rising to new life…' (Third Eucharistic Prayer, *ASB*).

One introductory sentence to the *ASB* Communion service comes from Paul's letter to the Philippians: 'It has been granted to us that for the sake of Christ we should not only believe in him,

but also suffer for his sake' (Philippians 1:29).

The Christ who is with us, and in us, shares our suffering—and the bread and the wine in our bodies remind us that we are the body of Christ. Paul says that he received his teaching about Holy Communion direct from the risen Christ.

For I received from the Lord what I also delivered to you, that the Lord Jesus on the night when he was betrayed took bread, and when he had given thanks, he broke it, and said, 'This is my body which is for you. Do this in remembrance of me.' In the same way also the cup, after supper, saying, 'This cup is the new covenant in my blood. Do this, as often as you drink it, in remembrance of me.' For as often as you eat this bread and drink the cup, you proclaim the Lord's death until he comes.

SB

Seeing Jesus

Some Greeks . . . went to Philip . . . and said, 'Sir, we want to see Jesus.'
Philip went and told Andrew and the two of them went and told Jesus.
Jesus answered them, 'The hour has now come for the Son of Man to
receive great glory. I am telling you the truth: a grain of wheat remains no
more than a single grain unless it is dropped into the ground and dies. If it
does die, then it produces many grains. Whoever loves his own life will lose
it; whoever hates his own life in this world will keep it for life eternal.
Whoever wants to serve me must follow me, so that my servant will be
with me where I am. And my Father will honour anyone who serves me.

Did the Greeks get to see Jesus? I'm sure
they did. But they couldn't see him very
clearly, because he had not yet died.
They could see Jesus the prophet and
teacher, Jesus the miracle worker. But to
see Jesus properly, to see his true glory,
we have to see his death. Then we see the
redeeming love of God in action, taking
the sins of human beings into itself, and
opening the way to eternal life. That is
why, in this Gospel, the cross is often
described as Jesus' glory.

It doesn't stop there, though. The
cross is not just something that happened to Jesus, but the pattern for our
lives. Jesus died to rise again to greater
glory, and in the same way, *we* have to be
ready to let our old lives, our old ways of
looking at the world, and of living for
ourselves, die as well. Then we can enter
into the new life that Jesus promises, and
in which we can see clearly who he is,
and what he has done for us.

A prayer

*Give me grace, Lord, to see you as you
are, and let the glory of the cross invade
and shape my life.*

MM

Love's extravagance

Six days before the Passover, Jesus went to Bethany, the home of Lazarus, the man he had raised from death. They prepared a dinner for him there, which Martha helped to serve; Lazarus was one of those who were sitting at the table with Jesus. Then Mary took half a litre of a very expensive perfume made of pure nard, poured it on Jesus' feet, and wiped them with her hair. The sweet smell of the perfume filled the whole house. One of Jesus' disciples, Judas Iscariot—the one who was going to betray him said, 'Why wasn't this perfume sold for three hundred silver coins and the money given to the poor?' He said this, not because he cared about the poor, but because he was a thief. He carried the money bag and would help himself from it. But Jesus said, 'Leave her alone! Let her keep what she has for the day of my burial. You will always have poor people with you, but you will not always have me.'

There are times when love leads to grand, extravagant gestures. 'I know I can't afford it, but...' Here Mary's love bursts out in the apparent waste of using expensive perfume to wash Jesus' feet. It raises the question which is still with us—is it better to spend money on Jesus directly, or to use the money for the good works Jesus tells us to perform?

Jesus doesn't answer the question. Instead, he takes the act as it was intended and more. Mary has been saving the perfume for a special occasion, and Jesus sees an unconscious prophecy of the anointing of his body for burial.

I think that it is Mary's love which answers Judas' question. What she did may or may not have been wise, but it sprang from an overwhelming love of Jesus. If we can say the same of our actions, we can be pretty sure that Jesus will accept them as they are meant.

A prayer

Lord Jesus, give me grace to love you without calculation, and to give to you without thought of reward, so that whatever others may say, my deeds will be for you alone.

MM

The sign of the kingdom

After Judas had left, Jesus said, 'Now the Son of Man's glory is revealed; now God's glory is revealed through him. And if God's glory is revealed through him, then God will reveal the glory of the Son of Man in himself, and he will do so at once. My children, I shall not be with you very much longer. You will look for me; but I tell you now what I told the Jewish authorities, "You cannot go where I am going." And now I give you a new commandment: love one another. As I have loved you, so you must love one another. If you have love for one another, then everyone will know that you are my disciples.'

Like Orthodox Jews today, the Jews of Jesus' day prided themselves on keeping the Law of God, the Torah. It was an act of obedience to God, and at the same time it was a sign to outsiders that here were the people of God. The most obvious signs (and the ones which almost all Jews stressed the most) were keeping the Sabbath, circumcision and food laws. These built a barrier around the chosen people and marked them out as special.

Christians soon dropped these signs, partly because they were a barrier that kept people out as well as a badge of belonging to God. But that didn't (and still does not) mean there was no way of telling who belonged to Jesus. There was one new law which all Christians must keep—to love. Of course, all the Jewish teachers would agree that love was the sign of God, but Jesus made it the *only* sign by which his people would be known to outsiders. It was the commandment which summed up all the others. If you want to see a follower of Jesus, look for love.

It's a tall order, isn't it? And none of us would claim to live up to it. But don't despair. Jesus called us his disciples—and that means 'learners'. A Christian is someone who is learning to love. We often fall down on the job, but as long as we remember what it is we are learning, we won't go too far wrong.

Think

On Jesus' definition, how much evidence is there for your Christianity?

MM

The servant king

So he [Jesus] rose from the table, took off his outer garment, and tied a towel round his waist. Then he poured some water into a basin and began to wash the disciples' feet and dry them with the towel round his waist. He came to Simon Peter, who said to him, 'Are you going to wash my feet, Lord?' Jesus answered him, 'You do not understand now what I am doing, but you will understand later.' Peter declared, 'Never at any time will you wash my feet!' 'If I do not wash your feet,' Jesus answered, 'you will no longer be my disciple.' Simon Peter answered, 'Lord, do not wash only my feet, then! Wash my hands and head, too!'

We all know this story, and we all know its basic point that Jesus sets us the example of humility and service. It is made even more significant when we realize that John does not mention the breaking of bread at the Last Supper where Jesus instituted the Holy Communion (instead, he mentions communion earlier, in chapter 6). So the message is that we who share together in the bread and the wine are to be each other's servants, in all humility.

We know the story well. But it is the hardest lesson to learn. For so many of us, our dignity and status are very important. We want to be looked up to, to be appreciated and respected. But that is really a sign of insecurity. We stand on our dignity because we are unsure of our worth. Jesus had another security. He knew that he was doing God's will, and so needed no other armour. He knew he was loved by God, and that gave him an infinite value just as we have value because God loves us.

And finally, the funny thing is that people who serve and look after the interests of others before attending to their own needs, usually find they are much more appreciated anyway. When my wife started her new job, she was told no to be too familiar with her staff or she would lose discipline. But she didn't take the advice. It seems that a boss who is approachable and caring can be respected too!

Reflect

Whom do you serve—your own pride, or the needs of others?

MM

Good Friday

So they took charge of Jesus. He went out, carrying his cross, and came to 'The Place of the Skull,' as it is called. (In Hebrew it is called 'Golgotha.') There they crucified him; and they also crucified two other men, one on each side, with Jesus between them ... Jesus knew that by now everything had been completed; and in order to make the scripture come true, he said, 'I am thirsty.' A bowl was there, full of cheap wine; so a sponge was soaked in the wine, put on a stalk of hyssop, and lifted up to his lips. Jesus drank the wine and said, 'It is finished!' Then he bowed his head and died.

Good Friday always seems a strange name for the most evil of days. On the face of it, many more evil acts have been committed than the murder of one wandering preacher—but I'm not too sure. Yes, this was an unjust killing and the destruction of a totally sinless person. But it was also the violent rejection of God himself. We may speak theologically of the rejection of God by humankind, but here we see it in all its awfulness, concentrated into one act of torture.

Yet at the same time it is indeed Good Friday, because here God takes on himself all that evil can do, all the concentrated rejection of good which people are capable of, and puts it to death. Jesus stands for us as the focal point of human sin, and takes it all on himself As we look at the cross, we are given a choice: to identify with those who crucify or with him who is crucified. To identify with Jesus is to hand over the burden of our sin, and let it die with him.

So in his apparent defeat, the death of his Son, God is victorious and Jesus is glorified. Life and death, good and evil, have clashed, and life wins—for death is put to death with Christ.

Meditate

See from his head,
his hands, his feet,
Sorrow and love
flow mingled down.
Did e'er such love
and sorrow meet,
Or thorns compose
so rich a crown?

Isaac Watts

MM

The waiting time

Early on Sunday morning, while it was still dark, Mary Magdalene went to the tomb and saw that the stone had been taken away from the entrance. She went running to Simon Peter and the other disciple, whom Jesus loved, and told them, 'They have taken the Lord from the tomb, and we don't know where they have put him!' Then Peter and the other disciple went to the tomb . . . Then the other disciple, who had reached the tomb first, also went in; he saw and believed. (They still did not understand the scripture which said that he must rise from death.) Then the disciples went back home.

Today is a hard day to celebrate. The joyful solemnity of Good Friday, with its blend of pain and victory, is over. Tomorrow we shall break out in joy as we celebrate the resurrection. But today we are in between—rather like the disciples in today's reading. They knew something strange was happening. The disciple Jesus loved (perhaps John, whose teaching lies behind this Gospel) believed—but what? That God was up to something, yes, but that Jesus was triumphant over death? Unlikely. He needed to see more before he could fully understand what Jesus had done, what it was that God had up his sleeve.

He was rather like many people who come to church. They come and enjoy the services, leaving refreshed and perhaps thoughtful, knowing that there is 'something there' but not yet really believing. They are unable to take the vital and decisive step into faith. They can see (probably) that God is up to something. It all begins to show a strange

and exciting pattern, but for them the picture has not yet become clear. They need the final meeting with Jesus. It will come.

Today is the waiting day. Waiting for God to act, for the resurrection light to shine. So today pray for all those who have not yet seen that light, but sense that it is there; for those who are waiting for faith, and who, with the dawning of Easter Day, may meet Jesus for themselves.

MM

A change of landscape

Now on the first day of the week Mary Magdalene came to the tomb early, while it was still dark, and saw that the stone had been taken away from the tomb. So she ran, and went to Simon Peter and the other disciple, the one whom Jesus loved, and said to them, 'They have taken the Lord out of the tomb, and we do not know where they have laid him.' Peter then came out with the other disciple, and they went toward the tomb. They both ran, but the other disciple outran Peter and reached the tomb first.

A friend of mine had a very frightening experience when he was a teenager. Walking home in the dark after a late party, he suddenly became aware that the landscape near his parents' house was 'all wrong'. A field that had been empty twelve hours earlier was now occupied by something that, on that cloudy starless night, appeared to be a castle-like building. Simon stood stock still for a moment as his mind attempted in vain to accommodate this logical impossibility. Then, seized by scalp-prickling horror, he sprinted away to the safety of home, only to learn from his amused parents that the 'castle' was actually a huge marquee, erected for some event on the following day.

Mary's experience was probably worse. The stone was gone, the soldiers were gone and the body was gone. It was *all wrong*, and it must have shaken her up. Mysterious empty tombs on dark nights are the stuff that Hammer films are made of. No wonder she ran to where Peter and John were, gasping out as she arrived the quite reasonable hypothesis that someone had moved the body. What an impact her news made on the disciples!

Bleary-eyed and unwashed, the Steve Ovett and Sebastian Coe of the New Testament hitched their skirts up and gave it everything they'd got. On the final bend John overtook Peter and was first to arrive at the tomb, where, ironically after all that explosive effort, he stopped abruptly and was unable to bring himself actually to enter it. What a tumult of emotions, questions and speculations must have filled the mind and heart of the disciple whom Jesus loved.

A question

Is there anybody or anything in the world or the universe that would make me run like that?

AP

Moments of truth

. . . stooping to look in, he saw the linen cloths lying there, but he did not go in. Then Simon Peter came, following him, and went into the tomb; he saw the linen cloths lying, and the napkin, which had been on his head, not lying with the linen cloths but rolled up in a place by itself. Then the other disciple, who reached the tomb first, also went in and he saw and believed; for as yet they did not know the scripture, that he must rise from the dead.

One of the most significant moments in my life occurred on the top of a double-decker bus when I was about ten years old. That morning I had read the words 'Everyone is I' in some obscure book, and I was frowningly anxious to work out what it meant. As the bus arrived in Tunbridge Wells and stopped at a zebra crossing, I looked down and, seeing an elderly lady making her laborious way from one side of the road to the other, the truth suddenly hit me. That lady was as important to herself as I was to myself. I was not *the* star-player in the universe, and the rest of the world's population were not bit-players in my life. The recognition changed my perception fundamentally.

A much more famous moment of recognition happened when Malcom Muggeridge, feeling cynical and sickened by commercialism and tourist exploitation at the (alleged) scene of Jesus' birth, gradually became aware of the way in which the faces of visiting pilgrims were quite transfigured by the idea that they were in the place where the great life began. Muggeridge saw a vital truth on that day and was deeply affected on a personal level.

Such moments of recognition impart knowledge that cannot be taught in normal ways and they change lives.

Here, in the empty tomb, Peter and John, gaze with growing awareness at the way in which the grave clothes are lying in an undisturbed position, as though the body had melted quietly away. In John's mind at least the awe-inspiring truth chimed like heavenly bells. It wasn't all over. The story was not finished. Somewhere, somehow—Jesus was alive.

A question

Have we told others about the significant moments of recognition in our lives? Perhaps we think they weren't spiritual enough.

AP

Blind grief

But Mary stood weeping outside the tomb, and as she wept she stooped to look into the tomb; and she saw two angels in white, sitting where the body of Jesus had lain, one at the head and one at the feet. They said to her, 'Woman, why are you weeping?' She said to them, 'Because they have taken away my Lord, and I do not know where they have laid him.' Saying this, she turned round and saw Jesus standing, but she did not know that it was Jesus.

Mary must have been pretty tough to withstand the traumas of this extraordinary day. When she got to the tomb, she experienced two encounters that my son would (with typical irreverence) describe as gob-smackers. The first was with the two angels.

When we read that Mary, still weeping, leaned down and saw two angels sitting in the tomb, then had a little chat with them, we tend to forget the drama and tension of the situation. This is partly due to the brevity with which the event is recorded, and partly to the dismal presentation of the Scriptures that we have allowed and endured for generations. Public readings of the Bible have been conducted in tones of such sepulchral monotony for so long now that there is a corporate perception of Biblical characters as two-dimensional, unemotional, cardboard cut-out figures who trot out their appointed lines in semi-anaesthetized voices. This distraught lady must have come very near to braining herself on the roof of the tomb when she saw these two strange figures who'd posted themselves at either end of the place where Jesus' body had lain. Did she know they were angels? I don't know: but such odd behaviour from human beings would have been no less alarming.

Perhaps the strength of grief overpowered fear, though. As soon as it became clear that these two beings knew nothing about the whereabouts of the body, Mary turned away to search elsewhere. How ironic that the angels asked their 'silly' question about why was she weeping because they could see Jesus standing behind her! Her sight was blurred by tears when she turned. She didn't recognize him.

A question

Do we grieve his absence when he stands before us?

AP

113

Getting excited

Jesus said to her, 'Woman, why are you weeping? Whom do you seek?' Supposing him to be the gardener, she said to him, 'Sir, if you have carried him away, tell me where you have laid him, and I will take him away.' Jesus said to her, 'Mary.' She turned and said to him in Hebrew, 'Rab-bo'ni!' (which means Teacher). Jesus said to her, 'Do not hold me, for I have not yet ascended to the Father; but go to my brethren and say to them, I am ascending to my Father and your Father, to my God and your God.'

I have seen films, pictures and mimes of this wonderful encounter, the second and most staggering of Mary's 'gobs-mackers'. In most of these presentations Jesus is standing like some product of the taxidermist's art, stiffly gesturing away a remarkably restrained Mary who has attempted to touch him in an elegant, saint-like manner. If it *really* happened like that let's all give up and go and become frog-worshippers. Chesterton made the point that believers and non-believers alike have great problems about genuinely accepting the fact that 'he became man'. The divine ordinariness of Jesus should be one of our greatest comforts. Instead, it's a serious stumbling-block to many, perhaps because it brings the reality of God so close that we are forced to respond from the heart, rather than from bits of our minds.

Do you really believe that Jesus was not smiling broadly when he asked Mary why she was crying and who she was looking for? Do you really think that Mary *didn't* throw herself at her beloved friend and master after he said her name in a way that was specially his? And do you not think he would have chucklingly retreated with both arms extended as he warned her that she must not touch him because he had not yet ascended to his Father ('not cooked yet' as a small friend put it)?

How we need some of this Mary-style excitement in the modern Church, the kind of excitement that follows real meetings with this real Jesus who is more down to earth than many of his followers.

Can you see her running and leaping, her eyes now wet with tears of joy, on her way to tell the disciples?

A prayer

We want to be excited, Lord.

AP

Who needs who?

On the evening of that day, the first day of the week, the doors being shut where the disciples were, for fear of the Jews, Jesus came and stood among them and said to them, 'Peace be with you.' When he had said this, he showed them his hands and his side. Then the disciples were glad when they saw the Lord. Jesus said to them again, 'Peace be with you. As the Father has sent me, even so I send you.' And when he had said this, he breathed on them, and said to them, 'Receive the Holy Spirit. If you forgive the sins of any, they are forgiven; if you retain the sins of any, they are retained.'

Neither John's perception of the truth, nor Mary's account of that first sparkling meeting, seems to have inspired any courage in the disciples. Here they are on the evening of that same Sunday, securely locked in for fear of the Jewish authorities tracking them down, probably discussing the day's events over and over again, but unable to do anything without the direct leadership and guidance of Jesus.

A lot of prayer-groups, churches and fellowships are in the same position. I've belonged to some of them. I've led one or two of them. Personally, I think it's far better to wait for Jesus to come, than to fabricate or role-play religious activity that is not authorized or commissioned. It's interesting to note that Jesus sends the disciples as he has been sent by the Father. In other words, he is asking for the kind of love and obedience that characterized his own ministry—a tall order for most of us without comfort and assistance of the Holy Spirit. William

Barclay points out how, from this speech, we learn that Jesus needs the Church, and the Church needs Jesus. Our failing groups might do well to abandon religion and invite Jesus to stand in their midst.

Once again the drama of the moment is rather inadequately expressed by the writer's assertion that 'the disciples were glad when they saw the Lord'. I'm quite sure that their responses varied from stunned silence to wild celebratory joy. These people were not stained-glass window types. Jesus was alive—anything was possible.

Questions

Do we believe that Jesus needs us? Do we need him?

AP

Staying honest

Now Thomas, one of the twelve, called the Twin, was not with them when Jesus came. So the other disciples told him 'We have seen the Lord.' But he said to them, 'Unless I see in his hands the print of the nails and place my finger in the mark of the nails and place my hand in his side I will not believe.'

I like the sound of Thomas. He may have been a bit of an Eeyore ('Let us also go, that we may die with him'), but he was honest and straightforward, and more than ready to commit himself when the evidence was clear. We could do with a few more like him in the Church today.

A friend of mine had to attend a foundation course run by a fellowship in the Midlands (attendance was compulsory for all prospective church members). The leader read out 1 John 3:6, and said it meant that anyone who became a Christian would stop sinning. My friend (a Christian for many years) interjected. 'You're not saying, are you, that Christians never sin? Because they do, don't they?'

Reproof, Christian forgiveness, humble disagreement and heavily veiled human annoyance met in the crinkly smile of the leader. 'If that's what the Scripture says,' he replied, 'then that must be the truth, mustn't it?' 'Well, I sin,' said my friend, 'don't you? And anyway, it says later on in the same letter that if we do sin—' 'I think we'd better agree to differ, friend,' interrupted the leader, 'we'll talk about it afterwards, OK?'

They did—and what horrified my friend was that it wasn't just a matter of mistaken teaching.

'Between you and me,' said the leader, 'of course Christians sin, but I didn't want to mislead all those new Christians on the course.'

Maybe Thomas was at fault for going off to be solitary with his grief (I would have missed Jesus' first appearance as well), but he stuck to his guns when faced with the emotional intensity of the others' experience. He wasn't going to say anything he didn't actually believe, however much he wanted it to be true. I like him.

A prayer

Father, help us to be honest and loving like Thomas, and help those of us who get a bit solitary, to be part of the Church, for your sake. We don't want to miss anything good!

AP

A message from the past

Eight days later, his disciples were again in the house, and Thomas was with them. The doors were shut, but Jesus came and stood among them, and said, 'Peace be with you.' Then he said to Thomas, 'Put your finger here, and see my hands; and put out your hand, and place it in my side; do not be faithless, but believing.' Thomas answered him, 'My Lord and my God!' Jesus said to him, 'Have you believed because you have seen me? Blessed are those who have not seen and yet believe.' Now Jesus did many other signs in the presence of the disciples, which are not written in this book; but these are written that you may believe that Jesus is the Christ, the Son of God, and that believing you may have life in his name.

Eight days after his first appearances Jesus stood among his disciples again, a real, touchable man. But the Bible doesn't say that Thomas did touch him, and I doubt if he bothered. That man standing in front of him, the man who had been at the front of his mind for the last eight days, as the other disciples endlessly discussed recent events, was Jesus. He was alive.

'My Lord and my God!' Thomas was as direct and uncompromising in his new-found belief as he had been in his doubt. As I said, Thomas (and all the others present behind those locked doors) were lucky. They met the risen Jesus and knew that death was somehow defeated. But now Jesus speaks a message through the passage of two thousand years to those of us who were not able to be there at the time.

'Blessed are those who have not seen and yet believe.' That's us, folks! We can meet the risen Jesus in the Bible, in personal or corporate prayer, and in the lives of others, but (except for a minuscule minority) we cannot meet him face to face as the disciples did. Jesus says we are blessed if we believe in him without that benefit. Let's face it, however good we may be at debating, it is only our personal experience of the risen Jesus that will convince others of the truth.

A reflection

Sceptic: Why did God create evil, then?
Disciple: I don't know, but Jesus came back to life . . .

AP

Life

You have been born anew, not of perishable seed but of imperishable, through the living and abiding word of God; for 'All flesh is like grass and all its glory like the flower of grass. The grass withers, and the flower falls, but the word of the Lord abides for ever.' That word is the good news which was preached to you.

In a bowl by my front window some white hyacinths are pushing up their heads in the heart of their green leaves, and soon they will be in full bloom and scenting the whole of the room with their fragrance. But soon after that they will be dead—the pure, white florets decayed into yellow sliminess and smelling nasty instead of sweet. Yes, next year they will bloom again, out in the garden, and for several years after that. But finally the glory of them will die away for ever. Like the glory of all our bodies and all flesh . . .

But there is a life that lasts for ever. It is the life of God, offered to us freely and in love. The creative word of God comes to us, almost as the Holy Spirit came to Mary at the birth of Jesus. 'The Holy Spirit will come upon you, and the power of the Most High will overshadow you; therefore the child to be born will be called holy, the Son of God.' Our response to the word of God has to be the same as Mary's: 'Let it be to me according to your word.' Then we shall be in the same relationship with God the Father as the unique Son of God—with our new life and new relationship possible because of the death of Christ. At Holy Communion, remember that you have a life in you which can never die and which is eternal. And be thankful.

Hold out your empty hands in faith . . . Take . . . eat . . . Drink this . . . all . . . of you . . . The body of Christ keep you in eternal life . . . The blood of Christ keep you in eternal life . . .

SB

Another betrayal

Peter was still standing there keeping himself warm. So the others said to him 'Aren't you also one of the disciples of that man?' But Peter denied it. 'No, I am not,' he said. One of the High Priest's slaves, a relative of the man whose ear Peter had cut off, spoke up. 'Didn't I see you with him in the garden?' he asked. Again Peter said 'No'—and at once a cock crowed.

No Christian can feel anything but sympathy for Peter. We have all denied Jesus at one time or another, by our words, or our failure to speak, or our deeds, or by our thoughts. Don't you recognize that sneaking wish that you were not a Christian—especially when facing a particularly attractive temptation? The niggling voice that says, 'If you could just forget about God for a little while?'

Peter did not deny Jesus out of a lack of love. If he had not loved Jesus, he would not have wept at his own betrayal, as the other Gospels tell us he did. He betrayed Jesus because this time fear outweighed his love. And haven't we too felt the pressure of fear, and been tempted to deny love because of it? It takes a special kind of strength to overcome that sort of fear. It is not a fear usually of physical danger, but a moral fear. Fear of being put on the spot, and it leads us to deny our friends and sometimes our God.

We need first of all to recognize and accept our weaknesses. Peter had been willing to fight, but surrounded with questioning enemies—perhaps more ready to mock than to attack-he crumbled. Yet I think it did him good. Knowing his weakness, he would be able to look for strength. For as Paul discovered, 'it is when I am weak that I am strong'. In our weakness, we have nowhere to turn but to God. We lose the temptation to go it alone, and as a result we are able to draw on the strength of God himself. It was that which in the end would allow Peter not only to stand up and follow Jesus, but to die for him.

Meditate

My grace is all you need, for my power is strongest when you are weak.

AP

Working and waiting

After this Jesus revealed himself again to the disciples by the Sea of Tiberias; and he revealed himself in this way. Simon Peter, Thomas called the Twin, Nathanael of Cana in Galilee, the sons of Zebedee, and two others of his disciples were together. Simon Peter said to them, 'I am going fishing.' They said to him, 'We will go with you.' They went out and got into the boat; but that night they caught nothing.

'Blow this for a game of soldiers—I'm going fishing!' This may not be an exact rendering of the Greek text, but I suspect it sums up Peter's feelings and attitudes. How long was a volatile character like him going to put up with hiding behind locked doors and waiting for something to happen? Jesus had said he was sending the disciples out to forgive and retain sins, empowered by the Holy Spirit, but somehow the 'Go!' had not yet been said. Perhaps, also, Peter was secretly troubled by his triple denial. Did it disqualify him? Was he forgiven? Would it ever be brought up? Peter was neither the first nor the last man to seek refuge from his anxieties in a day's fishing. They spent the whole night in the boat, but caught nothing. I bet they enjoyed it, though. A spot of hard physical effort can be an excellent antidote to the poison of emotional or spiritual turmoil. (This applies particularly to overweight, sedentary writers whose only exercise is eating.)

Whatever else was happening in the hearts of these disciples as they toiled with their nets, they must have been filled with a constant, buzzing excitement, an excitement that sprung from the knowledge that Jesus could turn up at any moment, in any place. Perhaps he would come walking across the surface of the water just as he had done before. Perhaps this time, Peter would keep his footing, join his master and do a little dance of joy with him across the Sea of Tiberias.

The Christian life at its best is like that, isn't it? Jesus can enter any situation, transforming it, and you and me. As the dawn breaks, that is what is about to happen to Peter.

A question

Am I watching for him? Do I expect him?

AP

Unconditional love

Just as day was breaking, Jesus stood on the beach; yet the disciples did not know that it was Jesus. Jesus said to them, 'Children, have you any fish?' They answered him, 'No.' He said to them, 'Cast the net on the right side of the boat, and you will find some.' So they cast it, and now they were not able to haul it in, for the quantity of fish. That disciple whom Jesus loved said to Peter, 'It is the Lord!' When Simon Peter heard that it was the Lord, he put on his clothes, for he was stripped for work, and sprang into the sea. But the other disciples came in the boat, dragging the net full of fish, for they were not far from the land, but about a hundred yards off.

If you want to know what the Christian faith is really about, this incident will provide as good an answer as any. It is about the kind of spontaneous, non-religious, extravagant love and affection that has motivated true followers of Jesus for generations.

At first, in the half-light of dawn, the disciples failed to recognize Jesus. As far as they were concerned he was a stranger who shouted advice from the shore (quite a common occurrence apparently), and very good advice it turned out to be.

Then, as the sky lightened and visibility improved, John happened to look towards the shore as he paused from his efforts for a moment, and something about the silhouette and stance of the solitary figure on the beach seemed terribly familiar.

'It's the Lord!' he whispered to Peter. Seconds later he must have been rocking in the slip-stream as his large piscatorial colleague, who had stayed only for as long as it took to throw some clothes on before leaping into the water and splashing his way towards Jesus. Thoroughly confused at that point about the meaning of Jesus' past ministry, uncertain about the present, totally ignorant of what the future might hold, and with the knotty issues of those three denials still unresolved, Peter just wanted to be with the person he loved. God grant us that same unconditional desire to be with Jesus.

A prayer

Father, help us to recognize Jesus when he helps us with ordinary things. We want to love him as much as Peter did.

AP

God in his own world

When they got out on land, they saw a charcoal fire there, with fish lying on it, and bread. Jesus said to them, 'Bring some of the fish that you have just caught.' So Simon Peter went aboard and hauled the net ashore, full of large fish, a hundred and fifty-three of them; and although there were so many, the net was not torn. Jesus said to them, 'Come and have breakfast.' Now none of the disciples dared ask him, 'Who are you?' They knew it was the Lord. Jesus came and took the bread and gave it to them, and so with the fish. This was now the third time that Jesus was revealed to the disciples after he was raised from the dead.

I have already mentioned, in connection with Mary's first sight of her risen master, the divine ordinariness of Jesus. Here, in this little scene on the beach, the same quality is even more dramatically evident. How wonderful that God doesn't approach such moments in his own history as though he was an epic film producer. No stirring music, no cast of thousands, no apocalyptic visions in the sky. The risen Jesus—God himself, the glory of the universe—was cooking breakfast for his friends. Real and solid, he nudged the fire into more effective life and moved his head to avoid getting smoke in his eyes. Ordinary. Peaceful.

Like waking up after a nightmare, a real encounter with God nearly always feels like a blessedly reasing return to the familiar and warm sensation of true reality. That's why it's so important to make it clear to non-believers that they are not being asked to give their hearts to some alien, far-away, irrelevant concept.

They might be more willing to give their hearts to a God who knows how to get an open fire going without matches or paraffin. This is the world *he* made. He and it are parts of the same reality.

Do you feel ignorant sometimes when you read the Bible? I often do. That's why I had to find out what other writers thought about the significance of the 153 fish that were caught by the disciples, and I was amazed at the number of complex explanations that have been suggested over the years. Do you think they just enjoyed counting their big catch, do you? Is that a possible explanation? No—too ordinary, eh?

A question

What is 'real life'?

AP

It has to be said

When they had finished breakfast, Jesus said to Simon Peter, 'Simon, son of John, do you love me more than these?' He said to him, 'Yes, Lord; you know that I love you.' He said to him, 'Feed my lambs.' A second time he said to him, 'Simon, son of John, do you love me?' He said to him, 'Yes, Lord, you know that I love you.' He said to him, 'Tend my sheep.' He said to him the third time, 'Simon, son of John, do you love me?' Peter was grieved because he said to him the third time, 'Do you love me?' And he said to him, 'Lord, you know everything; you know that I love you.' Jesus said to him, 'Feed my sheep. Truly, truly, I say to you, when you were young, you girded yourself and walked where you would; but when you are old, you will stretch out your hands, and another will gird you and carry you where you do not wish to go.' (This he said to show by what death he was to glorify God.) And after this he said to him. 'Follow me.'

A young friend phoned me last year to describe a visit she had made to her grandmother in Germany. The old lady is matriarchal, stubborn and full of strong opinions—a force to be reckoned with. My friend, Greta, is a considerable force in her own right, but on this particular occasion she wasn't feeling very sure about anything. Since her baby son had died she had been struggling back to some level of hopefulness. Grandmother had clearly decided that the process would be accelerated by a detailed analysis of Greta's faults, weaknesses and recent failures, and that she would be the one to do it. Greta listened to this barrage of criticism until she just couldn't take any more. 'Even if that's all true, Gran,' she said, 'why don't you say nice things as well? Why don't you tell me you love me? That's what I need to hear.' 'Tell you I love you?' said her grandmother. 'I don't need to tell you that. It goes without saying.' But it didn't. Love needs to be spoken and heard. Peter needed to express his love for Jesus. His words sealed the total commitment that was being asked of him if he was to follow his master to the death.

A thought

God needs to be told that he's loved.

AP

Never mind him

Peter turned and saw following them the disciple whom Jesus loved . . . When Peter saw him, he said to Jesus, 'Lord, what about this man?' Jesus said to him, 'If it is my will that he remain until I come, what is that to you? Follow me!' The saying spread abroad among the brethren that this disciple was not to die; yet Jesus did not say to him that he was not to die, but, 'If it is my will that he remain until I come, what is that to you?' This is the disciple who is bearing witness to these things, and who has written these things; and we know that his testimony is true. But there are also many other things which Jesus did; were every one of them to be written, I suppose that the world itself could not contain the books that would be written.

It's a little wearying to see that misunderstandings in the Christian Church began as long ago as this. And we've been pretty consistent ever since, haven't we? How on earth did the health and wealth movement ever gain credence in the eyes of anyone who has actually read the New Testament? How have we managed to get so confused and puzzled and divided on issues such as healing and tongues and denominationalism and Communion and how to arrange the chairs?

There is, however, no misunderstanding at all about Jesus' response to Peter's question: 'Never mind him—I'll sort him out. You follow me.' Isn't it difficult to allow other people to be what they are without commenting or wanting to modify their behaviour? Jesus was quite clear about these two disciples. Peter was to be a shepherd to the followers of the Saviour, and John was to be a witness to the things that Jesus had done and said. Both of these tasks were essential and each was assigned to an individual specially chosen by God.

So much to be done, but so much power and guidance available if we are willing to follow. The final verse of the book emphasizes the limitless scope of Jesus' activity in our world.

A prayer

Father, help us to be humble enough to appreciate and value the work that others do for you. We need each other so much. Teach us how to make the Church strong.

AP

Pentecost, power & presence

Jesus is alive! Christ is risen! But the Christian faith is not only about something almost unbelievably wonderful that happened two thousand years ago. It is about the Spirit of the risen Christ living in our hearts—transforming us, and mending the image and likeness of God in which the human race was created and which each one of us has broken.

Christianity isn't about keep a set of rules or a code of ethics. It is about the life of God in the soul of man. A power and a provision beyond anything we could imagine—and so great that many Christians still don't really believe it or experience it. This is what is written in one of the New Testament letters:

Simon Peter, a servant and apostle of Jesus Christ, to those who through the righteousness of our God and Saviour Jesus Christ have received a faith as precious as ours. Grace and peace be yours in abundance through the knowledge of God and of Jesus our Lord. His divine power has given us everything we need for life and godliness through our knowledge of him who called us by his own glory and goodness. Through these he has given us his very great and precious promises, so that through them you may participate in the divine nature and escape the corruption in the world caused by evil desires.

2 Peter 1:1-4 (NIV)

So for eight weeks now we look at different readings on the power and the presence of God-with-us. At the start of Matthew's Gospel it says that ' "The virgin will be with child and will give birth to a son, and they will call him Immanuel"—which means, "God with us" ' (Matthew 1:23). Jesus was 'God-with-us'. The Holy Spirit is also God-with-us—now, in the 1990s. In that passage from the second letter of Peter he talked about the great and precious promises of God. Here is a promise which Jesus made:

'If a man is thirsty, let him come to me and drink. Whoever believes in me, as the Scripture has said, streams of living water will flow from within him.' By this he meant the Spirit, whom those who believed in him were later to receive. Up to that time the Spirit had not been given, since Jesus had not yet been glorified.

John 7:37–39

Father, Son and Spirit

'Truly, truly, I say to you, he who believes in me will also do the works that I do; and greater works than these will he do, because I go to the Father. Whatever you ask in my name, I will do it, that the Father may be glorified in the Son; if you ask anything in my name, I will do it. If you love me, you will keep my commandments. And I will pray the Father, and he will give you another Counsellor, to be with you for ever, even the Spirit of truth, whom the world cannot receive, because it neither sees him nor knows him; you know him, for he dwells with you, and will be in you.'

A man in my church has gone through a great deal of anguish because of the words 'he who believes in me will do the works that I do; and greater works than these will he do...' He feels that he ought to be doing greater works than Jesus, and that the reason why he isn't is that he doesn't believe enough. But we aren't just individuals. We are members of the body of Christ.

On the Day of Pentecost when the apostle Peter spoke to the crowd, three thousand people were added to the just-born Church. But Peter wasn't just an individual. He was a member of the body of Christ and his gift was that of an apostle. He didn't live his life in isolation. He shared it with the rest of the apostolic band and with the disciples of Jesus. On the Day of Pentecost Peter did greater works than Jesus had ever done. But Peter was the preacher, and the Holy Spirit of Jesus worked in people's hearts.

At Holy Communion today we shall hear the words: 'We are the body of Christ. In the one Spirit we were all baptized into one body...' The Holy Spirit empowers the body of Christ. One member does one thing, and another member another. The power flows into all of us a Jesus promised: '... you shall receive power when the Holy Spirit has come upon you, and you shall be my witnesses in Jerusalem and in Judaea and Samaria and to the end of the earth.' For us that means that we shall first of all be witnesses where we live—and then our witness will spread out like the ripples from the centre of a pool.

SB

Some gifts of God

Before the Day of Pentecost, the disciples' track record for bravery was not good. On the night before Jesus died, instead of giving him the support he longed for, they fled in fear. On Easter Day, they were still terrified. Yet on the Day of Pentecost, we find these same men preaching with power and boldness, witnessing with courage and in a way which was readily understood by citizens of a variety of countries and giving spiritual direction to thousands of new converts. How had this change come about?

What seems to have happened was that, on the Day of Pentecost, when they were 'baptised with the Holy Spirit' in the way Jesus had promised, a whole new chapter of their lives began. It was the beginning of the era which Jesus foretold when he promised that the day would come when they would be able to do the same works that he performed in his earthly ministry—and even greater works:

'I tell you the truth, anyone who has faith in me will do what I have been doing. He will do even greater things than these, because I am going to the Father . . . And I will ask the Father, and he will give you another Counsellor to be with you for ever-the Spirit of truth . . . You know him, for he lives with you and will be in in you.'

What seems to have happened is that, on the Day of Pentecost, the mantle of Jesus fell on the disciples in rather the same way as the mantle of Elijah fell on Elisha (2 Kings 2:1–18). The result was that they found that they were empowered by the Spirit to speak and think and act in the same life-changing way as Jesus.

Peter reminds us, in his Pentecost sermon, that we can enjoy a similar empowering: 'In the last days, God says, I will pour out my Spirit on all people' (Acts 2:17).

The question is, do we want a fresh touch of God's Spirit? Do we want our prayer and our service to be re-vitalized?

A prayer

Breathe on me breath of God,
Fill me with life anew,
That I may love what Thou dost love
and do what Thou wouldst do.

Edwin Hatch

JH

The Spirit guides

Just before he ascended to heaven, Jesus commissioned his disciples to spread the good news of his Kingdom throughout the world. Left, as they were, without their Master's physical presence, the disciples would need guidance about who was to go where and when. Luke makes it clear that the Holy Spirit is a guiding Spirit. In the Acts of the Apostles he demonstrates how the Holy Spirit has a whole variety of ways of making the will of God known. Sometimes he speaks in an unmistakable way:

Now an angel of the Lord said to Philip, 'Go south to the road—the desert road—that goes down from Jerusalem to Gaza.' So he started out, and on his way he met an Ethiopian eunuch, an important official in charge of all the treasury of Candace, queen of the Ethiopians. This man had gone to Jerusalem to worship, and on his way home was sitting in his chariot reading the book of Isaiah the prophet. The Spirit told Philip, 'Go to that chariot and stay near it.'

The result of this Spirit-engineered encounter was that this Ethiopian government minister was wooed into God's Kingdom. Meanwhile the Spirit was leading Philip in an even more curious way. Having baptized the newly-converted Ethiopian:

The Spirit of the Lord suddenly took Philip away, and the eunuch did not see him again ... Philip, however, appeared at Azotus and travelled about, preaching the gospel in all the towns until he reached Caesarea.

Later in Luke's book, we read of the Holy Spirit giving further specific instructions: 'While they were worshipping the Lord and fasting, the Holy Spirit said, "Set apart for me Barnabas and Saul for the work to which I have called them ..." The two of them, sent on their way by the Holy Spirit, went down to Seleucia and sailed from there to Cyprus' (Acts 13:2, 4).

A project and a prayer

Read Acts 8:26–40, Acts 13 and Acts 10:9–11:30—preferably with a map of the world the disciples knew in front of you. Notice how the Holy Spirit made known to the disciples where they should go and when. Pray that you may similarly tune in to the Spirit's insistent, guiding voice.

JH

The Spirit glorifies Jesus

Waiting can be exciting or frustrating, draining or re-energizing. It depends who or what we are waiting for. Waiting often creates in us an emptiness.

During the days that lay between Jesus' Ascension and the Day of Pentecost, the Holy Spirit seems to have created such an emptiness in Jesus' disciples. The mystics call this longing a *capax Dei*, a capacity for God. The Holy Spirit did this so that the disciples should be filled with the fullness of Jesus' own life. As Jesus himself reminded them, his Spirit's mission on earth is to make Jesus' presence and teaching real to us. He always focuses the spotlight on Jesus, not on himself. He always inspires us to worship, praise and glorify God's Son:

'The Helper will come—the Spirit, who reveals the truth about God and who comes from the Father. I will send him to you from the Father, and he will speak about me . . . When . . . the Spirit comes . . . he will give me glory, because he will take what I say and tell it to you.'

Nothing has helped me to recognize this servant-role of the Holy Spirit more than a certain icon: the Icon of the Holy Trinity. This was painted by the Russian iconographer, Andrei Rublev in an attempt to give the Russian people a glimpse of God's love. In the icon, the three members of the Holy Trinity: the Father, the Son and the Holy Spirit, are represented as angels sitting round a table. Jesus sits in the centre with the Father on his left and the Holy Spirit on his right. Every time I gaze at this icon, I realize afresh that the Holy Spirit's eyes and gestures are giving glory to Jesus. It is as though he is saying, 'Don't concentrate on me. I'm only the footman. Let me introduce you to the Master, Jesus himself.'

A project

Find a copy of Rublev's Icon of the Holy Trinity. Gaze at it through a ring: a real ring or one made with your thumb and index finger. Look first at the figure on your right, the Holy Spirit. Let him introduce you to Jesus. See what happens.

JH

The Spirit transforms us

One of the Holy Spirit's tasks is to spread deep down inside the believer an awareness of the felt love of God. Many Christians, myself included, can testify that this is what seemed to happen to them when they were 'baptized with the Holy Spirit'. They no longer gave only intellectual assent to the fact that God is love. They knew it. His liquid love had trickled from their head into their heart.

Another of the tasks of the Spirit of Jesus (that is the way the Holy Spirit is described in Acts 16:7) is closely linked with this. It is to transform us into the likeness of Jesus who is love personified.

Paul reminds us that, if this is to happen, two things are necessary. One is that, just as mirrors or windows facing the setting sun glow and change colour as they are bathed in the beauty of the sun's rays, so we must turn away from self and the world towards the glorified Christ so that we reflect his radiance. The other is that just as light and warmth, rain and dew work a quiet, hidden miracle on a tree, causing it to bear luscious fruit, so the Spirit of Jesus, if we co-operate with him, quietly cultivates in our lives characteristics which resemble the personality, attitudes and actions of Jesus.

We, with our unveiled faces reflecting like mirrors the brightness of the Lord, all grow brighter and brighter as we are turned into the image that we reflect; this is the work of the Lord who is Spirit.

The Spirit produces love, joy, peace, patience, kindness, goodness, faithfulness, humility, and self-control.

Galatians 5:22–23 (GNB)

The miracle of transforming love seems to happen in this way. As we make Jesus the centre of our lives, he floods us with his Spirit, the Spirit of love. This affects our entire life: our relationship with God, our relationships at home and at work, in the Church and in the community. Gradually, it gives birth to uncharacteristic humility and patience, kindness and gentleness, peace and joy—and self-control.

A prayer

Gracious Spirit, dwell in me!
I myself would gracious be;
And with words that help and heal
Would Thy life in mine reveal . . .

Thomas Lynch

JH

The Spirit convicts

The Holy Spirit floods us with the love of Jesus, with love for Jesus and love for his world. The Holy Spirit also transforms us into the likeness of Jesus. No wonder Jesus told his disciples to wait in the city until they were baptized with his life-giving Spirit.

But the Spirit of Jesus has another task too. Jesus reminded his disciples of this on the night before he died:

It is to your advantage that I go away, for if I do not go away, the Counsellor will not come to you; but if I go, I will send him to you. And when he comes, he will convince the world concerning sin and righteousncss and judgement: concerning sin, because they do not believe in me . . .'

After the disciples were baptized with the Holy Spirit on the Day of Pentecost, we see Peter preaching with uncharacteristic power. Luke records the result of his revolutionary sermon. His congregation of some three thousand people were 'cut to the heart'—convicted of the sin of unbelief. Such a phenomenon is a sure sign that the Holy Spirit is at work.

He works similarly in our own lives: highlighting personal sin until we come to the place of repentance. Then he delights to cleanse us and fill us afresh with the love of God.

Hiring a holiday car on one occasion illustrated, for me, the *gentle* but persistent way with which the Holy Spirit convicts. My husband was driving this unfamiliar vehicle one sunny morning when a shrill, intermittent sound startled us. It seemed to be coming from the car's mechanism. When we slowed down, the noise stopped. When we accelerated, the persistent buzz began again.

Eventually the penny dropped. There was nothing wrong with the car as we had feared. The alarm was simply a reminder that we were exceeding the speed limit!

Because the Spirit of Jesus is a *Holy* Spirit, he is like an in-built alarm system alerting us when there are impurities which need to be dealt with: self-centredness, lack of love, unbelief . . . But his revelations of sin are always shown against the backcloth of God's love.

For prayer

May the fire of the Holy Spirit burn up the dross in our hearts and set them on fire with zeal for your service.

JH

What happened?

Archbishop William Temple once wrote: 'It is no good giving me a play like *Hamlet* or *King Lear*, and telling me to write a play like that. Shakespeare could do it; I can't. And it is no good showing me a life like the life of Jesus and telling me to live a life like that. Jesus could do it; I can't. But if the genius of Shakespeare could come and live in me, then I could write plays like that. And if the Spirit of Jesus could come and live in me, I could live a life like that.'

On the Day of Pentecost the Spirit of Jesus enveloped the disciples in such a way that these once-timid men, among other things, were preaching authoritatively, expounding the Scriptures skilfully, prophesying powerfully, communicating in languages they had never learned, healing the sick and demonstrating wisdom and discernment in tricky pastoral situations. They were exercising, from the word go, the gifts which the Holy Spirit gives for the up-building of Christian fellowships:

There are different gifts, but the same Spirit . . . To one there is given through the Spirit the message of wisdom, to another the message of knowledge by means of the same Spirit, to another faith by the same Spirit, to another gifts of healing by that one Spirit, to another miraculous powers, to another prophecy, to another distinguishing between spirits, to another speaking in different kinds of tongues, and to still another the interpretation of tongues. All these are the work of one and the same Spirit, and he gives them to each one, just as he determines.

Thousands of Christians today are testifying to the good news that the Holy Spirit is still giving to his Church gifts of revelation: words of wisdom and knowledge—flashes of insight which, apart from the Spirit, would have remained hopelessly hidden from the human mind and senses. Christians are still receiving that special love-language with which the believer communicates to a loving God—the gift of tongues. And the Spirit has not stopped entrusting us with the gift of healing. We still live in the era of the Holy Spirit.

For meditation

Supernatural living through supernatural empowering is at the very heart of New Testament Christianity.

Jim Packer

JH

Temptation

For the word of God is living and active. Sharper than any double-edged sword, it penetrates even to dividing soul and spirit, joints and marrow; it judges the thoughts and attitudes of the heart. Nothing in all creation is hidden from God's sight. Everything is uncovered and laid bare before the eyes of him to whom we must give account. Therefore, since we have a great high priest who has gone through the heavens, Jesus the Son of God, let us hold firmly to the faith we profess. For we do not have a high priest who is unable to sympathise with our weaknesses, but we have one who has been tempted in every way, just as we are—was yet without sin. Let us then approach the throne of grace with confidence, so that we may receive mercy and find grace to help us in our time of need.

God knows our hearts through and through. He knows our hopes and our dreams and our desires. He knows all the good things about us and all the bad things. The generous and loving side of us and the mean and nasty side. He sees it all and sooner or later we shall see it all. But it is all right to see it, because then we can set about praying in the right way. Jesus our high priest is right there at the throne of God interceding for us. He knows what it's like to be human and he knows what it's like to be us. So we can go to God and get help—whatever we have done and whatever our problem is.

A way to pray

Be aware of yourself in the presence of God, and let the word of God enter you, like a sword cutting into your heart and your mind. Reflect on what it says . . . about loving your enemies . . . about loving your neighbour . . . about feeding the hungry . . . about holiness and purity . . . Ask the Spirit to show yourself as you are . . . Then go to the throne of the universe just as you are . . . Know that Jesus is there, your high priest . . . Ask for grace, and receive the help he gives you . . .

SB

The Shepherd

The Lord is my shepherd, I shall not want. He maketh me to lie down in green pastures: he leadeth me beside the still waters. He restoreth my soul...

This is the best-loved of all the Psalms, and we shall look at it for three days. We sing it at our weddings and at our funerals and the words bring us comfort and joy. We always think of it as the Shepherd Psalm, but the Shepherd is also the Guide and the Host. It has just one theme, that God is sufficient for all our human need.

Flocks in the Middle East follow the shepherd, who leads them into the pastures where they will find just the food they needed. And whatever is happening to us right now is just the food that we need—even though we might not like the taste of it very much.

The shepherd is in the process of restoring 'my soul', which often means 'my life' or 'myself'. God restores and renews *me*. A few years ago I watched them restoring Michelangelo's marvellous ceiling in the Sistine Chapel. They were half way through and the colours at one end were dark and the colours at the other bright. The dirt and grime of the years had dulled the original painting, now all the figures were being stored to their original glory. In God's original design he created us in his own image and likeness. But as one of the confessions puts it: 'we have marred your

image within us'. God can restore it to the original design. The Shepherd God has glorious plans for his sheep!

A reflection

Wherever he may guide me,
No want shall turn me back;
My Shepherd is beside me
And nothing can I lack.
His wisdom ever waketh,
His sight is never dim;
He knows the way he taketh,
And I will walk with him.

A.L. Waring

Accept the place the divine providence has found for you, the society of your contemporaries, the connection of events.

Ralph Waldo Emerson

SB

The Valley of the Shadow

He leadeth me in the paths of righteousness for his name's sake. Yea, though I walk through the valley of the shadow of death, I will fear no evil: for thou art with me; thy rod and thy staff they comfort me.

Often we don't know which way to turn. But the Shepherd guides his sheep— sometimes through the ordinary circumstances of their lives and sometimes through a special call. When we hear the voice of the Shepherd we know it: 'Your ears shall hear a voice behind you saying, "This is the way, walk in it", if you turn to the right hand or if you turn to the left.' Then one day we hear the voice calling us home. A man I know has just heard that call . . . into the valley of the shadow of death. I don't think he will fear any evil there, because he knows God. And unlike many people he has never been afraid to talk about death.

In my book *Drawing Near to the City: Christians speak about dying*, I wrote this: 'The psychiatrist Franz Perls said that we are afraid to live because we are afraid to die. Ernest Becker won the Pullitzer Prize for 1974 with his book *The Denial of Death*: "The idea of death, the fear of it, haunts the human animal like nothing else; it is a mainspring of human activity designed largely to avoid the fatality of death, to overcome it by denying in some way that it is the final destiny for man." . . . Leonard Bernstein in his Harvard lectures on music through the centuries said that the twentieth century is full of the sound of death, insisting that we listen to it in one way if we won't listen to it in another—because in our century death is the one thing that we refuse to speak about.' But not everyone refuses, and that book is by people who have been willing to speak. It does seem to be gloriously possible to walk through the valley of the shadow of death and of deep darkness, shepherded and guided by the one who is the light of the world.

SB

The Host

Thou preparest a table before me in the presence of mine enemies: thou anointest my head with oil; my cup runneth over. Surely goodness and mercy shall follow me all the days of my life; and I will dwell in the house of the Lord for ever.

Banquets and meals with God are right at the heart of Christianity, rooted in its Jewishness. Jesus has meals with his friends (and with other people's enemies), and Holy Communion itself is a meal, in which Christ is the Host and the Bread and the Wine. Heaven itself is going to be a marriage supper, and we are going to eat it with God and reign with him for ever and ever.

A friend of mine was a most marvellous host, and he and his wife (an equally marvellous hostess) used to call their house the Logan Inn. He produced the most superb wines in generous measures and she cooked the most delicious meals. But it wasn't just the food and drink that their friends went for. It was being made to feel totally at home and enormously welcome. Beethoven symphonies filled the house with loud, glorious music as we got ready for dinner, and when we came downstairs an enormous log fire was burning in the grate. When he died I had the privilege of giving the funeral address—and I finished with words from G.K. Chesterton, speaking of the inn at the end of the world where God himself will be the host.

To think about

Comradeship and serious joy are not interludes in our travel: but our travels are interludes in comradeship and joy, which through God shall endure for ever. The inn does not point to the road, the road points to the inn. And all roads point at last to an ultimate inn—and when we drink again it shall be from the great flagons in the tavern at the end of the world.

G.K. Chesterton

SB

Born for love

Having purified your souls by your obedience to the truth for a sincere love of the brethren, love one another earnestly from the heart. You have been born anew, not of perishable seed but of imperishable through the living and abiding word of God; for 'All flesh is like grass and all its glory like the flower of grass. The grass withers, and the flower falls, but the word of the Lord abides for ever.' That word is the good news which was preached to you. So put away all malice and all guile and insincerity and envy and all slander. Like newborn babes, long for the pure spiritual milk, that by it you may grow up to salvation; for you have tasted the kindness of the Lord.

All creatures have the same nature as their parents, whether the creature is a tiny blackbird chick just hatched out a turquoise spotted egg, or a foal that stands on its legs and nuzzles its mother only minutes after it is born, or a human baby, totally dependent for life on another human being. Christians, born again of the Spirit of God, have the nature of God. And the nature of God is love. It is impossible for a real Christian not to love, because the new nature growing within her (or him) is the same as God's nature. But the new nature has to grow, just as a baby has. The new-born Christian is to thirst for the pure spiritual milk of the 'word'. That isn't just the Bible. It is all things that have to do with the Word, who is God himself. The Word that went forth from God on the first day of creation ... the Word who was 'in the beginning with God' ... the Word that the whole of creation declares about the glory of God without even speaking a word. The Word of the Lord abides for ever—and it is through that Word that the Christian is born.

A prayer

Living Lord God, help me to nourish your life in me—and to thirst for all things that flow from you, the living Word. Help me to live—to love you and my neighbour and myself, with the love that flows from your heart of love.

SB

Challenged

Prayer and life go together. Jesus made this very clear to Peter when he challenged him to:

'Feed my lambs.'

I once met a shepherd boy in Nazareth. His task was to look after his father's flock of seventeen lambs: to find grass for them even in drought, to watch them lest they strayed, to protect them from danger of wild animals or thieves, to lead them to their pen at night. He held in his arms a new-born lamb. 'Just twelve hours old,' he told me. 'He's mine.' He fed this lamb with a bottle. When it was tired, he carried it. When it bleated anxiously, he caressed it. And he had already given it a name. It was this kind of caring Middle Eastern shepherd Jesus had in his mind when he commanded Peter to feed the lambs of the Kingdom. Jesus knew that on the Day of Pentecost, thousands would turn to him. In a world which was soon to persecute Jesus' followers, these men and women would be as vulnerable as new-born lambs. They would need nourishing with spiritual milk, and protecting from their enemy, Satan.

'Put yourself into their skin,' Jesus seems to say to Peter. 'Bring them to maturity. Strengthen them.' Young Christians today are equally vulnerable. Growing up as they do in a culture where Christian values are scorned rather than upheld, they are increasingly confused. We have a responsibility to feed them. We may be in a position personally to encourage young people and new Christians to live life God's way. If not, we can still support God's beginners through prayer.

For prayer

Think of a person who has recently turned to Christ. Or think of a child known to you or a teenager. Or think of someone you know who has influence over such people: parents, teachers, clergy, writers, broadcasters. Lift the person in your mind to God. Ask him to supply their needs. Ask him, too, whether you might be able to help in some way.

JH

Charged

Feed my lambs. That's the challenge Jesus gave Peter and which we examined yesterday. Just as that challenge applies, not just to Peter, but to all of us, so does the further charge which Jesus gave Peter:

'Take care of my sheep.'

The flock of God needs feeding at every stage of their growth. Teenagers need to be helped through the transition to adulthood. Couples in love need to be helped to make the transition to marriage. Married people need to be shown how to make the transition to parenthood or, alternatively, supported through the traumas of childlessness should parenthood be denied them. Middle-aged couples need to be encouraged to let their children go—to try life their own way. Widows and widowers need to be supported so that they can face life without their loved one. Single people need to be assured that they are not second-class citizens but of great value to God and his Church. A niche needs to be found where their unique contribution can be given and received with thanksgiving. All this, and more, is included in Jesus' charge to Peter: 'Take care of my sheep'—give to the adults all they need for sustenance and growth. That's a tall order. What makes the task even more daunting yet even more of a

privilege is the reminder that Peter is to be Jesus' under-shepherd. 'Feed my sheep.' Just as Jesus charged Peter, so he charges us with the care of certain adult sheep and he expects us to know where the pastures are where they can graze to their heart's content and be nourished. Sometimes we will be able to help them personally. At other times it will be our prayers which build them up. And on other occasions we will put them in touch with other people who can best help them.

For meditation

Listening to God and listening to others are indivisible.

JH

Death's defeat

Martha said to Jesus, 'If you had been here, sir, my brother would not have died. Even now I know that whatever you ask of God, God will grant you.' Jesus said, 'Your brother will rise again.' 'I know that he will rise again,' said Martha, 'at the resurrection on the last day.' Jesus said, 'I am the resurrection, and I am life. If a man has faith in me, even though he die, he shall come to life; and no one who is alive and has faith shall ever die. Do you believe this?' 'Lord, I do,' she answered; 'I now believe that you are the Messiah, the Son of God who was to come into the world.'

Death overturns all our assumptions about our own lives. It spells the end of plans, dreams and hopes. Faced with the reality of death, faith itself falters. Martha's brother is dead, and Jesus failed to come in time. Yes, of course she believes in the final resurrection; yes, of course she believes—even now—in the power of Jesus, and in his special rapport with God. But there is a note of doubt. The faith that Jesus' confidence demands ('your brother will rise again') is not there. It is not complete trust in Jesus.

So Jesus will go on to bring Lazarus back to life, to show that he himself is, as he said, true life. In the presence of Jesus, death cannot triumph. Yet we know that Lazarus will still die again. This is not the complete conquest of death, just a fore-taste of what is to come. It is necessary for Martha and her sister. It is a necessary demonstration that Jesus' words are to be trusted. But even then it is not the real sign.

The real conquest of death comes when Jesus dies—and rises. Not to return for a time to this world, but real resurrection, which passes into eternal life with God. The real conquest of death for us does not lie in this world, but in union with Jesus. This is what we celebrate in Holy Communion. We share there in Jesus' death, and look for the real triumph of life which comes only when we trust in him.

JH

The God who comes

On my first trip to New Zealand, I visited a church which has been built by Maoris on the edge of a beautiful lake. After I had fingered the carved pulpit with its inlay of mother-of-pearl, I knelt down to pray. When I opened my eyes, I noticed something I hadn't spotted earlier: etched on the picture window in front of me was a figure of Jesus dressed in the kind of cloak traditionally worn by Maori chiefs. Because this window looks out onto the lake, it looked as though 'the Maori Christ' was striding across the blue water making a bee-line for me. I gasped. Jesus seemed so life-like. So real. And he was smiling at me.

A photograph of this 'Maori Christ' now hangs in my study. It reminds me of a basic, biblical truth: that God is the God who comes.

For forty days between his Resurrection and his Ascension, Jesus came to each of his disciples in turn. He detected their despondency and determined to turn their gloom into joy. And, as we shall remind ourselves between now and Ascension Day, he continues to come to us. He wants to convert our sadness into overflowing joy. That is why he gives us this invitation:

'Here I am! I stand at the door and knock. If anyone hears my voice and opens the door, I will come in and eat with him, and he with me.'

Jesus' invitation comes to us just as we are. There is no need for us to conjure up a particular kind of emotion before we invite him into our home, our innermost being or our community. He loves us just as we are.

A meditation

Imagine that Jesus is standing outside the place where you live. He is knocking at the door. You go to it and invite him in.

Notice whether you give him a warm welcome or a reluctant one. Take him on a conducted tour of this home which represents your life. Watch his reaction as he moves from room to room or corner to corner. Is there anything you want to say to him? How does he respond? If you would like him to take up residence, tell him that and show him where he can stay.

JH

To the despairing

Yesterday, we reminded ourselves that God is the God who comes; that he comes to us just as we are. He comes whether we are happy or sad, expecting to see him or believing that his love has evaporated.

Today, we place the spotlight on the way he came to Mary and turned her grief into inexpressible joy:

> **Mary stood outside the tomb crying. As she wept, she bent over to look into the tomb and saw two angels in white, seated where Jesus' body had been, one at the head and the other at the foot. They asked her, 'Woman, why are you crying?' 'They have taken my Lord away,' she said, 'and I don't know where they have put him.' At this, she turned round and saw Jesus standing there, but she did not realise that it was Jesus. 'Woman,' he said, 'why are you crying? Who is it you are looking for?' Thinking he was the gardener, she said, 'Sir, if you have carried him away, tell me where you have put him, and I will get him.' Jesus said to her, 'Mary.'**

Mary must have been in the depths of despair as she made her way to the tomb. She had no way of knowing what we now know: that she was about to enjoy a fresh encounter with Jesus. What she did know was that the One around whom her life had resolved had been wrenched from her. What she also knew was that the absence of her Beloved had left her with an aching emptiness—an inconsolable loneliness.

But just as the dawn crept up on Mary, so did Jesus. And just as Jesus crept up on Mary, so he delights to creep up on us when we are in despair. He comes even when, because of bereavement or long-term illness, onset of dependency or unemployment, we seem to have been stripped of even the ability to pray. When he comes, his presence floods every nook and cranny of our life, bathing it with light and love and joy—despite our circumstances.

A prayer

Loving Lord, shed the radiance of your love today on all who struggle with the darkness of despair. Into your love, in particular, I hold . . .

JH

Faith for fear

The prophet Isaiah promises that the Messiah will comfort all who mourn, giving them beauty for ashes, gladness instead of mourning and 'the garment of praise instead of a spirit of despair' (61:3). Yesterday, we saw how Jesus did this for Mary. On the same first Easter Day, Jesus' unexpected appearance in the Upper Room brought about a similar miracle. This time he appeared to his terrified disciples turning their fear into faith:

On the evening of that first day of the week, when the disciples were together, with the doors locked for fear of the Jews, Jesus came and stood among them and said . . . 'Peace be with you! As the Father has sent me, I am sending you.' And with that he breathed on them and said, 'Receive the Holy Spirit.'

The disciples were as much locked into their fear as, physically, they were locked into the Upper Room. But just as Jesus found a way through the locked doors and windows, so he gained access to their turbulent emotions, breathing into them his shalom, that deep sense of well-being which only he can give, and his Holy Spirit, his own energy.

Like the disciples, we sometimes find ourselves filled with fear: fear of physical pain or separation from loved ones, fear of death or dying, redundancy or poverty, spiders or snakes. Many Christians, when they find themselves riddled with such fears, cane themselves so that they are full of guilt as well as fear. But there is no need to be so harsh with ourselves. The risen Lord is the God who comes to us just as we are. As he came into the disciples' fear, so he will come into ours and change it into the new wine of faith.

A prayer

Risen Lord Jesus, as you met Mary in the garden and as you consoled your disciples in the Upper Room that same Easter Day, so come, today and every day, to the bereaved, the depressed, and the fearful; renew their hope, rekindle their love, reassure them that you are the God who comes, that you always come in love.

JH

The bewildered blessed

In one of her novels, Elizabeth Goudge describes a certain doctor: 'He did not believe in capricious fortune but in a carefully woven pattern where every tightly stretched warp thread of pain laid the foundation for a woof thread of joy.' An interweaving of joy and pain: life is like that. The disciples who walked from Jerusalem to Emmaus on that first Easter Day were to discover this in an unforgettable way. The pain which was to form the foundation for their joy was their inability to make head or tail of the events of the last week of Jesus' life. As they tramped along the dusty road, they poured out their perplexity, not realizing that the one who listened was the one of whom they spoke:

'Jesus of Nazareth . . . was a prophet, powerful in word and deed before God and all the people. The chief priests and our rulers handed him over to be sentenced to death, and they crucified him; but we had hoped that he was the one who was going to redeem Israel. And what is more, it is the third day since all this took place. In addition, some of our women amazed us. They went to the tomb early this morning but didn't find his body. They came and told us that they had seen a vision of angels, who said he was alive.

Then some of our companions went to the tomb and found it just as the women had said, but him they did not see.'

Jesus tramped beside them, absorbed their hopelessness, answered their many questions and then blessed these battered disciples by revealing himself to them. As they shared a few moments of intimacy at the meal table, the penny dropped. They saw that 'the stranger' was Jesus.

Just as Jesus drew alongside his baffled disciples, so when our hopes are dashed or when we find ourselves incapable of understanding why circumstances have taken curious and unexpected turns, he draws alongside us, blessing us in our bewilderment in such a way that our pain becomes the warp through which he weaves a woof of unimaginable joy.

For prayer

Pour out to Jesus any problems that perplex you. Be aware that he listens, cares and wants to bless you.

JH

Devoted to doubters

In his poem *The Little Black Boy*, William Blake reminds us that God delights to come to us in love:

Look at the rising sun: there God does live,
And gives His light, and gives His heat away,
And flowers and trees and beasts and men receive
Comfort in morning, joy in the noonday . . .
And we are put on earth a little space
That we may learn to bear the beams of love.

Thomas had to learn the hard way how to bear the beams of divine love. Thomas was absent when Jesus defied the locked doors and windows on Easter Day and he scoffed when he was told that Jesus had risen. He even prided himself in refusing to stoop to the gullibility of the others:

'Unless I see the nail marks in his hands and put my finger where the nails were, and put my hand into his side, I will not believe it.'

Jesus not only refused to reject his cynical disciple, he subjected himself to each of Thomas' outrageous requests:

A week later his disciples were in the house again, and Thomas was with them. Though the doors were locked, Jesus came and stood among them and said . . . to Thomas, 'Put your finger here; see my hands. Reach out your hand and put it into my side. Stop doubting and believe.'

Jesus so beamed his love on Thomas that he dispelled his doubt and drew from his disciple the most profound statement of faith anyone had yet made: 'My Lord and my God!' No one else had ever called Jesus God.

Like Thomas, most of us find our hearts hardened by doubts from time to time and the impression is sometimes given that God's love for us is withheld until we return to fullness of faith. Nothing could be further from the truth. Jesus is devoted to doubters. Just as he loved Thomas enough to show him his nail-pierced hands and wounded side, so he burns through the frightening fog of our uncertainties with his beams of love, longing that our doubts should become a basis for a joyous, humbling rediscovery of faith.

A prayer

Just as I am . . . I come.

JH

Jesus freely forgives

When someone we love hurts or rejects us, our instinctive reaction is to recoil from them or to determine to punish them. We might even find that our love for them has turned to hatred because hate is love hurting.

Because we react in that way, when we have failed God we expect him to react towards us with similar coldness and aggression. It takes some of us a long time to accept that even when we have hurt him, God continues to beam his love onto us.

Jesus' dealings with Peter after the resurrection underline this. After his threefold denial of Jesus on the night before the crucifixion, Peter must have felt that he had forfeited all right to God's love. Yet such was his love for Peter that Jesus appeared to him within hours of his resurrection. We are not told what happened when Jesus met Peter somewhere in Jerusalem on Easter Day (see Luke 24:34). What we are told is that Jesus continued to beam his love on Peter in such a way that Peter's hardness was melted and he learned to express love for his master all over again:

When they had finished eating, Jesus said to Simon Peter, 'Simon son of John, do you truly love me more than these?' 'Yes, Lord,' he said, 'you know that I love you.' Jesus said, 'Feed my lambs.' Again

Jesus said, 'Simon son of John, do you truly love me?' He answered, 'Yes, Lord, you know that I love you.' Jesus said, 'Take care of my sheep.' The third time he said to him, 'Simon son of John, do you love me?' Peter was hurt because Jesus asked him the third time, 'Do you love me?' He said, 'Lord, you know all things; you know that I love you.' Jesus said, 'Feed my sheep...'

What Jesus did for Peter—understanding him, forgiving him, healing him, reinstating him—he longs to do for us. That is why he died on Calvary's cross.

Reflect

You must come to God as you are: 'sinful, spiritually handicapped and disabled in many ways... And you accept these handicaps and disabilities because he accepts you... as you are'

James Borst

JH

Sacrifice

Then Jesus said to his disciples, 'If anyone would come after me, he must deny himself and take up his cross and follow me. For whoever wants to save his life will lose it, but whoever loses his life for me will find it. What good will it be for a man if he gains the whole world, yet forfeits his soul? Or what can a man give in exchange for his soul?'

When Jesus told us to take up our cross and follow him he wasn't telling us to carry a heavy weight around in order to build up our muscles and get spiritually fit. He was telling us to follow him to death. That is what crosses were made for, so that people could be crucified on them. It was an agonizingly painful death—and Jesus here is calling us to a death of our old selfish self, which will be very painful.

In the profoundest sense of all we have already died. We can say with St Paul: 'I have been crucified with Christ and I no longer live, but Christ lives in me. The life I live in the body, I live by faith in the Son of God, who loved me and gave himself for me' (Galatians 2:20).

So in our human bodies we live out the life of Christ in us. He gave himself for us, so in our lives now we give ourselves in love to our neighbours and our enemies and the whole world. That self-giving love is nothing less than a sacrifice and we speak of it as such after receiving the bread and wine of Holy Communion. Sometimes we shall find our sacrifice a joy. Sometimes it will be nothing less than a crucifixion.

A prayer

Almighty God, we thank you for feeding us with the body and blood of your Son Jesus Christ. Through him we offer you our souls and bodies to be a living sacrifice...
'The body of Christ keep you in eternal life.'

SB

Jesus is alive

Unwinding is one of the hardest things in the world for some of us. So we come to prayer tense and tired—unable to concentrate. It helps some of us to begin our prayer time by simply saying the name of Jesus over and over to ourselves or to repeat several times God's invitation through the Psalmist: 'Be still and know that I am God.' When we do this, we quieten down and familiar Bible truths take on a new meaning. Like this little cameo Mark paints of the disciples on Easter Day:

They were mourning and crying.

The loss of someone you love is a stunning blow. Tears might flow freely. You might find yourself unable to think straight or to make decisions. The disciples had actually watched Jesus dying on the cross. The memory must have seared itself deep into their minds and imagination. They had watched, too, while Joseph of Arimathea had wrapped the lifeless body in a linen cloth, placed it in an empty tomb and rolled the stone across the entrance of the cave for safety. Then they had retreated behind locked doors where they could give vent to their grief in private. Unlike us, Jesus' companions did not know the punch-line of the story—that Jesus was to emerge from that tomb. Alive. So when he did rise from the dead, Jesus faced the task of converting them, one by one, from sorrow to joy. As we observe how he did this, we may find ourselves curiously changed. For though we do know the punch-line (that Jesus conquered death) many of us still find it easier to identify with Christ's suffering than to bring our emotions into harmony with his resurrection joy. This means that Jesus is now faced with the task of converting us from sorrow to joy—or, to borrow a phrase of Gerard Manley Hopkins, he has to teach us what it means to have Christ 'Eastering in us'.

For prayer

Ask God so to Easter in you that you may be thrilled with resurrection joy.

JH

Tender and compassionate

Before you pray, relax. First clench your fists and tense every muscle in your body. Then, starting from your toes and moving upwards, relax your muscles and open your hands as a sign that you are open to God and his Word. Be still like this for a few minutes before you read on. Because his disciples were so weighed down with grief Jesus had to convert them, one by one, from sorrow to joy. As we watch him doing this, we learn a great deal about the nature of the risen Lord we worship. Take, for example, his treatment of the disciples who were rejecting as nonsense the claim made by some of the women that they had seen the Lord: 'When they heard that Jesus was alive and that [Mary] had seen him, they did not believe it' (Mark 16:11); 'But they did not believe the women because their words seemed like nonsense' (Luke 24:11). Luke highlights the tenderness and compassion with which Jesus melted their hardness and dealt with the sin of unbelief. He shows how Jesus came personally to them proving his identity by showing them the hands and feet which still bore the tell-tale marks of the nail-prints:

'Why are you troubled, and why do doubts rise in your minds? Look at my hands and my feet. It is I myself. Touch me and see . . .' When he had said this he showed them his hands and feet.

The result? The reason for their unbelief changed: 'They still did not believe . . . because of joy and amazement' (Luke 24:41). Many of us find it equally difficult truly to believe some of the claims Jesus made but we need never despair about this. Jesus is the same 'yesterday, today and for ever'. And just as he persisted in breaking down the barriers which prevented the disciples from believing, so, when our faith grows cold for any reason, with the same sort of tenderness and compassion, he woos us back until love for him and trust in him flowers once more.

A prayer

Search my heart, O God. Melt with the warmth of your tender love any unbelief you unearth there.

JH

Patient

The disciples should have anticipated the resurrection of Jesus. After all, several passages in the Old Testament predict that the Messiah would rise from the dead. And Jesus himself had warned them many times that he would die and then on the third day, he would rise again. Even so, they failed to understand. And even when Jesus appeared personally to them and showed them his hands and his feet, as we saw yesterday, 'They still did not believe' (Luke 24:41). Some teachers might have given up at this stage. But not Jesus. He loved them so much and so longed that they would grasp the truth that he persisted:

He said to them, 'This is what I told you while I was still with you: Everything must be fulfilled that is written about me in the Law of Moses, the Prophets and the Psalms.' Then he opened their minds so they could understand the Scriptures.

What Jesus taught them that day was not new. Rather he underlined familiar truths in such a way that, at last, their minds were able to contain them.

We are even more privileged than the disciples. We have the Old Testament and the New to reveal to us everything we need to explain the mysteries of our faith. Even so, sometimes we find ourselves riddled with doubt. At such times, it is good to be assured of God's patience; of his longing to reveal to us as much of the mystery as we need to grasp. He does this in a whole variety of ways: through sermons, through discussions, through notes like these, through nature, through books, through meditation, through circumstances—even through pain ... He takes the initiative in making his ways plain—not through newness but through 'nowness'. Immediacy. Our responsibility is simply to be receptive and to allow ourselves to be worked on by God.

For meditation

Be still. Look back. Ask yourself: 'What has God been trying to show me about himself recently?'

JH

Gentle

Love is patient. Love is kind. That's what St Paul claims and no one demonstrates this more than Jesus himself. Most pastors would have given up on Thomas when he made that preposterous and presumptuous claim:

'Unless I see the scars of the nails in his hands and put my finger on those scars and my hand in his side, I will not believe.'

But not so Jesus. Jesus loved Thomas. More than anything else, he wanted this disciple to be certain that his master really had risen from the dead. And so Jesus answers Thomas' prayer, comes to him personally and invites him to gaze at his hands and thrust his own hand into Jesus' wounded side. Did the other disciples look on scandalized? Probably. Most of us are not good at respecting the sincere doubts which assault others. But Jesus understood and he cared more about Thomas' welfare than the doubts he was expressing. And Jesus' perseverance and gentleness won the day. It broke through the hard crust of cynicism and drew from the doubting disciple the most profound profession of faith that anyone had yet uttered in the presence of the resurrected Jesus.

'My Lord and my God!'

Not even Mary had yet called Jesus 'God'. Thomas is the disciple whom many of us most resemble. We, too, resist, question, refuse to give way lest we are found to be gullible. We demand proof. Fellow Christians grow weary of our scepticism. We separate them with our questions and fears. But just as Jesus read the heart of 'doubting Thomas', so he reads our doubts, detects the love and hurt that lie behind them and, when the time is ripe, he comes to us, melts our hardness and with his customary gentleness, chides us with a twinkle in his eye: Stop doubting and believe!

A prayer

Lord, I do believe. Help my unbelief.

JH

Forgiving

God is compassionate. He is 'slow to anger, abounding in love and faithfulness, maintaining love to thousands...' So writes the author of the book of Exodus (34:6–7). Jesus highlighted these truths when he appeared to his friends after the resurrection. He also demonstrated how forgiving he was. Of all the disciples, Peter must surely have been the one who suffered most after the death of Jesus. How often, I wonder, did he turn over in his mind the fact that he had slept in Gethsemane's garden instead of supporting Jesus in prayer as his master begged to be spared the indignity and pain of the cross? How often did he recall the blasphemous way in which he had denied all knowledge of Jesus? How often did he watch in slow motion an action-replay of that moment when, while the cock let out his blood-curdling crow, Jesus turned to him with such hurt in his eyes? Yes. Peter must have felt a complete and utter failure and continued to weep bitter tears as he re-lived his cowardice. No wonder he had difficulty in coming to terms with the fact that Jesus might have risen from the dead. But such is the overflowing forgiveness of the crucified Jesus that he chose to come personally to Peter. Luke gives us only the bare bones of the encounter:

'The Lord has risen and has appeared to Simon.'

Did Peter fall at Jesus' feet and grovel when he met Jesus in Jerusalem? Possibly. Such failure often fills people with fear as well as guilt. But just as Jesus prayed for Peter and released him from the guilt and the effect of his failure, so he delights to restore us to full fellowship with the Father.

For meditation

Think of a time when you have failed God. Then put yourself in Peter's shoes as, for the first time, he sees Jesus standing beside him. What does Jesus do? What does he say?

JH

Loving

Even when we've been forgiven by God, it is easy to fall into the trap of believing that we have forfeited our right to serve him in any major way. On such occasions, we can draw comfort from Jesus' further encounter with Peter. This encounter came to life for me one day when I was sitting on a tiny beach beside the Sea of Galilee. This beach, it is believed, marks the place where Jesus cooked breakfast for his disciples after the resurrection and where he brought fresh hope to Peter. To commemorate Peter's re-commissioning, a most moving statue has been erected on this spot. The statue represents Peter acknowledging his unworthiness by kneeling at Jesus' feet and reaching out empty, helpless hands to him while gazing adoringly into his Master's face. Jesus, meanwhile, is laying one hand on Peter's head in blessing while holding in the other a shepherd's crook which, clearly, he is about to give to his contrite disciple. John records the story which prompted the sculptor to produce this masterpiece:

Jesus said to Simon Peter, 'Simon son of John, do you truly love me more than these?' 'Yes, Lord,' he said, 'you know that I love you.' Jesus said, 'Feed my lambs' . . . 'Take care of my sheep.'

Love does not dominate, it cultivates.

Love does not crush, it restores. Love is what Jesus is. And here we see his love in action. Just as Jesus took time and trouble to build up his battered and bruised disciples, so he comes to us in the aftermath of our failures and discouragements and asks us: 'Do you love me?' Then he affirms us by showing us just what our new vocation is to be.

For meditation

Respond to Jesus' question: Do you love me?

JH

153

A prayer of St Paul

I remember you in my prayers and ask the God of our Lord Jesus Christ, the glorious Father, to give you the Spirit, who will make you wise and reveal God to you, so that you will know him. I ask that your minds may be opened to see his light, so that you will know what is the hope to which he has called you, how rich are the wonderful blessings he promises to his people, and how very great is his power at work in us who believe. This power working in us is the same as the mighty strength which he used when he raised Christ from death and seated him at his right hand in the heavenly world.

In some churches a deeply symbolic piece of ritual takes place on the evening of Ascension Day. Up until then the great Easter candle has been in the sanctuary—near to the Communion table. On Good Friday the light of the world went out. But on Easter morning it shone out of the tomb, and after the resurrection the risen Christ showed himself to his followers over forty days. Then he went away again; they didn't know his presence in that form any more.

So on the evening of Ascension Day the Easter candle is carried out of the church. It has been my task as a deacon to do that, and always when I have lifted it up and carried it high—out of the church—I felt a deep desolation. I didn't want it to go! But the purpose of this separation was to bring about a deeper closeness and a deeper union. Something far, far better than the physical presence of Jesus, or even the presence of the risen Christ, was on its way.

But in the meantime there was an emptiness to experience ... and a waiting for the new.

A way to pray

Think of what you feel like when someone you love goes away: perhaps for a few weeks, or perhaps in the separation of death. Imagine the Easter candle leaving the church ... symbolizing the light going out of your life. Tell God what you feel like. Don't jump ahead too quickly to the wonder of Pentecost and the giving of the Holy Spirit to live within you. Can you still believe even in your own experience of emptiness and darkness? Dare you still hope in the God who loves you?

SB

The gift of contemplation

Over the past few days we have reminded ourselves that God is the God who comes, that Jesus underlined this in the weeks following his Resurrection, that during those forty days, he fulfilled Isaiah's promise and gave his disciples gladness instead of sadness. Joy displaced the despair of his bereaved, bewildered, guilt-ridden and doubting disciples.

But Jesus' appearance to the disciple he loved, John, assures us that it is possible to be grief-stricken and despondent but at the same time so open to God that even though we do not see or hear him, yet we become deeply aware of his living presence.

In chapter 20 of his Gospel, John recalls how, early on Easter morning, Mary startled himself and Peter with the news that Jesus' body had been removed from the tomb. Peter and John raced to the garden. John reached the tomb first but stayed on the threshold while Peter ran straight inside:

He saw the strips of linen lying there, as well as the burial cloth that had been around Jesus' head. The cloth was folded up by itself, separate from the linen. Finally the other disciple, who had reached the tomb first, also went inside. He saw and believed. (They still did not understand from Scripture that

Jesus had to rise from the dead.)

John does not say that he enjoyed an encounter with Jesus. What he implies is that, through the gift of contemplation, he 'saw' the risen Lord with the inner eye of faith. For contemplation sees beyond words and concepts and symbols, and even though it cannot grasp to the full their meaning, it enters into the reality they represent. Contemplation goes further. As it stops to gaze, it is awakened to the mystery of God's presence even though God remains hidden.

Just as John saw and believed without fully understanding the mystery he contemplated, so Jesus invites us to receive the gift of contemplation which will enable us to join the throng of those who are blessed because, although they have not seen the risen Lord with their physical eyes, they have seen him with the eye of faith—and believed and worshipped.

For meditation

By love can he be caught and held, but by thinking never.

The Cloud of Unknowing

JH

Jesus brings joy

The risen Christ must have been fun to be with. He sprang so many surprises on his disciples—like the morning he cooked breakfast for them on the shore of the Sea of Galilee.

Seven of the disciples had spent the night out on the lake—fishing. They had caught nothing. As dawn broke, Jesus appeared on the seashore and suggested that they should throw their nets out of the other side of the boat. While they worked, he busied himself by barbecuing fish for their breakfast:

When they landed, they saw a fire of burning coals there with fish in it, and some bread. Jesus said to them, 'Bring some of the fish you have just caught. Simon Peter climbed aboard and dragged the net ashore. It was full of large fish, 153, but even with so many the net was not torn. Jesus said to them, 'Come and have breakfast.' None of the disciples dared ask him, 'Who are you?' They knew it was the Lord. Jesus came, took the bread and gave it to them, and did the same with the fish.

These seven disciples were skilled fishermen but that morning they must have been discouraged and exhausted. What fun Jesus must have had preparing for them a whole string of surprises: his unscheduled visit, the unexpected haul of fish and the welcome meal. How they must have laughed as they enjoyed that meal together on the shore.

Just as Jesus surprised his disciples and injected them with such joy, so he creeps up on us when we are in the middle of the most mundane or exacting task, and gives us the sustenance of his smile of love. He overshadows someone with his presence as they do the washing up. As the writer concentrates on a piece of work, he gives inspiration. As two married people work at their relationship, he fills them with a new and deep love for each other and they experience resurrection joy.

To mull over

Resurrection as a present miracle does not deliver us from the unevenness and turmoil and fragmentariness of being human. The miracle is to be found precisely within the ordinary round and daily routine of our lives.

H.A. Williams, *True Resurrection*

JH

Ascension Day

Two days ago, we saw how, through the gift of contemplation, our inner eye can see the invisible and believe what we cannot understand. The Ascension of Jesus is one of those mysteries which needs to be contemplated rather than studied.

To contemplate simply means 'to look at', to gaze, or, as a friend of mine puts it, 'to gawk'. If, at the same time as we gawk, we picture the events we are pondering as vividly as we can, using what C.S. Lewis called 'our baptised imagination', an event like the Ascension will always present us with fresh insights.

Piecing together the fragments of information the Gospel-writers provide us with, we know that on Ascension Day, Jesus prepared his disciples for this final post-resurrection appearance by inviting them to meet on a certain mountain-top. When he arrived they worshipped him. In response he gave them certain promises: the gift of power through the baptism of the Holy Spirit, the privilege of being his international envoys, his personal blessing. It was while he was blessing them that the cloud received and hid him, taking him from them. They were awed—overwhelmed with the kind of deep-down joy which sometimes accompanies an unforgettable spiritual experience.

But what the disciples did not know as they watched the cloud which contained God's glory was what was happening to Jesus in the heavenly realms. Paul describes it:

[God] raised him from the dead and seated him at his right hand in the heavenly realms, far above all rule and authority, power and domination, and every title that can be given, not only in the present age but also in the one to come. And God placed all things under his feet and appointed him to be head over everything for the church, which is his body, the fulness of him who fills everything in every way.

A project

Imagine that you are standing on the mountain-top with the disciples. Watch the cloud receive Jesus. Picture him being greeted by his Father and the angels. Let God unfold hidden truths. As he opens your heart and mind to the conquering King, ask yourself, 'How do I want to worship the ascended Jesus?'

JH

Waiting

Someone has rightly said that the stops as well as the starts of life are ordained by God. On Ascension Day, Jesus told his disciples to 'stop':

'Do not leave Jerusalem, but wait for the gift my Father promised, which you have heard me speak about. For . . . in a few days you will be baptised with the Holy Spirit.'

Many Christians, after they have enjoyed an encounter with God, cannot contain their joy. They tell all and sundry what they have seen and heard and felt.

It would have been easy for the disciples to do that on Ascension Day. After all, they had a scoop of a story: they had witnessed the end of Jesus' life on earth and his sensational re-entry into heaven. But Jesus cautions them—wait in the city, he says—then travel to the ends of the earth to spread the good news.

They needed to be empowered by the Spirit. That was one reason why they were told to wait. If they had rushed from the mountain-top to Jerusalem or Galilee, their witnessing would have been garbled and ineffective.

Waiting also gave them time to assimilate their three years with Jesus, time to relish and make sense of them; to put together the pieces of the jigsaw.

Waiting almost certainly deepened their longing for that 'something more' Jesus had promised. They loved and trusted Jesus, so although they could not have known how the Holy Spirit would come to them, what they did know was that his coming would equip them in some way for the task to which Jesus had called them.

Just as Jesus told his disciples to 'wait', so he begs us to build into the senseless rush of our over-busy lives, 'godly pauses'—times when we still ourselves, assimilate and relish God's gifts and open ourselves to him so completely that we reach out for the 'something more' he is always offering us.

A project

Today and every day, make five minutes to watch an action replay of the past twenty-four hours. Select from the video playing on the screen of your mind only the good things that have happened to you. Relish them. Give God thanks for them.

JH

Prepare for Pentecost

I used to puzzle over Luke's observation that, having witnessed Jesus' Ascension, the disciples were filled with *joy*. How, I wondered, could they part from their master and experience joy and not pain? After all, at most railway stations and airports, when friends and relatives bid each other farewell, their eyes are filled with tears.

One Ascension Day, I realized that the reason why the disciples were so joyful was that they understood the radical difference between a disappearance and a departure. As Louis Evely points out, 'A departure causes an absence, a disappearance inaugurates a hidden presence.' On Ascension Day, Jesus did not depart from his disciples in the sense that he deserted them; he simply disappeared. And he had prepared them for this disappearance:

'I will ask the Father, and he will give you another Counsellor to be with you for ever—the Spirit of truth . . . I will not leave you as orphans; I will come to you.'

Here Jesus is not only preparing his friends for his inevitable disappearance but promising that when he goes, the Holy Spirit, the third person of the Godhead, will come to them as a gift from the Father. This Holy Spirit is the Holy Paraclete—the one who is called by God to draw alongside us and to help us in any kind of need. He is the Comforter, the Counsellor, the Strengthener, the Enabler of God's people. (All this is wrapped up in that word 'Paraclete' or 'Counsellor'.) And although the Holy Spirit is a separate person from Jesus— he is 'another' Counsellor—the Greek word Jesus uses for 'another' literally means one of the same kind—of the same divine nature and with the same aims as himself. When the Holy Spirit takes up residence inside us, therefore, it is as though, in some mysterious way, Jesus himself fills us with his own eternal fullness.

On Ascension Day, did the Holy Spirit remind the disciples of this teaching Jesus had given them just before he died? Was this why his disappearance filled them with joy and not grief? We don't know. What we do know is that through his Spirit, Jesus wants to indwell us.

A prayer

Spirit of the Living God,
Fall afresh on me.

JH

The Holy Spirit's task

On Ascension Day, Jesus told his disciples to wait in Jerusalem until they were empowered by the Holy Spirit. Yesterday we observed who the Holy Spirit is: the third person of the Holy Trinity, separate from but linked with Jesus. Today and for the next few days, we examine some aspects of the Holy Spirit's mission. Paul mentions one:

God has poured out his love into our hearts by the Holy Spirit, whom he has given us.

Love is what God is. And love has to communicate itself. From the beginning of time, God has demonstrated his love for man and woman. But we have been slow to grasp that love. Even though Jesus died to show us the lengths to which love is prepared to go, we still have difficulty in absorbing the amazing fact that God loves each of us uniquely. It is the Holy Spirit's task, not simply to convince us that God loves us, but so to spread this love in our innermost being, that we feel its warmth, tenderness and compassion. This inner awareness and certainty of God's love is what motivates us to respond. When we know God loves us, it inspires us to love him in return.

One way of showing God we love him is to worship him through hymns and choruses, spoken prayers and psalms or the silent prayer of loving attentiveness. This two-way love-affair between the believer and God is brought about by the Holy Spirit. It is the nub of true prayer.

And such prayer which springs from love from God and love for God gives birth to something else: love for God's world. A study of the life of Jesus quickly reveals how intensely he loved rich and poor, intellectuals and the uneducated alike. He was filled with compassion for them, quite literally taking upon himself their frustrations and sorrows. The Holy Spirit's task is so to work in the deep places of our lives that we will not be content simply to worship nor just to pray. We shall beg to be shown how to take the love of God into a desperately needy world.

A project

As you read the newspaper or watch the news today, pray: 'Lord, how can I help to rescue your world?'

JH

Invaded by the Spirit

When the day of Pentecost came, they were all together in one place. Suddenly a sound like the blowing of a violent wind came from heaven and filled the whole house where they were sitting. They saw what seemed to be tongues of fire that separated and came to rest on each of them. All of them were filled with the Holy Spirit and began to speak in other tongues as the Spirit enabled them. Now there were staying in Jerusalem God-fearing Jews from every nation under heaven. When they heard this sound, a crowd came together in bewilderment, because each one heard them speaking in his own language. Utterly amazed, they asked: 'Are not all these men who are speaking Galileans? Then how is it that each of us hears them in his own native language? ... we hear them declaring the wonders of God in our own tongues!' Amazed and perplexed, they asked one another, 'What does this mean?' Some, however, made fun of them and said, 'They have had too much wine.'

Jesus' followers prayed and waited for the promised Holy Spirit. His arrival was unmistakable! Things began to happen. The wind filled the house, and the Spirit's presence could be felt all round them. Flames were seen on each individual, and each person was touched. They began to speak in 'tongues'. God gives this gift to many Christians today, either a known language to convey God's message, or unknown words to enrich prayer. A clergyman I know once spoke in tongues during a sermon. An amazed visitor in the congregation asked 'How does he know High German?' God used this means to catch the person's attention. The people praised God freely as they 'declared his wonders'. (I was a Christian for many years before the Spirit's fresh touch gave me real joy in worship.) Reactions were mixed—honest enquiry or sceptical mocking.

The same happens nowadays. The Spirit does not always work so dramatically. He may come more like a breeze than a gale. But when he comes we shall still see clear evidence of his powerful activity.

A way to pray

Dare you ask God to release his Spirit in you? Can you let him choose how he does it?

RG

The Bible comes alive

Then Peter stood up with the Eleven, raised his voice and addressed the crowd: 'Fellow Jews and all of you who live in Jerusalem. Let me explain this to you; listen carefully to what I say. These men are not drunk . . . It's only nine in the morning! No, this is what was spoken by the prophet Joel: "In the last days, God says, I will pour out my Spirit on all people. Your sons and your daughters will prophesy, your young men will see visions, your old men will dream dreams . . . I will show wonders in the heaven above and signs on the earth below . . . And everyone who calls on the name of the Lord will be saved."'

Do you remember Peter's cowardice when Jesus was on trial? Three times he denied any association with Jesus. What a transformation when the Spirit came! In the face of charges of drunkenness he stood up with the other eleven disciples and preached a bold, impromptu sermon. He first addressed the mockers: 'No, we are not drunk. The Spirit has come.'

The Spirit gave Peter a new understanding of Scripture. He quoted first from the prophet Joel and later on from Psalms 16 and 110. He proclaimed that their new experience was fulfilling Joel's words that the Spirit would be poured out on all believers, not just on a select few (as in the Old Testament) . Peter expected the prophecies, visions, dreams, wonders and signs that all follow in the Book of Acts.

The Spirit enabled Peter to recall whole passages of Scripture. The Jews were strong on memorizing—and we can take a leaf out of their book. We can learn parts of the Bible by heart, ready for the Spirit to prompt us in times of need. The Spirit also enhances our own love of Scripture. He can give us a new hunger for the Bible and new joy and understanding in reading it.

A prayer

Blessed Lord, who caused all holy Scriptures to be written for our learning: help us to hear them, to read, mark, learn and inwardly digest them that, through patience and the comfort of your holy word, we may embrace and for ever hold fast the hope of everlasting life, which you have given us in our Saviour Jesus Christ.

The Collect for the second Sunday in Advent, ASB

RG

Peter's message

'Men of Israel, listen to this: Jesus of Nazareth was a man accredited by God to you by miracles, wonders and signs, which God did among you through him, as you yourselves know. This man was handed over to you by God's set purpose and foreknowledge; and you, with the help of wicked men, put him to death by nailing him to the cross. But God raised him from the dead, freeing him from the agony of death, because it was impossible for death to keep its hold on him . . . God has raised this Jesus to life, and we are all witnesses of the fact. Exalted to the right hand of God, he has received from the Father the promised Holy Spirit and has poured out what you now see and hear.'

After responding to the mockers Peter spoke about the heart of his good news, Jesus: who lived, died, rose and ascended.

Jesus who lived. 'Jesus of Nazareth' was human, but 'accredited by God': divine power was demonstrated in his works. Peter reminds his hearers that Jesus' deeds were not mere hearsay; even those who had not watched Jesus' deeds could see their effects. *Jesus who died.* 'You . . . put him to death.' Peter puts the responsibility for the cross onto his hearers, along with the traitor Judas and the jealous Jewish and Roman leaders. Yet behind these men was 'God's set purpose and foreknowledge'. Isn't it utterly amazing? God knew from the beginning that human disobedience would spoil his good creation. Yet he actually used human wickedness in his divine plan to redeem human wickedness. *Jesus who rose.* Immediately after the crucifixion the disciples must have

been altogether confused and discouraged. But then they saw Jesus alive and on one occasion 'he appeared to more than five hundred . . . at the same time' (1 Corinthians 15:6). So the resurrection became a linchpin of the apostles' preaching. *Jesus who ascended.* After they had waited in Jerusalem, as he told them to just before the Ascension, Jesus fulfilled his promise that his followers would be enriched when he left them and the Spirit came to them.

A reflection

Peter wrote later that we should be ready to explain our faith to everyone who asks us about it (1 Peter 3:15). Are you more ready to speak about church activity—or about Jesus who lived, died and rose, and whose Spirit is resident in your life?

RG

A challenge to commitment

'Therefore let all be Israel be assured of this: God has made this Jesus, whom you crucified, both Lord and Christ.' When the people heard this, they were cut to the heart and said to Peter and the other apostles, 'Brothers, what shall we do?' Peter replied, 'Repent and be baptised, every one of you, in the name of Jesus Christ for the forgiveness of your sins. And you will receive the gift of the Holy Spirit. The promise is for you and your children and for all who are far off—for all whom the Lord our God will call.' With many other words he warned them; and he pleaded with them, 'Save yourselves from this corrupt generation.' Those who accepted his message were baptised, and about three thousand were added to their number that day.

Peter's sermon, inspired by the Holy Spirit, was direct and hard-hitting. The hearers were 'cut to the heart' by the words and by the Spirit, whom Jesus had said would 'convict the world of guilt' (John 16:8). Their cry was 'Help! What are we to do?' Peter's answer was quite clear. *They had to repent.* Repentance means a change of direction. If they were to receive forgiveness for sins they needed to turn round from those sins. *They had to be baptized.* This was a public declaration of the commitment of their wills and hearts. *They would be given the Holy Spirit.* That is the right of all people who commit themselves to Jesus' way. Peter said that the promise was for his hearers, for their children and for all whom God would call. This does not mean that the children of believers are automatically children of faith; they, like others who will hear about Jesus, are each responsible for their own commitment, even if they have been baptized as infants. Personal response *and* baptism are important Christian foundations, whichever happens first.

A question

How does this passage challenge you?

RG

A living fellowship

They devoted themselves to the apostles' teaching and to the fellowship, to the breaking of bread and to prayer. Everyone was filled with awe, and many wonders and miraculous signs were done by the apostles. All the believers were together and had everything in common. Selling their possessions and goods, they gave to anyone as he had need. Every day they continued to meet together in the temple courts. They broke bread in their homes and ate together with glad and sincere hearts, praising God and enjoying the favour of all the people. And the Lord added to their number daily those who were being saved.

Daily growth in our church! That would be exciting—so long as we were flexible, willing to change to accommodate the growth. What were the marks of this church in Jerusalem which 'enjoyed the favour of all the people' and attracted so many to join the believers? *They devoted themselves*... That implies whole-hearted commitment... *to the apostles' teaching*... These new believers were hungry to learn from Old Testament Scripture and from all the apostles had learnt from Jesus... *to the fellowship* ...They were not individualistic in their faith, as many of us are ...*to the breaking of bread*... The Eucharist was central. They had no church buildings but met for worship in their own homes... *to prayer*... This apparently included formal, traditional prayer in the temple and public Christian worship in the temple courtyard as well as solo and corporate prayer in their homes.

Everyone was filled with awe... They had a great awareness of God's presence and reverence for him. *There were many miracles*... The disciples had watched Jesus, and now, empowered by the Spirit, they copied him. *They held their possessions loosely*... They did not say 'mine' but 'ours'. *They shared meals together with glad and sincere hearts*... They loved being together in joy and openness. *They were full of praise*...

A reflection and a prayer

Think: *How far does my life and my church's life match up to those early Christians?*

Pray: *Most merciful Redeemer, Friend and Brother, may we know you more clearly, love you more dearly, and follow you more nearly, day by day.*

Richard, Bishop of Chichester

RG

A miracle of healing

One day Peter and John were going up to the temple at the time of prayer—at three in the afternoon. Now a man crippled from birth was being carried to the temple gate called Beautiful, where he was put every day to beg from those going into the temple courts. When he saw Peter and John about to enter, he asked them for money. Peter looked straight at him, as did John. Then Peter said, 'Look at us!' So the man gave them his attention, expecting to get something from them. Then Peter said, 'Silver or gold I do not have, but what I have I give you. In the name of Jesus Christ of Nazareth, walk.' Taking him by the right hand, he helped him up, and instantly the man's feet and ankles became strong. He jumped to his feet and began to walk. Then he went with them into the temple courts, walking and jumping, and praising God. When all the people saw him walking and praising God, they recognised him as the same man who used to sit begging at the temple gate called Beautiful, and they were filled with wonder and amazement at what had happened to him.

Imagine the scene, and put yourself in the place of the lame man. Think how he felt as he was carried to his regular begging spot; as he asked for money; as he was told to get up and walk; as Peter took his hand; as he went into the temple courtyard; as the crowd watched in amazement. Take pen and paper (later, if you can't do it now), and 'be' the cripple writing your diary that evening. Use this to sense the power of Jesus making an impact on your life.

This man had been incapacitated for forty years. That fact encouraged me ten years ago when I was struggling with the effects of lifelong pain and anger—and I was over forty years old. I thought 'If God could heal that man, he can change me!' He did. The power of Christ is still active.

This morning I prayed for the same power to overcome a chronic bad habit left over from childhood.

For prayer

Talk to God about anything that has troubled you for many years, and ask for the power of Christ for change.

RG

Weakness and power

The priests and the captain of the temple guard and the Sadducees came up to Peter and John while they were speaking to the people. They were greatly disturbed because the apostles were teaching the people and proclaiming in Jesus the resurrection of the dead. They seized Peter and John, and because it was evening, they put them in jail until the next day. But many who heard the message believed, and the number of men grew to about five thousand.

Peter and John had gone to the temple for the formal time of prayer. Some might have thought that a major miracle was enough excitement for one day. But Peter was immediately ready to talk to the gathering crowds about Jesus. He reminded them plainly that they were responsible for killing Jesus, 'the author of life'. But this Jesus was raised from the dead by their nation's God and it was 'by faith in the name of Jesus' that the cripple was healed. 'When God raised up his servant he sent him first to you to bless you by turning each of you from your wicked ways' (Acts 3:26). Peter sets us an example in his readiness to seize any opportunity to talk about Jesus, and in the boldness and clarity of his message.

The reactions to his preaching were strong. On one hand hundreds more joined the crowd of believers. On the other hand there was strong antagonism. That is always so. The more clearly the gospel is preached, the more it divides followers from sceptics. The opposing groups had different motives. Look again to see why they were 'greatly disturbed'.

The priests would have been fearful of losing their authority with the ordinary people. The Christians threatened them as much as Jesus did. The Sadducees would have been outraged by any suggestion that the resurrection could be true. And the captain of the temple guard would have been concerned for security and order in the temple precincts—and probably for his own job security too. So out of their weakness they used their power to imprison the apostles.

A reflection

Think about yourself, your priorities and your fears. Then consider each of the people in this story, and decide whom you are most like. Peter? The new believers? The priests? The Sadducees? The captain?

RG

Three in One

Recently a barrister friend of mine told me about another barrister who works in the same chambers and who is a Christian. She is highly intelligent, but she can't understand the Trinity. The early Christians didn't have to, because the word was never used until three hundred years later. But perhaps those early Christians had an even tougher problem. They were nearly all Jews, and the great summary of their belief, the *Shema*, was carved on their hearts and said aloud to their children:

'Hear O Israel: the Lord our God, the Lord is one. You shall love the Lord your God with all your heart, and with all your soul, and with all your might. And these words which I command you this day shall be upon your heart; and you shall teach them diligently to your children, and shall talk of them when you sit in your house, and when you walk by the way, and when you lie down, and when you rise.'

But those first Jewish Christians knew that in Jesus they had gloriously encountered God, and seen what Bishop John Robinson called so beautifully 'the human face of God'. Therefore they worshipped the risen Christ and also prayed to him. But that wasn't the end of their difficulty or of their wondering delight, because next they encountered God dwelling gloriously within their own hearts—in a way that had never been known before. So this was God in a third manifestation—the Holy Spirit. Different from Jesus, and different from the One whom Jesus called Father. But it was still the same God, and God was still One.

The only way to begin to comprehend the mystery is to pray it. So sit still in your chair and ask God to reveal himself to you as he is. Worship the Creator God who made the world... and think of the galaxies spinning in space... and a tree you know... and all growing things. Think of living creatures... dogs and cats and elephants, and the faces and voices of people you love. Then remember Jesus, walking the roads of Galilee two thousand years ago and telling those wonderful stories: the prodigal son, the lost sheep, the good Samaritan... and then dying on a cross, rising from the dead, and ascending into heaven: and worship him and talk to him. Finally, be aware of the Holy Spirit of God within you—and marvel and worship again.

SB

Weakness and courage

The next day the rulers, elders and teachers of the law met in Jerusalem ... They had Peter and John brought before them and began to question them: 'By what power or what name did you do this?' Then Peter, filled with the Holy Spirit, said to them: ' ...If we are being called to account today for an act of kindness shown to a cripple and are asked how he was healed, then know this ... It is by the name of Jesus Christ of Nazareth, whom you crucified but whom God raised from the dead, that this man stands before you healed ... Salvation is found in no-one else, for there is no other name under heaven given to men by which we must be saved.' When they saw the courage of Peter and John and realised that they were unschooled, ordinary men, they were astonished and they took note that these men had been with Jesus ... [The leaders then conferred on their own] ... Then they called them in again and commanded them not to speak or teach at all in the name of Jesus. But Peter and John replied, 'Judge for yourselves whether it is right in God's sight to obey you rather than God. For we cannot help speaking about what we have seen and heard.'

The Jewish leaders were in a quandary. They had hoped at Jesus' death would end their difficulties. Now they found themselves facing new problems! They knew the healing was real and that 'all the people were praising God for what had happened' (v. 21). Two ordinary men stood before them, and the whole group of leaders was floored.

A promise

'When they arrest you, do not worry about what to say or how to say it. At that time you will be given what to say, for it will not be you speaking, but the Spirit of your Father speaking through you.'

Matthew 10:19–20

A prayer

Lord Jesus, I confess that I fail in my courage to speak for you, and in ... [fill in your own words]. Please fill me with your Spirit, that I may be more like Peter and John, and more ...

RG

Bold prayer

On their release, Peter and John went back to their own people and reported all that the chief priests and elders had said to them. When they heard this, they raised their voices together in prayer to God. 'Sovereign Lord,' they said, 'you made the heaven and the earth and the sea, and everything in them. You spoke by the Holy Spirit through the mouth of your servant, our father David: "Why do the nations rage and the peoples plot in vain? The kings of the earth take their stand and the rulers gather together against the Lord and against his Anointed One." Indeed Herod and Pontius Pilate met together with the Gentiles and the people of Israel in this city to conspire against your holy servant Jesus whom you anointed. They did what your power and will had decided beforehand should happen. Now, Lord, consider their threats and enable your servants to speak your word with great boldness. Stretch out your hand to heal and perform miraculous signs and wonders through the name of your holy servant Jesus.'

Set free, Peter and John returned to their friends; 'They told us to stop preaching.' Most of us would spend hours discussing the situation, but they immediately prayed. Notice how they praised God: *Sovereign Lord*: God is in total control. *You made*: He is Lord of all creation. *You spoke by the Holy Spirit*. I believe they had in mind the whole of Psalm 2, which continues, 'The One enthroned in heaven laughs ... he rebukes them in his anger ...' God is Lord over all rulers. *Your power and will had decided*: Even the conspiracy against Jesus was in God's eternal purpose. Now notice their requests.

Enable your servants to speak: even though it was Peter's preaching that put them in prison! *Stretch out your hand to heal*: even though it was a miracle that started the fuss. Then, 'After they prayed, the place where they were meeting was shaken. And they were all filled with the Holy Spirit and spoke the word of God boldly.' (v. 31)

A reflection

Consider how you are feeling now. How does that make you want to pray?

RG

The danger of deceit

Now a man named Ananias, together with his wife Sapphira, also sold a piece of property. With his wife's full knowledge he kept back part of the money for himself, but brought the rest and put it at the apostles' feet. Then Peter said. 'Ananias, how is it that Satan has so filled your heart that you have lied to the Holy Spirit and have kept for yourself some of the money you received for the land? Didn't it belong to you before it was sold? And after it was sold, wasn't the money at your disposal? What made you think of doing such a thing? You have not lied to men but to God.' When Ananias heard this he fell down and died. And great fear seized all who heard what had happened.

This dramatic story follows a passage that concentrates on the Christians' generosity with their possessions. Many of them sold property and entrusted the money to their leaders to use for the poor. Let's imagine Ananias and Sapphira talking together: S. People are asking why we haven't given away any of our lands. A. Aren't they ours to do with what we want? S. We could sell one of the fields and give part of the cash. A. And then pretend it was all we got from the sale.

How easily one suggestion leads to the next! In this story we see *The downward pull of human sin*: Greed and deceit characterize this couple. Peter recognized their right to ownership; his concern was their lies. *The reality of Satan*: When Ananias and Sapphira yielded to temptation they gave Satan an opportunity to enter their lives. Satan grabs any crack of human sin as an open door. Some people ignore his very existence; others blame him for everything that goes wrong. Both extremes are mistaken, but be warned of his activity. *The power of the Holy Spirit:* Jesus often knew what was in people's hearts. Peter, filled with the Spirit, had the same gift (which Paul calls a 'message of knowledge' in 1 Corinthians 12:8). God used it to convict Ananias of his sin.

A thought

Ananias was guilty; fear of God's judgment brought on his fatal heart attack. The Church's fear was godly fear; that leads to repentance and change.

RG

God's mighty power

The apostles performed many miraculous signs and wonders among the people. And all the believers used to meet together in Solomon's Colonnade. No one else dared join them, even though they were highly regarded by the people. Nevertheless, more and more men and women believed in the Lord and were added to their number. As a result, people brought the sick into the streets . . . and all of them were healed. Then the high priest and all his associates . . . were filled with jealousy. They arrested the apostles and put them in the public jail. But during the night an angel of the Lord opened the doors of the jail and brought them out. 'Go, stand in the temple courts,' he said, 'and tell the people the full message of this new life.'

The Jewish leaders were determined to shut up the apostles—literally, in jail, and metaphorically, to keep them quiet. God had other ideas! *He exercised his power to heal.* We remember the crowds that thronged round Jesus. Power to heal did not end with Jesus—nor with the apostles. God still heals today, though such an intensive period of miracles is occasional, not all the time. *He continued to draw people to follow Jesus* through preaching and through miracles. *He sent an angel to free them from prison.* This, too, reminds me of Jesus in the Gospels. 'An angel of the Lord came down from heaven and, going to the tomb, rolled back the stone' (Matthew 28:2). The power that freed Jesus is the same power that freed the apostles—and the same 'incomparably great power' is available 'for us who believe,' says Paul (Ephesians 1:19). *He emboldened them to keep preaching despite the authorities' opposition.*

A prayer

Father, I find it hard to believe these things can happen nowadays. To be honest, I'm scared. But I do want your Spirit to fill me, and to overflow in the way I live and the way I speak.

RG

Unstoppable witnesses

At daybreak they entered the temple courts, as they had been told, and began to teach the people. When the high priest and his associates arrived, they called together the Sanhedrin—the full assembly of the elders of Israel—and sent to the jail for the apostles. But on arriving at the jail, the officers did not find them there . . . [They were found in the temple courts, teaching the people, and brought before the Sanhedrin and the High Priest.] 'We gave you strict orders not to teach in this name,' he said. 'Yet you have filled Jerusalem with your teaching and are determined to make us guilty of this man's blood.' Peter and the other apostles replied: 'We must obey God rather than men! The God of our fathers raised Jesus from the dead—whom you had killed by hanging him on a tree. God exalted him to his own right hand as Prince and Saviour that he might give repentance and forgiveness of sins to Israel. We are witnesses of these things and so is the Holy Spirit, whom God has given to those who obey him.'

Have you ever tried bobbing for apples? The buoyancy of the apple makes it almost impossible to hold down. The apostles were rather like that apple! However hard the Jewish authorities tried to check them from preaching they could not do it. Peter's words show us why they were so unsquashable. They were single-minded in their allegiance. 'We must obey God rather than men.' They knew it was God's power that 'raised Jesus from the dead' and 'exalted him to his own right hand.' They were witnesses. They had first-hand experience of Jesus' resurrection and ascension. They had been given the Holy Spirit.

A prayer

Lord God, I pray that I might know the hope to which you have called me, and the riches of your glorious inheritance in the saints, and your incomparably great power in us who believe: a power which is like the working of your mighty strength, which you exerted in Christ when you raised him from the dead and seated him at your right hand in the heavenly realms.

Based on Ephesians 1:17–23

RG

173

Expediency and wisdom

When they heard this, they were furious and wanted to put them to death. But a Pharisee named Gamaliel, a teacher of the law, who was honoured by all the people, stood up in the Sanhedrin and ordered that the men be put outside for a little while. Then he addressed them: 'Men of Israel, consider carefully what you intend to do to these men. Some time ago Theudas appeared, claiming to be somebody, and about four hundred men rallied to him. He was killed, all his followers were dispersed, and it all came to nothing. After him, Judas the Galilean appeared in the days of the census and led a band of people in revolt. He too was killed, and all his followers were scattered. Therefore, in the present case I advise you: Leave these men alone! Let them go! For if their purpose or activity is of human origin, it will fail. But if it is from God, you will not be able to stop these men; you will only find yourselves fighting against God.'

The council members were understandably furious. They were the leaders and the experts on theological matters; they expected to be revered and obeyed. Now these uneducated followers of Jesus were accusing them of murder, constantly defying them, and attracting more and more followers through preaching apparent blasphemy. Killing them seemed the obvious way out. But among them was a wise, even-tempered man. Gamaliel knew that God was sovereign and that his good purposes would be worked out. Gamaliel's argument was simple. 'Wait and see what happens. If this is just a human revolt it will fade, as the others did. If it is of God'—as Gamaliel probably believed— 'we do not want to be on the wrong side.' What wise words for precaution against panic reactions!

A way to pray

Meditate on those words of Gamaliel and ask yourself: Is God really in control? Can he be trusted one hundred per cent? What anxiety in my life now should I deliberately ask him to control?

RG

Move with the Spirit

...Right then three men who had been sent to me from Caesarea stopped at the house where I was staying. The Spirit told me to have no hesitation about going with them. These six brothers also went with me, and we entered the man's house. He told us how he had seen an angel appear in his house and say, 'Send to Joppa for Simon who is called Peter. He will bring you a message through which you and all your household will be saved.' As I began to speak, the Holy Spirit came on them as he had come on us at the beginning. Then I remembered what the Lord had said, 'John baptised with water, but you will be baptised with the Holy Spirit.' So if God gave them the same gift as he gave us, who believed in the Lord Jesus Christ, who was I to think that I could oppose God?

The living God is always pouring out his love and himself into improper places and improper people—and the rigidly religious find it disturbing and upsetting. They would prefer God to behave like a tidy canal, staying within the banks which they have dug, and directed where they have chosen. But instead the river of life flows just where it chooses. It floods its banks in glorious abandon and abundance, and the desolate deserts of the earth start to blossom and bear fruit. Isaiah prophesies that one day, 'The earth shall be filled with the knowledge of the Lord as the waters cover the sea' (11:9), and in 49:6 of the same book God speaking through Isaiah says, 'It is too light a thing that you should be my servant to raise up the tribes of Jacob ... I will give you as a light to the nations, that my salvation may reach to the end of the earth' (49:6). Now it was happening. God was giving himself to Gentiles as well as to Jews—and not doing it in the proper order! Pouring out himself in the baptism of the Spirit *before* they had gone through the procedures—and doing it even as Peter was in the process of preaching. First the baptism of the Holy Spirit—and then the baptism of water. You can read all about it in Acts 10.

SB

175

Spiritual administrators

In those days when the number of disciples was increasing, the Grecian Jews among them complained against the Hebraic Jews because their widows were being overlooked in the daily distribution of food. So the Twelve gathered all the disciples together and said, 'It would not be right for us to neglect the ministry of the word of God in order to wait on tables. Brothers, choose seven men from among you who are known to be full of the Spirit and wisdom. We will turn this responsibility over to them and will give our attention to prayer and the ministry of the word.' This proposal pleased the whole group. They chose Stephen, a man full of faith and of the Holy Spirit; also Philip, Procorus, Nicanor, Timon, Parmenas, and Nicolas from Antioch, a convert to Judaism. They presented these men to the apostles who prayed and laid their hands on them.

The apostles knew where their priorities lay, in prayer and preaching. But they were concerned for the good of the community and they were willing to delegate responsibility. It is noticeable that they did not make autocratic decisions but they consulted the whole congregation.

What qualities would you look for in those who were to be practical, caring administrators? Most of us would probably seek gifts of organization and social concern. What did the apostles look for? 'Men who are known to be full of the Spirit and wisdom.' That should be the prime aim of any of us who want to serve God in any capacity, whether in an upfront 'spiritual' ministry or in washing dishes, singing in the choir, as PCC members or sidespersons, in the church or in daily employment. We are prone to separate the 'sacred' from the 'secular', instead of submitting our lives to him as a whole. If we are 'full of the Spirit' we will consult him often during the day, whatever our occupation.

The names of the men chosen are all Greek names. Care was taken to choose those who would be trusted to be fair to everyone who had felt neglected. That shows wisdom.

A reflection

What lessons does this passage have for those who are Church leaders? What encouragements for those who do the 'ordinary' jobs?

RG

Christlikeness

Now Stephen, a man full of God's grace and power, did great wonders and miraculous signs among the people. Opposition arose, however, from members of the Synagogue of the Freedmen (as it was called) Jews of Cyrene and Alexandria as well as the provinces of Cilicia and Asia. These men began to argue with Stephen, but they could not stand up against his wisdom or the Spirit by whom he spoke. Then they secretly persuaded some men to say, 'We have heard Stephen speak words of blasphemy against Moses and against God.' So they stirred up the people and the elders and the teachers of the law. They seized Stephen and brought him before the Sanhedrin. They produced false witnesses, who testified, 'This fellow never stops speaking against this holy place and against the law. For we have heard him say that this Jesus of Nazareth will destroy this place and change the customs Moses handed down to us.' All who were sitting in the Sanhedrin looked intently at Stephen, and they saw that his face was like the face of an angel.

Stephen was chosen by the congregation to serve food to the widows. He soon showed that he had gifts to use in other ways. As I read about Stephen I see in this Christian one who was very much a Christ-man. There are several remarkable similarities between Stephen and his master. If you can find time during the week, underline in your notes some of the phrases that remind you of Jesus.

Do you know anyone of whom you might say that his face, or her face, 'is like the face of an angel'? If we want to reflect the love and beauty of Jesus we start where Stephen started; he was 'full of the Spirit'. If we open ourselves to the Holy Spirit he will reveal Jesus to us and gradually make us more like our master.

A reflection

Now the Lord is the Spirit, and where the Spirit of the Lord is, there is freedom. And we, who with unveiled faces all reflect [or contemplate] the Lord's glory, are being transformed into his likeness with ever-increasing glory, which comes from the Lord, who is the Spirit.

2 Corinthians 3:17–18 (NIV)

RG

Angry blame

'You stiff-necked people, with uncircumcised hearts and ears! You are just like your fathers: You always resist the Holy Spirit! Was there ever a prophet your fathers did not persecute? They even killed those who predicted the coming of the Righteous One. And now you have betrayed and murdered him—you who have received the law that was put into effect through angels but have not obeyed it.' When they heard this, they were furious and gnashed their teeth at him.

Stephen was accused by false witnesses of speaking against the temple, the law and their customs. So the high priest asked him whether these complaints were true. His reply took his hearers through the early history of their own nation, from Abraham's call to leave Mesopotamia through to Solomon building the temple. His theme was the repeated misunderstanding and rejection received by Joseph, Moses and others. His hearers listened patiently; Stephen clearly knew his ancient history. So long as he was speaking about others they were not touched; but as soon as he confronted them directly they were convicted—and they were furious.

It is easy to point a finger at other people. But a hand that points a forefinger at another has three other fingers pointing back at the person doing the pointing. 'If any of you is without sin, let him be the first to throw a stone at her,' said Jesus to those who brought him a woman accused of adultery. Honesty made them gradually disappear. When

we see that we are as much to blame as others we can react in two ways. We can turn our guilt into anger, as these men did against Stephen. Or our guilt can lead us to confession, repentance and finding God's forgiveness.

A confession

Before you use this confession, read it through. Then stop and think honestly how it applies to you, so that you can be specific and genuine in your prayer.
Lord, I think of the times when I have blamed others when I was guilty myself.
Please forgive me for my unfairness, especially when others have been hurt by it. Show me where I should apologize or make restitution.

RG

Christlike death

But Stephen, full of the Holy Spirit, looked up to heaven and saw the glory of God, and Jesus standing at the right hand of God. 'Look,' he said, 'I see heaven open and the Son of Man standing at the right hand of God.' At this they covered their ears and, yelling at the top of their voices, they all rushed at him, dragged him out of the city and began to stone him. Meanwhile, the witnesses laid their clothes at the feet of a young man named Saul. While they were stoning him, Stephen prayed, 'Lord Jesus, receive my spirit.' Then he fell on his knees and cried out, 'Lord, do not hold this sin against them.' When he had said this, he fell asleep. And Saul was there, giving approval to his death.

Stephen was filled with the Holy Spirit. The Spirit gave him a rare experience, a vision of the majesty and glory of God and of the Son of Man (an Old Testament name for the Messiah). His death, like that of Jesus, was ugly and cruel. Yet through the Spirit he behaved like Jesus, forgiving those who hurt him and entrusting his spirit to God. It is the same Spirit who can transform our own prayer and worship, to help us sense the glory of the almighty God. It is the Spirit who helps us to forgive those who wrong us and to trust our whole lives to him.

The members of the Sanhedrin were shaken by the events of recent months. But they were sincerely convinced that Stephen was blaspheming in his claim to see God; so they were obeying the Jewish law in stoning him—no doubt delighted to have the final excuse for their anger to boil over in killing him. It is possible to be sincere but utterly wrong—especially when our emotions want to convince us that we are right. Saul only played a small part in this event, but Luke's mention of his presence implies that it made a significant impact on him and played a part in his subsequent conversion.

A way to pray

Look back at the Bible reading for the last three days. In what ways would you like to be like Stephen? Then, in prayer, open yourself to God to change you.

RG

Creatures of the night

'God so loved the world that he gave his only Son, that everyone who has faith in him may not perish but have eternal life. It was not to judge the world that God sent his Son into the world, but that through him the world might be saved. No one who puts his faith in him comes under judgement; but the unbeliever has already been judged because he has not put his trust in God's only Son. This is the judgement: the light has come into the world, but people preferred darkness to light because their deeds were evil. Wrongdoers hate the light and avoid it, for fear their misdeeds should be exposed. Those who live by the truth come to the light so that it may be clearly seen that God is in all they do.'

When I was a little boy, I hanged my teddy bear. Gruesome, but not unusual in little boys. Unfortunately, the rope took the paint off the banister, so I blamed my small brother, and he got spanked. Once we do one wrong thing, we are usually led into covering it up with a lie. Then we cover that by lying to ourselves, rather than face unpleasant facts—especially when they are more serious than damaging the paint-work. That is why repentance is so difficult. We can develop a habit of hiding from ourselves. And the bigger our sins, the harder we lie and the harder it is to face the truth.

Love demands that we face that truth. We cannot love without being honest or receive love without being open. So when the love of God comes into the world in Jesus, it faces no only glad acceptance, but bitter denial.

This is not only true of people faced with their first offer of the gospel. As we follow Jesus, we are called to be honest with him and with ourselves. We are called not to hide in the shadows but to let his light shine on us to show up the areas where we most need his help. That can be a painful thing, like antiseptic on a wound. But it is what we need for our healing.

Pray

Batter my defences Lord; shine out light through the cracks in my armour of falsehood, and draw me closer into your healing love.

MM

Ask for anything

If you remain in me and my words remain in you, then you will ask for anything you wish, and you shall have it. My Father's glory is shown by your bearing fruit; and in this way you become my disciples. I love you just as the Father loves me; remain in my love. If you obey my commands, you will remain in my love, just as I have obeyed my Father's commands and remain in his love. I have told you this so that my joy may be in you and that your joy may be complete. My commandment is this: love one another, just as I love you.

It seems a sweeping promise—to ask for anything, and get it. Does it mean that Christians can always be sure of getting the right Christmas presents? Surely there is a catch? Well, yes there is, but that's not the best word for it. Jesus cannot mean that if we ask for something sinful, we will get it, and that rules out a lot of things. He is not offering prayer as a means of getting anything we covet, even if what we want is good in itself. Instead, he is describing the end result of a life of prayer—an end that I, for one, am far away from!

'Anything' must mean anything that is in line with our relationship with God. As we've seen, that rules out immoral or wicked things. But it goes deeper than that. Prayer can never force God to do things. He always remain in charge. So the kind of prayer which is always sure of its answer is the prayer which grows out of a deep awareness of God's will out of a deep relationship with him.

As we come to know God better, we become more and more aware of what he wants—and our prayers reflect that. So we pray more as he wants, and our prayers are answered more often. It is not that our prayers have become more powerful, but that we see his will more clearly. Prayer is God's way of inviting us into his plans, and about becoming involved in what God is doing.

A prayer

Pray for a deep awareness of God, and a clearer vision of will.

MM

Love in action

For six weeks now we shall look at the heart of Jesus' teaching—which is inseparable from his actions. Love in action showed us and told us how to love. He touched the untouchables, and talked to people whom the rest of society had pushed out to the edges. Like the Samaritan woman—who had had five husbands and was currently set up with a live-in lover. Jews weren't supposed to talk to women in public at all, let alone an unrespectable woman such as this one. But Jesus not only talked with her. He talked theology with her—and she ended up the conversation a new person. Not because of the theology, but because she met Jesus and drank the living water that he offered her by the well.

The Sermon on the Mount sums it all up—and people sometimes say that they aren't Christians but they believe in the Sermon on the Mount. But they can't have read it—or if they have they must have done it with their minds totally closed to what it says. It is the most radical piece of teaching in history—and apart from the Spirit of Jesus living in us we shall never even begin to live it out in the world.

As we read about love in action in Jesus we can know that he is showing us what God is like and also what we are meant to be like:

> You have heard that it was said, 'Love your neighbour and hate your enemy.' But I tell you, Love your enemies and pray for those who persecute you, that you may be sons of your Father in heaven. He causes his sun to rise on the evil and the good, and sends rain on the righteous and the unrighteous. If you love those who love you, what reward will you get? Are not even the tax collectors doing that? And if you greet only your brothers, what are you doing more than others? Do not even pagans do that? Be perfect, therefore, as your heavenly Father is perfect.

Matthew 5:43–48

The commands of God

My son, do not forget my teaching, but keep my commands in your heart, for they will prolong your life many years and bring you prosperity. Let love and faithfulness never leave you; bind them around your neck, write them on the tablet of your heart. Then you will win favour and a good name in the sight of God and man. Trust in the Lord with all your heart and lean not on your own understanding; in all your ways acknowledge him, and he will make your paths straight. Do not be wise in your own eyes; fear the Lord and shun evil. his will bring health to your body and nourishment to your bones.

This is an apt passage for us as we study the Scriptures, because by reading the Bible we are doing just what we are being told to do. It is Wisdom who is speaking, and the one through whom the world and its creatures were made knows just how human creatures need to run their lives in order to be healthy and happy. 'The claim that some behaviour patterns lead to human health and happiness while others do not—simply because of the way people are made—surely merits a hearing from a generation which faces the global threat of Aids. Perhaps this lay behind the embarrassment of an anonymous psychologist who cares for many Aids patients, when he was asked by a journalist, 'If we had played by New Testament rules on sexual behaviour, would we have ever had an epidemic?' 'Of course not,' he replied, 'but, for God's sake, don't quote me on that!' (Dr Caroline Collier, *The Twentieth-Century Plague*, Lion Publishing).

Reflect

How different would the world be if all the people in it remembered what God has told them to do and they did it ... in their family lives ... in their sex lives ... in their business lives ... in their eating ... in their drinking ... in their motoring ... How different would my own life be if I really obeyed the maker's instructions? Did God give his commands to make us happy or to spoil our fun?

SB

Copy-cats

'In very truth I tell you, the Son can do nothing by himself; he does only what he sees the Father doing: whatever the Father does, the Son does. For the Father loves the Son and shows him all that he himself is doing, and will show him even greater deeds, to fill you with wonder. As the Father raises the dead and gives them life, so the Son gives life as he chooses. Again, the Father does not judge anyone, but has given full jurisdiction to the Son; it is his will that all should pay the same honour to the Son as to the Father. To deny honour to the Son is to deny it to the Father who sent him.'

After healing a paralysed man on the Sabbath, Jesus is asked what authority he has to ignore the law against working on the Sabbath. His answer is that he does only what he sees his Father doing. The image in the opening verses is probably drawn from the kind of apprenticeship Jesus would actually have had in the carpenter's shop at Nazareth. The son learnt his trade by copying exactly what his father did.

In the same way, as Son of God, all Jesus' work is copied from what God does. Not only in healing the sick, but also in bringing (eternal) life. This is important. Sometimes Christians are tempted to see Jesus as the friendly saviour, and God as the distant judge. Jesus becomes a sort of defence against God. But that cannot be true. The proper way of looking at it is the one John gives us. Jesus copies his Father so closely because Jesus is *God's* way of bringing salvation.

In a smaller (but still important) way,

the idea of copying God applies to us as well. When we put our faith in Jesus we are brought into that father/child relationship with God. We too become God's apprentices. Like all normal apprentices, we will make mistakes, but the important thing is to keep our eyes on what our Father s doing, and act the same way.

Pray

Father, open my eyes to what you are doing in the world. Wherever I see you at work, give me grace to work with you and for you.

MM

The living Word

'The Father who has sent me has borne witness on my behalf. His voice you have never heard, his form you have never seen; his word has found no home in you, because you do not believe the one whom he sent. You study the scriptures diligently, supposing that in having them you have eternal life; their testimony points to me, yet you refuse to come to me to receive that life.'

Yesterday we saw Jesus' defence of his actions as simple obedience to God. But what evidence can he offer that he can know God's will so well? The answer is that God himself is Jesus' witness. He has testified for Jesus. Not by direct speech, or by appearing bodily, not even by Jesus' own prophetic words, since Jesus is not believed, God has spoken of Jesus through the Jewish Scriptures (our Old Testament). So Jesus issues a challenge to the religious leaders of his time: look at the Bible, and prove me wrong!

That might seem easier said than done. We often hear it said that you can prove anything from the Bible. In fact though, you can't. What you can do, is read only the bits that prove your case, or read it with your mind already made up. Jesus' words here are a challenge to us as we read these Bible notes. How do we come to the Bible? Do we come expecting to prove our own opinions, or to have them challenged by the word of God? Do we come already knowing what it must say? I remember a Bible study in which a difficult verse got the comment, 'Of course, it can't really mean that, or

what we believe would be wrong!' In fact, there's always the chance that what we believe is at least incomplete.

The answer, of course, is to read the Bible with the desire to learn, and to hear God speak to us. To read it with prayer and meditation, ready to be shown something new. Without that attitude, all the Bible knowledge in the world is useless; it's just so much information. But with that attitude the Bible becomes the living word of God, to teach challenge and encourage us.

Think

Just what do you want from your Bible reading? Pray about that and ask God to speak to you.

MM

Food for life

Jesus said to them, 'I am the bread of life. Whoever comes to me will never be hungry, and whoever believes in me will never be thirsty . . . I have come down from heaven, to do not my own will, but the will of him who sent me. It is his will that I should not lose even one of those he has given me, but should raise them all up on the last day.'

This year I have heard dozens of complaints about the weather. Either it is too hot, or else it is too cold. While shopping today, it was made quite clear to me that the thing to have is a compact-disc player. Last year it was a video recorder, and the year before that a home computer. It seems that whatever we have, weather or goods, it isn't *quite* what we truly want.

The same holds true on a deeper level. No matter how loving our parents, we wish they were more understanding. No matter how close wife or husband, we sometimes wonder whether we would have been happier with someone else. At the deepest point of our souls, it seems that there is a dissatisfaction which we cannot fill, not with property, or money, or love. There is always something missing. There is a hunger, a thirst.

Then along comes Jesus with those incredible words: 'Whoever comes to me will never be hungry . . . will never be thirsty.' Jesus is claiming to be the one who can satisfy, finally and forever that deepest and most hidden longing in our hearts.

Why? Because the longing is, in the end, for God. It is a desire to return to a home we have forgotten but never replaced—to be at one with the one who made us to love him and know him. It is the longing for heaven, where Jesus came from, and to which he promises to raise us up. Once we come to him, we may still feel that longing, but at last we can know that it will be fulfilled. Because he has come to satisfy the hunger, and to take us home.

Meditate

You have made us for yourself, O God, and our hearts are restless till they find their rest in you.

St Augustine

MM

Jesus the real thing

'In very truth I tell you, unless you eat the flesh of the Son of Man and drink his blood you can have no life in you. Whoever eats my flesh and drink my blood has eternal life, and I will raise him up on the last day. My flesh is real food; my blood is real drink. Whoever eats my flesh and drinks my blood dwells in me and I in him.'

We've all seen the adverts for a certain American fizzy drink, which tell us that it is 'the real thing'. The idea is that there are many imitators, but only the original stuff has the true flavour. The same sort of idea is in these verses. Many things claim to fill the deepest needs of our lives, but only the God who meets us in Jesus can really fit the bill.

He meets our needs, not by any sort of magical formula, but by entering into a deep and rewarding relationship with us. We live in him and he in us. Being a Christian is not just about getting the creeds and doctrines and forms of worship just so. It is about getting to know Jesus; about letting him become friend and brother, teacher and lover.

Like any friendship, our love affair with God has to be worked at and nourished. We have to feed it. At the centre of that relationship is the act of worship we call, amongst other things, the Eucharist, Communion, or Mass. It is I time when we feed on him, and are being filled with his love and mercy, his self-sacrifice and spiritual refreshment. It is a time for getting close to Jesus and sharing in his life.

At Communion

Imagine the bread dissolving within us, being absorbed into our bodies. Think of the presence of Jesus within us— becoming one with us, and filling us with his love.

Imagine the wine being absorbed into our blood, flowing through our veins. Think of the strength of Jesus running through us, filling us with energy, and power to do his will. Praise God for the life he shares with us.

MM

Too much to stomach

On hearing [these things], many of his disciples exclaimed, 'This is more than we can stand! How can anyone listen to such talk?' Jesus was aware that his disciples were grumbling about it and asked them 'Does this shock you? Then what if you see the Son of Man ascending to where he was before? It is the spirit that gives life; the flesh can achieve nothing; the words I have spoken to you are both spirit and life. Yet there are some of you who have no faith.'

While it isn't mentioned by the other Gospel-writers, it is quite possible that some of Jesus' disciples left him as they began to understand more of his teaching. But John has more in mind. He is writing at a time when the Church is becoming divided, especially by people (called Docetists, from the Greek word for 'seem') who could not believe that Jesus was truly human. The incarnation was too much to swallow. How could God have really come down from heaven? (Which is what this chapter of the Gospel says he did.) Surely Jesus must have only seemed to be human?

Once again we see the big mistake of limiting God to our ideas. John's answer here is that they are thinking in purely human terms (the 'flesh' which cannot give life). Instead, they must be open to God who speaks to the spirit.

Today we have to remember that the gospel is still offensive to many people. It attacks their self-esteem. (I remember a man who left his church after many years when he finally got the message that he was considered a sinner!) It upsets their view of the world and their beliefs about what is and is not important. To others it merely sounds quaint and old-fashioned.

There are times when we have to accept that and avoid the temptation to water down our faith so that it is more palatable. John could have gone down that road, but he knew that in the end nothing would be left. Better to hold fast to the amazing fact that in Jesus, God truly has visited us.

Reflect

If the Christian faith does seem strange, is that really remarkable? Would the God who created all that exists really be expected to do anything that isn't incredible?

MM

Hope and despair

From that moment many of his disciples drew back and no longer went about with him. So Jesus asked the Twelve, 'Do you also want to leave?' Simon Peter answered him, 'Lord, to whom shall we go? Your words are words of eternal life. We believe and know that you are God's Holy One.'

There is a delightful simplicity about Peter's answer. Yet it covers a deep truth. If we don't have Jesus, what do we have left? A friend of mine, after many years of discipleship, claims to have lost his faith. He says that his work and his family life and his desire to help others are as strong without God as with him. I'm sure he's right. But that's as far as he can take it. If I ask him what purpose he has in life; what he will do, or what he will be worth, if he loses his job or family or strength, he has no answer. When I ask whether he will have more than memories when his elderly parents die, he can only say, 'No'.

After all, without God what do we know about life? The existence of our planet becomes an accident. That it can support life is an unlikely chance. We come into the world by chance, we die leaving nothing that will last more than a few years.

The greatest curse of all is that still we cannot shrug off the feeling that there is purpose in the world, that we *do* have a value above what we do or give or have.

But there is no need to take that road. In Jesus we do see the Holy One of God, who comes to show that there is purpose because we were made to love and serve God, that we have value because God made us and loves us enough to die for us. We don't have to turn our back on a scientific view of the world, for underneath it we can see that reality is not about mechanical accidents, but about love and creativity. Jesus truly has the words of eternal life, for they give us hope and meaning in the face of despair and emptiness.

Think

No matter what I do, or have, I have value, because God values me.

MM

Love!

One of the teachers of the law came and heard them debating. Noticing that Jesus had given them a good answer, he asked him, 'Of all the commandments, which is the most important?' 'The most important one,' answered Jesus, 'is this: "Hear, O Israel, the Lord our God, the Lord is one. Love the Lord your God with all your heart and with all your soul and with all your mind and with all your strength." The second is this: "Love your neighbour as yourself." There is no commandment greater than these.'

They weren't new, these two commandments that Jesus said were the greatest. They were there right back in the Pentateuch (Deuteronomy 6:4–5 and Leviticus 19:18 if you want to look them up). 'Love your neighbour as yourself...' isn't about a narcissistic self-love but about a healthy self-love. If we are hungry we will feed ourselves, and if we are thirsty we will get ourselves something to drink. This is the most basic love of all—and when we dare to find out who is hungry and who is thristy we shall probably ask the question that produced the story of the Good Samaritan: 'Lord, who is my neighbour?' And we might like the answer as little as Jesus' listeners when he gave it.

But what about the commandment to love God? What does that really mean and how do we do it? To love with all our hearts means to love with the whole of our being. To love with all our understanding means to use and exercise our mind and our thinking in the process. And to love with our all our strength means to bend all our energy to our loving. But what does it mean to love? Love is not an emotion and not a feeling of delight or rapture (though sometimes that can be the result of loving). To love God is quite simply to do the will of God. Jesus said in the Gospel of John, 'If you love me, keep my commandments.' We use our heart in commitment to them— our mind in discovering and exploring them—and the whole of our strength in performing them.

SB

190

All the thirsty people

Jesus, tired by the journey, sat down by the well. It was about the sixth hour. When a Samaritan woman came to draw water, Jesus said to her, 'Give me something to drink.' His disciples had gone into the town to buy food. The Samaritan woman said to him, 'You are a Jew. How is it that you ask me, a Samaritan, for something to drink?'—Jews, of course, do not associate with Samaritans. Jesus replied to her: 'If you only knew what God is offering and who it is that is saying to you, "Give me something to drink," you would have been the one to ask, and he would have given you living water.'

Nowadays we hear quite a lot about groups of Christians marching around the edge of a town or part of a city 'claiming it for the Lord'. One hopes that they get involved with the centre of such areas as well. A friend of mine was asked to run a house for homeless men in the East End of London when he was still very young. Each night he set off in the dark to seek out places where these men (many of them alcoholics) settled for the night. Sometimes he was so frightened that he turned round and ran home again. He was only a part-time coward, though. He persisted, and the project thrived. He took Jesus to people who might not have met him otherwise.

Here we see Jesus taking himself into an area that Jews normally avoided like the plague. He did not walk round it; he walked into it.

Having despatched the disciples (why did it take twelve men to collect the groceries?), he then defied convention even further by not only speaking to a Samaritan woman, but actually asking her for a drink. Like the homeless men that my friend visited on their own ground, she was curious about the motivation for this unusual behaviour. The answer in both cases was the same. Jesus had come, bringing the water of life. It is not easy to go into places that are unfamiliar or threatening in some way, but if we want to follow Jesus, that is what will happen. It may be the people next door, it may be the pub down the road, it may be deepest Borneo, but if he calls us, we either go—or disobey.

A prayer

Lord, am I avoiding anyone or anywhere that you want me to visit? I need courage. Please give it to me when I need it, so that I can take you to those who need living water.

AP

Unpoisoned water

'You have no bucket, sir,' she answered, 'and the well is deep: how do you get this living water? ... Jesus replied, 'Whoever drinks this water will be thirsty again; but no one who drinks the water that I shall give him will ever be thirsty again: the water that I shall give him will become in him a spring of water, welling up for eternal life.' 'Sir,' said the woman, 'give me some of that water, so that I may never be thirsty or come here again to draw water.' 'Go and call your husband,' said Jesus to her, 'and come back here.' The woman answered, 'I have no husband.' Jesus said to her, 'You are right to say, 'I have no husband'; for although you have had five, the one you now have is not your husband. You spoke the truth there.'

Sometimes self-indulgence and sin appear very much more attractive than the path of virtue, especially when it is the path of arid, bloodless duty. Six years ago, when a stress-related illness forced me out of work and my world was collapsing around me, I wrote these words:

Who made these poison pools in
desert lands
So sweet and cool?
A welcome lie,
The chance to die with water on my lips.
I've seen how others try to die
Unpoisoned in the sun,
I do not think that I can do as they
have done.

In this passage, Jesus is offering clean, healthy, running water to replace both the poisoned water of negative behaviour and the aridity of loveless virtue.

In the case of the Samaritan woman, it is her predilection for a broad choice of close gentlemen friends that constitutes the poisoned water that will kill her in the end. What a mind numbing shock it must have been when this rather impressive stranger's innocent-sounding suggestion was followed by such an accurate stab of insight.

God understands our failings. He knows the weaknesses that are responsible for bad decisions and developments in our lives. But the living water is still on offer, water that will purify our minds and bodies and make virtue a by-product of joy.

A prayer

Lord, I know you will not be soft with me when straight speaking is needed. Let us meet and talk. You will tell me what is not clean in my life, and I shall ask you for living water to wash it away.

AP

He lives in our hearts

'I see you are a prophet, sir,' said the woman. 'Our fathers worshipped on this mountain, though you say that Jerusalem is the place where one ought to worship.' Jesus said: 'Believe me, woman . . . the hour is coming—indeed is already here—when true worshippers will worship the Father in spirit and truth: that is the kind of worshipper the Father seeks. God is spirit, and those who worship must worship in spirit and truth.' The woman said to him, 'I know that Messiah—that is, Christ—is coming; and when he comes he will explain everything.' Jesus said, 'That is who I am, I who speak to you.'

The Samaritan woman's religious understanding was sketchy and intuitive, but on one point she was quite clear. 'The Christ is coming and he will explain everything.'

One summer holiday we entertained seventeen Russians to a barbecue in our garden on a Saturday evening. Our guests were in a party mood. They had come to England as tourists, but, because of a breakdown in communications at an early stage the local man who had organized the trip mistakenly believed them to be seventeen youth leaders on a fact-finding tour. Frequent, inexplicable trips to scout troops, schools and youth clubs had left the Russians completely bewildered and just a little resentful. Now, with their host's eccentricities explained, they danced and sang under our apple trees, determined to enjoy themselves.

'What do you think about God?' I asked one of them through an interpreter, thinking that I could predict his answer.

'We have no education in God,' he replied, 'but'—and he thumped his barrel chest—'he lives in our hearts.'

Can you understand what I mean when I say that I envied that man slightly? In this part of the world it may be that we have too much education in God, and not enough simple awareness of his presence with us. Like my Russian, the Samaritan woman was in possession of one simple, certain truth: 'The Christ is coming . . .'

Imagine the heart-stopping amazement that this woman must have felt when the man who had already proved his power to her said, 'You're right, and I'm him—I've come.'

A thought

Is there such a thing as a more sophisticated faith? How does the tension between intelligence and simplicity help or hinder us? Are we too ready to assume that some groups, races or religions know nothing of Jesus?

AP

Come and see Jesus

At this point his disciples returned and were surprised to find him speaking to a woman, though none of them asked, 'What do you want from her?' or, 'What are you talking to her about?' The woman put down her water jar and hurried back to the town to tell the people, 'Come and see a man who has told me everything I have done; could this be the Christ?' This brought people out of the town and they made their way towards him. Meanwhile, the disciples were urging him, 'Rabbi, do have something to eat'; but he said, 'I have food to eat that you do not know about.'

We are told that when the food buying committee came back from whatever the Samaritan equivalent of Tesco's was, they were surprised to find their master talking to the Samaritan woman, but that they declined to comment. Some people suggest that this indicates sensitivity and tactfulness on the part of the disciples, but I doubt it. We hear in another part of the Gospels that they were afraid to tell Jesus what they were discussing because it might make him angry. It seems much more likely that they were simply beginning to learn that if he was doing something, however strange, it must be worth doing, and the best thing they could do was to co-operate.

The principle holds good today. Find out what God is doing and join in, as a friend of mine put it recently, and don't ask unnecessary questions.

The Samaritan woman, in defiance of many modern three-point sermons on outreach, now rushes off full of excitement to evangelize before she gets round to repenting. Whenever and wherever the power of Jesus is genuinely manifested we are bound to see this kind of natural, spontaneous spreading of the good news that Jesus has come. She simply could not contain herself, and soon the sheer infectiousness of her enthusiasm brought a congregation out to the well.

We say we are in the decade of evangelism (a fact which must excite God greatly!) but if what we are doing is devising and organizing events, then asking God if he would care to help with the chairs or the refreshments, or some other little task not yet allocated, we shall get nowhere. Jesus himself, his power and his love, must be at the very centre and forefront of our efforts, exciting people so much that they rush off to tell others.

A prayer

Help us to follow you unquestioningly, Lord, and to keep you at the front of all we do.

AP

Passion and privilege

So the disciples said to one another, 'Has someone brought him food?' But Jesus said: 'My food is to do the will of the one who sent me, and to complete his work. Do you not have a saying: Four months and then the harvest? Well, I tell you, look around you, look at the fields, already they are white for harvest! Already the reaper is being paid his wages, already he is bringing in the grain for eternal life, so that sower and reaper can rejoice together. For here the proverb holds true: one sows, another reaps. I sent you to reap a harvest you have not laboured for. Others have laboured for it; and you have come into the rewards of their labour.'

I have never been very good at talks that are based on three points beginning with the same letter, but this passage is about priorities, passion and privilege.

Fired by this productive encounter with the gentile world, Jesus refuses the food that the disciples have brought, and re-asserts his chief priority, which is obedience. Notice that his 'food' is not seeing thousands of people converted, or sick people healed, but simply to do the will of the one who sent him. It is about relationship. What is our priority?

The passion in this section is unmistakable. The time has come for the harvest to be brought in, and Jesus is filled to the brim with Holy Spirit excitement at the urgency and the wonder and the power and the splendour of God's salvation plan nearing its climax. What is our passion?

The privilege is for the disciples and for us. We are fellow-labourers with Jesus himself in the fields that have been planted and tended by the prophets, and died for by our friend, brother and king. An immense amount of work has been done by others. Now it is our turn. Into our hands is placed a shining sickle of love and truth and judgment. The harvest is waiting for us. Does it feel like a privilege?

The challenge of this passage is immense. If we are only playing at Christianity, it will have no appeal for us at all. There is a powerful symbolic message in Jesus' refusal of earthly food in favour of spiritual sustenance. It suggests and invites a commitment that will remove our fundamental dependence on the things of this world. I find that quite frightening, don't you?

A prayer

Lord, we want to share your passion and your priorities. We are weak and blind. Open our eyes to your power and our great privilege.

AP

She told them about Jesus

Many Samaritans of that town believed in him on the strength of the woman's words of testimony, 'He told me everything I have done.' So, when the Samaritans came up to him, they begged him to stay with them. He stayed for two days, and they said to the woman, 'Now we believe no longer because of what you told us; we have heard him ourselves and we know that he is indeed the Saviour of the world.'

This Samaritan woman must have been quite something! She obviously set up a very dynamic little one-woman mission team, probably standing on a Samaritan soap-box in the market-place and describing her vivid encounter in graphic detail. If present-day Christian publishers had been around at the time, she would undoubtedly have been snapped up to write one of those testimony paperbacks that begin with the old life (five husbands) and end with the new life (one-woman mission team ... and so on). Clearly her audiences did not condemn her on hearing about her lurid past, so presumably the new life in her was powerful indeed.

Nor did she make the mistake that many evangelists and Church leaders do nowadays, of drawing her listeners to herself instead of to Jesus. They insisted on seeing for themselves, and having seen him, they wanted to keep him, as I am sure we all would. They were then able to say, as one hopes and prays that all converts will be able to say eventually: 'You told us about him, but now we've met him for ourselves, and we know who he is.'

The most any of us can hope for, whatever our dreams of spiritual progress may be, is to become an effective signpost pointing to Jesus. Generally speaking, signposts are not required to pontificate about means of transport or the way in which passengers should position themselves. They simply point the way.

I cannot help feeling that this little period of time spent in a Samaritan town must have been a pleasant respite for Jesus. He had left Judaea to avoid the Pharisees, and here, in the middle of a country that the Jews despised, he found acceptance and a warm response among Gentiles. Perhaps it is not surprising that, in a certain parable, the hero was a Samaritan.

Reflect

Is our new life more dynamic than the old one? Do we draw people to us or to Jesus? Do we mind our own business after that? Could Jesus relax with us for a while?

AP

A way to pray

St Francis of Assisi (1181–1226) was the son of a rich cloth merchant. One day, when he was in a ruined church, he heard the voice of God saying, 'Go and repair my house'. He and his first disciples lived in poverty and went round preaching, working and serving the needy. They had an infectious love for God, and the little band grew into the vast order of Franciscan friars. Francis loved the whole of creation and all God's creatures, and there are stories of him preaching to the birds and taming a wolf.

Franciscan spirituality (and spirituality is simply the practice of spiritual things) is very popular among ordinary people who like to do things for others, and this is a good and effective form of prayer. This is a practical spirituality and today's Bible passage comes from what has been called the practical Book of James.

Is anyone among you suffering? Let him pray. Is any cheerful? Let him sing praise. Is any among you sick? Let him call for the elders of the church, and let them pray over him, anointing him with oil in the name of the Lord; and the prayer of faith will save the sick man, and the Lord will raise him up; and if he has committed sins, he will be forgiven. Therefore confess your sins to one another, and pray for one another, that you may be healed.

Suggestions

Think of someone you know who is old or sick, and then go and visit them. Think of someone you know who is unhappy. What could you do to help? Think about the people who have Aids—and perhaps talk with other people about what you could do to help.

SB

197

The light of the world

'You are the light of the world. A city set on a hill cannot be hid. Nor do men light a lamp and put it under a bushel, but on a stand, and it gives light to all in the house. Let your light so shine before men, that they may see your good works and give glory to your Father who is in heaven.'

It is a dull winter afternoon and I have just been out to buy some biscuits because some people are coming to tea. As I walked down my road, and into Nutley Lane where the shop is, all the little houses were in darkness, with their windows shut tight. But then, through one of the windows, I saw a lamp shining. The light shone out into the street, and I could see the cosiness of the tiny room inside...

Now, two hours later, my visitors have come and gone. Beth, Hannah and Nicholas (who is three) and their mother, Maureen. I lit the log fire, and as the flames took hold we all watched— Nicholas most intently of all, with his eyes wide open and hardly blinking. The drawing power of fire and light is enormous—and even a tiny light can shatter the darkness of a vast area.

As the disciples of Jesus we are the light of the whole world—a tiny flame in a vast darkness. Light attracts people. It shows them the way in the darkness. And when our light shines out through the things we do they will see a small shining of the glory of God.

The word 'good' that Jesus used to describe our 'works' means good, beau-

tiful, winsome and attractive, not a tight-lipped, disapproving do-gooding. That will never glorify God.

For reflection

Thou art Fire and Light
Give us hearts of flame!
Make us to burn like beacons
In defiance of ancient Night
Make us braziers in the cold
streets of the cities,
Make us lamps in Thy sanctuaries,
Make us candles to the Sacred Heart.
The World is lost, and is looking
for the Way.

M. Farrow

SB

The whole of the law

'Think not that I have come to abolish the law and the prophets; I have come not to abolish them but to fulfil them. For truly, I say to you, till heaven and earth pass away, not an iota, not a dot, will pass from the law until all is accomplished. Whoever then relaxes one of the least of these commandments and teaches men so, shall be called least in the kingdom of heaven; but he who does them and teaches them shall be called great in the kingdom of heaven. For I tell you, unless your righteousness exceeds that of the scribes and Pharisees, you will never enter the kingdom of heaven.'

Some people say that Matthew invented this bit of the Sermon on the Mount to please the Jews. But that is a way of getting themselves off the hook, and escaping from the real, life-giving demands of the law. Jesus was not referring to the endless, impossible definitions of the scribal law, such as a burden (which wasn't to be carried on the Sabbath) being 'food equal in weight to a dried fig, enough wine for mixing in a goblet, milk enough for one swallow, honey enough to put on a wound...' (W. Barclay). The essential Old Testament law was the Ten Commandments, written on tablets of stone.

But the New Testament law is internal, written on our hearts. The new law of love, and it is possible to live in love because the Spirit of God lives in us. Augustine of Hippo's famous definition of the new law is 'Love God, and do what you like'. But that will never include breaking any of the Ten Commandments. We can be forgiven if we do, but

they still define what love is. One way to read them is as promises. As if God says to us: 'If you walk by faith, with the Spirit of my Son in your heart, you will have no other gods before me; you will not make yourself a graven image and bow down to it; you will not take my name in vain; you will remember the sabbath day to keep it holy; you will honour your father and your mother; you will not kill; you will not commit adultery; you will not steal; you will not bear false witness against your neighbour; you will not covet your neighbour's house, or her husband or his wife, or anything that is your neighbour's' (Exodus 20:3–17).

SB

If you are angry

'You have heard that it was said to the men of old, "You shall not kill; and whoever kills shall be liable to judgment." But I say to you that every one who is angry with his brother shall be liable to judgment; whoever insults his brother shall be liable to the council, and whoever says, "You fool!" shall be liable to the hell of fire. So if you are offering your gift at the altar, and there remember that your brother has something against you, leave your gift there before the altar and go; first be reconciled to your brother, and then come and offer your gift. Make friends quickly with your accuser, while you are going with him to court, lest your accuser hand you over to the judge, and the judge to the guard, and you be put in prison; truly, I say to you, you will never get out till you have paid the last penny.'

All of us would prefer to be shouted at in anger than murdered. But the sin of anger is the same sin as murder, like a poisonous plant that starts small and grows to full size. Jesus is not using the word for the anger which suddenly blazes up and just as suddenly dies down. He is using a different word, describing 'anger become inveterate. It is the long-lived anger; it is the anger of the man who nurses his wrath to keep it warm; it is the anger over which a person broods, and which he will not allow to die' (Barclay).

That sort of anger can speak out in bitter words. It calls a brother or a sister a So-and-so (*raca*), a word of contempt and despising. That can end in the hell of fire. Gehenna, the rubbish dump outside Jerusalem where fire was always burning through spontaneous combustion, and worms and maggots bred on the decaying food. Brooding, despising anger refuses to forgive or to apologize. But one day it may be too late.

A prayer

Father, forgive me my sins, in the same way and to the same extent that forgive those who sin against me. May I ask forgiveness from other people and you when I sin against them.

SB

Adultery

'You have heard that it was said, "You shall not commit adultery." But I say to you that every one who looks at a woman lustfully has already committed adultery with her in his heart. If your right eye causes you to sin, pluck it out and throw it away; it is better that you lose one of your members than that your whole body be thrown into hell. And if your right hand causes you to sin, cut it off and throw it away; it is better that you lose one of your members than that your whole body go into hell.'

Anger is the same sin as murder and lust is the same sin as adultery. Lust means 'an intense or unbridled sexual desire'. There is a total difference between looking at a woman (or a man) lustfully and looking with natural enjoyment. Pornography is about looking and lusting. The person in the photograph is depersonalized the woman, the boy, the little girl or the man.

Some people in our society are fighting against pornography. They see it for what it is. But adultery is hardly seen as a sin at all. Even some so-called Christians do it. They call it loving, and when their marriage gets tough they spend some of their time in the marriage bed and some in another, softer bed. They soothe their consciences by remembering the first half of what Jesus said to the woman taken in adultery: 'Neither do I condemn you'. But he went on. 'Go your way, and sin no more.' Adultery is forgivable. So is any sin. But all sin damages the sinner, and once the damage is done it may be irreparable.

Jesus is not telling us literally to pluck out our eye when it lusts, or to cut off any part of us which causes us to sin like Origen, who mutilated himself into a eunuch. This is simply a Jewish way of dramatic exaggeration to make the point. It is a call to spiritual action to mortify our sins: to take up our cross daily and follow Christ not on a country walk round the Lake of Galilee, but to death.

To think about

What is your attitude to adultery, to lust and to pornography? What is Jesus' attitude? Are they the same? If not, who has got it wrong?

SB

Divorce

'It was also said, "Whoever divorces his wife, let him give her a certificate of divorce." But I say to you that every one who divorces his wife, except on the ground of unchastity, makes her an adulteress; and whoever marries a divorced woman commits adultery.'

A Jew could divorce his wife if she put too much salt in his supper. Deuteronomy 24:1 writes of a man divorcing a wife 'because he has found some indecency in her', and according to the Rabbis in the liberal school of Hillel one form of indecent behaviour as over-salting a man's food. There were others, such as talking to men in the streets, brawling, and going outside with her head uncovered. Rabbis from the stricter school of Shammai said that indecency meant unchastity.

In the Greek world at the time of Jesus there were three classes of women. Demosthenes wrote, 'We have courtesans for the sake of pleasure; we have concubines for the sake of daily cohabitation; we have wives for the purpose of having children legitimately, and of having a faithful guardian for all our affairs.' In the Roman world the *paterfamilias* could not only divorce his wife but set up his own court and condemn her to death. Marriage was despised. To try to rescue it taxes were imposed on the unmarried, who were not allowed to inherit anything. Children were seen as a disaster, and those who had them were given special privi-

leges. There were as many divorces as there were marriages. Juvenal tells of a woman who had eight husbands, Martial of a woman who had ten. Think of the wonder it must have been for the woman at the well of Samaria to meet Jesus. He knew she had five husbands, and wasn't married to her current lover. But he still offered her living water.

Later in this Gospel (19:16) Jesus quotes Genesis: '. . . a man shall leave his father and mother and be joined to his wife, and the two shall become one flesh.' Divorce is an amputation.

A prayer

Lord Jesus Christ, you have shown us the right way. But when we get it wrong, and those whom we love get it wrong, still come to us in your love to forgive us, and to heal our broken hearts.

SB

'Yes' or 'No'

'Again you have heard that it was said to the men of old, "You shall not swear falsely, but shall perform to the Lord what you have sworn." But I say to you, Do not swear at all, either by heaven, for it is the throne of God, or by the earth, for it is his footstool, or by Jerusalem, for it is the city of the great King. And do not swear by your head, for you cannot make one hair white or black. Let what you say be simply "Yes" or "No"; anything more than this comes from evil.'

On the face of it this passage doesn't seem to have much to say to us. But if we have ever lived or worked with a liar then it will have. The background to it is that the Rabbis were as permissive about oaths as they were about divorce. The Old Testament said things like, 'When a man vows a vow to the Lord . . . he shall not break his word.' But they said that so long as a vow didn't include the name of the Lord, then whoever had made the vow needn't be so particular; it could be broken.

Jesus, as ever, went to the heart of the matter and told us to be the sort of people whose word can be trusted, people who speak the truth. Pilate slithered away from it with his sophisticated question, 'What is truth?' But in ordinary life we know perfectly well what it is, and when we speak it it transforms our relationships. It has to be done in love. And we don't necessarily have to speak the whole truth and tell someone just how upset we are with them. We can reserve that for God.

Consistently to lie to a person is ultimately to destroy the relationship. Even white lies make it shallow. 'Do you like my dress?' someone asks us, and perhaps we think it makes her look like mutton dressed as lamb, or a woman of the streets! Could we say, in truth and in love: 'Well, I'm not sure it's totally you! It doesn't seem to make the most of the person that you are and that I like'?

Ask yourself

How much does the truth matter to you? Do you tell it, as best you can? Do you tell so called 'white lies', which still aren't the truth? Do you think Jesus ever told them? Then pray: Lord Jesus, help me to be a woman of truth, a man of truth, like you.

SB

A way to pray

Augustine of Hippo (354–430) came back to the Christian faith after a spiritual struggle, during which his mother Monica prayed for him. In a garden he heard a voice saying, *'Tolle, lege'*—'Pick up and read'. So he picked up the Bible, and came to God through the words that he read.

In the Augustinian method of prayer we use our creative imagination to transpose the Bible into today. We think of the Bible as if it was a personal letter to us, and we imagine what a biblical scene would be like if it happened today.

When Jesus was at table in his house, many bad characters—tax-gatherers and others—were seated with him and his disciples; for there were many who followed him. Some doctors of the law who were Pharisees noticed him eating in this bad company, and said to his disciples, 'He eats with tax-gatherers and sinners!' Jesus heard it and said to them, 'It is not the healthy that need a doctor, but the sick; I did not come to inite virtuous people, but sinners.'

Think about what that passage is really saying, and let it sink into your heart. Imagine who would be there round the table with Jesus if that happened today. Who are the people in our society that we disapprove of and look down on? Shut your eyes, and see it happening... and imagine yourself sitting there at the table with them. Tell God what you think and what you feel. Be still... What is God saying to you through this?

The house of the soul

O Lord, the house of my soul is narrow; enlarge it, that you may enter in. It is ruinous. O repair it! It displeases your sight; I confess it, I know. But who shall cleanse it, to whom shall I cry but to you? Cleanse me from my secret faults, O Lord, and spare your servant from strange sins.

Augustine of Hippo

SB

The second mile

'You have heard that it was said, "An eye for an eye and a tooth for a tooth." But I say to you, Do not resist one who is evil. But if any one strikes you on the right cheek, turn to him the other also; and if any one would sue you and take your coat, let him have your cloak as well; and if any one forces you to go one mile, go with him two miles. Give to him who begs from you, and do not refuse him who would borrow from you.'

If the Sermon on the Mount was a range of mountains, then today and tomorrow we should be on its highest peak or, rather, looking at them rather warily from a long way off. Some of us are still struggling round in the foothills. Jesus is calling us to climb Mount Everest: to love our enemies (we shall do that tomorrow!) and not to resist evil. Almost impossible demands, humanly speaking, and we are not sure if we want to go quite that far.

Jesus is talking about retaliation and personal revenge and saying, 'Don't take it'. Don't even resist those who wrong you (REB). Let it hit you. Don't hit back and don't retaliate. And if a Roman soldier makes you carry his kit for a mile, which the law allows him to, carry it for a second mile. If we don't hit back then we have stopped that particular evil in our own body in a very small way as Jesus 'bore our sins in his own body on the tree' (1 Peter 2:24). If we give an extra mile freely, not under compulsion, then we shall experience a new quality of freedom and the person we do it for will experience a new quality of loving. It won't be that we walk at their side looking smug. Instead we shall look happy knowing just a little of the blissful happiness the Beatitudes promise us.

To think about

Who is the man or woman who wrongs you physically or perhaps emotionally? Imagine a scene in which they do wrong you—but in which you don't resist them—and think of Jesus there in the room with you. Then perhaps think of someone who forces you to do what you don't want to do and work out how you could go the second mile in love and freedom.

SB

Love your enemies

'You have heard that it was said, "You shall love your neighbour and hate your enemy." But I say to you, Love your enemies and pray for those who persecute you, so that you may be sons of your Father who is in heaven; for he makes his sun rise on the evil and on the good, and sends rain on the just and on the unjust. For if you love those who love you, what reward have you? Do not even the tax collectors do the same? And if you salute only your brethren, what more are you doing than others? Do not even the Gentiles do the same? You, therefore, must be perfect, as your heavenly Father is perfect.'

So here we are on the most glorious height of the Sermon on the Mount. Loving his enemies is what God does—and the reward for loving ours is to be like God. This particular word for love means 'unconquerable benevolence, invincible goodwill' (Barclay). It is to want the very best for our enemy, and to pray that he or she will be blessed and happy.

In *The Hiding Place*, Corrie ten Boom tells how in a church in Munich a former SS guard came up to her, and she recognized him as the man who had watched her and her sister in the shower room in Ravensbruck as they were processed. Now he came up to her to thank her for the wonder of her message: 'To think that He has washed *my* sins away.' He bowed and held out his hand. But she couldn't even lift hers. Angry, vengeful thoughts flooded into her mind and even when she prayed for forgiveness for them she still couldn't move. So she prayed again. 'Jesus, I cannot forgive him. Give me Your forgiveness.' Then, as she took his hand, the most incredible thing happened. 'From my shoulder along my arm and through my hand a current seemed to pass from me to him, while into my heart sprang a love for this stranger that almost overwhelmed me. And so I discovered that it is not on our forgiveness any more than on our goodness that the world's healing hinges, but on His. When He tells us to love our enemies He gives, along with the command, the love itself.'

SB

In secret

'Beware of practising your piety before men in order to be seen by them; for then you will have no reward from your Father who is in heaven. Thus, when you give alms, sound no trumpet before you, as the hypocrites do in the synagogues and in the streets, that they may be praised by men. Truly, I say to you, they have received their reward. But when you give alms, do not let your left hand know what your right hand is doing, so that your alms may be in secret; and your Father who sees in secret will reward you . . .

'When you pray, you must not be like the hypocrites; for they love to stand and pray in the synagogues and at the street corners, that they may be seen by men. Truly, I say to you, they have received their reward. But when you pray, go into your room and shut the door and pray to your Father who is in secret; and your Father who sees in secret will reward you.'

People don't always like the idea of rewards. They say they are mercenary. But rewards are an inescapable part of life, and since Jesus spoke about them perhaps we shouldn't be higher-minded than he was. A reward is what we get for doing something—the inner satisfaction of seeing another person happy because of what we have done, or playing Elgar's Cello Concerto beautifully because we spent many years developing our gift and practising.

The hypocrites get their rewards of admiration from other people but no rewards from God. No answers to prayer, because it wasn't real prayer. Real prayer, that flows out of our secret heart straight to the heart of God, is always answered. Real giving is a reflection of God, and we are more blessed in our giving than our receiving. We are enlarged, and there is more of our self to give, and more of our money. Yet to give in secret will not mean we drop five-pound notes through people's doors in the middle of the night, for fear that if we signed a cheque they would know it was us. We just have to keep quiet about it.

Consider

How do you give and how do you pray? What rewards do you desire?

SB

When you fast

'And when you fast, do not look dismal, like the hypocrites, for they disfigure their faces that their fasting may be seen by men. Truly, I say to you, they have received their reward. But when you fast, anoint your head and wash your face, that your fasting may not be seen by men but by your Father who is in secret; and your Father who sees in secret will reward you.'

Not if! When! 'When you fast', said twice. We're to fast in secret, like our giving and our praying, and we shall get a reward for this as well. But what will this reward be, and why do we have to fast anyway? I must be honest and confess that I never have and also confess that writing these notes on the Sermon on the Mount is being very salutary and very uncomfortable. I am having to change my behaviour in several different ways and now it looks as if sometimes (and secretly) I shall have to fast.

One thing fasting seems to achieve is to set us free from our appetites, which mostly in the Western world are rather large. We get addicted to food, whether it is peanuts or chocolate or just eating, and our appetite controls us rather than our controlling it. Fasting could teach us to discipline ourselves, and an occasional day's fast would improve our health and de-toxify our system. Fasting makes more sense of feasting—and even to miss lunch by accident can make supper taste even better.

But the spiritual reward for fasting is that we pray more effectively. Those who do it say they experience great clarity of mind and insight, and it seems to have a purifying effect on their inner spirit.

Jesus himself fasted for forty days in the wilderness immediately after his baptism and before he began his public ministry.

To think about

When you will fast . . . and what you think it might do for you.

SB

Your treasure

'Do not lay up for yourselves treasures on earth, where moth and rust consume and where thieves break in and steal, but lay up for yourselves treasure in heaven, where neither moth nor rust consumes and where thieves do not break in and steal. For where your treasure is, there will your heart be also. The eye is the lamp of the body. So, if your eye is sound, your whole body will be full of light; but if your eye is not sound, your whole body will be full of darkness. If then the light in you is darkness, how great is the darkness!'

According to William Barclay a 'sound' eye literally means a 'generous' eye and the word for evil regularly meant 'grudging'. So Jesus is speaking of the difference between a person who looks at situations and people and is drawn to give and a person who looks and grudges and doesn't give.

Professor Sir Norman Anderson tells a story about a rich woman who died and went to heaven. She was received politely by St Peter, ushered in through the pearly gates, and told she would be taken to her heavenly house. As they walked down the street St Peter pointed to an enormous, magnificent mansion. 'That belongs to your gardener', he told her and the woman thought happily to herself, 'Well, if that's just my gardener's house, whatever will mine be like?'

Then they came to it, right at the end of the road, and St Peter led her towards a tiny wooden hut. 'Here your are,' he said, 'this is yours.' 'But how can it be?', she said, 'when my gardener's house is so beautiful and so big?' 'Well,' said St Peter,

'I'm afraid it was the best we could do with what you sent to us.' The theology and imagery of heaven might not be quite correct, but the point of the story is right. 'You can't take it with you,' someone said, 'but you can send it on ahead.'

To think about

What are you building in heaven?

SB

Only one master

'No one can serve two masters; for either he will hate the one and love the other, or he will be devoted to the one and despise the other. You cannot serve God and mammon. Therefore I tell you, do not be anxious about your life, what you shall eat or what you shall drink, nor about your body, what you shall put on. Is not life more than food, and the body more than clothing? Look at the birds of the air: they neither sow nor reap nor gather into barns, and yet your heavenly Father feeds them. Are you not of more value than they? And which of you by being anxious can add one cubit to his span of life?'

The Aramaic word *mammon* simply used to mean material possessions. It comes from a word which means 'to entrust', and so *mamon* was the wealth which a man entrusted to someone to keep safe for him. But Barclay says that over the years it came to mean 'that in which a man puts his trust', and then *mamon* was spelt with a capital M and came to be regarded as nothing less than a god.

Our god is the power in whom we trust, and the one that we worship and serve. A man I know spent all his working life worrying about what would happen to him when he retired, and he put more and more money into pension funds. He wore a worried expression and old clothes, because he didn't want to waste money on new ones.

Jesus is saying to us, 'Don't put your trust in money—put it in your heavenly Father. He feeds the birds and he will feed you'—which isn't to say that we are to sit around and do nothing. The black-bird who lives in my garden works quite hard most of the day towing worms out of the grass. But they are there for him to eat, and he doesn't stockpile them for the future.

A spiritual exercise

Do what Jesus suggested. Really look at the birds, and the beauty of their feathers and at the beauty of the flowers . . .

SB

A way to pray

Ignatius (1491–1556) was a soldier. He was wounded in battle, and a badly treated broken leg left him walking with a limp for the rest of his life. He wrote the Spiritual Exercises, a way of praying to become spiritually fit. He was the founder of the Jesuits.

Ignatius taught a way of praying which makes the Bible come alive. We use our imagination to see the original event in our mind's eye, and as we do so we ask God to meet with us and speak to us.

So, before you read about Jesus calling his first disciples by the Sea of Galilee, pray now that God will guide you and help you to use your imagination. Ask that he will bless you as you use this way of praying.

Perhaps you could begin by imagining yourself standing on the seashore of a place that you know, with the waves lapping at your feet, and the blue sky overhead... Then, before you start to read, be still for a moment in silence...

Jesus was walking by the Sea of Galilee when he saw Simon and his brother Andrew on the lake at work with a casting-net; for they were fishermen. Jesus said to them, 'Come with me, and I will make you fishers of men.' And at once they left their nets and followed him. When he had gone a little further he saw James son of Zebedee and his brother John, who were in the boat—overhauling their nets. He called them; and, leaving their father Zebedee in the boat with the hired men, they went off to follow him.

After you have finished reading shut your eyes and look at what you see. Then think about what is happening in the scene in front of you—and just listen.

Now consider what you have discovered from this. Talk with God about what you are thinking and feeling—perhaps out loud, just as if you were talking to one of your friends. Then bring this time of prayer to an end with 'Our Father'.

SB

Don't worry

'And why are you anxious about clothing? Consider the lilies of the field, how they grow; they neither toil nor spin; yet I tell you, even Solomon in all his glory was not arrayed like one of these. But if God so clothes the grass of the field, which today is alive and tomorrow is thrown into the oven, will he not much more clothe you, O men of little faith? Therefore do not be anxious, saying, "What shall we eat?" or "What shall we drink?" or "What shall we wear?" For the Gentiles seek all these things; and your heavenly Father knows that you need them all. But seek first his kingdom and his righteousness, and all these things shall be yours as well. Therefore do not be anxious about tomorrow, for tomorrow will be anxious for itself. Let the day's own trouble be sufficient for the day.'

If we worry, there can be something wrong with our relationship with God. And since none of us ever trusts in that way all the time, then we are going to worry for some of the time.

But we need to look at whatever we are worrying about and examine it, as it were, in the presence of God, and tell him all about it.

Then we must listen because there will be an answer. Today's passage is part of the answer.

Another part might be 'You eat too much, my child—or drink too much—or have quite enough clothes and don't need any more—and what about my children who haven't got food or clothes or houses or medical supplies?' It might be 'Cut up your credit card and throw it away.' It might be 'Don't let the world around you squeeze you into its own mould.'

A spiritual exercise

Read the passage again—slowly and prayerfully ask God to speak to you through it.

SB

Ask, seek, knock

'Ask, and it will be given you; seek, and you will find; knock, and it will be opened to you. For every one who asks receives, and he who seeks finds, and to him who knocks it will be opened. Or what man of you, if his son asks him for bread, will give him a stone? Or if he asks for a fish, will give him a serpent? If you then, who are evil, know how to give good gifts to your children, how much more will your Father who is in heaven give good things to those who ask him! So whatever you wish that men would do to you, do so to them; for this is the law and the prophets.'

Jesus is teaching us here about the need to persist in prayer. We aren't just to ask once. The tense is the 'present continuous': 'keep on asking, keep on seeking, and keep on knocking'. We are praying to a father who will never mock us or make fun of our prayers. But it seems that those prayers are necessary to God in order to get his will done in the world. If it was going to happen automatically, Jesus would not have told us to pray 'Your will be done'.

If we want to know what the will of God is in a particular situation, Jesus gives us the Golden Rule of Christianity—a totally new piece of teaching, which no one had ever taught before. 'Whatever you wish that men would do to you, do so to them.' It simplifes life enormously if we put ourselves in the shoes of the hungry, the poor, the lonely and even the bad-tempered and nasty. If we were like that, how would we want the other person to treat us?

To think about

How persistent are your prayers? Think of a person you know who is in need and put yourself in his or her shoes. What action would you then like 'you' to take.

SB

213

The two gates

'Enter by the narrow gate; for the gate is wide and the way is easy, that leads to destruction, and those who enter by it are many. For the gate is narrow and the way is hard, that leads to life, and those who find it are few.'

Some people who say they believe in the Sermon on the Mount have never really read it. Today's passage is uncompromising. One way leads to life, the other way leads to destruction. Not very acceptable teaching in today's Church, especially in England. What we have done is to cut out of the Gospels most of the tough, hard things.

A few extreme liberal scholars would say that Jesus didn't say any of them anyway it was the early Church, or the Gospel-writers. But even in the ordinary Church, sayings like today's, about the different endings of the different roads, are not taken very seriously, and the body of Jesus' teaching has had the bones of it removed so that it can hardly stand up.

There are two ways and two doorways, and we can choose which one we go through. The easy way is 'broad, spacious, roomy'. The hard way is narrow, and every day we have to carry our cross along it and die.

But the broad way leads to destruction and the narrow way leads to life, and Jesus has told us what the way is and how to get on to it. 'I am door. If anyone enters by me he will be saved' (John 10:9); 'I am the way, the truth and the life' (John 14:6).

To think about

Which way are you on? Are you walking the way of life, with Christ? 'I have come that they might have life, and have it more abundantly . . .'

SB

How to judge

'Judge not, that you be not judged. For with the judgment you pronounce you will be judged, and the measure you give will be the measure you get. Why do you see the speck that is in your brother's eye, but do not notice the log that is in your own eye? Or how can you say to your brother, "Let me take the speck out of your eye" when there is the log in your own eye? You hypocrite, first take the log out of your own eye, and then you will see clearly to take the speck out of your brother's eye. Do not give dogs what is holy; and do not throw your pearls before swine, lest they trample them under foot and turn to attack you.'

Jesus is not telling us to put all our critical faculties into suspension. If a man has abused his child, or raped a woman, or killed someone through drunken driving, we aren't supposed to purse up our lips and say loftily, 'It's not for me to judge him'—as if it didn't matter what the man had done. What we are required to do is have the same attitude to him as we would do ourself, if we had done the same thing. If you or I should ever drive a car when we had too much drink (or perhaps even any, according to the experts) inside us, and then injure someone, we wouldn't just shrug our shoulders and say, 'Ah well, that's life'. We should be ashamed and very sad. We would long for forgiveness, and we would want our life somehow to be restored to us with some sort of quality and value. We might never be able to put right the injury we had done to the other person, but we would want to do all we could. We would need help with that, and loving friends who still stuck by us

and didn't give us up.

Perhaps we are simply to do for the offender what we would like him to do for us if we were in his shoes—and somehow suffer with him in his sin. And even if it is only a speck in his eye, it still has to be taken out. But we shall see better how to get it out when we realize how frail we are and then take the log out of our own eye.

To think about

How do you react when someone else does something wrong—and how do you talk about them?

SB

A tree and its fruit

'Beware of false prophets, who come to you in sheep's clothing but inwardly are ravenous wolves. You will know them by their fruits. Are grapes gathered from thorns, or figs from thistles? So, every sound tree bears good fruit, but the bad tree bears evil fruit. A sound tree cannot bear evil fruit, nor can a bad tree bear good fruit. Every tree that does not bear good fruit is cut down and thrown into the fire. Thus you will know them by their fruits. Not every one who says to me, "Lord, Lord," shall enter the kingdom of heaven, but he who does the will of my Father who is in heaven. On that day many will say to me, "Lord, Lord, did we not prophesy in your name, and cast out demons in your name, and do many mighty works in your name?" And then will I declare to them, "I never knew you; depart from me, you evildoers." '

Jesus is talking here about false teachers and he uses two metaphors. First of all wolves disguised as sheep—and they might take us in for a bit. But then he changes the metaphor to trees. 'A wolf may disguise itself; a tree cannot. Noxious weeds like thorns and thistles simply cannot produce edible fruit like grapes and figs' (J. Stott). On the day of judgment the trees that didn't bear good fruit will be cut down and since we recognize the trees by their fruit, what is it?

First, there's the teacher's character, and when we see the fruit of the spirit we can trust that here is a good teacher: 'and the fruit of the Spirit is love, joy, peace, patience, kindness, goodness, faithfulness, gentleness, self-control'. But the actual teaching itself is also 'fruit', and if it denies the great doctrines of our faith then it is suspect. But if we are troubled by what some say, for instance, about the resurrection, let us read what the New Testament writers say about it. They have no doubt that it took place. But it was a great mystery—and not just the coming to life again of a dead body.

SB

Wise and foolish

'Every one then who hears these words of mine and does them will be like a wise man who built his house upon the rock; and the rain fell, and the floods came, and the wind blew and beat upon that house, but it did not fall, because it had been founded on the rock. And every one who hears these words of mine and does not do them will be like a foolish man who built his house upon the sand; and the rain fell, and the floods came, and the winds blew and beat against that house, and it fell; and great was the fall of it.' And when Jesus finished these sayings, the crowds were astonished at his teaching, for he taught them as one who had authority, and not as their scribes.

At this very moment the man next door, Charlie, is digging the foundation for his new house. He has three other men and a mechanical digger to help him, and the foundations are being cut over a metre deep and half a metre wide into the clay soil. Then tomorrow thirty tons of concrete will be poured into the trenches to make a rocklike foundation for the new, and quite small, house to stand on. When it is built the strong west winds that blow in our part of the country will never be able to shift it.

But what are the winds that might blow us over—if we don't have our foundation on the rock that is the teaching of Jesus?

Perhaps they are the winds of God that will test our lives on the last day, when all that we have made of the house of our life will stand in the presence of the God who is wind and fire, and who has committed the judgment to the man Christ Jesus.

The Sermon on the Mount sums up all of Christ's teaching. It can change our whole world if we follow it. But we shall only be able to follow the teaching if we follow the Teacher.

SB

A way to pray

Theresa of Lisieux was a Carmelite nun who is commemorated on 1 October each year. Her 'little way' of performing every small action simply for God has been an inspiration to countless people ever since her death in 1897, and so has her autobiography, *The Story of a Soul*. She wrote it because her Reverend Mother told her to. Theresa had been sitting by the fire on a winter evening in the convent telling some of the other nuns about her childhood—and the things she said were of such interest that, almost laughingly, Mother Agnes said 'I order you to write them down.'

So Theresa dedicated her manuscript to Mother Agnes, and wrote 'It is just for you that I am going to write down the story of the little flower which Jesus has picked...' That may sound syrupy to us, but it is her way of speaking—and it can lead us deeper into God. She says that all the flowers which he made are beautiful, and that the particular glory of a rose doesn't take away the glory of a tiny violet with its smell, or the glory of an ordinary daisy. She saw that if the lesser blooms wanted to be greater ones, then nature would lose much of her glory, and 'there would be no little flowers to make a pattern over the countryside. And so it is with the world of souls, which is his garden. He wanted to have great Saints, to be his lilies and roses, but he has made lesser Saints as well; and these lesser ones must be content to rank as daisies and violets, lying at his feet and giving pleasure to his eye like that. Perfection consists simply in doing his will, and being just what he wants us to be' (*Autobiography of a Saint*, trans. Ronald Knox).

I have been crucified with Christ; it is no longer I who live, but Christ who lives in me; and the life I now live in the flesh I live by faith in the Son of God, who loved me and gave himself for me.

Praying

Think of yourself as a flower or a tree or a vegetable growing in the garden of God. What are you? Do you realize that God delights in you—whether you are an oak tree or a cabbage or a buttercup? How will you grow for God? Then think of all the things you will be doing today... and imagine yourself following Theresa's little way, and doing them all for Jesus... What difference would it make?

SB

The true shepherd

Truly, truly, I say to you, he who does not enter the sheepfold by the door but climbs in by another way, that man is a thief and a robber; but he who enters by the door is the shepherd of the sheep. To him the gatekeeper opens; the sheep hear his voice, and he calls his own sheep by name and leads them out. When he has brought out all his own, he goes before them, and the sheep follow him, for they know his voice. A stranger they will not follow, but they will flee from him, for they do not know the voice of strangers.

It used to be fashionable to say that there are no parables in John's Gospel, and certainly there are no homely little stories like the Prodigal Son. But in illustrations like today's reading, we can hear the familiar style of Jesus' parables, drawing on everyday life to make a telling and challenging point.

The Middle Eastern shepherd had a close relationship with his sheep; he knew all of them by name, and they could recognize his voice. He was their defender and provider. That's what Jesus is like. There are, and always have been, many offers of salvation going about. They come in the form of religions and superstitions. How do we know which one to accept?

Jesus claims to be the true shepherd, not because he has a better offer (though he does!) but because he has a deep and abiding love for each of his sheep. He knows each one of us by name. He has gone to the cross to bring us back to God. His claim is the claim of love. Once we accept his claim on us, and get to know him, we ourselves find that nothing else will do. In the uncertainties of daily life we can learn to hear his voice, and, following it, find the right path through the maze of decisions and problems that face us. He knows us and we know him.

A prayer

Thank you, Lord for the love you have for me. Thank you, that knowing me inside and out, you still love me and call me to follow you.

MM

Apprentices

Jesus said to them, 'Truly, truly, I say to you, the Son can do nothing of his own accord, but only what he sees the Father doing; for whatever he does, that the Son does likewise. For the Father loves the Son, and shows him all that he himself is doing; and greater works than these will he show him, that you may marvel. For as the Father raises the dead and gives them life, so also the Son gives life to whom he will.

Here we have a parable in disguise. One of the saddest things about fatherhood in our society is that our children have little opportunity to learn by watching how Dad does things. In Jesus' time it was different. The son was usually his father's apprentice. He learnt his trade by watching and helping Dad. It was in image that Jesus' hearers would instantly recognize. Jesus was the apprentice, learning by copying what his Father was doing. And in fact, many scholars believe that the original form of this saying was more clearly a parable about an apprentice.

So when Jesus healed on the Sabbath, he did so because he saw his Father constantly at work to bring life and healing. When he taught about the kingdom, he did so because he heard the word of God calling his people to repentance. When he went to the cross, he did so because he saw the love of God reaching out to take the effects of evil on to himself.

Jesus came to bring us, too, into the family of God. We are called to be children of God, and God's appren-tices. We are called to see the work of God, and to copy it, however poorly, in our lives. When we see God's love, we are called to love. When we hear God's word we are called to share it. When we feel God's compassion we are called to show it. It isn't always easy to see where God is at work, or to know exactly how he is going about it. But then, an appren-tice must watch carefully, which for us means prayerfully.

A prayer

Father, open my eyes to see you working, and help me make that work my own.

MM

Keep going!

In a certain city there was a judge who neither feared God nor regarded man; and there was a widow in that city who kept coming to him and saying, 'Vindicate me against my adversary.' For a while he refused; but afterward he said to himself, 'Though I neither fear God nor regard man, yet because this widow bothers me, I will vindicate her, or she will wear me out by her continual coming.'

It is never easy for the poor to get justice. They cannot afford lawyers to plead for them, and the judges themselves usually belong to the privileged classes who are seen by the poor as their exploiters. That remains true today, and how much more so it must have been in Jesus' day. So at once we can identify with and admire the determination of the widow—traditionally the poorest of the poor. She wears the judge down by her pestering.

But wait a minute. Who are we meant to see as the judge? God? Yes. It's a daring comparison, but isn't it so true? Don't we pray, and pray again, and seem to get no answer? Doesn't God himself seem to be unjust; on the side of whatever causes our misfortune? Everyone who has ever prayed that their loved one might not die, that their home might not be repossessed, and seen the prayer fail, knows that God is the unjust judge. Yet, says Jesus, if even a wicked man can be forced, by sheer exasperation, to do good, surely the good God will hear our prayer.

It's a tantalizing parable, because we know that the prayer is not always answered. At least, not in the way that we want. But if God is so much greater and better than the man in the parable (and surely he is) then we cannot give up on prayer. We must keep at it, knowing that whatever the outcome, our prayer is heard, and heard by the God who is love.

A prayer

Pray—not for understanding, but for faith; not for what we want, but for what is best; not for comfort, but for courage. 'And will not God vindicate his elect, who cry to him day and night?' (Luke 18:7)

MM

Certain help

Which of you who has a friend will go to him at midnight and say to him, 'Friend, lend me three loaves; for a friend of mine has arrived on a journey, and I have nothing to set before him'; and he will answer from within, 'Do not bother me; the door is now shut and my children are with me in bed; I cannot get up and give you anything'? I tell you, though he will not get up and give him anything because he is his friend, yet because of his importunity he will rise and give him whatever he needs.

This parable is almost the same as the parable of the unjust judge. The visitor's request is bound in the end to be successful. On the other hand, it is even more forceful in making the point about God's goodness. The parable is a single question; 'Which of you can imagine this situation?' The answer is, no one.

It was unthinkable that such a request for hospitality would be refused. Everyone knew that the day's bread would be used up by night-time. Yet the demands of hospitality were sacred. Anyone with spare bread would never think twice about lending some, to have it replaced in the morning. And even if the unthinkable happened, and the request was at first refused, persistence would pay off. The man with bread could never face his neighbours if the news of his stinginess got out. So the point of the parable is that God's goodness and care for his people is as automatic and reliable as the request for bread for a guest. As we say yesterday, it doesn't always seem that way. But dare I suggest that sometimes we spend too much time agonizing, and not enough trusting?

God has shown us his love—above all in Jesus, but in many daily ways as well—and there are times when he expects us to take it on trust. The attitude Jesus is asking for here is the simple realization that God's failure to care is like the failure of village hospitality to his hearers—unthinkable.

A prayer

Thank God for his care, and make a conscious decision to trust your life to him.

MM

Master of the house

When the unclean spirit has gone out of a man, he passes through waterless places seeking rest; and finding none he says, 'I will return to my house from which I came.' And when he comes he finds it swept and put in order. Then he goes and brings seven other spirits more evil than himself, and they enter and dwell there; and the last state of that man becomes worse than the first.

A shivery sort of parable; a story of spooks and horrors. Yet to Jesus' listeners it was an everyday tale. They believed more firmly than we do in demons and their ability to take over a human life. I suspect they knew more than we do. But the point is not really about exorcism, and the danger of relapse, though it includes that. It is about who controls our life.

A human life, says Jesus, is meant as a dwelling place. It can be the abode of God and good, or the devil and evil. And the picture he paints is one we are really familiar with. Do you remember the days, perhaps long ago, when being a Christian was a joy and delight? Temptations slid off easily and the call to follow Jesus brooked no delay. Now we labour heavily, and sins we thought behind us are back and worse than ever. The road looks long, and there are plenty of good reasons to put off the good we know we ought to do.

I hope you don't know that feeling— but many of us do. And part of the reason is that we have pushed God to the back of our minds and down our list of priorities.

He has come in and tidied the house, but we let it be empty. So all the old horrors flow back in.

The remedy is simple. We have to accept that we are not our own people. We are God's. And that means we are wholly his, and he is all that counts. Once we realize that, the way may still be hard, but it is full of joy and the assurance of his presence.

A meditation

Be filled with the Spirit.

Ephesians 5:18

MM

The salt of the earth

'You are the salt of the earth; but if salt has lost its taste, how shall its saltness be restored? It is no longer good for anything except to be thrown out and trodden under foot by men.'

Salt is the stuff that brings out the flavour of things—sprinkled over a bag of chips or added to a pan of potatoes. If we forget to add it when we put them to boil they never taste the same afterwards, even if we add salt when we mash them. Salt doesn't just bring out the flavour of things. It stops them going bad. It was the great preservative of the ancient world, and even today people rub salt into their meat to stop it going bad, and hang salted fish out in the sun to dry.

So as Christians we are to bring out the real taste of people and to stop the world's corruption. Two things, that happen because of who we are. Like Christ (to some degree) and he brought out the real taste of people. As he loved them and accepted them, they changed: Matthew the corrupt tax-collector into an honest one who gave money to the poor instead of robbing them; the woman who'd had five husbands and a live-in lover into a witness for Christ and something of a theologian. They had found their true self—the person they were meant to be and that God had created them to be. In old-fashioned language, their souls had been saved. Their sick souls or selves had been made whole and healthy—from *salve*, or

health ... But it isn't only individual souls that are sick and need to be healed. Society is sick as well, and if it isn't to go off like rotten fish then it needs help. As Christians we are to rub salt into it and stop its decay. Perhaps in the west some of us have lost some of our salt-ness. Salt doesn't actually change its nature, but it gets contaminated. Then it is useless.

To think about

As you go through today, think about what salt does to things. Think about bringing out the flavour of food, of people: about stopping food going off, of society going rotten. Think about particular people, particular issues. Think about how salty you are and your church is, and how effectively the salt is doing what it is meant to do.

SB

Corrie ten Boom's praying

Thou art my hiding place and my shield: I hope in thy word.

A Christian man once said to me, fairly angrily, 'You don't know what it's like to be in prison ...' Neither did he, physically. He was speaking of a prison he had once experienced because of a dreadful predicament he had been landed in. He was entitled to complain, because I had never allowed him to know much of my own inner pain. But I did know just a little of the sort of prison that he was talking about: I had wept scalding, bitter tears because for much of my life my own fears, shyness, upbringing and uncertainty had locked me up within myself, and I simply didn't know how to get free.

We can't speak of any experience we haven't had (or that we have had but are not willing for other people to know about) and we can only speak of the presence of God in any situation where we have really known it. What most of us can say about what God can do for us is limited. But what Corrie ten Boom can say isn't limited. She knew the hurt and rejection of a broken love affair, which is common to most of us. But she can also speak out of what has probably been the most terrible experience of human beings on this earth—apart from the man Christ Jesus on the cross. She endured the horror of the concentration camp at Ravensbruck with her sister Betsy—an incredible woman, who actu-ally pitied the prison guards for being as they were, and was awesomely Christ-like in the way she prayed for their forgiveness.

Many of you who read these notes will know Corrie ten Boom's amazing book *The Hiding Place*. Out of the depths of her knowledge of God in the awful-ness of Ravensbruck she gives us this prayer:

*Thank you, Lord Jesus
that you will be our hiding place,
whatever happens.*

In a few moments of courageous imagin-ing, will you think of the worst things that could ever happen to you? Feel their awfulness and ugliness. Then say that prayer of Corrie ten Boom out loud. Learn it—and in the weeks and years ahead pray it over and over again.

SB

How God remakes and mends us

In a fascinating phrase in the letter to the Christians at Ephesus Paul says that 'We are God's work of art, created in Christ Jesus to live the good life as from the beginning he had meant us to live.' (Ephesians 2:10 JB). We are going to spend some time considering ourselves as God's work of art, and then look at the letter which the phrase comes in (although in a different translation).

There is a unique relationship between the artist and a work of art, the creator and the created—and we are not just pieces of stone passive under the hand of the sculptor, like the marble which Michelangelo transformed into that beautiful and much-loved statue of David. We can cooperate or not, as we choose. Some of the work will hurt us, but in the end it will be worth it.

The New Testament prayers which we look at at the end of our four weeks will help us to put up with the suffering and also, together with all the saints (who in the New Testament are all Christians) 'to grasp how wide and long and high and deep is the love of Christ, and to know this love that surpasses knowledge.' In the carving out of the work of art that is us one of the things that will happen is that day by day our capacity for God will increase, and our vision of God will grow clearer.

A long time ago I prayed the following prayer. 'Lord, whatever it costs you and whatever it costs me, I want to be the best that I can be for you.' I wasn't thinking of the cost to God-in-Christ of dying on the cross. What I was praying for was his working in me and over me to enable me to change. And I wasn't voluntering myself as a candidate for some dreadful disease. Simply for the inevitable suffering of having to deny myself and follow him. And I didn't have in mind to become a great saint like Teresa of Avila—a great oak tree of a saint. But I wanted to be the best blackberry bush that I could be for God—beautiful leaves, delicious fruit for people and for birds (and a home for birds to nest in, like the temple of God). Very ordinary—and fairly prickly!

God's work of art

For the next few days we shall be considering ourselves as God's work of art, and discover how we have to work as fellow-artists with God.

But God loved us with so much love that he was generous with his mercy: when we were dead through our sins he brought us to life with Christ—it is through grace that you have been saved—and raised us up with him and gave us a place with him in heaven, in Christ Jesus. This was to show for all ages to come, through his goodness towards us in Christ Jesus, how infinitely rich he is in grace. Because it is by grace that you have been saved, through faith; not by anything of your own, but by a gift from God; not by anything you have done, so that nobody can claim the credit. We are God's work of art, created in Christ Jesus to live the good life as from the beginning he had meant us to live.

When a woman and a man have a child they are creating her (in one sense) through their loving act of procreation, and a good mother and father love their daughter simply because she is theirs. As she grows up they will do all they can to help her develop into a mature, loving human being. You could say that she is their 'work of art'. But she will share in the work. She will listen to what they say (some of the time!) and let their wisdom and their words shape and form her life. But she has the freedom to disobey them—and if she decides to go off into a far country and be a prodigal daughter she will in one sense be dead. If she comes home again they might say, 'This our daughter was dead and is alive again; was lost and is found.' And in the far country the 'work of art' may have got damaged—but love will restore it.

Now will you read that passage from Ephesians out loud and, substitute 'me' for 'us' and 'I' for 'we', to let the truth of it penetrate deep into your heart. Let your mind dwell on the fact that you are God's work of art. Think of Michelangelo, working year after year on the Sistine Chapel ... Think of the satisfaction and delight to the artist and to other people ... Remember that you and the Holy Spirit within you are partners in creating the work of art that is you. 'God is at work in you, both to will and to work for his good pleasure' (Philippians 2:13). God's work of art is more valuable than the Sistine Chapel or the whole world.

SB

You are . . . You shall be . . .

Yesterday we were thinking and praying about ourself as God's work of art. In today's Gospel reading Jesus says to Peter something on the same lines: that the transforming presence of God with us will release and develop the person we have it in us to be.

> John was standing with two of his disciples when Jesus passed by. John looked towards him and said, ' There is the Lamb of God.' The two disciples heard him say this and followed Jesus . . . One of the two who followed Jesus after hearing what John said was Andrew, Simon Peter's brother. The first thing he did was to find his brother Simon. He said to him, 'We have found the Messiah' (which is the Hebrew word for 'Christ'). He brought Simon to Jesus, who looked at him and said, 'You are Simon son of John. You shall be called Cephas' (that is, Peter, the Rock).

In the Bible a person's name stands for his nature and his character. Matthew's Gospel quotes Isaiah's prophecy of the Messiah: 'Behold, a virgin shall conceive and bear a son, and his name shall be called Emmanuel', which means, 'God with us' (Matthew 1:23). The man who is 'God with us' tells Simon what lies ahead: 'You shall be called Peter, the Rock.' In the Old Testament, God is the Rock strong and utterly reliable, and a great, cool shadow for tired and weary travellers to hide in under the fierceness of a Middle Eastern sun.

One day Peter would be like that, and it would happen through his friendship with Jesus. Jesus knew what he could do with Peter. 'He knew his weakness. He knew his instability. He knew his potentialities; that in that human personality were residential things that make for greatness. The strength was there only potentially; the durability was not there; but He knew Himself. He knew what He would do with that shaly, shifting sort of stuff. He could transmute it into rock' (G. Campbell Morgan, *The Parables and Metaphors of Our Lord*).

Now sit in silence and let what you have read sink in. Re-read it and reflect on it. Listen to the voice of God with you and within you. 'You are . . . You shall be . . .'

SB

Testing you . . .

We are still thinking about ourselves as God's work of art. God who is the artist loves it and works on it to make it the best it can be. Then he will be satisfied and delighted and so shall we—not in a boastful way, but deeply pleased that we have become what God wanted us to be. But the way to the best is a hard way. Even Jesus 'learned obedience through what he suffered' (Hebrews 5:8), and that is the way that we shall learn it.

All the commandment which I command you this day you shall be careful to do, that you may live and multiply, and go in and possess the land which the Lord swore to give to your fathers. And you shall remember all the way which the Lord your God has led you these forty years in the wilderness, that he might humble you, testing you to know what was in your heart, whether you would keep his commandments, or not. And he humbled you and let you hunger and fed you with manna, which you did not know, nor did your fathers know; that he might make you know that man does not live by bread alone, but that man lives by everything that proceeds out of the mouth of the Lord.

When Jesus was in the wilderness Satan tempted him to satisfy his own hunger and turn stones into bread. But even after forty days without food Jesus held on to the truth that man does not live by bread alone—and came through the test undefeated . . . Our physical longings and hungers are one of the man arenas for our testing. The Western world titillates our sexual appetites through all its media, and when we say 'no' to adultery or fornication it can be a severe form of suffering. But by the act of refusal we develop spiritual muscle, which is the whole point of the testing. We are God's work of art—perhaps like a ballet dancer devoted to the perfection of her art. She gives all that she has to the art, but in the end she knows it was worth it—and so do those who watch her.

As you pray, will you remember what was the worst time of testing in your life, and really think about it? What did God teach you through it, and what did you learn through it? What sort of trials and testings are you going through at the moment . . . in your family . . . your business . . . your friendships . . .? Read the passage from Deuteronomy out loud, and realize that whatever it is you are going through God intends it for your ultimate good.

SB

His glory

When the Church was in the process of recognizing which books were specially inspired by God and which weren't (like experts deciding which £5 notes come form the Bank of England), some Christians accepted books in 'the Apocrypha' because they were in the Greek version of the Old Testament, but others disagreed. Yet even these last saw them as useful reading for the Christian life. This passage helps as we think of ourselves as God's works of art.

I will remind you of the works of the Lord, and tell what I have seen. By the words of the Lord his works come into being and all creation obeys his will. As the sun in shining looks on all things so the work of the Lord is full of his glory . . .

That is a lovely passage to use for a meditation. So let it remind you that you are one of 'the works of the Lord . . .' The psalmist says that we are 'Fearfully and wonderfully made . . .' Consider how amazing your body is . . . Sit quietly . . . and think about each part of it, from your head to your toes . . . from your brain to your muscle system, that enables you to wiggle your toes.

You are one of the living creatures who has come into being through God's creative word . . . spoken right back at the beginning of creation . . . 'By the words of the Lord his works come into being . . .' and the work of art that is you is being formed as you let it shape into the wonderful human being that you have it in you to be . . . To listen is to let the word soak in to you like the sunlight . . . the light that shines out of Scripture, and the glory that shines out of the whole of creation—even the damaged or hurt parts—which can point us to the freedom to choose good or bad that has been built into our world.

'We all, with unveiled face, beholding the glory of the Lord, are being changed into his likeness from one degree of glory to another, and this comes from the Lord who is the Spirit' (2 Corinthians 3:18). Think of yourself as God's work of art . . . being changed into his likeness, from one degree of glory to another . . . and rejoice that 'the work of the Lord is full of his glory . . .'

SB

A good crop of beans

All the beans in the world don't grow into bean plants. They aren't meant to. Beans are for food, and the whole point of the planting is a good harvest for people to eat... either the shelled beans with their polished skins cooked into a tasty stew, or the whole green pod boiled and perhaps served up shining with oil and flavoured with garlic. But some other plants produce more beans than others...

[Jesus] said in a parable, 'A sower went out to sow his seed; and as he sowed, some fell along the path, and was trodden under foot, and the birds of the air devoured it. And some fell on the rock; and as it grew up, it withered away, because it had no moisture. And some fell into good soil and grew, and yielded a hundredfold... Now the parable is this: The seed is the word of God... And as for that in the good soil, they are those who, hearing the word, hold it fast in an honest and good heart, and bring forth fruit with patience.'

These days I am too busy, but I used to grow green, climbing beans. When it was nearly time for dinner I would go down the garden to pick them... and when there was lots of them I liked it. It wasn't that my family and I would have enormous helpings and eat them all ourselves. We would give them away to friends. But a gardener is deeply satisfied when she or he has a good crop...

We are still thinking of ourselves as God's work of art. Will you imagine yourself as a climbing bean plant... still God's work of art, but this time the divine artist is a gardener.

The bean plant needs food and fresh air, rain and sunshine. You need food... the bread and wine of Holy Communion... the milk and the meat that is the word of God. You need the air that is the breath of God, the Holy Spirit... the Spirit who is softening, refreshing rain... he has poured down for you abundant rain, the early and the latter rain, as before (Joel 2:23). And shining over everything you need the warmth of the love of God, so that you grow up into the light into your full glory... Will you work out now how to get all that you need to grow?

SB

Perfect in weakness

A friend of mine is an alcoholic. He will never be able to say 'I was an alcoholic...' It is something that he lives with... always. He says that it's like being a sinner... the weakness is always there, right at the heart of us... but there is a power that will help us at each moment not to drink and not to sin...

I will move on to the visions and revelations I have had from the Lord. I know a man in Christ who... was caught up into paradise and heard things which must not and cannot be put into human language... In view of the extraordinary nature of these revelations, to stop me from getting too proud I was given a thorn in the flesh, an angel of Satan to beat me and stop me from getting too proud! About this thing, I have pleaded with the Lord three times for it to leave me, but he has said, 'My grace is enough for you: my power is at its best in weakness.' So I shall be very happy to make my weaknesses my special boast so that the power of Christ may stay over me, and that is why I am quite content with my weaknesses, and with insults, hardships, persecutions, and the agonies I go through for Christ's sake. For it is when I am weak that I am strong.

The strength isn't give to us once for all in a great big surge of power so that we know we are strong... like inheriting a fortune and knowing we are rich. It is give to us moment by moment... for whatever it is we have to do or to resist doing... God doesn't finish the work of art and send it off on its own... he's at work within it, 'to will and to do of his good pleasure'... He relates to it all the time... within it as its true life, its creator and its lover... but never overriding its free will to choose life and love and a moment-by-moment relationship with him... Our weakness is exchanged for his strength... and isn't only saints like Paul who can experience the glory of the transaction. My friend who is an alcoholic experiences it every day of his life.

Meditation

Will you consider now where you need to exchange your weakness for God's strength? We don't like admitting that we are weak... it seems feeble. But it is rather like admitting that we have sinned... it's only then that we know the joy of forgiveness.

SB

A way to pray

And though the Lord give you the bread of adversity and the water of affliction, yet your Teacher will not hide himself any more, but your eyes shall see your Teacher. And your ears shall hear a word behind you, saying, 'This is the way, walk in it,' when you turn to the right or when you turn to the left.

Prayer isn't just what we say to God. It is also what God says to us. So we have to listen. This dialogue between 'Me and God' was given to me by Bridget Hill, but I cannot find out who wrote it because a year ago she died.

Me   I am listening, Lord. (louder).
        I *am* listening, Lord
God No, you're not . . .
Me   Yes, I am. I am listening Lord.
God No, you're talking . . .
Me   Well, what must I do?
God Listen.
Me   But nothing happens when I do. And I don't believe anything is going to happen.
God Oh yes. *Something* will happen.
Me   Why is it so hard? I'll try again. I'm listening, Lord . . . (Pause)
God Why are you in such a hurry?
Me   I'm not. At least—am I? I have a great deal to do—and there isn't much time and
God interrupts.
        You have all the time there is. You are not so busy as you think you are. You are frightened.
Me   Frightened?

God Frighted of being alone. Frightened of remembering. Frightened of thinking. Frightened of giving all. Frightened of what I might say.
Me   Yes, I am. I am. But what can I do?
God Perhaps nothing. Have you asked what *I* can do?
Me   What *can* you do?
God All that needs doing.
Me   Who are you?
God I am the one you are running away from. Sit down and be at peace. And learn what I can do . . .

An exercise

Sit quietly with your hands on your knees for five minutes and listen. There will probably be a hundred things going on inside your head . . . But go on listening . . . and you are very likely to hear the still, small voice of God speaking to your heart.

SB

233

Neither do I condemn . . .

Today is the last day that we are thinking about ourselves as God's work of art. The story of the woman taken in adultery appears in John's Gospel in different places . . . and scholars think this may be because at one stage the Church found it so shocking that they left it out. Respectable 'churchianity' (as opposed to the real thing) joins in the complaint of the scribes and Pharisees: 'This man eats with tax gatherers and sinners'. But those unlikely candidates are going to be God's works of art just as much, and just as gloriously, as St Peter, St Paul and Mother Teresa . . .

Early in the morning, when Jesus is teaching in the temple, the scribes and Pharisees bring in a woman and make her stand in the middle.

. . .they said to him, 'Master, this woman was caught in the very act of adultery. In the Law Moses has laid down that such women are to be stoned . . . What do you say about it?'

We may know the next thing that happens. Jesus bends down and writes with his finger on the ground. Then he speaks to the men: 'Let him who is without sin among you cast the first stone . . .' and they go away, on by one, beginning with the eldest. Jesus is left alone with the woman standing before him. He looks up and says to her 'Woman, where are they? Has no condemned you?' She answers, 'No one, Lord.' Then come words that have rung like a peal of joy through the centuries ever since: 'Neither do I condemn you; go, and sin no more.' Another work of art is being created by its Saviour God.

He comes, with feet deliberate and slow,
Who counts a contrite heart His sacrifice.
(No other bidders rise to stake their claims,
He only on our ruins set a price.)
And stooping very low engraves with care
His Name, inedible, upon our dust;
And from the ashes of our self-despair
Kindles a flame of hope and humble trust.
He seeks no second site on which to build,
But on the old foundation, stone by stone,
Cementing sad experience with grace,
Fashions a stronger temple of His own.

Patricia St John, *The Alchemist*

SB

A tough training

Recently I saw a television programme about two young skaters who passionately wanted to be world champions. They skated exquisitely already, and the speed and grace of their performance lifted my heart up in sheer delight... But they spent hours every day practising... to produce an even better performance and perfect their technique. It was a tough training programme set up by their coach and there was no other way to the top.

Joseph was on his way to the top, and his training was going to be incredibly tough.

Now Joseph was well built and handsome, and ... [Potiphar's] wife cast her eyes on [him] and said, 'Sleep with me.' But he refused, 'Look,' he said ... 'my master does not concern himself with what happens in the house, having entrusted all his possessions to me ... He has exempted nothing from me except yourself, because you are his wife. How could I do anything so wicked, and sin against God?' ... But one day when ... none of the men of the household happened to be indoors, she caught hold of him by his tunic and said, 'Sleep with me.' But he left the tunic in her hand, took to his heels and got out ... She kept his tunic by her until his master came home. Then she told him ... 'The Hebrew slave you brought to us burst in on me to make a fool of me. But when I screamed, he left his tunic beside me and ran away.' When his master heard his wife say, 'This was how your slave treated me,' he became furious. Joseph's master had him arrested and committed to the gaol where the king's prisoners were kept.

Joseph must have wept bitter tears. First being sold into slavery, and now this... It must have seemed so unfair.. to do the right thing and then be put in prison. An incredibly tough training... but one day it would take him right to the top... not just as a ruler in Egypt but as a human being.

To meditate on

Count it all my joy, brethren, when you meet various trials, for you know that the testing of your faith produces steadfastness. And let steadfastness have its full effect, that you may be perfect and complete, lacking in nothing.

James 1:2–3

SB

Looking over the gifts

Blessed be the God and Father of our Lord Jesus Christ, who has conferred on us in Christ every spiritual blessing in the heavenly realms. Before the foundation of the world he chose us in Christ to be his people, to be without blemish in his sight, to be full of love; and he predestined us to be adopted as his children through Jesus Christ. This was his will and pleasure in order that the glory of his gracious gift, so graciously bestowed on us in his Beloved, might redound to his praise. In Christ our release is secured and our sins forgiven through the shedding of his blood. In the richness of his grace God has lavished on us all wisdom and insight. He has made known to us his secret purpose . . . that the universe, everything in heaven and on earth, might be brought into unity in Christ.

At a wedding reception the presents are unpacked and displayed. The guests examine them a little enviously, and the new couple plan just where to put them and how to use them. After a few years, some are taken for granted, some have fallen into disuse and others have disappeared. Exactly who gave what fades from memory.

Something like that can happen in the Christian life. We start with wonder at the great things God has done for us. He has forgiven our sins, brought us into his chosen people, made us a part of his amazing plan to restore a broken world to himself. And all of this he has given to us freely, graciously. But after a time we forget. We begin to suspect that repeated sins aren't really forgiven (or even forgivable). 'Father' becomes a formal prayer word instead of a joyful recognition of a new place in God's family.

So Ephesians begins with a reminder of God's free gifts to us. Look them over, it says, and take stock of all that you have through God's love.

Meditate

Read over the list of what God has given us. Think what it means, and give thanks.

MM

Double vision

In Christ indeed we have been given our share in the heritage, as was decreed in his design whose purpose is everywhere at work; for it was his will that we, who were the first to set our hope on Christ, should cause his glory to be praised. And in Christ you also—once you had heard the message of the truth, the good news of your salvation, and had believed it—in him you were stamped with the promised seal of the Holy Spirit; and that Spirit is a pledge of the inheritance which will be ours when God has redeemed what is his own, to his glory and praise.

At times I am accused of having a blinkered view of the world because of my Christian belief. My usual answer is that I see the world not through blinkers, with too narrow a view, but through 3-D glasses which give everything an extra dimension.

Christians see the world like everyone else—we are part of it, and firmly rooted in it, and only a fool would suggest otherwise. We are part of the sorrow and joy of the world. But we also see a hidden depth, for we have been marked out as belonging to eternity. The Spirit of God has become a part of our lives (however poorly we may respond to his prompting) to promise us a future of peace and joy and open our eyes so that behind the events of the world we see the working of God.

Often our vision is clouded, and it is hard to see how God is at work in the world, or to believe fully in the promised future. Yet in our prayer and worship, and those unexpected moments which sneak up on us from time to time to fill our hearts with wonder, we see enough to know that the promise is real. We see enough to live our lives in the light of that promise, and in trust in the God whose purpose is everywhere at work.

Pray

Bring to God those things which hurt and puzzle us, where we cannot see him at work. Pray not for understanding, but for trust, and remember those things where the vision of God does shine through.

MM

Catching the vision

I never cease to give thanks for you when I mention you in my prayers. I pray that the God of our Lord Jesus Christ, the all-glorious Father, may confer on you the spiritual gifts of wisdom and vision, with the knowledge of him that they bring. I pray that your inward eyes may be enlightened, so that you may know what is the hope to which he calls you, how rich and glorious is the share he offers you among his people in their inheritance, and how vast are the resources of his power open to us who have faith.

Yesterday we took up one of the themes of this opening section of Ephesians and thought about the new vision which knowing God brings. Yet such a vision of God is not something that arrives fully developed, or the writer wouldn't pray that his readers would get it. It comes with time, and it is the gift of God himself.

It is God's gift, because only he can reveal himself to us. So part of the work of the Holy Spirit, who is God's down-payment on all that is yet to come, is to open our eyes to how God works, and to fix our thoughts on him—the gifts of vision and wisdom which bring knowledge of God.

It is something which comes with time, because we often (perhaps always) resist what God wishes to do in our lives. Perhaps we resist out of fear, preferring the apparent safety of what we know and are against the strange (though better) promise of what we shall have and be. Perhaps we resist out of a perverse desire to cling to things which we know are wrong, but still find enjoyable or profitable. The very heart of Christian life is the struggle to turn our lives towards God and to co-operate with his Holy Spirit, whether in prayer or lifestyle or attitudes. The great thing is, though, that the slightest change of direction is likely to catch us up in the rush of the Spirit, like stepping into the path of an avalanche. We are called to cooperate with him, but he does most of the work!

Meditate

Put before God those things you think may be getting in his way. Tackle them one by one, and ask for his help.

MM

Power source

[God's] mighty strength was seen at work when he raised Christ from the dead, and enthroned him at his right hand in the heavenly realms, far above all government and authority, all power and dominion, and any title of sovereignty that commands allegiance, not only in this age but also in the age to come. He put all things in subjection beneath his feet, and gave him as head over all things to the church which is his body, the fullness of him who is filling the universe in all its parts.

The resurrection is the foundation stone of Christian faith. By it, God revealed not only his own power to raise the dead but also showed Jesus to be right in his teaching and mission. It is not just that God raises the dead, but that he raised *this* man from the dead. Without the resurrection, Jesus would be insignificant.

There have been many religious teachers and leaders, both good and bad. Jesus would have been just one more—but the resurrection changes that. Many people have died for their beliefs, both good and bad. Jesus would have been just one more martyr to a cause—but the resurrection changes that. In the resurrection, the power of God has reached into the world to declare that Jesus truly is all that he claimed—the Saviour of the world. By the resurrection, God has declared that Jesus is the Lord of the Church and all creation.

Yet there is even more. Because the risen Lord is our Lord, we too can tap into the power that raised him. In our prayer and worship, in our striving to do his will in the world, we are not thrown back on our own resources. Instead, the power of God himself becomes the driving force of our lives, our work and our witness. The new life we begin with Christ is the beginning of a life which has already conquered death, and because of that we need fear nothing.

Pray

Lord God, open my eyes to the power that is available to me and to your Church and teach me to expect great things from you.

MM

The Vine

'I am the true vine, and my Father is the vinedresser. Every branch of mine that bears no fruit, he takes away, and every branch that does bear fruit he prunes, that it may bear more fruit. You are already made clean by the word which I have spoken to you. Abide in me, and I in you. As the branch cannot bear fruit by itself, unless it abides in the vine, neither can you, unless you abide in me. I am the vine, you are the branches. He who abides in me, and I in him, he it is that bears much fruit, for apart from me you can do nothing.'

The vine was a symbol of Israel. In the temple at Jerusalem, on the entrance to the innermost shrine—the holy of holies, where the presence of God dwelt—was a great, golden vine. The prophets say that Israel is the vine that God has planted—and that he planted it to bear fruit.

'I am the true vine . . .' I am what Israel is meant to be—always in a relationship of love with her creator, always doing the will of God, always loving God and loving her neighbour. Now the people of God were so be so intimately related to God that they would live in him, and he would live in them. These later chapters of John say that in several ways—and this way says it by using the picture of the vine. We cannot be closer to something than to be a branch of it—joined to it in a living union, and with its life-giving sap flowing through us. Then, and only then, shall we bear the fruit that God desires us to bear—and when we are fruitful he will prune us to make us more fruitful. All the circumstances of our lives are the instruments for the pruning—and when things get hard, and when we are hurting, it helps to remember that.

The way to abide in the vine is not to struggle. It is to be aware. To sit still and think about it—to imagine a vine (or an apple tree if we are not very sure what a vine looks like). Jesus said, 'I am the true vine'. We can say to ourselves, 'I am a branch of the true vine', and we can sit still and let the truth and the wonder of that sink right into the depths of our heart.

SB

The wrath of God

You once were dead because of your sins and wickedness; you followed the ways of the present world order, obeying the commander of the spiritual powers of the air, the spirit now at work among God's rebel subjects. We too were once of their number: we were ruled by our physical desires, and did what instinct and evil imagination suggested. In our natural condition we lay under the condemnation of God like the rest of mankind.

The wrath, or condemnation, of God must be one of the most unpopular subjects for modern preaching. We feel uneasy suggesting that the loving God could be angry or could ever condemn anyone. When we are faced with a passage like today's, we are tempted to skip over it to verse 4: 'God is rich in mercy . . .' But if we do, we are unfair to the biblical message, and unfair to the greatness of God's love.

The full extent of God's love can only become apparent in the light of human sinfulness. A love which ignores wrong-doing is not a Fatherly love but the vague affection of a senile great-grandparent. So the writer pulls no punches here. People who do not turn to God are not simply neutral: they are rebels against God who are part of a world system which owes its allegiance to the devil.

That seems a bit strong, doesn't it? After all, we all know plenty of nice unbelievers. And the world contains much goodness and beauty. Yet at the same time we see great evil in the world, and our minds reel under the enormity of some of it. It would be good to think that such terrible things are done only by a few inhuman monsters. But the truth is even more terrible. Much of the time the great evils are committed by ordinary 'nice' people like us, and often they fail to see the horror of what they do.

We need to take the fact of human evil and rebellion seriously both to understand the extent of God's love and the reality of the need for salvation.

Think

What signs do we see around us (and in us!) of rebellion against God?

MM

The depth of love

But God is rich in mercy, and because of his great love for us, he brought us to life with Christ when we were dead because of our sins; it is by grace you are saved. And he raised us up in union with Christ Jesus and enthroned us with him in the heavenly realms, so that he might display in the ages to come how immense are the resources of his grace, and how great his kindness to us in Christ Jesus. For it is by grace you are saved through faith; it is not your own doing. It is God's gift, not a reward for work done. There is nothing for anyone to boast of; we are God's handiwork, created in Christ Jesus for the life of good deeds which God designed for us.

Yesterday we began to take seriously the reality of sin and human enmity with God. But we don't think about sin just to make ourselves feel bad. Instead, it gives us some idea of the greatness of God's love which reaches out not just to those who love him, but to his enemies. Even more, God doesn't expect us to earn a place with him. He offers us a new start absolutely freely. That's what the word 'grace' means.

It's the complete reversal of what most people imagine. We are not told to be good so that we can get to heaven. Instead, we are offered heaven on a plate, and so are expected to be good. Of course, it seems unfair. It means that the very worst people have the same offer of salvation as the very best. But then, that's what love is about. God's love doesn't draw any line beyond which someone is too awful to bother with—and I find that very comforting!

On the other hand, doing good does count. It isn't the way to earn salvation, but it is the way to express the new life that we are given. When we put our trust in God, we become new, with new aims and a new lifestyle which God calls us to.

Meditate

Read today's passage slowly and carefully. Try to grasp something of the love of God, and of the greatness of the gift he has given us so freely—but not without cost to himself.

MM

God's ancient people

Remember then your former condition, Gentiles as you are by birth, 'the uncircumcised' as you are called by those who call themselves 'the circumcised' because of a physical rite. You were at that time separate from Christ, excluded from the community of Israel, strangers to God's covenants and the promise that goes with them. Yours was a world without hope and without God. Once you were far off, but now in union with Christ Jesus you have been brought near through the shedding of Christ's blood.

As members of a new religion, it was tempting for the first readers of Ephesians to behave as though they were the first to discover faith in God, and to imagine that they were free to make up their doctrines as they went along. The writer reminds them that there has been a nation that knew God for thousands of years—the Jews. The new Church was part of a history in which God had been working for longer than they could imagine.

Tragically, Christians have often forgotten their Jewish origins, and the great debt that they owe to the original people of God, whose Messiah is also the Saviour of the world. Whatever we think of the status of Jews who reject Jesus (and opinions differ) we cannot ignore the special place they have with God, or the great debt which we owe them.

In fact, Ephesians suggests that to be a Christian is to be brought into the people of Israel, rather than to be something separate. In Jesus, God has fulfilled his promise that all the world will be able to know the God of the Jews.

As Christians, we must remember this, for in the past the Church has persecuted the Jewish people in a way that denies all that God has said about his special people. Even worse, we see today the return of anti-semitism in Europe and need to be on our guard against any such views in the Church.

Pray

Think of the history of Israel through the Old Testament to Jesus' day, and try to grasp something of God's great plan of salvation, and the people he used to bring it about.

MM

Breaking barriers

For [Christ] is himself our peace. Gentiles and Jews, he has made the two one, and in his own body of flesh and blood has broken down the barrier of enmity which separated them; for he annulled the law with its rules and regulations, so as to create out of the two a single new humanity in himself, thereby making peace. This was his purpose, to reconcile the two in a single body to God through the cross, by which he killed the enmity. So he came and proclaimed the good news: peace to you who were far off, and peace to those who were near; for through him we both alike have access to the Father in the one Spirit.

From a Gentile point of view, the Jews were an unsociable and exclusive group, having little to do with their pagan neighbours and keeping strange and mysterious laws about food, the Sabbath and circumcision. From the Jewish point of view, Gentiles were idolaters and demon-worshippers with unsavoury morals and a corrupt lifestyle, as well as being unwelcome conquerors of Israel. The barrier between them was hard and fast.

Now, however, both Jews and Gentiles can meet as equal members of the people of God, bound together by a shared faith in Jesus. That faith broke down one of the firmest barriers in the ancient world. In fact, the early Christians soon discovered that Christ broke other barriers: in the Church, slave and free, men and women, discovered a new equality. That equality is based on God's grace. If all need salvation, who can claim to be superior to anyone else? So the gospel is not only about peace between God and his rebellious creatures; it is also a means of bringing peace between people who have been on opposite sides of the fence.

Look again at today's reading and ask whether the peace Jesus brings has really made an impact on your life.

Reflect

'Blessed are the peacemakers, for they shall be called the children of God.' How does our experience of the gospel help us to be peacemakers?

MM

God's new direction

Thus you are no longer aliens in a foreign land, but fellow citizens with God's people, members of God's household. You are built on the foundation of the apostles and prophets, with Christ Jesus himself as the corner-stone. In him the whole building is bonded together and grows into a holy temple in the Lord. In him you also are being built with all the others into a spiritual dwelling for God.

In today's reading the writer reminds us that the Church to which we belong–the whole people of God–is founded on the work and discipleship of those apostles and prophets whose insight into God's will and response to his call led them to take the gospel outside of Judaism. The first Christians were all Jews, and many simply saw Jesus as the Saviour of the Jews. But some caught a new vision, that Jesus was for all. No doubt the writer is thinking mainly of Paul, 'the apostle to the Gentiles', but others caught the same vision. As a result, the Church grew and opened up the way for millions to follow Christ.

That change did not come about without opposition. Paul was caused great grief by Jewish Christians who could not share his views, but in the end the new vision prevailed, and here we all are, Gentiles almost every one!

It makes me wonder—how many new ideas and attitudes in Church have we looked at suspiciously? And how many people have benefited from them? Perhaps the thing that first attracted us to the Church was once frowned on by conservatives? Could it be that God still calls people to new visions, to break new barriers in the Church, in worship or evangelism? And could it be that many of us still fail to see what our founding apostles and prophets knew so well—that God always has something new up his sleeve?

Pray

Give me vision, Lord, to see your new works, and courage to perform them for you.

MM

Paul the apostle

With this in mind, I pray for you, I, Paul, who for the sake of you Gentiles am now the prisoner of Christ Jesus—for surely you have heard how God's gift of grace to me was designed for your benefit. It was by a revelation that his secret purpose was made known to me. I have already written you a brief account of this, and by reading it you can see that I understand the secret purpose of Christ. In former generations that secret purpose was not disclosed to mankind; but now by inspiration it has been revealed to his holy apostles and prophets, that through the gospel the Gentiles are joint heirs with the Jews, part of the same body, sharers together in the promise made in Christ Jesus.

In chapter 3 the letter to the Ephesians gives us a picture of Paul, imprisoned for his faith yet still dedicated to his mission as apostle to the Gentiles.

In verse 1 he says he is a prisoner of Christ (see Philemon 1). It means that it is his Christian faith that landed him in gaol. But it also means that the one who really has hold of him is not his human warder but Jesus. There are times when I would rather not be a Christian. Sometimes the struggle seems too much, and I'd rather let go and stop trying to do what God demands. Yet I can't. Deep down there is the awareness that something has hold of me which will not let go. People who try to turn their backs on their faith call it many things—guilt, conditioned ways of thinking, subconscious fear—but it is none of these things. It is God, who in Jesus Christ has taken hold of us, and will not easily let go.

When the times of doubt or spiritual tiredness pass, God is still there and has seen me through, and that is yet another thing to praise him for.

Think

Think about times when you have been tempted to turn away from God. How did he bring you back? Thank him for the way he stands by us, come what may.

MM

The fruit of love

'By this my Father is glorified, that you bear much fruit, and so prove to be my disciples. As the Father has loved me, so have I loved you; abide in my love. If you keep my commandments, you will abide in my love, just as I have kept my Father's commandments and abide in his love. These things I have spoken to you, that my joy may be in you, and that your joy may be full.'

The fruit that we bear on ourselves, who are branches of the vine, is love. It is the first on the list of the fruit of the Spirit in Galatians, and it is what the two great commandments are about.

Three directions for our love to flow in—to God, to our neighbour (not forgetting our enemy—loving her or him is an essential part of Jesus' transforming and radical teaching), and to ourself. As we abide in the vine who is Christ the love will flow through us in all those directions.

We shall know that we are loved ourselves. We shall become more and more aware of our preciousness and our enormous value to God. When we become aware of our own value, and know how enormously we are loved by God, that doesn't have the effect of making us vain. Not when it is the real thing. What happens is that we see other people in the same way. We are aware of their value and preciousness and uniqueness—and we want the same things for them that we want for ourselves.

If they are hungry we shall feed and if they are thirsty we shall give them some-

thing to drink. But that will only be the start of it. We shall want them to know God, and know the wonderful love of God, and the transforming power of Christ, and as the fruit of the Spirit that is love grows in us, we shall love God more with the whole of our being. He will satisfy our mind and our heart and our soul—and our strength will be poured out in our delighted worship and love for him.

The curious thing is that as we love we become more and more ourselves—and more and more like Christ. And the more we love the more the fruit of the true vine will be there for the whole world to eat... and the Father will be glorified. And our joy will be filled up and brimming over.

SB

Grace to share

Such is the gospel of which I was made a minister by God's unmerited gift, so powerfully at work in me. To me, who am less than the least of all God's people, he has granted the privilege of proclaiming to the Gentiles the good news of the unfathomable riches of Christ, and of bringing to light how this hidden purpose was to be put into effect.

Paul was convinced of the grace of God not because he found it as part of a creed or doctrine, but because he experienced it. Paul, the persecutor of the Church, was touched by the very one whose followers he hated. Few people could deserve it less; but then, grace is never deserved.

At the same time, Paul's conversion was not just for himself—it was also a call to a mission to share that grace with others. Jesus came to him to give him a job to do, and the same is true of all Christians. The job differs for each of us, but we can be sure of this—we do have a job to do. We may not be apostles, but all of us are witnesses to what God has done for us, and we all have good news to share.

Very often we are wary of telling others about our faith. Perhaps it is too 'evangelical' for our church tradition, or perhaps we feel that we are poor advertisements for Christ. Or we may simply feel too embarrassed about speaking of something that is so far out of most people's reckoning. None of that need worry us. The thing that counts is a willingness to tell the good news. If we are willing, we soon find that God himself provides opportunities. People begin to ask us—we don't have to force them up against a wall and make them listen!

Paul was willing because he was certain of what God had done for him. Are we?

Pray

Look back at the ways God has helped you over the years. Thank him for all that he has done and ask him to give you the opportunity to tell others about your faith.

MM

The universal Church

[God's purpose] lay concealed for long ages with God the Creator of the universe, in order that now, through the church, the wisdom of God in its infinite variety might be made known to the rulers and authorities in the heavenly realms. This accords with his age-long purpose, which he accomplished in Christ Jesus our Lord, in whom we have freedom of access to God, with the confidence born of trust in him. I beg you then, not to lose heart over my sufferings for you; indeed, they are your glory.

Today's reading gives the Church a staggering significance. It is the tool which God has chosen to reveal his plan of salvation to the world.

We need to recover that vision of the Church as God's instrument at work throughout the world. In Britain and Europe, and indeed through much of the developed world, it is easy to see the Church as a scattered group of defensive congregations with little to say to the modern world. We tend to stay in our local churches, and our vision of the Church is limited to our small group, and (even worse) our church building. So we easily become discouraged, and imagine that that is the truth of the matter.

Far from it! All over the world the Church is growing and new local churches are planted week by week. In some parts of the world the Church is all that stands between freedom and tyranny. And by belonging to our church we are a part of all this, united with millions of fellow Christians throughout the world, and indeed throughout time. So don't ever be tempted to be defensive. We are part of God's plan of salvation, and his instrument to spread the gospel.

Resolve

to keep up with what your fellow Christians are doing in the world. Pray for Church leaders who are in the news, and for the overseas work your church supports. Remember that the Church of God is far greater than the little group to which you belong.

MM

Learning to pray

I thank my God every time I remember you. In all my prayers for all of you, I always pray with joy because of your partnership in the gospel from the first day until now, being confident of this, that he who began a good work in you will carry it on to completion until the day of Christ Jesus. It is right for me to feel this way about all of you, since I have you in my heart; for whether I am in chains or defending and confirming the gospel, all of you share in God's grace with me. God can testify how I long for all of you with the affection of Christ Jesus. And this is my prayer: that your love may abound more and more in knowledge and depth of insight, so that you may be able to discern what is best and may be pure and blameless until the day of Christ, filled with the fruit of righteousness that comes through Jesus Christ—to the glory and praise of God.

For four days we are looking at four beautiful prayers from the New Testament so that we can learn how to pray better. Paul was in prison, but it didn't stop him praying. He was full of joy before God for the Philippians, and he prayed that their love would keep on growing. And as it grew, the Philippian's knowledge of God and of what was right would grow as well. It seems strange to connect love with knowledge—but if we have ever seen a parent spoiling a child then we shall make the connection. Love wants the very best for whoever it loves (and also for its enemy), and only mature love knows what is best.

A prayer

Lord, teach me how to pray like Paul. Show me what is best for the people you have put in my heart to pray for. But let me never forget that even you can't make them good by force—only be love. So help me to love them with a love that keeps on growing, and help me to pray for them.

SB

That you may know

For this reason, ever since I heard about your faith in the Lord Jesus and your love for all the saints, I have not stopped giving thanks for you, remembering you in my prayers. I keep asking that the God of our Lord Jesus Christ, the glorious Father, may give you the Spirit of wisdom and revelation, so that you may know him better. I pray also that the eyes of your heart may be enlightened in order that you may know the hope to which he has called you, the riches of his glorious inheritance in the saints, and his incomparably great power for us who believe. That power is like the working of his mighty strength, which he exerted in Christ when he raised him from the dead . . .

We are trying to improve our prayer life, so let's compare it with Paul's to see what changes we can usefully make in ours. Paul didn't just pray for people once. He prayed for them all the time, that the Father would fill them with the Spirit so that they would know him better, and light would shine in their hearts so that they would see the glory of all that God had given to them.

At the start of our Christian life, God makes his light shine in our hearts to give us 'the light of the knowledge of the glory of God in the face of Christ' (2 Corinthians 4:6). Just as the creation of the world began with the light shining in the darkness and was completed with 'Adam, the son of God' (Luke 3:38), so the new creation begins with the shinings and is completed with Jesus Christ, Son of Man and Son of God—'firstborn among the brethren'. The Christ who is born in us has to grow up to maturity— and the power of God that raised him from the dead will make that happen. Paul's prayer is that the Christians at Ephesus will experience it.

A prayer

Lord God, may I know your power—and may my church know it also. Shine in our hearts and shine in the world, so that people living in the darkness of sin and sorrow will come to the brightness of your shining and know your love and your forgiveness.

SB

A way to pray

The prayers that we are looking at in these four days are so superb that we can't do better than to make them our own and use them throughout the year. But it helps to reflect on each phrase in each prayer, so that is what we shall do today—very briefly because of lack of space.

'For this reason I kneel before the Father, from whom his whole family in heaven and on earth derives its name' (3:14–15). We can call God Father, or 'Abba', Daddy ... and all the people in this world and in the next who call him Father are our brothers and sisters.

'I pray that out of his glorious riches he may strengthen you with power through is Spirit in your inner being, so that Christ may dwell in your hearts through faith' (3:16–17). We can have an incredibly glorious power within us ... but it's the power of a person in us, the risen Christ, living in us in his Spirit.

'And I pray that you, being rooted and established in love, may have power, together with all the saints, to grasp how wide and long and high and deep is the love of Christ, and to know this love that surpasses knowledge—that you may be filled to the measure of all the fulness of God' (3:17–19). Deeply rooted in love we can have the power to know love—a love that's beyond words and knowledge, but one that we can know and experience—and then be filled with the love of God and with God himself right up to overflowing ...

'Now to him who is able to do immeasurably more than all we ask or imagine, according to his power that is at work within us, to him be glory in the church and in Christ Jesus throughout all generations, for ever and ever!' (3:20–21). No wonder there's such a shout of glory from Paul—and from us—because the possibilities and the promises are beyond all our imaginings. Read the prayer through now from the beginning, out loud. Name some people before God, then pray the prayer for them and include yourself in it as well.

SB

Forgiveness and fruit

For this reason, since the day we heard about you, we have not stopped praying for you and asking God to fill you with the knowledge of his will through all spiritual wisdom and understanding. And we pray this in order that you may live a life worthy of the Lord and may please him in every way, bearing fruit in every good work, growing in the knowledge of God, being strengthened with all power according to his glorious might so that you may have great endurance and patience, and joyfully giving thanks to the Father, who has qualified you to share in the inheritance of the saints in the kingdom of light. For he has rescued us from the dominion of darkness and brought us into the kingdom of the Son he loves, in whom we have redemption, the forgiveness of sins.

Our prayers start well and then fizzle out. But Paul's went on and on. And he kept on praying the same things. He asked God to fill the Colossians with a knowledge of his will—so that there were no gaps in their understanding and no places in their hearts and minds that didn't know what the will of God was. He asked that their lives would shine with the glory of God and be fruitful, as Jesus had told them to be: 'I am the vine; you are the branches. If a man remains in me and I in him, he will bear much fruit; apart from me you can do nothing... This is to my Father's gory, that you bear much fruit, showing yourselves to be my disciples' (John 15:5, 8).

Paul's prayer ends with great joy and thankfulness because of what has happened to him and to those he's praying for—and it has happened to all Christians too. We have all been rescued from the power of darkness and brought into the kingdom of light. The light of the world shines on us and in our hearts and gives us the power to love. We have all had our sins forgiven—so it isn't presumptuous to say that we know we are Christians. A Christian is a forgiven sinner whom God loves. Will you pray Paul's prayer again now for someone you know—and for yourself as well?

SB

About Prophets and About Priesthood

For the next six weeks we are going to look at two prophets and at the priesthood of Jesus. The first prophet is Jonah, who didn't want to be a prophet at all. When God told him to go to Nineveh he booked a place on a boat going in the opposite direction—and when in the end he did as he was told he ended up being very annoyed with God. Jonah wanted to see Nineveh blotted out for its bad behaviour. God wanted it to repent and be loved. One of the most fascinating books in the Old Testament. Someone read it aloud to me once, and I just laughed at Jonah's sheer human nastiness. Try it sometime! Adrian Plass' notes on Jonah were originally written for the Easter period, but death and resurrection are part of our Christian lives all the time, so are always relevant.

The priesthood of Jesus in the letter to the Hebrews can show us what priesthood is really about (and being a Christian is about being a priest—a member of a royal priesthood). All the trappings and ritual of the Jewish temple can be a superb visual aid for us to understand priesthood and how to enter in to the presence of God—and to discover that because we are 'in Christ' we are also (and always) living in the presence.

The prophet Ezekiel was shown visions of the glory of God which were so brilliant that he fell on his face—overwhelmed and awestruck. But he was made to get up so that he could be spoken to by God, and told to go and prophesy to people who were 'a nation of rebels'. Other visions showed Ezekiel the horror of their idolatry and sexual corruption—and he saw the glory of God rise up from the temple of God, where the acts of corruption were taking place, and depart from it.

Ezekiel wasn't a popular prophet, but then prophets never are. When they tell a nation what that nation doesn't want to hear then the establishment of the day tell them to be quiet and mind their own business. But it is their business, because it is God's business. A God who in the words of another prophet tells them very severely to change their evil ways: 'Cease to do evil, learn to do good; seek justice, rescue the oppressed, defend the orphan, plead for the widow' (Isaiah 1:16–17). Perhaps in our day the prophets would be crying out for oppressed minorities (or majorities), for the homeless, the mentally ill, and the aged.

The power of God

To keep me from becoming conceited because of these surpassingly great revelations, there was given me a thorn in my flesh, a messenger of Satan, to torment me. Three times I pleaded with the Lord to take it away from me. But he said to me, 'My grace is sufficient for you, for my power is made perfect in weakness.' Therefore I will boast all the more gladly about my weaknesses, so that Christ's power may rest on me. That is why, for Christ's sake, I delight in weaknesses, in insults, in hardships, in persecutions, in difficulties. For when I am weak, then I am strong.

The problem of a prayer that isn't answered is what we are looking at today. And it was an apostle who prayed it, pleading with God to give him what he wanted—and to take away what he didn't want. We don't know what it was, except that it hurt him and he didn't like it. But he doesn't tell us any more than that—and it is good that he doesn't. Because now we can apply what happened (and what didn't happen) to Paul to our own circumstances.

Paul prayed and pleaded and God didn't answer his prayer. Or that's what we might say. Yet 'No' is just as much an answer as 'Yes'. And God didn't just leave it at a stark 'No'. He made Paul a promise. 'My grace is sufficient for you, for my power is made perfect in weakness.' Then Paul must have turned to a different sort of prayer—in which he opened himself up to the grace and the presence and the power of Christ. And God did what he promised—so much so that Paul then started to boast about his weaknesses and to delight in them.

Reflect

Is there something that you long for God to take away from you? Something you have pleaded and prayed about and yet you are still stuck with? Could it be that God is saying to you what he said to Paul? If it is possible, then start to pray differently. Praise God for your weakness—and for his power. Then wait, expectantly, for his power to be made perfect in your weakness.

SB

Where now?

Now the word of the Lord came to Jonah the son of Amittai, saying, 'Arise, go to Nineveh, that great city, and cry against it; for their wickedness has come up before me.'

When I became a Christian, twenty-seven years ago, guidance was one of the items included in a sort of invisible evangelical kit-bag that was issued to all new recruits. From in front or from behind (depending on which Scripture was quoted) God would direct every step that we took. We would always know where to go and what to do because he would tell us.

I can't speak for others, but this subtle mis-teaching left me frequently paralysed (when God seemed to be saying nothing) and sometimes neurotic and twitchy (when a random thought invaded my mind). Did the Lord really want me to get a train to Walsall and give a blue cardigan to the first person that I met?

It was during this period that a friend told me he was being led to work in the Holy Land because every time he opened his Bible he found a reference to Israel.

It is precisely because the Holy Spirit *does* guide people clearly and specifically when necessary that we need to avoid the rather superstitious view of God's leading that prevails in many parts of the Church.

God's communication system is not based on some mouldy old hand oper-ated printer that produces documents too fuzzy to read. If he speaks to you—you'll know it!

Paul the apostle is a good model. He prayed constantly, made common-sense decisions, and was always ready to change his plans when a dream or a vision or a direct word from God told him he'd got it wrong.

Of course God is concerned with every step we take, but we're not involved in some ghastly spiritual version of *Come Dancing*. Jonah knew *exactly* what God wanted him to do. That's why he cleared off. On Palm Sunday Jesus knew exactly what God wanted as well. He didn't clear off, though. He entered Jerusalem knowing that death was inevitable.

A prayer

Lord, help me to stay close to you in prayer and study, so that our relationship affects all the decisions that I make. I trust that I will hear you clearly and specifically when necessary.

AP

Not my will . . .

But Jonah rose to flee to Tarshish from the presence of the Lord. He went down to Joppa and found a ship going to Tarshish; so he paid the fare, and went on board, to go with them to Tarshish, away from the presence of the Lord.

I wonder what Jonah did when he was not out being a prophet? Perhaps there was a sign over his door saying: AMITTAI AND SON—STICK WHITTLERS. Every now and then, as Jonah sat happily at home, whistling through his teeth and doing a spot of bespoke whittling, the Spirit of God would whisper in his ear and his heart would sink as he realized that it was time to move into prophet mode once again. Why had he got so fed up with it? What was the reason for his deliberate act of disobedience when he was told to go to Nineveh? We can't be sure—but we can guess.

My guess is that his lack of enthusiasm dated from the time when he began to realize that he would never be anything more than a messenger. It would have been quite exciting at first—rather exhilarating. How powerful it must have felt to threaten the enemies of Israel with the hammer of God as a consequence of their evil ways. Perhaps the first one or two failed to repent and suffered destruction as a result.

Then (as far as Jonah was concerned, anyway) the rot began to set in. Following the prophet's impressive forecast of doom and gloom, people repented, and Jonah began to sense that the God whose message he had delivered much *preferred* to forgive sinners. I guess Jonah felt a bit of a twit when this happened. All that ranting he'd done, and now God had changed his mind. Very hard to walk away keeping your back view dignified in those circumstances.

Unlike Clark Kent and Bruce Wayne, Jonah was not at all keen to don his super-prophet costume, not if he was going to end up feeling an idiot yet again.

God reserves the right to follow up our obedience in any way that seems fit. If we don't like it we can try to run away, but, as Jonah was about to discover, that doesn't always work.

A thought

Am I willing to have my cake but give up the right to eat it?

AP

Trouble for others

But the Lord hurled a great wind upon the sea, and there was a mighty tempest on the sea, so that the ship threatened to break up. Then the mariners were afraid, and each cried to his god; and they threw the wares that were in the ship into the sea, to lighten it for them. But Jonah had gone down into the inner part of the ship and had lain down, and was fast asleep. So the captain came and said to him, 'What do you mean, you sleeper? Arise, call upon your god! Perhaps the god will give a thought to us, that we do not perish.'

I find these verses a little disturbing. If I weren't doing these notes for other people I'd skip this bit and go on to something more comfortable. Can it really be true that my disobedience could cause a whole lot of trouble for folk who've done nothing wrong? Honesty compels me to admit that I know it to be true in my own life. I haven't gone down to Newhaven and taken ship to Dieppe to flee the will of God recently, but I have quite deliberately failed to tackle problems, heal relationships or perform tasks that should be top priorities in my life. The innocent fellow-travellers who suffer as a result are usually members of my family. Guilt makes me grumpy. Failure makes me fret. I become a little cloud, inflicting bad weather on my small part of the world.

In this account the little cloud called Jonah is lying, like a baby in its womb, down in the depths of the ship, hoping perhaps to hide in unconsciousness as so many of us do when we feel like fugitives.

What an awakening! The sensation of being dragged violently back into reality must have been dreadful—it always is. The fear and panic in the captain's voice, the sounds and movements of the storm, and the inescapable knowledge that God had taken the situation by the scruff of the neck and was shaking it until his disobedient servant fell out—all these things must have combined to become a waking nightmare for the prophet. The crew had dumped the cargo, a multi-faith prayer meeting had been held, everyone was quite terrified, and it was all Jonah's fault!

A question

Will I do what I'm told at last?

AP

Owning up

Then they said to him, 'Tell us, on whose account this evil has come upon us. What is your occupation? And whence do you come? What is your country? And of what people are you?' And he said to them, 'I am a Hebrew; and I fear the Lord, the God of heaven, who made the sea and the dry land.'

Isn't it difficult to own up sometimes? When I was about nine years old my father made a bow and arrow for myself and my brother, Ian, who was two years younger than me. He spent hours hunting in the woods for the right—absolutely straight—lengths of hazel, and then sat outside the shed on our allotment, trimming, cutting, tying, sharpening, and fashioning flights out of cardboard. Ian and I tried the weapon out. It worked marvellously. Later that day, when no one else was around, I did what I'd been wanting to do ever since I saw the completed implements. I fired the arrow as far as I possibly could. It was inexpressbily wonderful to drawback the string and feel the potential power in that strong, flexible length of hazel. When I released the arrow, it flew in a majestically huge and regular arc, curving up towards the sun, and curving down into a thick and quite impenetrable mass of undergrowth. That beautiful arrow was lost. I didn't tell anyone.

For some reason my father got it into his head that it was Ian who had lost the arrow. When I got to the allotment next morning Ian was in tears, and my father was angrily trying to make him confess. A block of ice gripped my heart as the crying and shouting escalated. Words crouched miserably just inside my mouth, too frightened to come out. Then my brother was clipped round the ear and I couldn't stand it any more. The smallest voice you ever heard in your life said, 'Dad, it wasn't Ian who lost the arrow, it was me.'

My father had used up all his anger on Ian, so I didn't get shouted at, but the ice took a long time to melt.

Poor old Jonah

A prayer

Lord, if there are things lodged in our hearts that chill us when we remember them, give us the courage to confess to the right person at the right time.

AP

Overboard

He said to them, 'Take me up and throw me into the sea; then the sea will quiet down for you; for I know it is because of me that this great tempest has come upon you.' Nevertheless the men rowed hard to bring the ship back to land, but they could not, for the sea grew more and more tempestuous against them . . . So they took up Jonah and threw him into the sea; and the sea ceased from its raging.

This is a very heart-warming story, don't you think? I like the sound of the fellows on this ship. The whole of their profits had gone overboard with the cargo, they'd been buffeted and terrified by an appalling storm, but they still tried as hard as they could to avoid throwing the author of their misfortunes into the sea. Of course, they must have been a little puzzled. Did this powerful, weather controlling God *really* want them to throw his prophet into the ocean? Wouldn't he be angry with them? They failed to understand, just as Peter failed to understand when he provoked the famous 'Get thee behind me, Satan' speech from his master, that, in the context of God's planning and special knowledge, negative events and circumstances are sometimes essential. As we think tomorrow about Jesus' horrendous death on the cross, this central truth becomes very evident, but enlightenment usually comes only by hindsight.

I got thrown overboard a few years ago, when illness left me with no job, no church, and no prospects. If you had suggested to me then that this was all part of God's plan for me I would have gone for your throat. I guess that as Jonah travelled the short distance from the ship's rail to the boiling sea, he must have reflected that he had known better days. But he knew God better than I did when my crisis happened. I don't doubt that he was very frightened, but there is a sort of wry awareness in his brave assertion that the tempest would abate if the sailors threw him over the side.

'Maybe I'm going to drown,' he might have said to himself as he hit the water, 'but I have an awful feeling that I'm going to Nineveh . . .'

A reflection

We are not really capable of assessing the divine perspective on any situation or circumstance. Perhaps its more useful to develop trust and obedience than insight.

AP

The screaming moment

And the Lord appointed a great fish to swallow up Jonah; and Jonah was in the belly of the fish three days and three nights. Then Jonah prayed to the Lord his God from the belly of the fish, saying, 'I called to the Lord, out of my distress, and he answered me; out of the belly of Sheol I cried, and thou didst hear my voice. For thou didst cast me into the deep, into the heart of the seas, and the flood was round about me; all thy waves and thy billows passed over me.'

When the scribes and Pharisees asked Jesus for a sign, he told them that the only sign they'd be given was the sign of the prophet Jonah.

On the day that we call Good Friday, Jesus allowed us to 'throw him overboard' so that the storm of God's displeasure would not destroy us. He spent three days in a place that was far darker and more dismal than the belly of a whale. From the cross he cried out his desolation and anguish to his Father, whose back was turned on his son for that one screaming moment in eternity. Unlike Jonah, Jesus was innocent. He went where he was told, said what he was told, and died when he was told.

I have to say that I don't understand the crucifixion. I accept that this is more a measure of my understanding than a comment on the crucifixion, but I suspect that many others will identify with my lack of comprehension. I don't mean that I can't see the basic logic of somebody taking the blame and being punished for what I have done and not done; nor am I saying that I don't accept or appreciate the power of what Jesus did. How could I? The wordless truth and significance of the cross is in my bones, and in the bones of every suffering body or situation that ever was. I think I mean that there is a great mystery enshrouding that strange, cosmic event, and that I prefer the mystery to half-baked, glib explanations of what was going on.

What about Jonah? I wonder if he knew what this dark, wet, heaving environment was. We shall never know for certain, but one thing's clear enough from the prophet's impassioned prayer there's nothing like being swallowed by a whale to stimulate revival!

A prayer

Thank you so much, Jesus, for being obedient.

AP

In spirit and truth . . .

Yesterday I realized that with human eyes it is impossible to see God. It was a deep awareness that suddenly took a hold of me, and I was seized with a sort of holy dread... awe mixed with excitement. And at every moment of knowing that I also knew that there is a different, far more glorious way of seeing. I found myself worshipping. I had known the truth in my head but now I was experiencing it in my heart—in delight and wonder. It is the truth that Jesus revealed to the woman of Samaria.

'...But the hour will come—in fact is here already—when true worshippers will worship the Father in spirit and truth: that is the kind of a worshipper the Father wants. God is Spirit, and those who worship must worship in spirit and truth. The woman said to him, 'I know that Messiah—that is, Christ—is coming; and when he comes he will tell us everything.' 'I who am speaking to you,' said Jesus, 'I am he.'

God is everywhere (which is not at all the same as saying that every *thing* is God). In Christ 'all things hold together' (Colossians 1:17)—so faith can see the glory of God streaming out of all things, and worship. Christ can meet us through all things—Christ the Word of God, who 'reflects the glory of God and bears the very stamp of his nature, upholding the universe by his word of power' (Hebrews 1:3). St Paul writes of 'Christ in you, the hope of glory' (Colossians 1:27). The Spirit of Christ can totally indwell matter—and totally indwell us as fire indwells iron. The difference in kind makes the indwelling possible.

Will you sit quite still for a few moments, looking at all the things around you, and meditate on what Jesus revealed to the woman of Samaria about true worship?

Reflect

Earth's crammed with heaven,
And every common bush afire with God;
But only he who sees, takes off his shoes,
The rest sit round it, and pluck
blackberries...

Elizabeth Barrett Browning,
Aurora Leigh

SB

Raging at God

'The waters closed in over me, the deep was round about me; weeds were wrapped about my head at the roots of the mountains. I went down to the land whose bars closed upon me for ever; yet thou didst bring up my life from the Pit, O Lord my God.'

I sometimes find myself thinking rather dark thoughts, especially on the day before Easter Sunday. When I read these words of Jonah, spoken from the belly of the whale, I suddenly remembered that horrible incident some years ago (widely covered by the media at the time) when a young Italian boy was trapped at the bottom of a disused well. Attempts to rescue the poor lad went on for days with the whole world watching via newspapers and television. Everywhere, people prayed that he would be brought up alive from the pit. But he wasn't. He died at the bottom of the well while his mother wept at the top.

I raged at God. I hated God. I told God what I thought of his weakness or his cruelty or whatever it was that prevent him from doing something so obvious, especially in the face of such a barrage of prayer from every corner of the globe.

'You must have seen him!' I raved. 'How could you watch him go through that and not do anything about it? How? Tell me!'

I won't bother trotting out the statutory answers to these questions. I know them. I've used them when others have asked me about such things, and they're not really satisfactory. Two things help me.

First, the God I meet through Jesus weeps and hurts and cares and loves. I've grown to trust him despite getting so angry with him. That isn't an answer—it's a relationship.

Secondly, I take heart from the experience of the disciples on the night following Jesus' death. I believe that they too must have raged at God, unable to believe that he could have allowed such a cruel, pointless, waste of a life that had so much to offer. How could a loving Father stand by and watch as his Son was nailed to a piece of wood between two criminal scum? What a mess! What a waste! What a dark night of tears. Nothing would ever mean anything again.

Then came the dawn.

A prayer

Hold my hand, Lord, it's dark.

AP

263

Solid ground

And the Lord spoke to the fish, and it vomited out Jonah upon the dry land.

As soon as God had had a chat with this very cooperative whale the creature obligingly deposited Jonah on dry land, and, for the first time since leaving Joppa harbour, the prophet felt solid ground beneath his feet.

This is what Easter is all about. Until Jesus rose quietly but triumphantly from the dead, the world was an island in creation that sank beneath the feet of every man and woman as soon as their mortal bodies became too old to function. The resurrection redefined solid ground. Now, death is no longer relevant, because we can be admitted into the true reality of eternal life with Jesus in the place where he lives with his Father. As soon as death had been overcome, a return to Eden—spiritual and physical—became possible.

All that and chocolate eggs as well!

I've rarely been able to celebrate Easter on Easter Day, but I do celebrate it on all those occasions when, like Jonah, I am rescued yet again from some whale of a problem that is about to digest me into nothingness. I know I am saved once and for all, but every now and then the resurrection principle acts as a structure within my confusion and I know I'm saved all over again.

One of the few occasions when my mood matched the day was an Easter Sunday five years ago, when I attended the morning service in Norwich Cathedral, one of my all-time favourite buildings. It was one of those incomparable spring mornings full of rippling light and hope. The place was packed, the singing was wonderful, and the prayers seemed to buzz and resonate with the will of God. The deep bass note of tradition and the high and beautiful living presence of the Holy Spirit made my heart soar. Tears filled my eyes and I, who have almost never raised my arms in worship in the most informal situations, suddenly wanted to thrust my open hands as high into the air as high as they would go in the middle of a formal Anglican cathedral service. I didn't. I wish I had done. I was an Easter chicken. I bet, if the truth were told, there was a whole flock of us there that day.

A prayer

Thank you for setting our feet on the mainland. May Easter be always in us.

AP

Completing the loop

Then the word of the Lord came to Jonah the second time, saying, 'Arise, go to Nineveh, that great city, and proclaim to it the message that I tell you.'

Poor old Jonah! If he had gone to Nineveh when he was first told to, he wouldn't have ended up in the mess he found himself in and having to hear God give him exactly the same order as before. The prophet's personal rebellion had been nipped in the bud before it had the chance to get going. No doubt he was relieved and grateful to be saved from a blubbery death, but as he squelched off in the direction of this stronghold of the national enemy, all the old misgivings must have settled over him like a shadow.

But how thankful we should be that God *does* organize and allow these 'loops' in our lives. Have you done a loop? I have. On at least one occasion in my life I have deliberately taken a direction that is opposed to the will of God. One day I shall write a book with the title, *Life in the Loops*. These little drifts and diversions are almost always interesting (ask Jonah!) but they become progressively more hollow, unsatisfying, or just plain dangerous more dangerous, indeed, than those things that the world fears most. I don't know if Jonah really believed that he could escape God by changing his geographical position, but a greater and more horrible permanent fate would have resulted from real separation from the Creator.

Yes, the good news is that God will sort our mistakes and wrong turnings out. He would never have taken us on in the first place if he wasn't prepared to cope with the inevitable dips in our behaviour and response. (Most of the prophets were temperamental, awkward, passionate people who wouldn't last two minutes in most of our modern churches.)

The bad news is that the job we've been given doesn't change. As far as God is concerned, completing the loop means 'business as usual'.

Off to Nineveh!

A prayer

Thank you, Lord, that you rebuke us when we get in a mess, but that you don't give up on us.

AP

Into action

So Jonah arose and went to Nineveh, according to the word of the Lord. Now Nineveh was an exceedingly great city, three days' journey in breadth. Jonah began to go into the city, going a day's journey. And he cried, 'Yet forty days, and Nineveh shall be overthrown.'

Do you get the impression, as I do, that Jonah slipped straight into top prophesying gear as soon as he actually reached Nineveh? Prophets and evangelists are like that in my experience. They may moan or complain or even become sullenly uncommunicative at times (modern ones as well as Old Testament ones) but as soon as they start to do what they are called and born to do there's no stopping them. A sort of spiritual professionalism takes over. Vanity and vulnerability take a back seat as God drives his message into the listeners. I'm quite sure that Jonah's warning to the citizens of Nineveh was not even slightly diluted by his reluctance to be there. His 'ministry' was part of him, which is more than can be said for many of us.

I know at least two people who have spent most of their lives denying (or trying to deny) a part of themselves that God has almost certainly been wanting to use for years.

One of them is a very talented artist who, when he became a Christian more than thirty years ago allowed the climate of Christian disapproval that befogged art at the time to dissuade him from continuing with his career as a painter. He has recovered from this foolishness now, but many years were wasted as he tried to pretend that this essential part of him had been painlessly amputated, and that he didn't care. God cared. If Jonah had been ordered to paint pictures he would have been wasting his time at Nineveh.

My other friend is a musician—a cellist. This chap has wanted to 'do something for the Lord' for ages. He gets quite depressed when things don't seem to work out. He's just beginning to realize—with some amazement—that what the Lord wants is some really good cello-playing, and not just 'Christian stuff'.

Painting, prophesying or playing the cello—whatever is right is all right.

A question

Are we doing what we are?

AP

And the power of fear

And the people of Nineveh believed God; they proclaimed a fast, and put on sackcloth, from the greatest of them to the least of them. Then tidings reached the king of Nineveh, and he arose from his throne, removed his robe, and covered himself with sackcloth, and sat in ashes. And he made proclamation and published through Nineveh, 'By the decree of the king and his nobles: Let neither man nor beast, herd nor flock, taste anything; let them not feed, or drink water, but let man and beast be covered with sackcloth, and let them cry mightily to God; yea, let every one turn from his evil way and from the violence which is in his hands. Who knows, God may yet repent and turn from his fierce anger, so that we perish not?'

How could one disobedient little prophet have such a dynamic effect on such a huge community? In scale and depth of response this mission of Jonah's makes a Billy Graham rally look like a Quaker meeting in a telephone box. How did he do it? Well, first of all, of course, he didn't do it. His threat of destruction after forty days carried the authority and authenticity of the Holy Spirit, yet another lesson for all of us that it is both pointless and perilous to claim that we speak for God when we are only guessing.

Secondly, and precisely because the prophecy was so convincing, the citizens of Nineveh were clearly terrified. Modern evangelism tends to major on the attractiveness of God's love for us, and the logical desirability of being reunited with our Creator, and we need those emphases to counteract the influence of the Pharisees who surround us, but fear has a long and respectable pedigree in the history of God's dealings with men and women. Why? Quite simply because God knows that for those who do not belong to him there is a lot to be frightened of. If someone whom you love is in danger you warn them, and you hope against hope that they will save themselves.

The people of this city threw themselves into repentance wholeheartedly, inspired and commanded by their king, who ordered a suspension of all normal activities while everybody turned to God.

A question

This kind of head–heart–body repentance is rare today. Why?

AP

Unless you become . . .

When God saw what they did, how they turned from their evil way, God repented of the evil which he had said he would do to them, and he did not do it.

In a recent article my wife described an occasion when, after working in Germany for a few days, I flew into Heathrow, arriving at about seven o'clock in the evening. Bridget drove up to meet me, bringing our two younger sons with her. Joseph, aged twelve, and David, aged eleven, knew how much I would be looking forward to seeing them. They pushed to the front of the waiting crowds so that their shining faces would be the first thing I saw as I came out of the green channel with my luggage. It was such a pleasure for me to see them there.

The God who so freely forgave these Assyrian penitents, and who describes himself through Jesus as a Father, takes a similar pleasure in our confident awareness that he wants to see us. Not because we have earned his affection, nor for any other motives of personal pride, but because, like Joe and David at the airport, we know that he loves us with a passion that is graphically illustrated in the story of the prodigal son. Let's not get smug about the rotten old sinners in Nineveh. We all need to go through the repentance door if we want to be hugged by God.

What sort of door is the repentance door? I found a clue recently. A few miles along the coast from us there's a place called Jungle Tumble. It's a highly coloured maze of tunnels, ladders, netting and plastic balls—a little paradise for children who want to enjoy the ecstasy of physical abandonment. Recently we took four-year-old Katy and eleven-year-old David to visit this place that we'd heard so much about. When we arrived we discovered that only children under a certain fixed heights were allowed. Katy was little enough. David was too big. What to do? Fortunately the lady in charge invited David to duck his head under the bar. 'Look,' she said, 'now you're small enough!'

We bow our heads and become a bit smaller before we enter joy.

A reflection

Chesterton said, 'A man is never so tall as when he bows.'

AP

The way in

Jesus said, 'In truth, in very truth I tell you, I am the door of the sheepfold. The sheep paid no heed to any who came before me, for these were all thieves and robbers. I am the door; anyone who comes into the fold through me shall be safe. He shall go in and out and shall find pasturage.'

One of the oldest formulas for Christian prayer goes something like this: to the Father, through the Son, in the power of the Holy Spirit. Prayer is a process which involves us with each person of the Trinity. As Jesus taught us, we pray to God the Father, and our prayer is assisted and powered by the help of the Spirit. But we pray through Jesus. It is Jesus who makes true prayer possible.

As a human being, Jesus is one with us, sharing our weaknesses and temptations, identifying with our sorrows and joys. As God, he is the one who can lift us up to the presence of God, letting us overcome our human limitations—or rather, overcoming them for us. As God and man, his death on the cross opened up a way into the presence of God, as he became the bridge across the gaping chasm that would otherwise separate us from the Father. Jesus, you might say, has one foot on each side of the gap; the human with us, and the divine with the Father.

It is as we identify in faith with him, that we are able to cross the gap ourselves; in this life through prayer, and in the life to come, in person. Jesus, as he puts it in today's reading, is the door; the door between worlds.

This is one reason why prayer is so important. It is our way of overcoming human limits as we enter the presence of God. So never cease to pray, for in prayer we are caught up in the work of Jesus, who brings us into the presence of the Father by the power of the Spirit.

MM

Getting cross with God

But it displeased Jonah exceedingly, and he was angry. And he prayed to the Lord and said, 'I pray thee, Lord, is not this what I said when I was yèt in my country? That is why I made haste to flee to Tarshish; for I knew that thou art a gracious God and merciful, slow to anger, and abounding in steadfast love, and repentest of evil. Therefore now, O Lord, take my life from me, I beseech thee, for it is better for me to die than to live.'

Well, who's an angry little prophet, then? Jonah is very bold with God, isn't he? Mind you, he must have known him very well. It reminds me of the way one of my sons used to respond to being told off when he was very small. After a minute or two of my parental raging he would look me in the eye and say triumphantly, 'Anyway, you love me, so you'll be nice to me in a minute . . .' I wouldn't recommend that as a way of responding to the wrath of God, but I'm glad David knew I loved him, and I find the interchange between Jonah and God a refreshingly real and familiar one. The prophet is doing a real Basil Faulty here, furious that God has done exactly what he feared he would do. He's forgiven them! Huh!

It's interesting to note that God did not insist on Jonah sharing his intention or motivation as far as Nineveh was concerned. He simply wanted him to do as he was told. Jesus made exactly the same point in his parable of the two sons. One said he would do what was asked of him, but didn't. The other got stroppy and refused to obey, but then went and did what he'd been told.

Similarly, when Jesus called Zacchaeus down from his tree, the little man wasn't required to sort his attitudes and behaviour out before nipping home to sort a meal out. Again and again throughout Scripture the same point is made. Those who love God are those who obey him.

Now it was time for Jonah's little attitude problem to be sorted out.

Questions

Do I trust God enough to get cross with him? Do I love him enough to obey him?

AP

The incredible sulk

And the Lord said, 'Do you do well to be angry?' Then Jonah went out of the city and sat to the east of the city, and made a booth for himself there. He sat under it in the shade, till he should see what would become of the city.

I really like God in this story. I don't like him in all the Old Testament accounts, particularly the bits where mass killings are ordered, but I shall understand what that was all about one day. The thing I like in this story is that, having shown such compassion and taken such trouble with the enormous community at Nineveh, God now concentrates on one confused individual—Jonah.

If the prodigal son's elder brother is the heavyweight sulking champion of the New Testament, Jonah must be a front-line candidate in the Old. There he sits on the hillside, probably muttering about Joppa and ships and storms and whales and people not doing what they say they're going to do . . .

God tries to talk to him about it, but it seems that Jonah is one of those people who just can't understand anything without concrete examples or visible object lessons. The whale was the first and most dramatic one, but now it was time for something a little more agricultural. It has been most refreshing over the last few years to find that God does not have a set of unvarying procedures that he applies to anyone who comes within his orbit. In my own case, for instance, there have been times when my own rather negative expectations led me to predict a divine clip round the ear as a response to less than wonderful behaviour. In fact, because he knows and loves me, God has used encouragement and humour to lift me out of my lower self. Mind you, when the aforesaid clip round the ear is necessary he doesn't seem to have any qualms about applying it, and that's as it should be, even if I don't like it much at the time.

Jonah and you and I may be very different in outlook and personality, but don't worry—although we shall all finish up in the same place, a very individual and carefully designed route has been prepared for each of us.

A prayer

Thank you, Father, for loving me as an individual and planning things specially for me.

AP

271

The final lesson

And the Lord God appointed a plant, and made it come up over Jonah that it might be a shade over his head, to save him from his discomfort. So Jonah was exceedingly glad because of the plant. But when dawn came up the next day, God appointed a worm which attacked the plant, so that it withered. When the sun rose, God appointed a sultry east wind, and the sun beat upon the head of Jonah so that he was faint; and he asked that he might die, and said, 'It is better for me to die than to live.' But God said to Jonah, 'Do you do well to be angry for the plant?' And he said, 'I do well to be angry, angry enough to die.' And the Lord said, 'You pity the plant, for which you did not labour, nor did you make it grow, which came into being in a night, and perished in a night. And should not I pity Nineveh, that great city, in which there are more than a hundred and twenty thousand persons who do not know their right hand from their left, and also much cattle?'

My sulks are fairly fragile. If someone tickles me or says something absurd, my glum expression is likely to crack, and once I've smiled my sulk is usually ruined. Jonah, on the other hand, is so determined not to give an inch to God that he walks straight into the logical trap that is set for him. The writer of this book fails to record the prophet's response to the final, telling argument that one hundred and twenty thousand people must be as important as a plant, but I have no doubt that Jonah got the point. Perhaps the mention of cattle swung it in the end. A real waste!

A sad footnote to this story, recorded a few pages further on in the Old Testament in the book of Nahum, is that the people of Nineveh learned very little from their great deliverance. As far as we can tell they returned to their sins and were destroyed.

Jonah teaches me that obedience is essential; that God would rather forgive than punish; that he takes as much trouble with individuals as whole communities; and that he can be very humorous and nice.

A question

Do I share these attributes of God?

AP

Love speaks

In the past God spoke to our forefathers through the prophets at many times and in various ways, but in these last days he has spoken to us by his Son, whom he appointed heir of all things, and through whom he made the universe.

A friend and colleague of mine has just met the girl of his dreams—and he and I have been working several hundred miles away from where she lives. They keep in touch by telephone, and one day I found him on the top deck of our ship speaking into a mobile phone with a pleased expression on his face. Because he loves her so, he wants to speak to her (and the same is true of her). And because God loves us he wants to speak to us, and for us to listen. But love also wants to be in the presence of the beloved.

This Letter to the Hebrews tells us the ways in which God has spoken in the past and how he speaks in the present—in the past through the prophets, in the present through the Son. But it also tells us (and we shall look at this later on) how we can enter into the presence of the God who loves us, through the Son of God.

The writer says that it was through his Son that God made the whole of creation. The Prologue of John's Gospel says: 'In the beginning was the Word, and the Word was with God, and the Word was God. He was with God in the beginning. Through him all things were made; without him nothing was made that has been made.' (1:1-2) But the world that God created has gone wrong—or at any rate our planet earth has gone wrong (we don't know what might be happening in other worlds spinning round in the vastness of space). The people who live in our world have become separated through sin from the God who created them so that he could love them and they could love him back. So just as in the beginning God made all things through his Son, so through his Son he makes all things new and recreates our broken world.

A prayer

Lord God—you speak to me because you love me. Now I am going to be silent for a few minutes. Help me to listen to you.

SB

Exactly like God

The Son is the radiance of God's dory and the exact representation of his being, sustaining all things by his powerful word. After he had provided purification for sins, he sat down at the right hand of the Majesty in heaven.

As I look out of my window across the fields I can see a row of poplar trees with the sun shining on them. There is a hill behind them, but they are so tall that the tops of trees are against the pale-blue of the winter sky. The leaves fell off last month. But the glory of the poplar trees is in their unique shape just as much as their rustling leaves so that the sort of tree they are, and their essential nature, still shines out of them.

The glory that shone out of Jesus was the unique nature of God. When we look at Jesus we can see what God is like. We can see what Bishop John Robinson called so beautifully 'the human face of God'. When we look with the eyes of faith we see the Son of God, who sustains everything that is by his word of power; the divine energy that goes forth and holds in being the whole of the created universe, the universe that began when God spoke his word in the darkness and said, 'Let there be light!'

The writer of this letter says that the Son is the exact representation of the being of God like a seal stamped on wax. And the writer would know how Jesus lived his life on this earth as the friend of publicans and sinners and as the servant who washed the feet of his disciples. And as the one who forgave men and women their sins, and who died so that their sins could be forgiven.

'After he had provided purification for sins, he sat down . . .' This verse says in short what other chapters will say at length: that there is no need for any more sacrifices for sin. Jesus' work of sin-bearing is completed. As he said on the cross just before he died, 'It is finished!' So now he is sitting down.

A way to pray

Read this verse from Hebrews out loud and then be silent for two or three minutes being aware of the presence of God, and asking that the Spirit will reveal the glory of God to you . . .

SB

Friend and brother

In bringing many sons to glory, it was fitting that God, for whom and through whom everything exists, should make the author of their salvation perfect through suffering. Both the one who makes men holy and those who are made holy are of the same family. So Jesus is not ashamed to call them brothers. He says, 'I will declare your name to my brothers; in the presence of the congregation I will sing your praises.' And again, 'I will put my trust in him.' And again he says, 'Here am I, and the children God has even me.'

Jesus started something off so that we could enter into it and what he started was the Christian family. He is the unique Son of God—but God is 'bringing many sons to glory'—you and me and everyone who trusts in him. We are the children of God, so Jesus can say, 'Here am I, and the children God has given me', and we can say to God, 'Abba, Father', just as Jesus did.

Jesus did all that for us through his suffering. It was the only way it could happen. He was made 'perfect' through his suffering, and that word in the original Greek means that 'the thing or person so described fully carries out the purpose or the plan for which he or it was purposed and designed' (William Barclay). It was through his suffering that Jesus became a perfect mediator and a perfect sacrifice for sin. We shall look more deeply at these things as we go on in our study.

Prayer

Jesus, you are my friend and you are my brother, and through you I am a child of God. I rejoice that God is bringing many sons and daughters to glory and that I am one of them, because you suffered for me and died for me.

SB

Father, Son and Spirit

Philip said, 'Lord, show us the Father and that will be enough for us.' Jesus answered: 'Don't you know me, Philip, even after I have been among you such a long time? Anyone who has seen me has seen the Father. How can you say, "Show us the Father"? Don't you believe that I am in the Father, and that the Father is in me? The words I say to you are not just my own. Rather, it is the Father, living in me, who is doing his work. Believe me when I say that I am in the Father and the Father is in me ... If you love me, you will obey what I command. I will ask the Father, and he will give you another Counsellor to be with you for ever—the Spirit of truth.'

The Hebrew word *shema* means 'hear', and a Jewish father taught the faith to his family by saying 'Hear, O Israel: The Lord our God is one Lord; and you shall love the Lord your God with all your heart and with all your soul, and with all your might...' (Deuteronomy 6:4–5).

Jesus and his disciples would have had the Shema written on their hearts ever since they could hear and understand. But now Jesus was speaking of 'the Lord our God' who 'is one Lord' in three ways. 'Lord, show us the Father', pleads Philip—who must have heard Jesus talking to God as his father—and as Abba, or Daddy, in the intimate, trustful language of a child. But the Son has said to Philip that to know the Son is also to know the Father. Philip was seeing 'the glory of God in the face of Jesus Christ' (2 Corinthians 4:6)—but he wasn't seeing very clearly. The Son is not the Father and the Father is not the Son—and the works and the miracles that the Son did were the way to see more clearly

and to believe. The Son was going to the Father—and then neither Philip nor the other disciples would see him any more (except for a little while, after the resurrection and before he finally ascended to the Father). But then God the Holy Spirit would come to them—to be with them for ever. They wouldn't see him—but they would know him.

SB

He knows what it's like

For this reason he had to be made like his brothers in every way, in order that he might become a merciful and faithful high priest in service to God, and that he might make atonement for the sins of the people. Because he himself suffered when he was tempted, he is able to help those who are being tempted.

In the Walled City in Hong Kong, where Jackie Pullinger does the amazing work to which God has called her, drug addicts and junkies are going through the agony of 'cold turkey'–the pain of withdrawal from the drugs that their bodies cry out for in pain, because over the years they have grown used to the death-dealing, destructive 'high' that drugs give to a person.

But these addicts are not going through their agony on their own. At their side, supporting them and agonizing with them, are ex-addicts, who know what the pain is like. Now they are Christians, with a new power of joy within them the joy of the Holy Spirit, with whom Christ has flooded their hearts (and if you had seen the television programme you would have seen the joy of Christ shining out of them). These Christian men and women, filled with the Spirit, who were once in the terrible power of drugs, can help the new Christians who are going through the terrible pain of withdrawal. Whatever our pain is, and whatever our temptation is, Jesus will be there for us. He knows what it is like to be us except that he never sinned. It has been said that no one knows the full power of a temptation until they have resisted it to the very end. God knows what it is like to be a human being because he became one.

A way to pray

Think about a situation in your life that is hard—or a temptation that you are going through. Think about it and, as it were, feel it—and realize the presence of Jesus with you as you do so. Remember his sufferings, and his temptations, and ask him to help you in yours. Pray too for the drug addicts of the Walled City in Hong Kong as they come off drugs through the power of the Holy Spirit.

SB

We must not look back

For the word of God is living and active. Sharper than any double-edged sword, it penetrates even to dividing soul and spirit, joints and marrow; it judges the thoughts and attitudes of the heart. Nothing in all creation is hidden from God's sight. Everything is uncovered and laid bare before the eyes of him to whom we must give account.

As so often in this letter, the writer is helping people to understand their present situation by making them remember their past history (chapter 3). When the Jews had come out of Egypt in their great Exodus they had lost faith. They had come out of their old bondage as slaves but they had not entered into the promised land of freedom. They were in a wilderness, wandering round in circles, and hankering after the past.

This is what these Christian Jews seemed to be doing. So the writer urges them to listen to the voice of God, the Word of God. Their ancestors had hardened their hearts when God spoke. Now he was speaking again, of a place of rest, where they entered into the completed work of Christ (4:9–11). They did not have to work for their salvation. They simply had to enter into it by faith. But they must obey and the Word of God would penetrate their innermost being like a sword—seeing everything in their heart and judging it.

A reflection

Be quiet for a few moments—and reflect. Have you entered into the place of rest and assurance that this letter speaks of, so that you trust in the finished work of Christ on the cross? He bore your sins in his own body on the tree, and because of that God gives you himself and his forgiveness—out of his great love for you. Let what he says penetrate your heart— confident that it is love who holds the sword.

SB

Into the presence

Therefore, since we have a great high priest who has gone through the heavens, Jesus the Son of God, let us hold firmly to the faith we profess. For we do not have a high priest who is unable to sympathize with our weaknesses, but we have one who has been tempted in every way, just as we are yet was without sin. Let us then approach the throne of grace with confidence, so that we may receive mercy and find grace to help us in our time of need.

With today's passage we get to the very heart of the letter to the Hebrews its teaching about the high priesthood of Christ. The more we understand this the more we shall understand the real nature of Christian priesthood, and we need to know what that is so that we can live out our Christian lives according to the will and the amazingly glorious plan of God.

Next week we shall be looking at the plan of the Jewish tabernacle and at the various rituals which were performed in it.

We need signs and symbols and rituals to reveal reality to us. And the reality was (and is) that sinful men and women cannot just saunter into the holy and awe-ful presence of God. The high priest went into the Holy of Holies just once a year, carrying a sacrifice for the sins of the people. Then he came out again. But Jesus, our great high priest, has gone into the real presence of God on our behalf, and he is there for ever. One who has the same nature as us is there, for us, in the holy presence of God. So we can come to God with utter confidence, knowing that we are forgiven and understood, and that we have a merciful high priest. He will give us grace which is his presence and himself and his mighty power to help us in our own time of need.

Prayer

Lord Jesus Christ, help me to understand far more deeply what it means that you are our high priest (and my high priest), there in the presence of God for us (and for me) . . . always there. Spend a few moments meditating . . .

SB

The only perfect priest

Every high priest is selected from among men and is appointed to represent them in matters related to God, to offer gifts and sacrifices for sins. He is able to deal gently with those who are ignorant and are going astray, since he himself is subject to weakness. This is why he has to offer sacrifices for his own sins, as well as for the sins of the people.

The high priest who went into the presence of God on behalf of the people in the Old Testament was a sinner. He stood in the presence of God to represent men and women as they are. Because he was weak like the rest of humankind he could be sympathetic to their weaknesses and to their sins. He knew what sin was like because he himself sinned. He was one of them one of us. But he needed to be forgiven as well and the fact that he was a sinner detracted from the effectiveness of his intercessory work.

Sin spoils things. It spoils relationships, and it is always a failure in love. Anyone who is in the business of helping other people, whether professionally or simply as a friend, knows that some people seem to be much harder to deal with than others. It is often our own hang-ups and sins (and our failure to have dealt with our own weaknesses) which hinder our helping. If someone comes to us in real emotional pain because the person whom they love has rejected them, we shall not be able to help them very much if what their story does is to make the unhealed pain

of a rejection we have experienced well up and flood our consciousness with sadness and even resentment. The writer to the Hebrews is telling us about the weaknesses and sins of the Jewish high priest in order to show us how much better Jesus is at the job. Nothing we bring to him will ever perturb him ...

A prayer

Lord Jesus Christ, help me to know with total confidence that there is nothing that I have ever done, or can do, which will mean that you cannot function as my high priest ... bringing me to God ... bringing God to me ... forgiving all the sins I confess to you ... and loving me for ever and ever.

SB

After the suffering

During the days of Jesus' life on earth, he offered up prayers and petitions with loud cries and tears to the one who could save him from death, and he was heard because of his reverent submission. Although he was a son, he learned obedience from what he suffered and, once made perfect, he became the source of eternal salvation for all who obey him and was designated by God to be high priest in the order of Melchizedek.

The first verse of today's passage is very mysterious. It must be talking about the cries of Jesus to his heavenly Father in his agony in the Garden of Gethsemane. That means that God did not take away the suffering of death by crucifixion that Jesus faced. But after he had suffered he raised him from the dead. If that was true for the Son of God it will be just as true for us. God is unlikely to remove the suffering that we dread. But on the other side of the darkness there will be a shining victory and a blessed happiness.

If Jesus had to learn obedience through suffering there can hardly be any easier way for us to learn it. Even back in the Old Testament Job cried out of the darkness of his suffering, 'Though he slay me yet will I trust in him.' It is as we bow our head to the will of God in all the circumstances of our lives (even though they break our heart and we weep in desolation) that God takes all the things that are happening to us and works them together for good (Romans 8:28) for our good and for his glory. St Paul said that our 'slight momentary affliction is preparing for us an eternal weight of glory beyond all comparison' (2 Corinthians 4:17 RSV).

When it says that Jesus was 'made perfect' it means that 'all the experiences, the sufferings, through which Jesus passed perfectly fitted him to become the Redeemer and Saviour of men.' (William Barclay, *Hebrews*)

Lord Jesus Christ, you learned obedience through the things that you suffered and all the things that happened to you. Help me to learn obedience in the same way.

SB

Grow up!

The story which has been laid upon me to tell you about this matter is a long story, difficult to tell and difficult to grasp, for your ears have become dull. For, indeed, at a stage when you ought to be teachers because of the length of time that has passed since you first heard the gospel, you still need someone to tell you the simple elements of the very beginning of the message of God. You have sunk into a stage when you need milk and not solid food; for when anyone is at the stage of participating in milk feeding, he does not really know what Christian righteousness is, for he is only a child. For solid food is for those who have reached maturity, those who, through the development of the right kind of habit, have reached a stage when their perceptions are trained to distinguish between good and evil.

Have you ever said to someone who has provoked you by their irritating and infantile behaviour: 'Grow up!'? Those Christians were refusing to grow up— and many Christians in our day are doing the same. Today I have used William Barclay's translation of this passage, because it tells the tale so clearly. To refuse to grow up in our faith is pathetic and although God will forgive us for the sin of it he will not be pleased. Instead we shall be grieving the Holy Spirit.

Christian maturity has two sides to it. There is the maturity of a Christian character with the richness and the mellowness of a mature, good wine. We grow into that by using 'the means of grace'—prayer, fellowship with other Christians, Bible reading and study, and Holy Communion. These are the very things that the Bible Reading Fellowship exists to promote. The other side of

Christian maturity is our knowledge of our faith and our ability to share it.

Prayer

Lord Jesus Christ, help me to grow up— and show me where I am still a child. Forgive me for my refusal to grow—and help me to repent of my sin.

SB

Take, eat!

When the woman saw that the fruit of the tree was good for food and pleasing to the eye, and also desirable for gaining wisdom, she took some and ate it. She also gave some to her husband, who was with her, and he ate it. Then the eyes of both of them were opened, and they realised that they were naked; so they sewed fig leaves together and made coverings for themselves. Then the man and his wife heard the sound of the Lord God as he was walking in the garden in the cool of the day, and they hid from the Lord God among the trees of the garden. But the Lord God called to the man, 'Where are you?' He answered, 'I heard you in the garden, and I was afraid because I was naked; so I hid.' And he said, 'Who told you that you were naked? Have you eaten from the tree from which I commanded you not to eat?' The man said, 'The woman you put here with me—she gave me some fruit from the tree, and I ate it.' Then the Lord God said to the woman, 'What is this you have done?' The woman said, 'The serpent deceived me, and I ate.'

God tells us to eat some things and not to eat others—and eating is about something becoming part of us. In this story there were two trees, the tree of life and the tree of knowledge. Adam and Eve could have eaten the fruit of the tree of life, but they ignored it. The story describes the skew in human nature, which sees knowledge as the key to life and happiness.

But the truth is the other way round. Jesus said, 'I am the way, and the truth, and the life. No-one comes to the Father except through me' (John 14:6). It is life which leads us into truth and into knowledge: the eternal life which is a relationship with God. We are born again into the new life through the Spirit. Then we know the forgiveness of love, because he died for us on the tree of Calvary—the new tree of life. By faith we know the presence of Jesus in our hearts—and we strengthen our knowledge of that fact by doing what he told us to do, 'Take, eat, this is my body . . .'

SB

A priest for ever

...What we have said is even more clear if another priest like Melchizedek appears, one who has become a priest not on the basis of a regulation as to his ancestry but on the basis of the power of an indestructible life. For it is declared, 'You are a priest for ever, in the order of Melchizedek'... But because Jesus lives for ever, he has a permanent priesthood. Therefore he is able to save completely those who come to God through him, because he always lives to intercede for them.

The strange story of Melchizedek (in Genesis 14:18–20) is of a priest appearing to Abraham (the father of the Jewish race and also the father of the faithful). Abraham offered sacrifices to God through Melchizedek and—the Jews reasoned that because the Levitical priesthood was within Abraham (they would be his physical descendants)—that meant that they also offered sacrifices to God through Melchizedek. So his priesthood was superior to theirs. As well as that, there was no record of Melchizedek's death—so in one sense he had an 'eternal' priesthood. But he was only a type of the reality that was to come in Jesus.

Through Christ men and women have a priesthood that is always there. William Barclay says that the original Greek means that Jesus 'remains for ever' in two senses. The word means to remain in office so that he is always there to bring us to God and to bring God to us. It also means *to remain in the capacity of a servant*. He is always there to serve us and to do just what we need him to do. He is there in the presence of God endlessly interceding for us.

To think about

Think about the greatness and the holiness of God... and then reflect on the fact that Jesus is in the presence of God as the priest of men and women... knowing what it is like to be a human being... knowing what pressures we are under... knowing just what each one of us is going through right now, and knowing just what we need. And be thankful...

SB

The one in the middle

Such a high priest meets our need—one who is holy, blameless, pure, set apart from sinners, exalted above the heavens. Unlike the other high priests, he does not need to offer sacrifices day after day, first for his own sins, and then for the sins of the people. He sacrificed for their sins once for all when he offered himself. For the law appoints as high priests men who are weak, but the oath, which came after the law, appointed the Son, who has been made perfect for ever.

Jesus is the one in the middle. With one hand he touches the human race and with the other hand he touches God. Because he is 'truly God and truly man' he can hold on to your hand and also to the hand of God. He can bring you and me to God and God to us. He is 'set apart from sinners': different from us because he never sinned. But he knows just what it is like to be tempted—so as he holds on to us he can help us.

Jesus our high priest will always be there for us because he will never die—although once he died. Unlike the old order of priesthood he never needed to offer any sacrifices for his own sins. But he did offer a sacrifice for sins. Not his, but ours. When John the Baptist had seen him coming towards him he said, 'Behold the Lamb of God, who takes away the sin of the world.' Jesus offered himself, as the Book of Common Prayer says, as 'a full, perfect, and sufficient sacrifice, oblation (offering), and satisfaction, for the sins of the whole world'. The sacrifice was 'once for all'—so there is never any need, or any possibility, of any further sacrifice for sin. Therefore in the strict sense of the word Christians don't need 'priests' any more. We don't need mediators and we don't need sacrifices. We have a high priest who has made the only sacrifice we shall ever need, and who is always there for us—and with us.

Reflect

There is one God and one mediator between God and men, the man Christ Jesus, who gave himself as a ransom for all men. (1 Timothy 2:5–6 NIV)

SB

God's new plan

This is the covenant I will make with the house of Israel after that time, declares the Lord. I will put my laws in their minds and write them on their hearts. I will be their God, and they will be my people.

In one sense the whole Jewish system of sacrifices and priests, and tabernacles and covenants, was a failure. But in another sense it wasn't. It was like a doctor's diagnosis. It showed them (and us) that something was severely wrong with them that they couldn't put right themselves. 'It is not the healthy who need a doctor, but the sick,' Jesus said, (Luke 5:31), and the perfection that the Ten Commandments laid down showed the human race the severity of its sickness. At their heart the Ten Commandments are laws about loving God and our neighbour (and ourself). But they are outside us, written on tablets of stone, and we dismally fail to keep them. So God puts them inside us instead, and does it by giving us a new heart—like Christ's. Christianity is a mystical, spiritual religion, about the Spirit of Christ indwelling the human heart.

The Jewish system is a way for us to understand both the nature of God, who is holy, and also the nature and the work of Christ. The old covenant (or Old Testament) was an agreement that depended on us keeping our side of it. The new covenant (or New Testament) is the good news that God has acted in order to help us: to forgive us for not keeping it, and to give us a new nature so that we can.

Prayer

Lord God, I thank you for the stories and symbols of the Old Testament. Help me to think about them day by day, so that I understand more and more of your holiness (and my sinfulness) and realize the immensity of your love and the wonder of your amazing and perfect plan of salvation. Thank you!

SB

The perfect visual aid

Now the first covenant had regulations for worship and also an earthly sanctuary. A tabernacle was set up. In its first room were the lampstand, the table and the consecrated bread; this was called the Holy Place. Behind the second curtain was a room called the Most Holy Place, which had the golden altar of incense and the gold-covered ark of the covenant . . . The priests entered regularly into the outer room to carry on their ministry. But only the high priest entered the inner room, and that only once a year, and never without blood, which he offered for himself and for the sins the people had committed in ignorance. The Holy Spirit was showing by this that the way into the Most Holy Place had not yet been disclosed as long as the first tabernacle was still standing. This is an illustration for the present time, indicating that the gifts and sacrifices being offered were not able to clear the conscience of the worshipper. They are only a matter of food and drink and various ceremonial washings external regulations applying until the time of the new order.

At the front of the Most Holy Place there was a thick veil, or curtain, and the high priest could enter into that place only once a year, bearing the blood of a sacrifice. Then he came out again and sprinkled the blood over the people. To make the connection between this and the sacrifice of Christ we can simply turn to the Gospels, which tells us what happened at the very moment when Jesus died on the cross. 'With a loud cry, Jesus breathed his last. The curtain of the temple was torn in two from top to bottom . . .' (Mark 15:37–38) The Gospel writers were saying (in a way that every Jew would have understood) that a totally effective sacrifice had been for sin, and now the way into the presence of God was open for ever. Will you spend some time now meditating on what that means?

SB

The perfect sacrifice

When Christ came as high priest of the good things that are already here, he went through the greater and more perfect tabernacle that is not man-made, that is to say, not a part of this creation. He did not enter by means of the blood of goats and calves; but he entered the Most Holy Place once for all by his own blood, having obtained eternal redemption. The blood of goats and bulls and the ashes of a heifer sprinkled on those who are ceremonially unclean sanctify them so that they are outwardly clean. How much more, then, will the blood of Christ, who through the eternal Spirit offered himself unblemished to God, cleanse our consciences from acts that lead to death, so that we may serve the living God! For this reason Christ is the mediator of a new covenant, that those who are called may receive the promised eternal inheritance now that he has died as a ransom to set them free from the sins committed under the first covenant.

This Epistle started by saying that in the past God had spoken to us through the prophets and in various other ways. But now he had spoken through his Son. The Son was better than all the other ways. Better than angels and better than the prophets and better than the tabernacle. What today's reading is possibly saying (we cannot be sure) is that Jesus is the real tabernacle, the real place in which men and women meet with God. The old tabernacle was just a shadow of the real thing. The real thing and the real meeting place was Jesus, Son of God and Son of Man. The Son was also the real sacrifice.

The old animal sacrifices were only symbols of reality. The red heifer that was sacrificed on the Day of Atonement couldn't really take away sin but as people put their trust in God then the real sacrifice that was going to be made

(and in one sense had been made from all eternity—the New Testament speaks of 'the lamb slain from the foundation of the world') was effective for the forgiveness of their sins. God the Son offered himself to God the Father through God the Holy Spirit as a perfect sacrifice and if we put our trust in him then we are set free from the burden and bondage of our sins.

SB

The ever-open way to God

For Christ did not enter a man-made sanctuary that was only a copy of the true one; he entered heaven itself, now to appear for us in God's presence . . . Now he has appeared once for all at the end of the ages to do away with sin by the sacrifice of himself. Just as man is destined to die once, and after that to face judgment, so Christ was sacrificed once to take away the sins of many people; and he will appear a second time, not to bear sin, but to bring salvation to those who are waiting for him.

A man I know has just been into hospital for heart surgery. They put an instrument into the vein where the blood wasn't getting through to his heart and they unblocked it. Now the life-giving blood can flow again. And he can breathe again, far more comfortably. One day he may need to have the operation done again. The way for the blood to flow into his heart may get blocked again. But the way that Jesus has made for us to come to God will never get blocked again. And what Jesus has done will never have to be done again. The way into the presence of God is open for ever, and it was opened because he went into it (and takes us there with him if we have faith in him) through the blood of his own sacrifice.

Our three weeks with this letter to the Hebrews has to finish here, with the reminder that one day Christ will appear a second time, not to bear sin but to bring salvation to those who are waiting for him.

Prayer

Lord Jesus Christ, I thank you that through you the doorway into the Father's presence is always open for me to come through. May I live always within the presence, inside the Father's house—in you. Amen.

SB

The bread of life

'I am the bread of life. Your fathers ate manna in the desert and they are dead; but this is the bread which comes down from heaven, so that a person may eat it and not die. I am the living bread which has come down from heaven. Anyone who eats this bread will live for ever; and the bread that I shall give is my flesh, for the life of the world.'

Just before Easter Jesus had told his disciples that the hour had come for the Son of man to be glorified. 'His nature—which was also the nature of God—was going to shine out of him so that everyone could see the shining of the light. He said how it would happen. 'In all truth I tell you, unless a wheat grain falls into the earth and dies, it remains only a single grain; but if it dies it yields a rich harvest' (12:24 NJB). The harvest from the single grain of wheat who is Christ has been the bread of life for everyone in the whole world who ate it. 'Anyone who eats this bread will live for ever . . .'

There is bread for the body and bread for the soul, and this conversation in John 6 takes place after Jesus has fed the five thousand. That was with the ordinary, common barley bread the boy had given to Jesus along with the two little fishes. The boy gave up his lunch. Jesus gave up his life. When the crowds followed him round the lake he told them they had come for the wrong reasons: 'You are looking for me not because you have seen the signs but because you had all the bread you wanted to eat. Do not work for food that goes bad, but work for food that endures for eternal life, which the Son of man will give you' (6:26–27). They asked him what work it was that they had to do, and the answer was to believe in the one whom God had sent.

A reflection

When we eat the bread of Holy Communion the sacrament speaks to us of our human life sustained by ordinary food and our eternal life sustained by the Christ who is the bread of life.

SB

When the glory shines

God always shows us his glory through familiar things. Sometimes when John walked along his road to the station, looking into people's gardens and enjoying the roses he would suddenly find his heart caught up in worship. The experience would only last a moment, but he would go into the rest of the day feeling different and somehow in tune with everything. That is how it is for most of us.

Martin Buber, the Jewish philosopher, said that all our relationships, even with things, should be personal. We should relate to nothing as an 'it'. A table ... a tree ... a sparrow or a bus conductor ... they are all 'Thou', and God is the 'Eternal Thou'. And Buber said that every 'Thou' can be for us a gateway through to the Eternal Thou. We can encounter God through every thing and every creature ...

As I looked at the living creatures, I saw a wheel on the ground beside each creature with its four faces ... They sparkled like chrysolite, and all four looked alike. Each appeared to be made like a wheel intersecting a wheel ... when the creatures rose from the ground, the wheels rose along with them, because the spirit of the living creatures was in the wheels. Spread out above the heads of the living creatures was what looked like an expanse, sparkling like ice, and awesome ... Above the expanse over their heads was what looked like a throne of sapphire, and high above on the throne was a figure like that of a man. I saw that from what appeared to be his waist up he looked like glowing metal, as if full of fire, and that from there down he looked like fire; and brilliant light surrounded him. Like the appearance of a rainbow in the clouds on a rainy day, so was the radiance around him. This was the appearance of the likeness of the glory of the Lord. When I saw it, I fell face down, and I heard the voice of one speaking.

Praying

Earth's crammed with heaven,
And every common bush afire with God;
But only he who sees, takes off his shoes,
The rest sit round it, and pluck
blackberries ...

Elizabeth Barrett Browning, Aurora Leigh

Will you pray the prayer that Moses prayed? 'Lord, I beseech you, show me your glory.'

SB

The glory

Once, when I was reading John Macquarrie's *Principles of Christian Theology*, I had an experience which totally surprised me. Academic books of theology are not where I expect to meet God. I read Macquarrie's comments on the revelation of the divine name—'I am what I am'... and I was suddenly so strongly aware of the presence and the glory of the living God that I had to cover my head with my duvet and hide. Somehow the glory came streaming through the words... and I was aware of the One 'who is and who was and who is to come' (Revelation 1:8).

As I write I have stopped for nearly half an hour... struggling to find words to describe the feelings of awe and dread and delight, plus the sense of knowing that this was what I was made for—to be in this relationship with this holy God. Wholly 'Other'—but whom we can know and who alone satisfies and quenches that divine longing and thirst within us.

Most of us only have little glimpses of the glory. Ezekiel had a stunning vision of it, and flat on his face before it he hears the voice of God.

He said to me, 'Son of man, stand up on your feet and I will speak to you.' As he spoke, the Spirit came into me and raised me to my feet, and I heard him speaking to me. He said: 'Son of man, I am sending you to the Israelites, to a rebellious nation that has rebelled against me; they and their fathers have been in revolt against me to this very day. The people to whom I am sending you are obstinate and stubborn. Say to them, "This is what the Sovereign Lord says." And whether they listen or fail to listen—for they are a rebellious house—they will know that a prophet has been among them. And you, son of man, do not be afraid of them or their words...'

A prayer

Lord God, the Israelites stand for all nations... all of us have rebelled against you. Help me not to rebel. Help my nation not to rebel. Show us your glory and speak to us. And may we listen to you... so that we might become a righteous nation, caring and compassionate and just, and holy.

SB

Hard porn and holiness

Ezekiel is looking at a new vision of the glory of the holy God, bright and shining. The church leaders are looking at dirty pictures in the darkness. The Spirit takes Ezekiel 'in visions of God to Jerusalem', where the elders of the house of Israel are in the temple.

Then he said to me... 'Son of man, do you see what they are doing, the great abominations that the house of Israel are committing here?'... So I went in and saw; and there, portrayed upon the wall round about, were all kinds of creeping things, and loathsome beasts, and all the idols of the house of Israel... Each (of the elders) had his censer in his hand, and the smoke of the cloud of incense went up. Then he said to me, 'Son of man, have you seen what the elders of the house of Israel are doing in the dark, every man in his room of pictures? For they say, "The Lord does not see us, the Lord has forsaken the land"'.

But the men were wrong. God did see. And God sees the evil of pornography in our generation. God's creatures are degraded... animals, women, men— even children. A million-dollar industry... and its tentacles reach out on to our television screens and our daily newspapers. In Britain 'Page 3 of The Sun' is a catchphrase, and people often give a knowing smile when they hear it... as into their mind's eye comes a picture of a young woman without most of her clothes. 'There's no harm in it', they say. Even churchgoers say it—to me, sometimes, when I have preached against it. But there is harm. The pornographers have depersonalized and degraded that woman and made her into an object—when God has created her a person in his own image and likeness.

A way to pray

What would you think and feel about a child being used as a model for pornographic pictures—implicitly or explicitly sexual? In the presence of the Holy One, pray... and ask to see our society through his eyes. Then go out into your day, or to your night's sleep, with a prayer for those involved in this evil industry... and think if there is anything you can do to fight the evil.

SB

Given up

Then he brought me to the entrance to the north gate of the house of the Lord, and I saw women sitting there, mourning for Tammuz. He said to me, 'Do you see this, son of man? You will see things that are even more detestable than this.' He then brought me into the inner court of the house of the Lord, and there at the entrance to the temple, between the portico and the altar, were about twenty-five men. With their backs towards the temple of the Lord and their faces towards the east, they were bowing down to the sun in the east.

In the very temple itself women and men were worshipping false gods. Tammuz was a 'god' of fertility. They said that when the vegetation died in the autumn he died—and they brought him back to life again in the spring by weeping and indulging in orgies of sexual immorality at fertility festivals in his honour. The men have deliberately turned their backs on the holiest of all, at the west end of the temple, and are facing east ... worshipping the sun instead of the sun's creator.

Men and women have given up the true God. The awe-ful judgment of God is to allow them to do it ... but not before pleading with them and calling on them (sometimes tenderly and sometimes fiercely) to come back to him God has given us free will We cannot be *made* to love—and if at the end some reject the love of God then the final judgment is that 'they will be shut out from the presence of the Lord' (2 Thessalonians 1:9). The presence of God now removes itself from the temple, and the judgment begins.

Now the glory of the God of Israel went up from above the cherubim ... and moved to the threshold of the temple. Then the Lord called to the man clothed in linen ... and said to him, 'Go throughout the city of Jerusalem and put a mark on the foreheads of those who grieve and lament over all the detestable things that are done in it.' As I listened, he said to the others, 'Follow him through the city and kill, without showing pity or compassion. Slaughter old men, young men and maidens, women and children, but do not touch anyone who has the mark. Begin at my sanctuary.'

SB

The man who loves sheep

I am looking out of my window on to a field filled with two dozen Shetland sheep... black and brown and white and all very woolly. The man they belong to is with them. He shepherds them in the day-time... into the section of the field where they are to eat (it has a fence down the middle and first they eat the grass in one half and then in the other). He shepherds them at night-time... shutting them safely into their wooden shed on cold winter evenings and when they are lambing. But the man whom they belong to doesn't keep them for their wool. He keeps them because he loves them... and as I look out of my window I can watch the relationship between him and his sheep.

The word of the Lord came to [Ezekiel]: 'Son of man, prophesy against the shepherds of Israel; prophesy and say to them: "This is what the Sovereign Lord says: Woe to the shepherds of Israel who only take care of themselves! Should not shepherds take care of the flock?... You have not strengthened the weak or healed the sick or bound up the injured. You have not brought back the strays or searched for the lost... I am against the shepherds and will hold them accountable for my flock. I will remove them from tending the flock... I myself will tend my sheep and make them lie down, declares the Sovereign Lord. I will search for the lost and bring back the strays. I will bind up the injured and strengthen the weak, but the sleek and the strong I will destroy. I will shepherd the flock with justice."'

God is speaking to Church leaders. But we are all shepherds in our own field... to our families, our friends, our workmates. We all have the task of loving and caring and feeding... giving all that is needed to grow and develop. For some of them we have to provide a safe place of shelter. The man I can see from my window does all that his sheep need. Do we?

A prayer

Lord Jesus Christ, you are the good shepherd and you gave your life for the sheep. Thank you that you did—and for all it cost you in tears and agony and pain—for me, and for the world that you love. I pray for the people who shepherd me. I pray for myself, and for the sheep that I am responsible for. Help all of us to be good shepherds.

SB

Really alive

Are there any situations in your life that seem absolutely hopeless? A broken relationship, perhaps... that once was alive and exciting, but now it's dead. Your church, perhaps... that never seems to have been alive, or if it was you weren't there to enjoy it. As you look at the situation you haven't much hope... only a deep sadness. That's how Ezekiel must have felt. But then God spoke to him in another vision—and in some churches it is read out on Easter Eve, the night before the resurrection.

The hand of the Lord was upon me, and he brought me out by the Spirit of the Lord and set me in the middle of a valley; it was full of bones... bones that were very dry. He asked me, 'Son of man, can these bones live?' I said, 'O Sovereign Lord, you alone know.' Then he said to me, 'Prophesy to these bones and say to them, "Dry bones, hear the word of the Lord!... I will make breath enter you, and you will come to life..." ' So I prophesied as I was commanded. And as I was prophesying, there was a noise, a rattling sound, and the bones came together, bone to bone. I looked, and tendons and flesh appeared on them and skin covered them, but there was no breath in them. Then he said to me, 'Prophesy to the breath; prophesy, son of man, and say to it, "This is what the Sovereign Lord says: Come from the four winds, O breath, and breathe into these slain, that they may live." ' So I prophesied as he commanded me, and breath entered them; they came to life and stood up on their feet—a vast army.

A way to pray

Shut your eyes and see the valley of dry bones... coming to life... see the breath of God breathing new life into the ones who had been dead... making them fully alive... Then hold your dead and hopeless situation... or someone else's... in the presence of God... and pray that he will put together the broken pieces and then breathe the breath of life into them.

*O, Breath of Life, come sweeping through us,
Revive Thy church with life and power.
O, Breath of Life, come, cleanse, renew us,
And fit Thy church to meet this hour.*

Elizabeth Porter Head

SB

Harvest, Love, and How to Listen and Speak to God

Harvest is about growing things reaching fruition—and then being harvested and used for whatever purpose they were planted. Wheat and corn are turned into bread or corflakes, and apples are eaten just as they are or baked in delicious pies. Jesus talked about the harvest—in the parable of the weeds:

'The kingdom of heaven is like a man who sowed good seed in his field. But while everyone was sleeping, his enemy came and sowed weeds aong the wheat, and went away. When the wheat sprouted and formed ears, then the weeds also appeared. The owner's servants came to him and said, "Sir, didn't you sow good seed in your field. Where then did the weeds come from?" "An enemy did this," he replied. The servants asked him, "Do you want us to go and pull them up?" "No," he answered, "because while you are pulling the weeds, you may root up the wheat with them. Let both grow together until the harvest. At that time I will tell the harvesters: First collect the weeds and tie them in bundles to be burned, then gather the wheat and bring it into my barn"' (Matthew 13:24–30 NIV).

The idea that God isn't going to provide a happy ending for everybody isn't very fashionable these days. But its unfashionableness doesn't mean that it isn't true. The truth according to the New Testament is that everyone who wants it can have a happy ending and eternal life. The offer is there. It is up to us to accept it—or not. In *The Great Divorce*, C.S. Lewis wrote that 'There are only two kinds of people in the end: those who say to God, "Thy will be done", and those to whom God says, in the end, "*Thy* will be done." All that are in Hell choose it. Without that self-choice there could be no Hell. No soul that seriously and constantly desires joy will ever miss it.'

In New Testament terms hell seems to be a final bonfire at the end of the age, in which the chaff is burnt and destroyed. 'The second death' it is called in the book of Revelation. Not something that goes on for ever, but a second and spiritual death after the death of our bodies. So as we think about harvest festivals we also think about the final harvest. We think about our present suffering and our future glory, and about the enormous and endless love of God—whose will is that we spend eternity in his presence in a mutual delight. There will be no problems of communication when we see him face to face and are like him. But now there are—so we end up this six weeks by looking at ways to listen to God and ways to speak to him.

All good gifts

'Harvest Thanksgiving' What's that? Some Christians in Singapore once asked me those questions when I mentioned to them our custom of celebrating God's goodness at harvest-time. Their questions made me think: Why *do* we have Harvest suppers and Harvest services? Where does the practice spring from? Are such celebrations still relevant in today's world? If so, what gifts please God? With harvest in the air, this week seems a good time to look at questions like these. The day before I began these notes, someone showed me the 'Creation jumper' she was wearing. God's creation gifts: the sun, the moon, land and sea, fish, fruit and vegetables, animals and birds had all been knitted into the design so that the jumper itself is a kind of celebration. It reminded me of an observation once made to Timothy:

The living God . . . generously gives us everything for our enjoyment.

I thought back to Genesis 1 where we see God hovering over what was to become planet earth and where we see him bring to birth light and darkness and all living creatures. I pondered on verse 29 where God says to the first man and woman: 'I give you every seed-bearing plant on the face of the whole earth and every tree that has fruit with seed in it. They will be yours food'—and I marvelled at the scope of his generosity.

Then I went to the supermarket. The shelves, as always, were bulging with luxuries as well as necessities. When I returned, I looked around my home—at the carpets and curtains, the pictures and treasures—and the books. And I echoed those words to Timothy. He has given me all this for my enjoyment. Suddenly, it seemed so right that once a year at least, in our church services we should place the spotlight on this generosity and give humble thanks for it.

An exercise

Close your eyes. Watch an action replay of the past 24 hours. Select from it memories of the good gifts God has given you. Relish them. Enjoy them. And then give him heartfelt thanks. Now open your eyes, look around your own home and ask yourself: 'Am I enjoying this as God intends?'

JH

Preparing for harvest

Think back to yesterday where we reminded ourselves that God is a generous giver. That is the back-cloth against which today's drama is acted out.

Because today we attend, in our imagination, the very first Harvest Thanksgiving Service on record. We read about this in Genesis 4 where we notice that two brothers attended this service: Cain, the farmer and Abel, the shepherd. From them we call learn what kind of attitude and gift brings God pleasure and what kind of gift brings him only pain.

Cain brought some of his harvest and gave it as an offering to the Lord. Then Abel brought the first lamb born to one of his sheep, killed it, and gave the best parts of it as an offering. The Lord was pleased with Abel and his offering, but he rejected Cain and his offering.

Imagine Cain's harvest crop: the grapes and pomegranates, the apples and pears the plums and figs, the honeydew melons and the water melons, the wheat and the barley. Watch him gleefully and greedily fill his barns. Then reflect on that telling phrase: 'Cain brought *some* of his harvest'—imagine him finding a few leftovers—like some bruised fruit and some straggly strands of wheat—and deciding to take these to the service of thanksgiving.

Then picture Abel holding and cherishing his new-born lamb. Watch as he examines it and, seeing how beautiful it is, longs to give it back to the giver. There is a generous barbecue for God. See the smoke curl up towards heaven and smell the roasting meat which, to God, was as fragrant incense.

And ask yourself why Abel's gift brought God great joy while Cain's gift brought only disappointment and sorrow. Was it because Abel's gift was a love-gift; a sign that Abel's life revolved around God not himself, while Cain's gift was brought out of duty and not gratitude—it showed that Cain's life revolved, not around God but around Cain?

Since this is one probable explanation for God's reaction, we would do well to let our harvest slogan read: Only the best for God.

A prayer

Lord God, may I be generous and not stingy. May my life so revolve around you that I may give generously—even recklessly—this harvest-time.

JH

God's promise

Harvest-time is a time for responding to God's generosity—and for expressing trust in the promise God made to Noah after the flood:

'Never again will I put the earth under a curse because of what man does... Never again will I destroy all living beings... As long as the world exists, there will be a time for planting and a time for harvest.'

There had been a moment in history when God was so horrified by the way sin was polluting his wonderful world that he resolved to destroy the planet. But his love for Noah, the one man whose whole life revolved around his Creator, dissuaded him from taking such drastic action. And at the end of the adventure, when Noah emerged from the ark, God gave a promise and a sign. He promised that never again would there be a world-wide failure of harvest and he spread across the sky the rainbow, his sign that he would remember this resolve never again to destroy all living beings.

Although the entire world never suffers the effects of wide-spread flooding or famine at one time, some parts of the world reel from these traumas regularly; others spasmodically. Not only in Africa, but in Asia, Poland and even in our own country, people live their lives on or below the poverty line. Countless are homeless. Thousands suffer the indignity of unemployment.

Our culture persuades us to accumulate possessions and wealth. Harvest-time challenges this contribution we are making to the injustice which today pollutes God's world. It persuades us to respond to God's love with sacrificial, generous giving. For some of us, it might be a sum of money, for others it might be possessions, like books (last year in the church I attend, realizing that Christians all over the world long for Christian books, we brought to the harvest services books of all kinds which Book Aid then shipped out to the people who will value them), for others it might be the gift of ourselves, or of a son or daughter whom we set free to serve God overseas or in one of the inner cities in our own country.

In prayer

We ask God to deliver us from apathy and to learn that real prayer gives birth to action.

JH

The example of Boaz

So far we have seen that harvest is a time for celebrating and a time for sacrificing; a time to enjoy God's good gifts and a time to meet the needs of others.

Boaz, who became the husband of Ruth, shows us how to enjoy life while supporting those God brings across our path. Ruth and her mother-in-law Naomi were not homeless but they were living below the poverty line. They never knew where their next meal was coming from. Naomi therefore encouraged her widowed daughter-in-law to go to the fields at harvest-time and to glean whatever she could. And Boaz, the wealthy landowner, spotted and supported her:

Then Boaz said to Ruth, 'Let me give you some advice. Don't pick up corn anywhere except in this field. Work with the women here; watch them to see where they are reaping and stay with them. I have ordered my men not to molest you. And whenever you are thirsty, go and drink from the water jars that they have filled' . . . At meal-time Boaz said to Ruth, 'Come and have a piece of bread, and dip it in the sauce.' So she . . . ate until she was satisfied, and she still had some food left over.

While to his workers, Boaz said:

'Let her pick [the corn] up even where the bundles are lying, and don't say anything to stop her. Besides that, pull out some corn from the bundles and leave it for her to pick up.'

The result of this sensitive giving was that both Ruth and Naomi had more than enough to eat and they overflowed with thanksgiving that their needs had been met.

At the same time, we see how Boaz was enjoying the harvest feast. (See Ruth chapter 3.) He knew how to celebrate and to sacrifice, how to throw a party and how to stay sensitively alongside those in need. He would have known how to respond to this plea (from the Cameroons):

We are all God's children.
I have knocked at your door
I have called to your heart
because I dream of a soft bed
because I am eager for a well-lighted house.
Why do you drive me away?
Open to me, brother!

Prayer

Teach me, Lord, how to feast and to fast—like Boaz.

JH

Sacrificial giving

When, at harvest-time or at any other time. we respond to God's love by giving sacrificially in the way we have seen Abel, Noah and Boaz doing, three things happen today as they did in Old Testament times. One is that pure pleasure is given to God: 'The Lord was pleased with Abel and his offering' 'The odour of the sacrifice pleased the Lord' (Genesis 4:4 and 8:21).

Another is that, through our generosity, people in need are reassured that God has not forgotten them: that he still loves them. So we find Ruth's mother-in-law marvelling at the amount of grain Ruth had gleaned:

**'Where did you gather all this? . . .
The Lord always keeps his
promises.'**

The third is that, because God is no man's debtor, we cannot out-give him. He rewards us. To Noah he gave the stunning symbol of the rainbow. To Boaz he gave the immense privilege of being a distant relative of his own Son, Jesus (see Ruth 4:17–22). To us he may give joy or peace or a deep sense of his approval and love.

This was brought home to me one year when I visited Poland. On the day when my husband and I were due to arrive, our host and hostess ran out of coffee and of tea and they had no money to replace these items. They wondered how they were going to feed their English guests.

A few hours before we turned up on the door-step, the postman delivered a parcel from my own home town. It had been sent by a friend of mine and it contained coffee, tea, washing powder, soap—the commodity items they could not buy for themselves. When they opened the parcel, the Polish people wept. 'It said to us that God has not forgotten us', they told me. 'And this happens time and time again.'

When I returned to England and told the sender of the parcel what had happened, she received her reward—that glow of happiness which comes from knowing that because we have responded to the prompting of the Holy Spirit, God and people meet and tell each other that they love each other.

A prayer

*Ask the Holy Spirit to show you what he
wants you to give this harvest.*

JH

302

A harvest Psalm

Sing to the Lord a new song; Sing to the Lord all the earth . . . Declare his glory among the nations, his marvellous deeds among all peoples. For great is the Lord and most worthy of praise . . . Splendour and majesty are before him; strength and glory are in his sanctuary. Ascribe to the Lord, O families of nations, ascribe to the Lord glory and strength. Ascribe to the Lord the glory due to his name; bring an offering and come into his courts.

Psalm 96 is a joy-filled song which is often sung at harvest-time. It was written for the thousands who thronged the streets of Jerusalem when the ark, the symbol of God's presence, was carried into the city. The song-writer begs the worshippers then and now to sing to God a 'new song'—a song which matches the freshness of God's love-gifts which are new every morning.

I find it easy to do this at harvest-time. As I gaze at the grapes and flower arrangements, smell the apples and the harvest loaf, feel the berries and the pumpkins, I am filled with the kind of wonder which says, 'I've never seen the church looking so beautiful'. And I mean it. The church really does seem to me more beautiful each year.

But the psalmist reminds us not only to look up but to look out; to let our praise flow not only in a God-ward direction but in an others-ward direction as well.

As we have seen in our observations of Boaz, one way of doing this is to make provision for the needy and so to show them that we care that they experience for themselves the wonder of God's love.

And the psalmist suggests that another way of ascribing to God the glory due to his name is by bringing into his courts a gift.

A meditation

Imagine that this psalm is a letter written today by God for you. Re-read it. Meditate on it. An act on it by looking up, giving thanks, stretching out a helping hand to someone in need and deciding what, for you, would be a worthy love-gift to bring to God this harvest-time.

JH

A harvest people

We began this harvest series by reminding ourselves that God is an abundant giver. We continued it by observing the need to balance feasting and fasting. And we saw how Abel brought pleasure to God by bringing him 'the fat pieces'. Today we come full circle: placing the spotlight once more on the generosity of God who gave us his 'fat pieces' in the form of his one and only Son. This gift, as Jesus once explained, is life-giving. Sustaining.

**Jesus declared, 'I am the bread of life. He who comes to me will never go hungry, and he who believes in me will never be thirsty . . . I am the living bread that came down from heaven. If anyone eats of this bread, he will live for ever. This bread is my flesh, which I will give for the life of the world . . .
Whoever eats my flesh and drinks my blood has eternal life . . . For my flesh is real food and my blood is real drink. Whoever eats my flesh and drinks my blood remains in me, and I in him.'**

The service of Holy Communion celebrates this self-gift of Jesus. 'Eucharist' means 'thanksgiving'. Every time we attend such a service it provides us with an opportunity to return to God humble thanks that he gave his Son so that we might live.

The service of Holy Communion also provides the setting where we may regularly receive the life-restoring food Jesus describes: his body and his blood. Christians down the ages have been divided about how the bread or wafer and the wine sustain us. But most would agree that in some sense the bread is Christ's body just as the wine is his blood and that this food nourishes and builds us up.

But the service does not end there. It moves us from thanksgiving, to feeding, to adoration and finally to making our personal response of love. And so it invites us to pray: 'Send us out in the power of your Spirit to live and work to your praise and glory.' In other words, having feasted at the banqueting table of God we go out to become harvest people—those who give to others the love God gives to them.

A prayer

Pray that we may be harvest people all the year round.

JH

The fruit of light

Therefore be imitators of God, as beloved children. And walk in love, as Christ loved us and gave himself up for us, a fragrant offering and sacrifice to God. But fornication and all impurity or covetousness must not even be named among you ... Be sure of this, that no fornicator or impure man, or one who is covetous (that is an idolater), has any inheritance in the kingdom of Christ and of God. Let no one deceive you with empty words, for it is because of these things that the wrath of God comes upon the sons of disobedience. Therefore do not associate with them, for once you were darkness, but now you are light in the Lord; walk as children of light (for the fruit of light is found in all that is good and right and true), and try to learn what is pleasing to the Lord. Take no part in the unfruitful works of darkness, but instead expose them.

Today we are looking at fruitbearing through an unusual image: the fruit of light, which is love. We are the beloved children of God. And just as little children imitate their parents as they learn to grow up, so we are to imitate God. We know what God is like, because Jesus showed him to us. We have seen the human face of God, and we know what is the will of God. This passage says what it *isn't*. Fornication and sexual impurity are out—and 'it has been said that chastity was the one new virtue which Christianity introduced into this world' (Barclay). True chastity is a way of loving our neighbour. The Church is fairly bad at getting its sexual teaching in line with the teaching of the Bible. In the Middle Ages it had a ludicrous attitude to sex within marriage. Bread and water for six months if anyone got any pleasure out of it. Now almost anything goes. I heard last week of a priest who a few years ago advised a worker in his mission to smoke, drink and sleep around a bit in order to get alongside the people.

As we come today to Holy Communion, perhaps we can present our bodies 'as a living sacrifice, holy and acceptable to God', which is our spiritual worship (Romans 12:1).

SB

305

No death penalty

There is therefore now no condemnation for those who are in Christ Jesus. For the law of the Spirit of life in Christ Jesus has set me free from the law of sin and death.

This is one of the greatest chapters in the Bible. It starts with our wonderful condition and state of grace 'in Christ Jesus'. St Paul has told us in chapters 6 and 7 how we have arrived at this state of grace. We haven't got what we deserve. God has given us something utterly different. 'For the wages of sin is death, but the free gift of God is eternal life in Christ Jesus our Lord,' (Romans 6:23).

In 1990 the media told us the tragic story of two teenage girls accused of smuggling drugs out of a country in the Far East and who were then sentenced to many years in prison. But the usual penalty in that country for drug trafficking is death. Terribly severe, but the effects of drug addiction are so terrible that it is a living death.

Perhaps we think it is terrible to say that 'the wages of sin is death'. But spiritual death is the inevitable consequence of sin, because sin separates us from God—and that is what 'death' means here. He loves us, but our terrible failure to love (which is what sin essentially is) makes union and communion with him impossible. Yet if we let the light of the love of God shine on us then it will show us not only your sins but also how to deal with them. Our baptism is the sacrament of a death (ours in Christ) and a new life (ours in Christ). We are in him and he is in us.

A prayer

Lord Jesus Christ, thank you that for those of us who live in you there is no condemnation. When the law of love points to my sin and says that I am guilty of not loving, then I can point to you on the cross and say, 'No death penalty for me——because Christ died for me.'

SB

Human nature and sin

For God has done what the law, weakened the flesh, could not do: sending his own Son in the likeness of sinful flesh and for sin, he condemned sin in the flesh, in order that the just requirement of the law might be filled in us, who walk not according to the flesh but according to the Spirit.

This is a great chapter, but it is also a difficult one. It is difficult because St Paul uses some words that don't mean what they seem to mean. 'Flesh' doesn't mean our skin. When Paul uses the word, 'he really means human nature in all its weakness, its impotence and its helplessness. He means human nature in its vulnerability to sin and to temptation. He means that part of man which gives sin its chance and its bridgehead. He means sinful human nature, apart from Christ and apart from God. He means everything that attaches a man to the world instead of to God,' (William Barclay, *The Letter to the Romans*, The Daily Study Bible, The Saint Andrew Press).

Jesus the Son of God had a human nature, just like ours, but St Paul says carefully that he was 'in the likeness of sinful flesh'. He had all the human desires that we have, and all the human hungers. But there was no sin in him—and the love that streamed between him and his Father like a river never got blocked by sin. In the mystery of the forgiveness of our sins, God 'condemned sin in the flesh'. The law passed the sentence of death, and Jesus suffered the death and the condemnation. We can walk out of the law court free—and with a new Spirit within us to live 'a new life according to his commandments' (Book of Common Prayer).

To consider

Sin is the putting of self in the centre where God alone should be. Sin is aching from the self instead of from God. It is falling short of the will and glory of God. Often it is more than that—it is setting one's will against God's will, consciously (where guilt is involved) or unconsciously (when the sinful consequences are equally disastrous).

George Appleton, *Journey for a Soul*, William Collins Sons & Co. Ltd.

SB

In tune with God

For those who live according to the flesh set their minds on the things of the flesh, but those who live according to the Spirit set their minds on the things of the Spirit. To set the mind on the flesh is death, but to set the mind on the Spirit is life and peace. For the mind that is set on the flesh is hostile to God; it does not submit to God's law, indeed it cannot; and those who are in the flesh cannot please God.

A person who lives 'in the flesh' cannot possibly live in tune with God, because the word 'flesh' actually means to live out of tune with God, and to have a will that is out of line with the will of God. We cannot sing out of tune and in tune at the same time. And to be 'in the flesh' is to sing out of tune.

But in the Spirit we do sing in tune with the will of God. We are in Christ, and the Spirit of Christ is in us, and now we can submit to God's law and do the will of God. We don't always, even once our new life has begun, but we can. Faith is the secret of it. In chapter 1 Paul writes, 'I am not ashamed of the gospel: it is the power of God for salvation to every one who has faith, to the Jew first and also to the Greek. For in it the righteousness of God is revealed through faith for faith; as it is written, "He who through faith is righteous shall live"' (Romans 1:16–17).

To be righteous is to be in a right relationship with God, with all our sins forgiven (and being forgiven every day) and with the Holy Spirit within us to help us to live a holy life of love. The last verse of Charles Wesley's marvellous hymn 'And can it be' sums it all up.

Reflect

No condemnation now I dread;
Jesus, and all in Him, is mine!
Alive in Him, my living Head,
And clothed in righteousness divine,
Bold I approach the eternal throne,
And claim the crown,
Through Christ my own.

SB

In a new field

But you are not in the flesh, you are in the Spirit, if in fact the Spirit of God dwells in you. Any one who does not have the Spirit of Christ does not belong to him. But if Christ is in you, although your bodies are dead because of sin, your spirits are alive because of righteousness. If the Spirit of him who raised Jesus from the dead dwells in you, he who raised Christ Jesus from the dead will give life to your mortal bodies also through his Spirit which dwells in you.

One day in Westminster Chapel Dr Martyn Lloyd-Jones asked us to imagine two fields next to each other with a hedge in between. One was the field of the flesh and the other was the field of the Spirit. When we became a Christian we moved out of one field into the other field. But sometimes in the field of the Spirit we behave just as we did in the field of the flesh. Then we start to doubt. Perhaps we aren't Christians at all? But we are. Our old bad habits will rear their heads. But now the Spirit of God lives within us, and even though our sin grieves him he never leaves us. Instead, he convicts us of our sin and shows us the Saviour. Then we are forgiven again and given another fresh start.

To think about

The first person to discover the resurrection of Jesus that morning was Mary Magdalene whose soul had once been possessed with seven devils. The resurrection of Jesus was a resurrection for such miserable persons as she, for ruined souls. To those who cannot grasp this meaning, resurrection remains an insoluble enigma, an empty falsehood, a prick of doubt. It is an ever-lasting secret. Not a few of us seem inclined to deny this miracle. If we are reluctant to accept sinners as friends, it means that we belong to the sceptics who deny the fact of resurrection. Let us, therefore, remember that the witness who saw the figure of Jesus the morning of his resurrection had been a prostitute.

Toyohiko Kagawa, Meditations, translated by Jiro
Takenaka, Harper and Brothers

SB

What we owe to God

So then, brethren, we are debtors, not to the flesh, to live according to the flesh for if you live according to the flesh you will die, but if by the Spirit you put to death the deeds of the body you will live. For all who are led by the Spirit of God are sons of God.

If we get into debt we worry. We owe something to somebody—and if we haven't got the money, then we can't pay. But the debt that Paul is talking about is different. It's a debt to take seriously, but not to worry about. God has given us the Spirit of Christ and the life of God is within us. 'I have been crucified with Christ; it is no longer I who live, but Christ who lives in me; and the life I now live in the flesh I live by faith in the Son of God, who loved me and gave himself for me' (Galatians 2:20). The Son of God makes us the sons and daughters of God, and the Spirit of God within us shows us how to live a Christlike life—and we owe it to him to do that. That's what our debt is. 'I appeal to you therefore, brethren, by the mercies of God, to present your bodies as a living sacrifice, holy and acceptable to God, which is your spiritual worship' (Romans 12:1). The loving actions that we do now with our bodies are the way that we worship and adore the God who loves us.

Consider

The word 'worship' comes from an old English word meaning worthship— giving to God his true worth as Creator, Redeemer, and indwelling Spirit. Worship is man's response to these divine activities. As we realize the greatness, the goodness and the 'allness' of God, we forget ourselves and our hearts break forth in praise. Yet worship is not just an expression in words or music or feeling, but the outgoing of our hearts and the acceptance of God as the governing reality of our lives. He becomes our chiefest good and our lives are henceforth offered to him in loving obedience.

*George Appleton, Journey for a Soul,
Willian Collins Sons & Co. Ltd.*

SB

Now I know I am

For you did not receive the spirit of slavery to fall back into fear, but you have received the spirit of sonship. When we cry, 'Abba! Father!' it is the Spirit himself bearing witness with our spirit that we are children of God, and if children, then heirs, heirs of God and fellow heirs with Christ, provided we suffer with him in order that we may also be glorified with him.

The Spirit in the heart of the Christian is the Spirit of the Son of God—and Jesus called his Father 'Abba'. It is the word that a little child uses—like our English word 'Daddy'. When we find ourselves crying out to God like that, we know that we have an inner witness to the truth that we are children of God.

Some years ago my father and I heard Dr Martyn Lloyd-Jones preaching on the doctrine of assurance. As he drove the car towards Hyde Park Corner my father was smiling. 'I know now that I'm a Christian,' he told me. 'You told me I was, and I didn't believe you. But now I know.' Next morning I took him in a cup of tea and he was sitting up in bed waiting for it and looking happy. 'When I woke up this morning I knew that something nice had happened. But for a moment I couldn't remember what. Then I did remember. I know now that I am a Christian.' Two years after that, just two months after his seventieth birthday, he died. He was quite sure that he was a Christian—a forgiven sinner and a child of God. His two favourite books in the Bible were the letter to the Romans and the Book of Revelation. He read them alternately over his morning tea and loved them—and as he read his faith grew deeper and stronger.

A story my father loved

The famous preacher D.L. Moody once said this to his congregation. 'One morning you will read in the paper, "Moody is dead." But don't you believe it! On that morning I shall be more alive than I have ever been.'

SB

God with us

If you love me, you will obey what I command. I will ask the Father, and he will give you another Counsellor to be with you for ever—the Spirit of truth. The world cannot accept him, because it neither sees him nor knows him. But you know him, for he lives with you and will be in you. I will not leave you as orphans; I will come to you . . . Because I live, you also will live. On that day you will realise that I am in my Father, and you are in me, and I am in you . . . If anyone loves me, he will obey my teaching. My Father will love him, and we will come to him and make our home with him.

Christianity is about the amazing truth that the God who made the galaxies, and who holds the stars and all things in being by his word of power, comes to live within the human heart. Yes, Christianity is about the forgiveness of sins and the love of God as well—but the God who is creator and lover wants to live in union and communion with every one of his human creatures. The God of the galaxies is also the God within, if we will have him. Jesus says to his disciples (and to us) 'If you love me, you will obey what I command . . .' What he commands us to do is to believe in him, and in the glorious truth that he loves us and died for us, and that (if we ask) he will forgive us our sins—everything we have ever done in the past, and the sins that we go on sinning in the present even though we long not to give in. And with the first forgiveness, which is the start of our Christian life, a wiping out of the past, and a beautiful new beginning, Jesus asks the Father for a Counsellor to be with us for ever. The Father hears his request and pours out the Holy Spirit on the Day of Pentecost to create the Church, and each of us needs our own personal Pentecost. If we don't know the glory of it, Holy Communion can help us. As we eat the bread and drink the wine we can know in faith that God-in-Christ comes to us and stays with us for ever.

SB

Waiting

I consider that the sufferings of this present time are not worth comparing with the glory that is to be revealed to us. For the creation waits with eager longing for the revealing of the sons of God; for the creation was subjected to futility, not of its own will but by the will of him who subjected it in hope; because the creation itself will be set free from its bondage to decay and obtain the glorious liberty of the children of God.

Most of us find it hard to wait for things. We wait impatiently for buses and wonder why they are so late. Then (in London) three Number 11 buses turn up in a convoy and we feel impatient with the bus company. We wait for a friend to arrive—or for a special letter to come through our letter-box. We wait for the end of term and the start of the holidays.

There is a lot in the Bible about waiting—and it is always about waiting with confident hope, because what we are waiting for is something that God is going to bring about. That makes our present sufferings far more endurable. In 2 Corinthians 2:17–18, St Paul says that those sufferings are effecting something good in us: 'this slight momentary affliction is preparing for us an eternal weight of glory beyond all comparison, because we look not to the things that are seen but to the things that are unseen; for the things that are seen are transient, but the things that are unseen are eternal'.

It isn't only we who wait. It is as if the whole of the creation is waiting and longing for things to be what one day they will be. The word translated 'eager longing' describes the attitude of someone 'who scans the horizon with head thrust forward eagerly searching the distance for the first signs of the dawn break of glory. To Paul, life was not a weary, defeated waiting; life was a throbbing, vivid expectation' (William Barclay, *The Letter to the Romans*). One day all created things will be caught up in Christ. There will be a glory beyond imagining, and everything will be set free from decay.

A way to pray

Think about the future and ask yourself what you are waiting for . . . waiting for in this life, and waiting for in the next life. Ask God to give you a glimpse of what the creation will be like when it is set free from decay.

SB

Groaning

We now that the whole creation has been groaning in travail together until now; and not only the creation, but we ourselves, who have the first fruits of the Spirit, groan inwardly as we wait for adoption as sons, the redemption of our bodies. For in this hope we were saved. Now hope that is seen is not hope. For who hopes for what he sees? But if we hope for what we do not see, we wait for it with patience.

Groaning is the sound of someone expressing their pain out loud, and making an agonized noise because they are hurting. The creation is hurting, and so are we. So we groan. But mostly we groan inside ourselves rather than out loud.

Sometimes we groan in our prayers, when the things that are happening to us or to someone we love are causing us deep distress. And it is all right to groan and all right not to enjoy our pain. We wouldn't be normal if we did enjoy it. But once we have done a certain amount of groaning in the presence of God we need to pray in a different way. The Psalmist shows us how. He has a conversation with himself 'Why are you cast down, O my soul, and why are you disquieted within me? Hope in God; for I shall again praise him, my help and my God' (Psalm 42:5).

We are waiting and hoping for our adoption as sons and for the redemption of our bodies, and as we wait and hope things happen to us. Paul tells of them in chapter 5 of Romans: 'We rejoice in our hope of sharing the glory of God. More than that, we rejoice in our sufferings, knowing that suffering produces endurance, and endurance produces character, and character produces hope, and hope does not disappoint us, because God's love has been poured into our hearts through the Holy Spirit which has been given to us' (Romans 5:2–5).

A way to pray

Read through Romans 5:2–5 again phrase by phrase. Ask God to show you how each thing leads on to the next. Pray that you might experience the love of God towards you as it is poured into your heart through the Holy Spirit.

SB

Praying for saints

Likewise the Spirit helps us in our weakness; for we do not know how to pray as we ought, but the Spirit himself intercedes for us with sighs too deep for words. And he who searches the hearts of men knows what is the mind of the Spirit, because the Spirit intercedes for the saints according to the will of God.

Because of the creation's suffering and our suffering there is a good deal of sighing and groaning going on in the world and in people. In this chapter 8 of Romans first the creation groans and sighs; then those in whom the Spirit dwells; and now the Spirit, as he prays within us. It isn't the world that he is praying for here, it's the saints. And they aren't the specially outstanding Christians like St Teresa of Avila and St John of the Cross and St Francis of Assisi. In the New Testament the saints are just ordinary Christians, like you and me. We all belong to a holy God, we all have the Holy Spirit dwelling in us, and therefore each one of us is 'a saint'.

But even saints aren't sure what to pray for other saints, so the Spirit prays. We don't know the words. But we do know the yearning and the aching that is happening within us. In that inner sighing we and the Spirit are praying 'Your will be done', for ourselves or for someone we love, and God the Spirit always knows what that will is. Often we are not sure. But then we can remember the Garden of Gethsemane, and the anguish of the Son of God as he prayed about his impending death on a cross: 'My Father, if it is possible, may this cup be taken from me. Yet not as I will, but as you will' (Matthew 26:39).

A way to pray

Pray for a situation in your own life, or in someone else's, that you don't know how to pray for. Let the Spirit pray within you, with sighs too deep for words, and feel the ache and the yearning inside you. Then simply pray 'Father, your will be done . . . '

SB

In everything God

We now that in everything God works for good with those who love him, who are called according to his purpose. For those whom he foreknew he also predestined to be conformed to the image of his Son, in order that he might be the first-born among many brethren. And those whom he predestined he also called; and those whom he called he also justified; and those whom he justified he also glorified.

What Paul says here is the most sublime statement of faith about our suffering that has ever been made. 'In everything God works for good with those who love him,' or 'in all things God works for the good of those who love him ...' If we lose our job or our money, if we fail our examination, if our husband or wife walks out on us, if the person we love doesn't marry us, or if we get put into prison (Paul was put there, and so was Joseph back in the Old Testament)—we know that in all those things God works for our good. And what is true in our suffering is also true in our happiness and in our successes—a happy marriage, a satisfying job, a business that flourishes. In all things and everything God works for good. He can use every single thing that happens to us to conform us to the image of his Son. That's what his purpose is—to make each one of us like Christ, all of us shining with the glory of God. That is our ultimate good. And God will work through all things to fulfil his good purpose for us.

A prayer

Lord God, it's hard to believe. That in all things you work for the good of those who love you. I do love you, Lord—though often my actions don't match up to my love. I remember now before you the things that I find hardest in my life— those things that I find it hardest to believe that you can work through for my good ... But Lord, I do believe ... Help thou my unbelief ...

SB

Paul argues our case

What then shall we say to this? If God is for us, who is against us? He who did not spare his own Son but gave him up for us all, will he not also give us all things with him ? Who shall bring any charge against God's elect? It is God who justifies; who is to condemn? Is it Christ Jesus, who died, yes, who was raised from the dead, who is at the right hand of God, who indeed intercedes for us?

In this most eloquent section of this marvellous chapter Paul tells out the praises of God in a series of dramatic questions—like a brilliant advocate addressing a jury. 'What then shall we say to this?' There is nothing we can say: only be stunned into silence by the wonder of it.

'If God is for us, who is against us?' Well some people are, and so is Satan. But God is so much greater that they simply don't count, not in the final reckoning.

'He who did not spare his own Son but gave him up for us all, will he not also give us all things with him?' The answer has to be yes. For the Son is 'the image of the invisible God, the firstborn over all creation. For by him all things were created, things in heaven and on earth, visible and invisible, whether thrones or powers or rulers or authorities, all things were created by him and for him. He is before all things, and in him all things hold together.' So when the Son is given for us, and given to us, we are given an inexpressible gift.

'Who shall bring any charge against God's elect?' Paul provides the answer to that one himself: 'It is God who justifies: who is to condemn? Is it Christ Jesus, who died, yes, who was raised from the dead, who is at the right hand of God, who indeed intercedes for us?' No, Christ won't condemn us. He is in the very presence of God praying for us.

A way to pray

Be still and reflect on the passage. Then lift up your heart and be thankful . . .

SB

With Christ for ever

Who shall separate us from the love of Christ? Shall tribulation, or distress, or persecution, or famine, or nakedness, or peril, or sword? As it is written, 'For thy sake we are being killed all the day long; we are regarded as sheep to be slaughtered.' No, in all these things we are more than conquerors through him who loved us. For I am sure that neither death, nor life, nor angels, nor principalities, nor things present, nor things to come, nor powers, nor height, nor depth, nor anything else in all creation, will be able to separate us from the love of God in Christ Jesus our Lord.

The dramatic questions and answers go on and become quite lyrical. Paul is glorying in the love of God and the act that nothing he can name in heaven or earth can ever separate us from it—if we are in Christ Jesus. That is where the chapter started—with the fact that there is no condemnation for those who are in Christ Jesus. No condemnation—and therefore no separation.

No wonder we read this passage so often at funerals, because it tells us (at a time when we urgently need to hear it again) about the wonder of the truth that in Christ even death can't separate us from the love of God. And one day all those who have died in Christ will meet again and love again—in perfect love. They will never be separated from the love of Christ—and therefore they will never be separated from one another.

A prayer

Thank you, Lord God, that there is no condemnation in Christ Jesus our Lord. I am so glad that your love is so strong that no person and no thing in heaven or earth, not even death itself, will ever be able to separate me from it. So nothing will ever be able to separate me from you, because you are love.

SB

The provision of God

Be careful to follow every command I am giving you today, so that you may live and increase and may enter and possess the land that the Lord promised on oath to your forefathers. Remember how the Lord your God led you all the way in the desert these for years, to humble you and to test you in order to know what was in your heart, whether or not you would keep his commands. He humbled you, causing you to hunger and then feeding you with manna, which neither you nor your fathers had known, to teach you that man does not live on bread alone but on every word that comes from the mouth of the Lord.

There is a brand of Christianity that says that when a person becomes a Christian then God makes all their enterprises successful. He won't. It simply isn't true.

Those who know about the spiritual life tell us that we are 'stripped', and it is in this process of stripping and suffering that God finds out (and so do we) how much we really love him. Job said, 'Though he slay me yet will I trust in him' (Job 13:15). But it is harder when we are still alive and our life is going agonizingly wrong. The job that we love comes to an end. The person that we cherish doesn't love us. We become ill— or someone close to us does.

What then? Do we cry out 'Why should this happen to me?' Or do we bow our heads to it and set about learning obedience through our suffering? There are, strictly, no second causes, because God created our world with all its possibilities for good and evil. But in all our suffering God is there with us. In *Making Sense out of Suffering* (Hodder & Stoughton), Peter Kreeft wrote that 'Suffering is not a problem requiring an answer but a mystery requiring a presence.'

To think about

What has caused most suffering in my life? Has this brought me closer to God—or have I somehow turned away from him into bitterness or unhappiness?

SB

Ways to listen to God

Through the written word

Love is what God is. And love aches to express itself. That is why the God of the Bible is a creative, communicative God who finds as many ways of showing love as there are people.

Because God is a talking God, and because, deep within each of us lurks the longing to hear him speak, for the next few days, we examine some of the ways in which God speaks. As a result, we should be better equipped to hear and understand him when he next whispers to our heart and ear.

Just as lovers express their love in writing: through poems and plays, sonnets, songs and love-letters, so God has written down his love for us. As St Augustine put it, the Bible is 'our letter from home'. But this letter is unlike any other letter we shall ever read. It possesses a peculiar power to penetrate our innermost being: to heal, to console, to challenge, to confront. J.B. Phillips found this when he made his paraphrase of the New Testament: 'Although I did my utmost to preserve emotional detachment, I found again and again that the material under my hands was strangely alive, it spoke to my condition in a most uncanny way.'

The Bible still speaks to our condition. And it always will as Isaiah reminds us:

As the rain and the snow come down from heaven, and do not return to it without watering the earth and making it bud and flourish . . . so is my word that goes out from my mouth: it will not return to me empty, but will accomplish what I desire.

Meditation

Read the whole of Isaiah chapter 55 as though it was written by God for you today. Read it slowly—several time if necessary. When a particular phrase or verse or word attracts you to itself, pause and put your Bible down. Repeat the phrase over and over again so that its truth trickles from your head to your heart. During the day, recall that phrase, repeat it again and ponder on it. This is the way we discover that the Word of God not only speaks to our condition, it challenges and changes our thinking and our lifestyle.

JH

Ways to listen to God

Through the living Word

God's written word, the Bible, worms its way right into the core of our being. But down the ages, as today, some people have ignored the written word and others have distorted its message. Even so love cannot be daunted. When one method of communication misfires, it finds another. So just as we resort to sign language when we find ourselves face-to-face with a deaf person or someone whose language is different from our own, so God sometimes uses signs and symbols to speak to us.

One such sign, as the writer to the Hebrews reminds us, is God's own Son:

In the past God spoke to our forefathers through the prophets at many times and in various ways, but in these last days he has spoken to us by his Son, whom he appointed heir of all things, and through whom he made the universe. The Son is the radiance of God's glory and the exact representation of his being, sustaining all things by his powerful word.

Jesus came, among other things, to show us what God is like.

The language of the life of Jesus is a vocabulary we need to master because many of us imagine God to be quite different from the way he is portrayed in Scripture. Some of us picture God as the divine sugar-daddy who exists to give in to all our wishes and whims and fancies. Others believe God to be a spoil-sport—intent on ensuring that we never enjoy life. Yet others feel that God is a punitive policeman: the big eye which always watches, waiting to pounce when we put a foot wrong.

We need to acknowledge what our feelings tell us about God and compare them with the Jesus of the Gospels who is Emmanuel, God with us.

A project

What do your feelings tell you God is like? Compare your findings with the picture of God painted by the life of Jesus. Ask this Jesus to release you from the trap of the false images of God which have held you in their grip and spoiled your relationship with him.

JH

Ways to listen to God
Through solitude and silence

Love communicates itself even across continents. Lovers and friends discover this when they are separated for some reason. The prodigal son discovered it, when, sitting in solitude in the pig-sty, the love of his father drew him as though by a magnet. Paul discovered it when, as a result of his missionary tours, he found his love for the converts to Christianity meant that he carried them in his heart wherever he travelled.

God's love, too, communicates itself wherever we are. We may run from him in suicidal panic as Elijah did and as Moses did before him, we may be unaware of his ways like the youth Samuel or we may be full of bitterness like Hannah, yet God will somehow find a way of showing us he loves us. And the best way to ensure that we hear that still, small voice is to take time to be on our own and to become still because God's voice is most clearly heard in solitude and silence.

Through Hosea God reminds us of this:

'I am now going to allure her; I will lead her into the desert and speak tenderly to her.'

We all need a desert place—somewhere which is as far removed as possible from our noise-polluted world; somewhere where we can encounter God afresh and regularly. 'If we are to witness to Christ in today's market places … If we are to be always available, not only physically, but by empathy, sympathy, friendship, understanding and boundless *caritas*, we need silence' (Catherine de Hueck Doherty, *Poustinia*).

A project

Find a place preferably in your own home to which you can retreat for prayer. Some people use a particular chair in their lounge. Others convert a spare bedroom into a prayer room. I have converted my loft into a tiny remote chapel. Let that place be your desert.

Thank God that he wants to speak tenderly to you there; that its stillness could be to your spirit what a good hearing aid or the ability to lip-read or sign is to a deaf person—the difference between being cut off from, or in touch with love.

JH

Ways to listen to God

Through nature

We have been teasing out ways in which God speaks today. He *does* still speak as Donald Coggan reminds us: 'Christians believe in a God who speaks. Ours is not a silent God, a God who sits, Sphinx-like, looking out unblinking on a world in agony.'

As we have seen, God speaks through the written word, the Bible, through the living Word, the life of his Son and through solitude and silence.

But God has another powerful sign language which has been celebrated by the psalmist and the prophets as well as by poets and artists down the centuries. It is the international language of nature. The psalmist put it this way:

The heavens declare the glory of God, the skies proclaim the work of his hands. Day after day they pour forth speech; night after night they display knowledge. There is no speech or language where their voice is not heard. Their voice goes out into all the earth, their words to the ends of the world.

Yes. Cumulus clouds, sun-sets and sunrises give us glimpses of the glory of God. And so does a butterfly with its gaudy wings.

A project

Take time to look carefully at God's creation in the next few days: the sky, some trees, flowers in the garden, houseplants, vegetables. Examine the colour, the shape, the texture. And ask yourself the question. What kind of a being must he be who could create colour and texture like this and distribute it though his world so liberally? Now write a hymn of praise to God, letting each line begin with 'You are . . .'

JH

323

Ways to listen to God

Through people

My husband and I once visited a country whose language we did not speak and whose alphabet was so different from ours that we could not read the signposts. Imagine our horror when we discovered that our hostess had been unable to meet us at the airport and that her home lay some eighty miles away! Few people at the airport spoke English and yet, by reading people's shrugs and smiles, frowns and gestures we managed to find our way to the tiny flat in the remote town where our hostess lived. People had helped us to find our way even though their directions had been wordless.

God speaks to us through the wordlessness of people. Jesus underlined this in the parable of the sheep and the goats when he reminded us that the homeless and the hungry, the sick, the poor and those in prison point to him and to ways of serving him.

He reminds believers that when he comes in all his glory, he will divide his followers into two groups. One group will rejoice to see him because they have spent their lives loving him:

'For I was hungry and you gave me something to eat, I was thirsty and you gave me something to drink, I was a stranger and you invited me in, I needed clothes and you clothed me, I was sick and you looked after me, I was in prison and you came to visit me.'

His puzzled followers will ask, 'Lord, when did we rescue you in these ways?' And he will make that memorable reply:

'Whatever you did for one of the least of these brothers of mine, you did for me.'

A prayer

Lord, may the truth of this parable change me so that, when I see and hear the cry of those in need I may see and hear you cry and respond with generous giving.

A project

Let articles and faces in your newspaper or on your television screen prompt you to pray and to give money or clothes to agencies like Oxfam, and Christian books to literature-starved people in Africa and Asia through Book Aid.

JH

Ways to listen to God

Through the imagination

Last week we saw how God speaks to us through needy people. But, of course, God also speaks to us through kind, gentle, sensitive people too. Think, for a moment, of the kindest person you have ever known. Close your eyes. Picture them. What was it about their behaviour that drew you to them? Thank God that they have given you a glimpse of a fraction of his love.

In doing that simple exercise, if you did it, you have used one of the most powerful listening tools each of us possesses: our imagination. In the West, many of us have been trained to ignore or even despise our imagination and that is a pity when it comes to meditating on Jesus' teaching, because Jesus was an Eastern teacher not a Western philosopher, and Eastern teachers appealed, very often, to the eye-gate and the ear-gate more powerfully than to the mind. And if we are truly to understand the innuendoes of Jesus' parables and pen-pictures, we shall need to engage our imagination.

Think, for example, of the story of the prodigal son in Luke 15. Jesus describes how the youngest son of a certain farmer demands that his father gives him his inheritance instantly. He then squanders it and ends up penniless and hungry. Sitting in the field feeding someone else's pigs, he comes to his senses and decides to go home:

'I will set out and go to my father and say to him: Father, I have sinned against heaven and against you. I am no longer worthy to be called your son; make me like one of your hired men.'

With our minds we can meditate on the folly of self-centred living and marvel at the generosity of a father whose love is strong enough to forgive and reinstate his son. This way we can glean a great deal from this story but new insights will come if we do the following exercise:

Read Luke 15:11–24. Imagine that you are the young man or the father. Enter into the story as fully as you can with all your senses, asking: 'What can I see and hear and smell and feel?' Let your imagination work for you. What has God shown you about himself or yourself?

JH

Bread of life

When they found Jesus on the other side of the sea, they said to him, 'Rabbi, when did you come here?' Jesus answered them, 'Truly, truly I say to you, you seek me, not because you saw signs, but because you ate your fill of the loaves. Do not labour for the food which perishes, but for the food which endures to eternal life, which the Son of man will give to you; for on him has God the Father set his seal.' . . . They said to him, 'Lord, give us this bread always.' Jesus said to them, 'I am the bread of life; he who comes to me shall not hunger, and he who believes in me shall never thirst.'

My favourite prayer is one which comes in the opening pages of St Augustine's Confessions: 'You have made us for yourself, O God, and our hearts are restless till they find their rest in you.' Augustine had lived a pretty carefree and self-indulgent life. But he had never really known satisfaction until he gave himself in faith to God. He went on to make many mistakes, as well as to be a bishop and theologian, but in all this his real source of peace was his knowledge of God.

It was that satisfaction of our deepest longings, that sense of peace at the heart of life, that John had in mind when he gave us the conversation of Jesus and the crowd who had been fed by a few loaves and fishes. Jesus had met their immediate hunger, but knew that their real hunger was far deeper. It was a hunger for meaning and purpose in life, a hunger for God.

Without God there remains a hole to be filled. With him, we may lack many things, but never the one thing that counts: real peace.

An exercise

As you come to worship and pray today, and especially to take Communion, bring before God all your deepest longings, and let him meet your hunger with the bread of life.

MM

326

Ways to listen to God

Through our emotions

When we listen to God in the ways I have been suggesting over the past few days, we shall find ourselves responding to him emotionally: with joy, maybe, as we delight in the wonders of his creation or with dismay at our seeming helplessness to put right the wrongs which give rise to unemployment, violence, starvation and the pollution of God's world.

We must learn to listen to these emotional reactions. Through them God speaks. They reveal to us more clearly than any other language whether our life revolves around self or around God. This revelation is important for two reasons. First, because although many of us believe that Jesus is our Lord, our lifestyle betrays that self still holds the reins. Secondly, because God has created us in such a way that true happiness will only be found by those who place God at the centre of their lives. Paul put this powerfully:

For to me, to live is Christ.

St Ignatius handed down to us a method of listening to God which enables us to establish on a regular basis whether Paul's testimony picks up an echo in our own heart. The prayer comes in four parts:
1.   We look back on the past 24 hours and pick out only the good things which have happened to us. We thank God for them.
2.   We look back on the same 24-hour period and ask God to show us where he has been at work in us. He often answers this prayer by pointing out our mood swings and suggesting we reflect on a particular emotion. By asking ourselves: 'Why was I feeling joyful at that particular time? Was it because God's kingdom was being extended in some way or because I was the centre of attention? Or, why was I feeling depressed? Was it because God's name was being brought into disrepute or because I was being neglected?', we discover who is at the centre of our universe: God or self.
3.   Where necessary, we confess our self-centredness and determine to change.
4.   We look ahead to the next 24 hours, anticipate where we shall need God's specific help and ask him for it.

A project

Try this method of prayer for yourself for the next week.

JH

Ways to listen to God

Through 'holy hunches'

Today we come to the end of our brief examination of ways to listen to God. But by now, I pray that our appetites have been whetted and that we have begun to experiment for ourselves finding that, indeed, God does speak.

People who make this discovery quickly learn that God is not man; that we must therefore allow him to be God. Among other things this means that we must beware of reducing him to a divine computer whose sole purpose in life is to make life easy for us. Christians who fall into this trap act as though all they have to do with their doubts and uncertainties is to feed their question or request into a God-shaped machine and instantly God will spew out his definitive instructions on a fast-moving printer.

But no! God is not like that and the more we go on to explore ways of listening to God, the more we shall discover that, just as, to become fluent in a language like Greek, you have to involve yourself with the customs and culture of Greek-speaking people, so to become fluent in this new language of listening, we have to become familiar with God's thought-patterns and longings. They are different from ours, as God reminds us through Isaiah:

'For my thoughts are not your thoughts, neither are your ways my ways,' declares the Lord. 'As the heavens are higher than the earth, so are my ways higher than your ways and my thoughts than your thoughts.'

One basic difference between ourselves and God is that, although we always struggle with the self-centredness with which we were born, God always serves; always gives. His one word motto seems to be OTHERS.

As we listen to him, it will not surprise us, then, if through 'holy hunches' we are prompted to telephone a certain person, visit someone, or send a cheque to a certain charity. As we act on these hunches, we quickly discover when they have been placed there by God because the help we give is so timely. God-sent.

A prayer project

Spend a few seconds now or later in the day listening for such 'holy hunches'. Act on them and see what happens!

JH

Ways to speak to God

As sons and daughters

'Father, hallowed be your name ... Ask and it will be given to you; seek and you will find; knock and the door will be opened to you. For everyone who asks receives; he who seeks finds; and to him who knocks, the door will be opened. Which of you fathers, if your son asks for a fish, will give him a snake instead? Or if he asks for an egg, will give him a scorpion? If you then, though you are evil, know how to give good gifts to your children, how much more will your Father in heaven give the Holy Spirit to those who ask him!'

A local schoolteacher was camping in Israel when he heard the little boy in the next tent calling for his father: 'Abby! Abby!' It is their word for Daddy, and God has sent the Spirit of his Son 'into our hearts so that we cry Abba'. That is how we are to speak to God ... using that most childish and intimate family name. We speak as little children but also as the sons and daughters of God. Children do not stay infantile ... they grow up and mature. Then we speak differently. Not so demandingly, perhaps.

In our relationship with our heavenly Father we can always go back to being little children and it can be enormously healing. And it is as little children that we inherit the kingdom. But as sons and daughters we can speak to God as adults—in the same way that Moses and God spoke:

'And the Lord spoke to Moses face to face, as a man speaks to his friend ...' Perhaps as sons and daughters we should also speak of our love ... which sometimes we find it embarrassing to speak about to our human parents. But if we can get through the embarrassment we shall be glad that we have spoken—to our mother and our father and to God.

Some of our speaking will be asking for things, and if we are mature we shall know that 'no' is an answer just as much as 'yes'.

A prayer

'How much more will your Father in heaven give the Holy Spirit to those who ask him!' So ask!

SB

Ways to speak to God

With confidence

Therefore, since we have a great high priest who has gone through the heavens, Jesus the Son of God, let us hold firmly to the faith we profess. For we do not have a high priest who is unable to sympathise with our weaknesses, but we have one who has been tempted in every way, just as we are—yet was without sin. Let us then approach the throne of grace with confidence, so that we may receive mercy and find grace to help us in our time of need.

There are some doors that I can knock on with absolute confidence. I know that the friend inside will be glad to see me—and will hold the door wide open and ask me to come in. Then I shall be offered something to drink and probably something to eat as well. Nearly all of us can go with confidence into a few places. But the marvel is that we can go to the throne of the universe with total confidence at any time.

The writer to the Hebrews is using the picture of the Jewish temple. The high priest could only go into the holiest of all, where the presence of God dwelt, once a year, bearing the blood of sacrifice. But now Jesus is the great high priest who has gone into the presence of God on our behalf through the blood of his own sacrifice. The way into the presence of God is not closed any more. It is open—for ever. So we can come to God with confidence. Like Wesley's marvellous hymn: 'Bold, I approach the eternal throne, And claim the prize, through Christ, my own.' Added to

that, our high priest and our mediator utterly understands our human weaknesses and temptations, because he has been through all of them—but without giving in to them. He understands us and loves us—and in any temptation or distress we can approach the throne of grace and get all the help we need. If we want it . . . and if we ask . . .

Praying

Go now with confidence to the throne of grace, through Christ our great high priest, and ask for any help that you need . . .

SB

Ways to speak to God

With groans

We know that the whole creation has been groaning as in the pains of childbirth right up to the present time. Not only so, but we ourselves, who have the firstfruits of the Spirit, groan inwardly as we wait eagerly for our adoption as sons, the redemption of our bodies. For in this hope we were saved. But hope that is seen is no hope at all. Who hopes for what he already has? But if we hope for what we do not yet have, we wait for it patiently. In the same way, the Spirit helps us in our weakness. We do not know what we ought to pray for, but the Spirit himself intercedes for us with groans that words cannot express. And he who searches our hearts knows the mind of the Spirit, because the Spirit intercedes for the saints in accordance with God's will.

Have you ever had such a heavy heart over someone that you cannot put it into words? A person whom you love, who is in some trouble or sadness or (worst of all) great sinfulness? Everywhere you go your heart aches, and you are in great heaviness of spirit. You are praying for the person—yet you don't know what to say or what to ask. If you have been through that experience you probably know it for what it is: the Spirit within you is interceding for the person on your heart 'with groans that words cannot express', and through the deep pain and groaning in you the Spirit is praying that the will of God will be done.

We can opt out of the pain if we want to—but then the costly work of intercessory prayer will not be done. When Christ hung in agony on the cross they called out to him: 'If you are the son of God, come down from the cross.' But if

he was to do the work of suffering for our sin, then he could not come down. He had to stay there and endure the agony for our sake.

A way to pray

You will know who it is that your heart aches for the most deeply. In the presence of God, feel the pain and the sorrow of it . . . and know that the Spirit is using your pain to intercede for the person you love 'with groans that words cannot express'.

SB

Ways to speak to God

In anguish and complaint

'Therefore I will not keep silent; I will speak out in the anguish of my spirit, I will complain in the bitterness of my soul. Am I the sea, or the monster of the deep, that you put me under guard? When I think my bed will comfort me and my couch will ease my complaint, even then you frighten me with dreams and terrify me with visions, so that I prefer strangling and death, rather than this body of mine. I despise my life; I would not live for ever. Let me alone; my days have no meaning.'

We can tell God everything that we are feeling. He knows all that we feel and all that we think anyway, and utterly understands us. But we still need to speak out. Not for his benefit but for ours. It is the truth that sets people free—so expressing the truth about our thoughts and feelings is a vital step on the way to our freedom and healing. Even God cannot do anything with our anger or our bitterness if we pretend that we are not angry, and not bitter. It is like confessing our sins. It is only when we recognize them and name them that we know the enormous relief of having them forgiven.

Until I was thirty years old I was never angry. Or at least, I never knew I was and never expressed it. Instead I had a series of agonizing bilious attacks, which knotted me and my stomach up in acute pain. Then, one day, I did get angry ... really angry ... and it was the day of my liberation, when my bilious attacks disappeared for ever. Now I express my anger (and all my other emotions) to God, just as Job did. At the end of the book God tells his friends that they got it wrong: 'You have not spoken of me what is right, *as my servant Job has*' (42:7). Job has spoken out plainly and openly to God. But the other side of the coin—the shining side—is that God has spoken plainly and openly to Job.

A way to pray

Try to get in touch with your feelings. Your disappointments ... your anger ... your sadness. Then 'feel them in the presence of God'—and tell him all about them. But then be quiet and listen. And go on doing this, day after day, for the rest of your life ...

SB

It is never too late

For the kingdom of heaven is like a householder who went out early in the morning to hire labourers for his vineyard. After agreeing with the labourers for a denarius a day, he sent them into his vineyard. And going out about the third hour, he saw others standing idle in the market place; and to them he said, 'You go into the vineyard too, and whatever is right, I will give you.' So they went. Going out again about the sixth hour, and the ninth hour, he did the same. And about the eleventh hour he went out and found others standing; and he said to them, 'Why do you stand here idle all day?' They said to him, 'Because no one has hired us.' He said to them, 'You go into the vineyard too.'

One of my jobs is that of chaplain to our local hospital. There I sometimes meet people who are having a sort of moral crisis. They find themselves helpless and with nothing to do—or that they can do. So they begin, perhaps for the first time, to think about God and to pray. 'But is it right?' they wonder. 'I've never thought about God before, or asked him for anything, or done anything for him. So how can I turn to him now, when I am in trouble?'

It's a fair question, and an honest one. Most of us don't believe in something for nothing, after all, and these patients don't want to try to cheat God. But they are wrong. The great thing about God is that he never asks why we turn to him (he knows!), but he accepts us all the same. It is the other side of the picture of the narrow door. It doesn't matter why or when we turn to God as long as we do it. He wants us that much.

Of course, once he has us, he will make demands, and he will make changes. Letting God in is the beginning of a process that never ends. C.S. Lewis once wrote that it was like getting a builder in to do up one room of a cottage and finding that he was demolishing the whole building to make a palace—the dwelling place of a king. But the first step is what counts.

A prayer

Pray for all those who tremble at the first step of faith.

MM

Ways to speak to God
In prayer for other people

...Since the day we heard about you, we have not stopped praying for you and asking God to fill you with the knowledge of his will through all spiritual wisdom and understanding. And we pray this in order that you may live a life worthy of the Lord and may please him in every way: bearing fruit in every good work, growing in the knowledge of God, being strengthened with all power according to his glorious might...

Putting our prayers for other people into words is a common way to speak to God. But sometimes we only do it at special times ... early in the morning or late at night. We read our Bible and then pray ... the usual pattern of the 'quiet time' and of the Benedictine *lectio divina* or 'sacred reading'.

But Paul prayed for people all the time, and Jesus told us to 'pray without ceasing'. Once we realize how much more there is to prayer than coming to God with a shopping list, then praying without ceasing becomes possible. It is a relationship that is there all the time. But we have to become aware of it and not run away from it. Such a relationship with such a great God can be fairly overwhelming. In the early years of my Christian life I would wake up in the morning and pretend that I wasn't awake. Quite absurd—because God knew I was. But I wanted some time on my own—away from the presence. Yet when I surrendered to it the sense of crowding totally disappeared, and God was as essential and present as the air

that I breathe and the warmth of the sun. Speaking to God for other people flows out of our continual relationship with him as naturally as apples grow on trees. But it does have to grow through various stages ... first the bud, then the apple blossom, and finally the ripe, sweet fruit.

A way to pray

When someone comes into your mind remember that God is with you ... and say 'Help John, Lord ... you know just what he needs' ... and then go on remembering John in the presence. If you know some of the great prayers of the Bible and the Church by heart, you will find yourself using their words as you pray. Use Paul's prayer for the Colossians for someone now ...

SB

Ways to speak to God

Through our tears

Thou hast kept count of my tossings; put thou my tears in thy bottle! Are they not in thy book? Then my enemies will be turned back in the day when I call. This I know, that God is for me. In God, whose word I praise, in the Lord, whose word I praise, in God I trust without a fear. What can man do to me?

Before he died I had the great privilege of having Fr Christopher Bryant, SSJE as my spiritual director. When we met I would tell him what was happening in my life, including my spiritual life. He would listen—in deep attention and (I could tell) in prayer.

One day I told him that when I prayed for one particular person I often found myself weeping—and Christopher Bryant nodded his head wisely: 'Yes', he said, 'the gift of tears. It is a gift that God has given to you, and it is a way of praying.'

'The rabbis had a saying: "There are three kinds of prayers, each loftier than the preceding—prayer, crying and tears. Prayer is made in silence; crying with raised voice; but tears overcome all things" ' (William Barclay).

We can pray for other people through our tears and we can pray for ourself. Once I was so sad about something that I even woke up in the morning weeping. In church that Sunday the whole service, in a quaint Puritan phrase, 'spoke to my condition', and one hymn even spoke about my tears.

We can speak to God through all our tears, and we shall always be heard.

Put thou thy trust in God,
In duty's path go on,
Walk in his strength with faith and hope,
So shall thy work be done.

Give to the winds thy fears,
Hope, and be undismayed:
God hears thy sighs and counts thy tears,
God shall lift up thy head.

Through waves and clouds and storms
His power will clear thy way:
Wait thou his time; the darkest night
Shall end in brightest day.

John Wesley (trans. from Paul Gerhardt)

SB

Ways to speak to God

Through body language

For the moment all discipline seems painful rather than pleasant; later it yields the peaceful fruit of righteousness to those who have been trained by it. Therefore lift your drooping hands and strengthen your weak knees.

Jesus, knowing that the Father had given all things into his hands, and that he had come from God and was going to God, rose from supper, laid aside his garments, and girded himself with a towel. Then he poured water into a basin, and began to wash the disciples' feet, and to wipe them with the towel with which he was girded.

It isn't true that actions speak louder than words, but they certainly speak *as* loudly, and the two have got to match. When Jesus washed his disciples' feet it matched what he had said about being a servant. The writer to the Hebrews knew that if a person stopped drooping and stood up straight they would feel a lot better and start to hope again. Like the lovely song from *Carousel* they sing at football matches: 'When you walk through a storm, keep your head up high, and don't be afraid of the dark. At the end of a storm there's a golden cloud, and the clear crystal song of a lark...'

What we do with our body is a language just as much as the words we speak—in our ordinary life and also in our prayer life.

In prayer workshops I ask people to experiment with their bodies as they pray: standing up with arms outstretched (as Moses prayed); sitting on a chair with head down and hands locked together (quite difficult to breathe!); looking upwards with the hands raised high; lying flat on the floor face downwards (a wonderful way to pray, either to worship or if things have got on top of us); and sitting on the floor by our bed or a chair with our head in our arms (like a child at its mother's knee).

Action

Will you experiment with all those ways ... and see what sort of prayer and attitude to God the actual bodily position evokes in you?

SB

Ways to speak to God

With laughter

When the Lord restored the fortunes of Zion, we were like those who dream. Then our mouth was filled with laughter, and our tongue with shouts of joy; then they said among the nations, 'The Lord has done great things for them.' The Lord has done great things for us; we are glad. Restore our fortunes, O Lord, like the watercourses in the Negeb! May those who sow in tears reap with shouts of joy! He that goes forth weeping, bearing the seed for sowing, shall come home with shouts of joy, bringing his sheaves with him.

Sometimes we think that God is someone we only turn to in times of trouble. When we get it hopelessly wrong we see him, as C.S. Lewis put it, as a sort of parachute—for use in an emergency. But when our relationship with God is as it is meant to be, it is a life spent in continual communion—enjoying each other's presence. (Do we dare to believe that God enjoys ours? It says he does . . . that 'The Lord delights in his people'——Psalm 149.) Then everything that we do, and all the emotions that we experience, happen in the presence of the God who lives within us through his Spirit.

So our joy and our laughter are ways to speak to God just as much as our tears, our groans, our complaints and our intercessions. Perhaps part of the joy in the laughter comes from the release of tension. The great dramatists knew how to relieve our pain in their tragedies . . . they suddenly give us the comic relief of laughter. Perhaps our own ability to

laugh at ourselves is a way of inner release and of growing towards wholeness. My father could never laugh at himself until he was 65, when he became a Christian. Then he began to see the funny side of himself. He even enjoyed it when we laughed at him, in great love and delight at his silliness in some of the things he did.

A prayer

Thank you for laughter, Lord. Thank you for the release that it gives. Help me to laugh at myself, and at other people . . . but tenderly, and in love.

SB

Words and actions

As he went on his way Jesus saw a man who had been blind from birth. His disciples asked him, 'Rabbi, why was this man born blind? Who sinned, this man or his parents?' 'It is not that he or his parents sinned,' Jesus answered; 'he was born blind so that God's power might be displayed in curing him. While daylight lasts we must carry on the work of him who sent me; night is coming, when no one can work. While I am in the world I am the light of the world.'

So often we wonder why God allows suffering. Some parts of the Bible (for instance, Deuteronomy) see it as direct punishment for sin. Others see that as too simple to fit the facts (Job and Ecclesiastes for example). For Jesus, the question seems to be irrelevant. The blind man is not an opportunity for an interesting discussion on the kind of sin that is punished from birth. It is an opportunity to help, and to show God's creative power (the man has never seen before, so this is more than a mere healing—it brings something new).

Of course, there is nothing wrong with thinking and debating. In the end, though, it is our actions which count. We will never have an answer to the problem of suffering (at least in this world), but like Jesus we have opportunities to bring to bear the light of the world.

After he is healed the blind man will be the centre of a storm, and a living parable of light and darkness. Jesus' action brings not only healing, but also awareness of God to those who are willing to see it. If he had just entered into debate with the disciples, he would have been only one more teacher who had his little say about the big problem. So, too, with us. We can talk about the love of God till we're blue in the face. But when we show it, it truly gets noticed. Once again, this is what it means to walk in the light.

Meditate

Let your light so shine before men that they may see your good works and glorify our Father in heaven.

Matthew 5:15

MM

Holding fast

The man who had been blind was brought before the Pharisees. As it was a Sabbath day when Jesus made the paste and opened his eyes, the Pharisees too asked him how he had gained his sight ... For the second time (the Pharisees) summoned the man who had been blind, and said, 'Speak the truth before God. We know that this man is a sinner.' 'Whether or not he is a sinner, I do not know,' the man replied. 'All I know is this: I was blind and now I can see.'

I am fairly well educated, quite able to speak in public, and don't mind a good argument from time to time. But there are still times when I feel as the man Jesus healed must have felt. Confused, bewildered, outclassed by the learned teachers of Scripture, and under pressure to explain away his incredible experience rather than acknowledge Jesus.

At times like that, I have no witty arguments, I feel tired and distressed, and all around me are people who simply laugh at my faith. The temptation is strong just to deny it as childish, old-fashioned, irrelevant. But I can't. Like the man who had been blind—like all Christians—my eyes have been opened.

Once we meet Jesus, we get a new way of seeing the world. God becomes important. Freedom from sin becomes important. We see a new reality which has been hidden until that moment. We may not be able to put it into words, because we are not poets or writers or preachers, but we know we have met Jesus, and that a new light has shone in our hearts.

The man in today's reading couldn't argue about Scripture like his questioners. He was not an expert on the Jewish Law. But one thing he knew: 'I was blind and now I can see.' That is something we can say too, and something we can hold on to. It has happened to us and nothing can remove that awesome fact.

Meditate/pray

Look back on your first encounter with God (if you can remember it). Think of the times he has opened your eyes to something new. These are real experiences of God. Thank him for them, and hold them fast.

MM

The Word Became Flesh and Dwelt Among Us

As we look ahead to Christmas we look again at the Word of God. In the wonderful prologue to the Gospel of John which is so often read out at Christmas it says that 'The Word became flesh and dwelt among us, full of grace and truth; we have beheld his glory, glory as of the only Son from the Father.' So we look at who and what the Word is—and then reflect on what we have read. Henry Wansbrough, who wrote these two weeks, suggests a way for us to pray them.

'Prayer about these passages needs thoughtful reading. Do not hurry. Just stop, reflect, re-read, refer back to the passage of Scripture addressed to you by the Lord, and talk to him about it. If the comment is helpful, reflect on it. If it is unhelpful, converse with the Lord about why it misses the point for you. The final nugget may be a little line to learn by heart and carry about during the day as a reminder and refresher of the time spent with God.'

Then we turn to two great chapters of Isaiah, and it is almost impossible for most of us to read them without hearing the glorious music of Handel's *Messiah*, with its soloists and its choruses singing out the praises of Christ. We hear the sorrowful tones of the contralto telling us that 'He was despised and rejected of men; a man of sorrows, and acquainted with grief.' When we hear that we see Jesus weeping in agony in the Garden of Gethsemane. We see Christ crucified suffering on the cross. Some scholars tell us that we ought to read Isaiah through Jewish and not Christian eyes—but that is almost impossible. Great events cast their shadows backwards—and to read these great chapters from Isaiah is to see the suffering of Jesus.

But then it is Christmas—with Mary and Joseph, the angels and the shepherds, and the final wonder of the child who was born in a stable. The word became flesh and dwelt among us—and we see the glory of God shining out of a helpless baby. Jesus Christ, who was born of Mary in a unique way—and who wants to be born in each one of us in a different way.

O holy child of Bethlehem,
Descend to us, we pray
Cast out our sin and enter in.
Be born in us, today.

'A Stable once had something inside it that was bigger than our whole world.'

C.S. Lewis, *The Last Battle*

'As I have loved you . . .'

'This is my commandment, that you love one another as I have loved you. Greater love has no man than this, that a man lay down his life for his friends. You are my friends if you you do what I command you. No longer do I call you servants, for the servant does not know what his master is doing; but I have called you friends, for all that I have heard from my Father I have made known to you. You did not choose me, but I chose you and appointed you that you should go and bear fruit and that your fruit should abide; so that whatever you ask the Father in my name, he may give it to you. This I command you, to love one another.'

If we can make the time for it, it would be a great nourishment and strengthening to our Christian life to take each phrase of today's Gospel and meditate on it separately before moving on to the next phrase.

We shall reflect on the enormous, total love that Christ has for us . . . to give his life for us. We shall spend some time wondering what it will mean for us to love one another like that—to give our life for our friends, our neighbours and our enemies. We shall reflect that Jesus calls us his friends . . . and realize what friendship means. A friend is someone we love to be with . . . that we have meals with . . . that we talk to about everything that is on our heart . . . and our friend talks to us about everything that is on theirs.

We shall reflect that Jesus has chosen us. We haven't applied for a job and been turned down. He chose us and then he appointed us—and the appointment and the job description is to go and bear fruit. We shall reflect on what the fruit is . . . and think about the fruit of the Spirit in our own life and see how far the fruit has to grow until it is ripe and mature. We shall reflect that we can ask the Father for anything that we need to that end—because to put that promise in its context is to be aware that it is about bearing fruit. The loveliest fruit of all. 'This I command you, to love one another . . .'

SB

God's creative Word

God said, 'Let the earth produce every kind of living creature in its own species: cattle, creeping things and wild animals of all kinds.' And it was so . . . God saw that it was good.

The Bible gives us a simplified picture of how the universe came to be, God supreme and smoothly issuing commands which are equally smoothly accomplished.

Is this a magical world, out of touch with reality? We know about the Big Bang, how countless millions of years ago something happened from which the universe as we know it came to be, and still continues to expand to unimaginable distances of light-years. Are the stories of creation untrue, then? No, they are simply another way of looking at the same facts.

The trees as we see them, the grass, the cornflakes in our packets, the spider's web in the corner—all came to be, and exist from moment to moment, because God wishes them to be so. If I cease to think a thought, that the girl's hair looks like strands of gold as she skips in the sunset, then that thought ceases to exist (even though the hair, the girl and the sunset all remain). Just so, if God should cease to create the trees, the grass, the cornflakes, the spider's web, and hold them in existence, then there would simply be nothing there.

The Big Bang was the beginning, but not *the* beginning. Perhaps, instead of the Big Bang and the creative Word of God, we should think of God's Great Roar, whose sound still continues, ebbing and flowing with the rhythms of the universe. But it was no meaningless roar, rather a thoughtful, loving and planned expression of thought, a Word. God created deliberately, with all the care of forming a Word. 'God spoke and it was so, and God saw that it was good.'

A reflection

By the Word of Yahweh the heavens were made, by the breath of his mouth all their array.

Psalm 33:6

HW

The prophetic Word

The word that came to Jeremiah from Yahweh as follows, 'Get up and make your way down to the potter's house, and there I shall tell you what I have to say.'

More than most of the prophets, Jeremiah seems to pluck the Word of the Lord out of the circumstances of his life.

He goes to watch the potter and sees God's message about Israel in the way the potter shapes different pots for different purposes.

He goes to the market and sees God's message in two baskets of figs, one ripe, the other putrid: just so, some of the members of God's holy people are good, some bad.

If we keep our ears and eyes open, the Word of the Lord may come to us in all kinds of guises: God's own fatherly criticism in the angry word of a colleague; the unfailing love of God in the affectionate word of a friend; God's warning in the shape of narrow escape; divine forgiveness in the acceptance of an apology. As we reflect on them we can see that all these are signs of God's love and care.

The Word of God is not just a spoken word, but can be heard in all the chances and encounters of daily life. We can pray about all the events of the day, reflect on them in the quiet of the evening. Blind and stubborn as we so often are, especially in the heat of action, we can share these events, these joys and setbacks, with the Lord, and see what Word of his they contain, what the Lord is trying to say to us.

A reflection

In the way of your instruction lies my joy, a joy beyond all wealth. I will ponder your precepts and fix my gaze on your paths.

Psalm 119:14–15

HW

God's Word of promise

As the rain and the snow come down from the sky and do not return before having watered the earth, fertilising it and making it germinate to provide seed for the sower and food to eat, so it is with the word that goes from my mouth.

In the Old Testament God's Word of promise is the backbone of his people's life, providing the structure and framework of all their thought and activity.

The promise to Abraham that his descendants should be as numerous as the sand on the seashore, the permanence of the protection which this implies, sustained Israel through all the vicissitudes of history. They were sure that God would deliver them—provided that they were faithful in their response to him.

Then the promise that David's line would not fail gave them confidence through the period of the monarchy. In the anguish of the Babylonian exile it was the promise of vindication, the messianic promise, which sustained them: the belief that in spite of their failure God would not desert them but would—in his own good time—transform the world and rid it of sorrow, suffering and death.

This hope was constantly reiterated by a succession of prophetic words. God's promise beat upon their ears age after age. So too for us, God's Word of promise sustains us. The meaningless death of an innocent loved one, betrayal by friends, personal failure and incompetence—whatever disaster befall, we still have God's promise to fall back on.

For those with Christian faith no disaster can be ultimate or permanent. God sustains the world. He can draw good out of evil. He promises never to desert those who put their trust in him. And his Word has power; it can never be invalidated. Just as with the Word of Creation, the mere speaking of it guarantees its accomplishment.

A reflection

Keep in mind your promise to your servant on which I have built my hope. It is my comfort in distress that your promise gives me life.

Psalm 119:49–50

HW

God's Word for himself: the Name of God

Then Yahweh passed before [Moses] and called out, 'Yahweh, Yahweh, God of tenderness and compassion, slow to anger, rich in faithful love and constancy, maintaining his faithful love to thousands, forgiving fault, crime and sin, yet letting nothing go unchecked.'

If you don't know somebody's name, you have little control over a person, as any teacher can tell from experience. So if you don't want to give yourself at all, just refuse to give your name.

At the beginning Abraham did not know the name of his Protector God, and often in the first stories of the Bible God refuses to give his name. It was only at the burning bush that the personal Name of 'Yahweh' was revealed, and even then it remained incomprehensible and perhaps meaningless. God would interpret it only as 'I am who I am'; this gives little away!

But later on, in the desert, when Israel has committed itself to God (and also fallen totally by its unfaithfulness over the golden calf) God does reveal the meaning of his Name. This is the gift by God of himself to his people, granting them a power over him, a pledge of intimacy and favour.

The revelation of the meaning of the Name is itself an act of love. It is as a God of mercy and tenderness, love and compassion that God makes himself known. This passage echoes down the Bible. It is quoted again and again within the Bible. That was how God came to be known as his love was revealed in all the aspects of its richness.

The actual name 'Yahweh' remains a mystery. To the Jews of recent times it is too sacred to be pronounced. Awe of God has taken precedence over loving intimacy. But the Name is still written, as a testimony of the abiding bond of love with Israel.

A prayer

I shall sing of the faithful love of Yahweh for ever, from age to age my lips shall declare your constancy, for you have said 'Love is built to last for ever.'

Psalm 89:1–2

HW

God's Word as Law

Had your Law not been my delight, I would have perished in my misery. I shall never forget your precepts, for by them you have given me life.

For most of us law is a restricting factor, defining the limits beyond which we may not go, restraining excesses and even cramping our style. For Israel in the Old Testament the Word of the Lord (which was his Law—and the Ten Commandments are called the 'Ten Words') was a delight.

Firstly, the Law was a revelation of God himself, communicating to Israel his own standards and requirements. The demands you make on people show the sort of person you are, and the demands God makes on his people show what he himself is. Especially is the case because the Law lays down the terms of the treaty or marriage contract between God and Israel. It details what sort of conduct in Israel is necessary for Israel to be God's people, to live together with God, to have God in their midst.

He cannot be in the midst of a people wholly foreign to him, and with a people wholly foreign to his ways there could be no bond. 'Be holy as I am holy' is not an arbitrary demand, but is a condition of associating with God. You must like the way your spouse behaves, and to encourage your spouse to behave in the way you find charming and lovely is itself an expression of love.

Secondly, the Law gives the people a chance to respond to God in this love, to show their own affection for God. So obedience to the Law is not a grim obligation, but a joyful response to God's initiative.

A reflection

Your commandments fill me with delight, I love them dearly.

Psalm 119:47

HW

He tented among us

The Word became flesh, he tented among us and we saw his glory, the glory that he has from the Father as the only Son of the Father.

The climax of the Prologue of John express the climax of history. 'Word' is the expression chosen by John to express the very real yet immaterial existence of that which exists within the divinity but is not identical with the Father, that which is in a vibrant relationship with God and is all that God is. And now—the opposite extreme—this is said to become 'flesh', a word regarded as far too coarse ever to be used in the polite conversation of previous generations!

The Word took on the full reality of human nature, with physical pain and pleasure, sexual desire and control, hunger and repletion, misery and delight, surprise and disappointment, the final agony and humiliation of death. Two hints remind us that this climax of history is also the fulfilment of Judaism.

First, the word translated 'tented' is used of dwelling in a tent, and recalls the tent of meeting in the desert during the Exodus, which remained the centre of God's presence among his people, the meeting-place of Israel with God. At the same time the word used in Greek has the same basic letters, so the same basic sound, as the Hebrew word for God's glory, *shekinah*; this must have been deliberate.

Secondly, 'we saw his glory' is an awesome phrase. The glory of God is so frightening that any human being flees in terrified reverence. No human being can see God and live; to see his glory is almost fearsome, driving anyone to hide in the dust or the crevices of the rock 'in terror of Yahweh, at the brilliance of his majesty' (Isaiah 2:19). This glory, though untamed, has now been made humanly visible in Jesus Christ.

A prayer

God, you are my God, I pine for you, my heart thirsts for you, my body longs for you, as a land parched, dreary and waterless. Thus I have gazed on you in the sanctuary, seeing your power and your glory.

Psalm 63:1–2

HW

Love your enemy

If you love those who love you, what credit is that to you? Even 'sinners' love those who love them. And if you do good to those who are good to you, what credit is that to you? Even 'sinners' do that. And if you lend to those from whom you expect repayment, what credit is that to you? Even 'sinners' lend to 'sinners', expecting to be repaid in full. But love your enemies, do good to them, and lend to them without expecting to get anything back. Then your reward will be great, and you will be sons of the Most High, because he is kind to the ungrateful and wicked. Be merciful, just as your Father is merciful.

Jesus said that the two great commandments from the Jewish Law were to love God and to love our neighbour as ourself—and the lawyer who asked him what were the greatest of all the commandments totally agreed with him. So do most people. But not with the commandment in today's passage. Most people resist it—and often do it by denial. 'But I haven't got any enemies,' someone will say, hopelessly out of touch with the truth and with their own inner feelings.

Well, I dare you to take Jesus' teaching seriously in just one area of life—the way you behave on the road. Thousands of people are killed or maimed on the roads of the Western world every year. So when you see someone drive very badly, will you pray for him—or for her? It might be a woman affected by her hormones, suffering from pre-menstrual tension, and statistically more likely in that condition to have an accident. It might be a man equally affected by his hormones, and by the aggressiveness that attaches to testosterone, and the younger the man the more powerufl the effect. But Christ can deliver us from hormonal mood-changes. And if all of us who are Christian drivers would obey Jesus' command to love our enemy just in this area of our lives then some of the destructiveness and death on the roads would stop.

It is the hardest command that Jesus ever gave us—and he is telling us to act like God. Will you pray that you may be able to love like that?

SB

Christ, the Word of the Father

In the beginning was the Word; the Word was with God and the Word was God ... The Word became flesh, he lived among us and we saw his glory.

The fourth Gospel opens with a prologue to set the scene of the whole Gospel. The theme of the Gospel is the revelation of the awesome divine glory of God made visible in Christ Jesus, and these few verses give the key in the magnificent imagery of a poem.

The first phase links back to the story of creation, 'in the beginning', placing the Word alone on the stage. Is this the first moment of creation, with God's creative Word poised to form the universe? Or is it the moment before creation, when the mysterious inner life of God existed alone in eternal timelessness?

John's writing is so rich and allusive that it is always rash to rule out entirely the possibility that both senses are meant. The translation of the second phrase is an impoverishment of the thought of the evangelist's Greek. He wrote 'the Word was towards God', suggesting a partnership, the Word turned towards God, receiving all from God, steadily and uninterruptedly in communication with God.

The third passage does not say that God and the Word are identical, the same being, but 'what God was, the Word was'. The Word has all the divine quality, power and substance. John chooses the expression 'Word' to convey the idea of identity in difference. My word expresses my thought, or indeed myself. It draws all its life from me, and needs to be continuously spoken by me. It is under my control and yet is not the same as myself, it has a certain being of its own, which yet is mine.

Just so with this Word of God, which has come among us and so made visible his glory.

A reflection

The grass withers, the flower fades, but the word of our God remains for ever.

Isaiah 40:8

HW

Christ, the 'Yes' of the Father

As surely as God is trustworthy, what we say to you is not both Yes and No. The Son of God, Jesus Christ, who was proclaimed to you by us . . . was never Yes-and-No; his nature is all Yes. For in him is found the Yes to all God's promises and therefore it is 'through him' that we answer 'Amen' to give praise to God.

Paul is replying to the charge of instability. It seems that the Corinthians had charged him with needlessly and capriciously changing his plans. He replies that his shares in the firmness of Christ, who is the firmness, the confirmation of God's promises. It is Christ who makes God's promises firm by bringing them to their fulfilment.

The clue to the full understanding of the richness of Paul's thought is that the Hebrew word for 'Amen' means strength, firmness, truth, stability— everything, in fact, that builds confidence and reliance. It is also, of course, the word used in public prayer, by which the listeners (by answering 'Amen') take on the prayer for themselves and confirm it as their own. So it is Jesus who provides us with the certainty of all God's promises. Just as in the public prayer of the Church there is a great chorus of 'Amen' to conclude a prayer and take it on board for everyone, so Jesus is the last word, who brings satisfaction and finality to God's Word of promise.

Paul may even by alluding to the fact that the great prayer of Christianity, the Eucharist, already in his time concluded 'through him', and received the response of the great 'Amen'. So, by this final 'Amen', we echo the fulfilment of God's promises in Jesus.

A prayer

. . .through him, with him, in him, in the unity of the Holy Spirit, all honour and glory is yours, almighty Father, for ever and ever. 'Amen'.

Eucharist Prayer, Roman Missal

HW

The two-edged sword

The Word of God is something alive and active. It cuts more incisively than any two-edged sword: it can seek out the place where the soul is divided from spirit, or joints from marrow, it can pass judgement on secret emotions and thoughts. No created thing is hidden from him; everything is uncovered and stretched fully open to the eyes of the one to whom we must give account of ourselves.

The author of the Letter to the Hebrews is referring to the passages of Scripture which provide the standards for his readers. They were faint-hearted and dissatisfied, looking over their shoulders at a situation they had left behind. Sternly, the writer reminds them that God has given us aims and guidance for our way of life, and that with him there is no deception.

How can we know God's will in the confusing hubbub of the market-place? Scripture does not provide easy, automatic answers. To jab at the Scriptures for an answer with the point of a pin is mere superstition, and tear a solitary text out of its context is not much better.

We need to understand, to love and to reflect on the Scriptures, recognizing that they reveal the mind and the power of their divine author. This is why they can be our judge: A human judge can be hoodwinked and deceived. A human partner in conversation can be flattered or diverted from the truth. But with a text that is the Word of God there is no deception. It speaks—and I have only myself to deceive.

But there is no point, because God cannot be deceived. And the Word of God is his instrument, his extended arm to me. The tenderness and forgiveness of God are all very well (and glorious). But only the blindest and most complacent Christian would even want to be free of judgment as well.

In the Gospels we see Jesus judging, or, rather, people judging themselves by their reaction to him, as they accept or reject him. As he is the Word of God, so we meet God's Word as we turn to the Gospels. As we read, in silence and in prayer, we hear the judgment of God.

A prayer

I have moulded myself to your judgments. I cling to your instructions, Yahweh, do not disappoint me. I run the way of your commandments.

Psalm 119:30–31

HW

Word of freedom

Is not this the sort of fast that pleases me: to break unjust fetters, to undo the thongs of the yoke, to let the oppressed go free, and to break all yokes? Is it not sharing your food with the hungry, and sheltering the homeless poor, if you see someone lacking clothes, to clothe him, and not to turn away from your own kin? Then your light will blaze out like the dawn and your wound be quickly healed over.

Unpopularity, persecution, mockery, failure held no fears for them. The prophets of the Old Testament proclaimed to their contemporaries how God saw the situation in their world. The Word of the Lord was that injustice was being done, that his people were enslaved.

Every now and then a figure appears in our world who speaks in the same way. William Wilberforce spoke out tirelessly, and eventually successfully, against the evils of slavery, which were simply accepted in the conventional world. A whole new frame of thinking was needed. In this century Martin Luther King was his successor, speaking out fearlessly for the rights of the oppressed black minority in the United States, and winning a whole new sensitivity by his death for his outspokenness.

In our generation perhaps it is Mother Teresa who speaks most clearly for the needs of the oppressed—in a way the conscience of the world. She speaks quietly too, and with tolerance but insistence. It is not necessarily the most strident voice which is most clearly heard.

A reflection

For as the rain and the snow come down from the sky and do not return before having watered the earth ... so it is with the word that goes from my mouth: it will not return to me unfulfilled.

Isaiah 55:10–11

HW

The imperishable seed

Your new birth was not from any perishable seed but from imperishable seed, the living and enduring Word of God. For all humanity is grass, and all its beauty like the wild flower's. As grass withers, the flower fades, but the Word of the Lord remains for ever. And this Word is the Good News that has been brought to you.

This passage from the First Letter of Peter is almost a meditation on what John's Gospel has to say about the Word. Jesus is the Word made flesh, come so that all people may have life. John's Gospel hovers over circles, with the flight of the eagle, round the precious concepts of the Word, truth and eternal life. 'Consecrate them in the truth,' prays Jesus at his Last Supper, 'your word his truth'. 'You have the words of eternal life,' cries Peter to Jesus, when many of the disciples cannot accept his teaching. 'I have come so that they may have life,' says the Good Shepherd, in contrast to the thief and the hireling.

What does it mean that this Word is the imperishable seed of eternal life? The world of Jesus was a world torn by strife, beset with disasters, a web of instability and insecurity. From this Jesus claims to set his followers free. The seed of life which he sows by the Word of his Good News cannot be lost or die. This is the essence of that faith which is commitment to him. Faith is no matter of believing this proposition or believing that dogma. It is a matter of trust, of whole-hearted commitment to him and to the promises of God which he mediates.

The instability of the world in which we live is no less than that of two thousand years ago. We may understand a little more about the cause of disease, disaster and death, but they still remain unavoidable, on a large scale or small. The only salvation remains to commit ourselves through thick and thin to the word of the Lord.

A prayer

True to your word, support me and I shall live; do not disappoint me of my hope.

Psalm 119:116

HW

353

The rider of the Apocalypse

And now I saw heaven open, and a white horse appear; its rider was called Trustworthy and True; in uprightness he judges and makes war. His eyes were flames of fire, and he was crowned with many coronets; the name written on him was known only to himself, his cloak was soaked in blood. He is known by the name, The Word of God.

The Book of Revelation offers a series of powerful, often frightening, images of conflict and bloodshed. These images predict the life of the Church down the ages. Christians are always in conflict with the powers of darkness and suffering from them, but secure in the knowledge that in the end neither those powers nor anything in the whole of creation will ever be able to separate them from 'the love of God, known to us in Christ Jesus our Lord' (Romans 8:39).

Several times in the course of descriptions of the conflict, the persecution suffered by God's faithful is said to be 'for the sake of the Word of God'. Just so, in Mark's Gospel, the Christian is exhorted to be true 'for my sake and for the sake of the Gospel'. Now, as the final scenes begin, we see the Word of God triumphant. This must be Jesus himself, personifying God's Truth and the Truth of the Gospel.

The powers of darkness nowadays may be there in external temptations to compromise, by dubious business partnership or by sexual infidelity. Or I shall encounter them within myself as I struggle to be true to my standards, to fulfil my resolutions, to be faithful to prayer, and to combat my faults.

This vision of the triumph of the Word of God, Trustworthy and True, must be an inspiration in our battle to be true to the Word which we have received. The fact that 'his cloak was soaked in blood' suggests that the rider did not himself escape unscathed. Primarily the blood is the blood of his enemies. But we cannot expect an easy triumph—nor to escape without wounds of failure and suffering.

A reflection

Your Word is a lamp for my feet, a light on my path.

Psalm 119:105

HW

Make way for Jesus

This is how John appeared as a witness. When the Jews sent priests and Levites from Jerusalem to ask him, 'Who are you?' he not only declared, but he declared quite openly, 'I am not the Christ.' 'Well, then,' they asked, 'are you Elijah?' 'I am not,' he said. 'Are you the prophet?' He answered, 'No.' So they said to him, 'Who are you? We must take back an answer to those who sent us. What have you to say about yourself?' So John said, 'I am, as Isaiah prophesied: a voice that cries in the wilderness: "Make a straight way for the Lord."'

'Who do you think you are, setting yourself up as some goody-goody with all this churchgoing? I know people who go to church, and they're no better than me. Lots of hypocrites . . .'

We've all heard something like that, though it may have been put in more (or less!) polite words. Who do we think we are with this religion stuff? And who do we think we are to tell people what is right and wrong, to stick our noses into other people's business? And why don't the bishops give the nation a clear moral lead—until they do, and then they are interfering in politics, or spoiling people's fun.

And if people are happy as they are, who are we to go bothering them with the gospel? Perhaps they just don't want that sort of thing?

There was one answer that John the Baptist gave, and one that we can give. We are a voice crying, 'Prepare the way of the Lord.' But we have an advantage that John never had. He looked forward to the coming of the Messiah. But we have met the Messiah and can call him by name—Jesus—just as he has called us by name and said, 'Follow me.' We are not better than others, but we have a better friend; one who is worth sharing and worth preparing ourselves and others to meet.

A way to pray

So in prayer and worship, as we meet again with him today, bring before him all those who don't yet know him, and ask for opportunities to be someone who, like John, prepares others to meet him too.

MM

Beautiful new clothes

Awake, awake, put on your strength, O Zion; put on your beautiful garments, O Jerusalem, the holy city; for there shall no more come into you the uncircumcised and the unclean. Shake yourself from the dust, arise, O captive Jerusalem; loose the bonds from your neck, O captive daughter of Zion.

Israel has gone to sleep, and God is calling to her to wake up and get dressed. The people of God must wake up to who they are and put on the beautiful clothes that their God (and husband) will give to them (his bride).

Yesterday I was in a shop watching a friend try on a beautiful bright yellow suit. She looked at herself in the mirror and smiled at her reflection. She had been feeling rather low, and new clothes can somehow lift our spirits up. An outward sign of leaving old things behind and making a new beginning. That is what God wants the people of God to do—and he buys the beautiful new clothes for us. We shall look at the cost of them later on. Today we shall just look at the clothes.

The daughter of Zion has been sitting in the dust. So she is dirty. Added to that there is a fetter round her neck. Unclean and un-free she is, and also powerless in her own strength. But the beautiful clothes that God will give to her (if she will put them on) will give her God's strength. Then she will be able to break her fetters and be what she is meant to be. Clean—and free—and holy.

A meditation

Imagine a bride sitting in the dust with a fetter round her neck. Imagine the husband who loves her giving her new clothes and strength. Then imagine her, in her beautiful clothes, at an Easter Parade—showing off the beauty and the glory of God in a world spoilt with the ugliness of fear, hate and hopelessness. A world that might lift up its head and dare to hope as it looks at the beautiful Easter clothes of the people of God. We wear them all the year round—for Christmas parties just as much as for Easter parades.

SB

Here am I, says God

For thus says the Lord: 'You were sold for nothing, and you shall be redeemed without money. For thus says the Lord God: My people went down at the first into Egypt to sojourn there, and the Assyrian oppressed them for nothing. Now therefore what have I here, says the Lord, seeing that my people are taken away for nothing? Their rulers wail, says the Lord, and continually all the day my name is despised. Therefore my people shall know my name; therefore in that day they shall know that it is I who speak; here am I.'

Chapters 40–55 of Isaiah are all about the servant of God, which Israel is supposed to be (as well as being the bride of God). But she hasn't been much good at either and she hasn't learned the lessons that she could have done from her sufferings. Because of the failure of the people of God, the name of God is despised.

Last week a friend told me about a Christian in his office who seemed to disapprove of life in general and of the people in the office in particular. But Jesus didn't disapprove of people. We can't imagine him going round with pursed lips and a sour face. He liked people—even people no one else liked. He went to parties with them—and told them the astonishing truth, and the very good news, that his Father God was just like him.

Isaiah says that God will act so that people will know just what he is like. They 'shall know my name', which is to know what the character and nature of God really is. But they won't just know

about him. They will know him in a personal relationship 'in that day'. 'Here am I,' God will say. God in action. God incarnate.

A reflection

'Here am I,' says God. He says it in his Word—'and the Word became flesh and dwelt among us' (John 1:14). God is still saying, 'Here am I'—in his Church and in his world, through 'Christ in you, the hope of glory' (Colossians 1:27). Reflect—what does your life say about God to those who know you—then pray that you will shine a bit brighter with the glory of God, and that all of us who are named with the name of Christ will do the same.

SB

Our God reigns!

How beautiful upon the mountains are the feet of him who brings good tidings, who publishes peace, who brings good tidings of good, who publishes salvation, who says to Zion, 'Your God reigns.'

Yesterday a friend told me of her despair and hopelessness. Years ago her father was paralysed in a car accident. He complains constantly and prays constantly, and God seems a million miles away. As she spoke I remembered Peter Kreeft's words, 'Suffering is not a problem requiring an answer but a mystery requiring a presence.' In the face of the father's complaining her mother behaves like a saint—but in fact she is an atheist. This is largely because a priest told her husband that his suffering was a punishment for his sin and she (rightly) refuses to believe in such a God.

But what if that man and that woman could believe that in spite of it all God is still reigning? What if in the darkness of his paralysis and his pain (the only part of him that isn't paralysed hurts all the time) he could know the presence of God with him? Always there. Always loving him. Always suffering with him. And yes, I know there can be miracles of healing. But not always. What if they could say with St Paul: 'So we do not lose heart. Though our outer nature is wasting away, our inner nature is being renewed every day. For this slight momentary affliction is preparing for us an eternal weight of glory beyond all comparison, because we look not to the things that are seen, but to the things that are unseen; for the things that are seen are transient, but the things that are unseen are eternal' (2 Corinthians 4:16–18).

A way to pray

Look at the world and at its pain. Be aware of your own heartache and hurts—and of the pain of the people you love, whether physical or emotional. An unhappy marriage. A life-threatening disease. Then affirm out loud the good news that 'Our God reigns'—even if you say it with tears in your eyes and hardly any hope in your heart. But go on saying it—and believing it—and let the light of that truth shine into other people's darkness as well as your own.

SB

Salvation that shows

Hark, your watchmen lift up their voice, together they sing for joy; for eye to eye they see the return of the Lord to Zion. Break forth together into singing, you waste places of Jerusalem; for the Lord has comforted his people, he has redeemed Jerusalem. The Lord has bared his holy arm before the eyes of all the nations; and all the ends of the earth shall see the salvation of our God.

Despair and desolation are transmuted into delight because of what God has done. The waiting of verse 5 comes to an end and is changed into singing. Death and negativity are replaced by life and fullness of being. God is victorious (and reigning) over all the darkness of death—and light and life can be had for the asking.

God is coming himself to Zion, to Jerusalem—but salvation won't stop there. All the ends of the earth are going to see it—and see what happens to a human being and to society when God enters in. I saw once what happened to one family when God entered into it. First the woman invited Christ into her heart, and then she prayed for her son and for her husband (who was an alcoholic) and also for her own and her husband's families. Then, slowly and gently, over a period of a few years, God entered into all their hearts. 'It's amazing,' she said, 'the whole of our family life is totally different. And it's just wonderful!' The husband's face shone with his new freedom—and as he spoke about it he would shake his head with wonder and then just smile with sheer happiness.

The Word of God enters into people—and the people of God tell it out and live it out—salvation for everyone to see.

A way to pray

Think of any despair in your own life, and in the life of other people you know. Think of the waste places—where things are dead, or where nothing ever grew— the places in your life, and in other people's lives, that are like a desert. Imagine the God of love entering into the despair, and into the desert. Imagine him entering into you, and into other people. What action would he take? What would Jesus do? Pray 'Your will be done, your kingdom come, on earth as it is in heaven . . .'

SB

A shining priesthood

Depart, depart, go out thence, touch no unclean thing; go out from the midst of her, purify yourselves, you who bear the vessels of the Lord. For you shall not go out in haste, and you shall not go in flight, for the Lord will go before you, and the God of Israel will be your rear guard.

God is calling his people to come out of captivity and to come home. The Jews were physically exiled from their own, God-given land. They were slaves in Babylon, where the inhabitants worshipped false gods. But the people of God are to be the slaves and the servants of God and obey only him. In a sense we live in exile all the time, in a world that neither knows God nor worships him. Instead it worships the gods of money, success and comfort. But we can still be at home in God even in the midst of 'a crooked and depraved generation, among whom [we] shine like stars in the universe as [we] hold out the word of life' (Philippians 2:15).

Those 'who bear the vessels of the Lord' were those from the priestly tribe, and they were to purify themselves. But all the people of Israel had been called to be priests—and in the Book of Exodus God told Moses of his plan and his purpose, and promised to guide them and to carry them: 'You have seen what I did to the Egyptians, and how I bore you on eagle's wings and brought you to myself. Now, therefore, if you will obey my voice and keep my covenant, you shall be my own possession among all peoples; for all the earth is mine, and you shall be to me a kingdom of priests and a holy nation' (Exodus 19:4–6). In the New Testament Peter picks up all those beautiful promises to the Jewish people and applies them to Christians.

A prayer

Lord God, help me—and all the members of your Church—to purify ourselves and to be the royal priesthood you have called us to be. So that we may bring men and women to you and you to men and women. Amen.

SB

A strange success story

Behold, my servant shall prosper, he shall be exalted and lifted up, and shall be very high. As many were astonished at him—his appearance was so marred, beyond human semblance, and his form beyond that of the sons of men—so shall he startle many nations; kings shall shut their mouths because of him; for that which has not been told them they shall see, and that which they have not heard they shall understand.

We would expect a servant of God to prosper. And for someone who has served God to be exalted and lifted up and very high sounds exactly right. Except to Christians, and to Jews after the gas chambers and the holocaust. Certainly Islam cannot believe that God would allow even one of his prophets to suffer, let alone the Son of God. So the Qur'an says that Jesus (whom Muslims regard as a prophet) was never crucified, but that God 'cast his likeness' on to someone else (Surah...)—and their tradition has it that this one was probably Judas.

The path of the prospering servant of God is exceedingly strange—and when people look at him they are astonished. Surely this one cannot be the servant of God—not looking like this, nailed to a cross and bleeding, and suffering this extraordinarily damaging thing. Looking at the awe-ful suffering, there's nothing to say. We're stunned into an appalled silence.

When it says 'my servant shall prosper,' that word implies "having the intelligence, insight and capability to bring to a successful conclusion what one wants to do" ' (*Servant Theology*). But only the Wisdom of God knows what has to be done and how to do it. And only the Word of God has the creative power actually to do it. So no wonder the New Testament writers said that their crucified God-in-Christ was both the Wisdom of God and the Word of God—living and dying in Jesus. To know what God is like, we have to look at Jesus.

A reflection

Think about the strangeness of the suffering of the servant of God. Think about Jesus as the Wisdom and the Word of God.

SB

The costly gift of love

Now one of the Pharisees invited Jesus to have dinner with him, so he went to the Pharisee's house and reclined at the table. When a woman who had lived a sinful life in that town learned that Jesus was eating at the Pharisee's house, she brought an alabaster jar of perfume, and as she stood behind him at his feet weeping, she began to wet his feet with her tears. Then she wiped them with her hair, kissed them, and poured perfume on them.

The Pharisee (whose name was Simon) got it hopelessly wrong and the woman got it exquisitely right. He was the expert in the law, and very religious. She was an ex-prostitute. But she loved Jesus and he didn't, and that was the explanation for all of it. To love God is to do the will of God—and use our heart, mind and energy in the process. It is the will of God that we should love him, and know him—and once we do know him the inevitable result is that we shall worship him. That is what this woman was doing. She stood behind Jesus to start with, but she didn't stay standing. She must have knelt—to wash his feet with her tears and to wipe them with her long, loose hair, the mark of a loose woman in those days. But this woman wasn't loose or lost any more. She had been found—and now she was adoring the one who had found her and forgiven her. One day he would pour out his life for her (and for all the sinners in all the world). She didn't know yet how great the cost would be for him to take and bear her sins into his own body on the cross of Calvary. But

her heart poured itself out in love towards him—and she poured out her costliest and most precious possession over his feet.

Today, when you eat the bread and drink the wine in the presence of Jesus, will you be self-righteous like Simon the Pharisee? Or worshipping and adoring like the sinful woman, delighting in the enormous love and mercy of God in Christ to you?

SB

The beauty of suffering

Who has believed what we have heard? And to whom has the arm of the Lord been revealed? For he grew up before him like a young plant, and like a root out of dry ground; he had no form or comeliness that we should look at him, and no beauty that we should desire him.

People could hardly believe their ears or their eyes. The things that Isaiah was saying cut across everything they had imagined and understood about God. Some people believed, and for them 'the arm of the Lord' (his power and his strength) was made known and the mystery was revealed. But it was an astonishing truth that was made known: that God is stretching out his arm to accomplish his will through the suffering of his servant. In the eyes of God the servant was like a beautiful, tender plant, delighting the gardener, and growing out of a dry, unfriendly environment. The suffering of the servant was the will of God, and the life—and finally the death—of the servant was the will of God. It was a hard thing to grasp.

God saw his beauty—but men didn't. St Paul had quite a struggle with the truth of the mystery of God. But the glory of it finally dawned on him like the blazing of the midday sun.

For the word of the Cross is folly to those who are perishing, but to us who are being saved it is the power of God . . . We preach Christ crucified . . . Christ the power of God and the wisdom of God.

(1 Corinthians 1:18, 23–24)

A reflection

Spend some time in the next twenty-four hours reflecting on your own attitude to suffering. Reflect on the suffering of Christ—reflect on any suffering you are going through yourself at the moment, or have endured in the past—reflect on the suffering of a person or a group of people of whom you know. Why do you think suffering happens—or is necessary? Connect your thinking and reflection with the verses from Isaiah that you have read over the past few days.

SB

We must look!

He was despised and rejected by men; a man of sorrows, and acquainted with grief; and as one from whom men hide their faces he was despised, and we esteemed him not. Surely he has borne our griefs and carried our sorrows; yet we esteemed him stricken, smitten by God, and afflicted. But he was wounded for our transgressions, he was bruised for our iniquities; upon him was the chastisement that made us whole, and with his stripes we are healed.

People didn't want to know him and they didn't want to look at him. They couldn't bear to look, because what was happening was in the deepest sense of the word 'unbearable'. One reason why we don't want to 'weep with those who weep' is that another person's pain can put us in touch with our own, which we may have been managing to deal with by denying it and pretending (quite unconsciously) that it doesn't exist. I suspect that the reason why young thugs beat up old people and even disabled people is that they themselves are terrified of being either old or disabled. It is all to do with not being able to bear the truth and reality of life. 'Human kind cannot bear very much reality,' wrote Eliot, and he hit the nail right on the head. Just as the Roman soldiers did when they were crucifying the servant of the Lord. Protestant Christians are not very good at contemplating the sufferings of Jesus. We often prefer to see an empty cross—not a crucifix with a tortured figure hanging there. 'It is all finished,' we say, and in one sense we are right. There

is no need for any more sacrifice for sin. God-in-Christ has done it all. But we need to contemplate in order to know the cost. To realize that our sins—and our sorrows—are finally dealt with by God-in-Christ taking the pain and the desolating separation of them into his own person.

A thought

We cannot dissociate ourselves from the people who crucified the servant of the Lord. They did it then, at that incredible moment in time. We do it all the time— as we hammer in the nails of unkind words to an old person or a child; the nails of nagging husband or a wife; the nails of despising the people of a different race. Reflect . . . and repent.

SB

He carried it for us

All we like sheep have gone astray; we have turned every one to his own way; and the Lord has laid on him the iniquity of us all. He was oppressed, and he was afflicted, yet he opened not his mouth; like a lamb that is led to the slaughter, and like a sheep that before its shearers is dumb, so he opened not his mouth.

In my Bible alongside today's reading there is a drawing of a sheep standing on a tiny ledge at the edge of a precipice. It is in great danger, and there is no way for it to rescue itself. Unless the shepherd lays on an astonishing rescue operation the sheep is facing a certain death. Isaiah is saying that God has done just what a good shepherd always does. He has laid on a rescue operation for all his lost sheep (and all of us are lost, or are until he has found us) that will mean life instead of death for us. But the cost is enormous. 'I am the good shepherd,' Jesus said. 'The good shepherd lays down his life for the sheep' (John 10:11).

Today's verses are very special to me, because it was through them that I discovered how my sins could be forgiven (and through Revelation 3:20 that I invited into my heart the one who forgave me and died in order to do it) . 'Do you realize that you are a sinner?' the Reverend John Collins asked me, looking at me with an immensely kind expression. 'Of course I do,' I told him. 'Hold out your hands,' John said, and on one of them he placed a heavy Bible. 'This hand is you,' he told me, 'and the Bible is your sin. Your other, empty, hand is Jesus. Now listen...' He read aloud to me, 'All we like sheep have gone astray; we have turned everyone to his own way; and the Lord has laid on him the iniquity of us all'—and as he said those last words he removed the heavy 'sin' from the hand that was me and put it on the hand that was Jesus. 'Now where is your sin?' he asked me. A child could have told him. 'It's on Jesus.'

A thought

Led like a lamb to the slaughter
In silence and shame,
There on Your back You carried a world
Of violence and pain.
Bleeding, dying, bleeding, dying...

Graham Kendrick

SB

He died for us

By oppression and judgment he was taken away; and as for his generation, who considered that he was cut off out of the land of the living,
stricken for the transgression of my people? And they made his grave with
the wicked and with a rich man in his death, although he had done no
violence, and there was no deceit in his mouth.

An innocent man suffering—and the
people who saw it didn't know what to
make of it. Isaiah asks a question in a way
that makes it plain what answer he
expects: 'Who considered that he was
cut off out of the land of the living,
stricken for the transgression of my
people?' The answer is 'No one—at the
time.' What Isaiah is talking about is
vicarious suffering, in which one person suffers on behalf of another. It is hard
to imagine how such a transaction can
actually take place, but perhaps forgiveness helps us to understand. If you injure
a friend (or an enemy) the only way for
you and that person to go on being
friends (or make friends) is for the
injured party to bear the pain of the
injury in his or her own person, and to
hold out to you the offer of a restored
relationship or a friendship that you
never knew before. I believe that the
mystery of the suffering of Christ is an
event something like that, magnified to
infinity. The Creator God who made our
world suffers the pain of the injury and
the hate that we inflict on him—and
every injury we do to any creature is a
sin against the Creator.

A reflection

*The world puts God-in-Christ to death—
and we cannot blame the Jews or the
Romans. We are all there hammering in
the nails and crying, 'Crucify him,
Crucify him!' We manage to kill the body
of the suffering servant—but God raises
him to life again. He comes to us again as
our friend and our lover, asking us to
respond to his love and to receive the
forgiveness he died to bring us. Day after
day after day . . .*

SB

He was made sin for us

Yet it was the will of the Lord to bruise him; he has put him to grief; when he makes himself an offering for sin, he shall see his offspring, he shall prolong his days; the will of the Lord shall prosper in his hand; he shall see the fruit of the travail of his soul and be satisfied; by his knowledge shall the righteous one, my servant, make many to be accounted righteous; and he shall bear their iniquities.

This astonishing suffering of the servant of the Lord is the will of the Lord. This is the way the sorrows of the world are going to be transmuted into joy. This is the way the sins of the world are going to be forgiven. And after he has made himself 'an offering for sin' he will see his sons and daughters. A strange progression, because the sin offering was always put to death. The bull offered on the Day of Atonement was killed, and the High Priest sprinkled its blood over he people. The Passover lamb was killed and eaten, and its blood put on the doorposts so that the angel of death would 'pass over' the house.

In Leviticus 5:14-19 a man who is guilty of sin 'shall bring to the priest a ram without blemish and the priest shall make atonement for him ... it is a guilt offering.' The guilt offering is a substitute for the guilty person. The one who is guilty is the one who ought to die—but God accepts a substitute. And when John the Baptist saw Jesus coming towards him at the start of his ministry he said, 'Behold, the Lamb of God, who takes away the sin of the world!' (John 1:29).

Just a few days ago someone told me how he resented God, because God was so cruel and condemning. I found myself with tears in my eyes, saying 'I can hardly bear what you say—and I am not blaming you, but you have got it hopelessly and utterly wrong.' God makes the innocent and obedient servant into the 'sin offering', and the ram without blemish pours out his life, and his blood, even unto death. But the picture of an unloving and angry Father pouring out his wrath on a loving and innocent Son is distorted.

A reflection

...in Christ God was [or, God was in Christ] reconciling the world to himself.

2 Corinthians 5:18–19

SB

He did it for us

Therefore I will divide him a portion with the great, and he shall divide the spoil with the strong; because he poured out his soul to death, and was numbered with the transgressors; yet he bore the sin of many, and made intercession for the transgressors.

Now the servant gets the reward for his suffering. As we saw yesterday, he 'shall see of the travail of his soul and be satisfied'. The satisfaction in the heart of God-in-Christ is that many are made righteous because the servant has borne the sin that was killing them.

The human race cannot deal with its own sin. We cannot work it off by doing good and acquiring 'merit'. We have earned death—the spiritual death which is separation from God. But God will give us spiritual life, if we want it: 'the wages of sin is death, but the free gift of God is eternal life, in Christ Jesus our Lord' (Romans 6:23).

The suffering servant of God won this life for us through his victory over the powers of evil in his death on the cross. 'He bore the sin of many, and made intercession for the transgressors.' It happened once for all on the first Good Friday morning. Jesus prayed for the soldiers who nailed him to his cross. 'Father, forgive them, for they know not what they do' (Luke 23:34). Then, three hours later, he died—and said in a loud voice that many believe was a cry of triumph: 'It is finished!' God-in-Christ was the offering for our sin. It happened in time on the first Good Friday. But 'the benefits of his death and passion' are there for us now through all of time.

A reflection

Through the death of Christ we can know the wonder and the relief of forgiven sin. We can know the wonder and the freshness of a new start and a new beginning. Not just once, but day after day after day. We can know that the Son of God still 'makes intercession for the transgressors'. All because he loves us— with a love that is stronger than death and that will never end.

SB

God and shepherds

And in that region there were shepherds out in the field, keeping watch over their flock by night. And an angel of the Lord appeared to them, and the glory of the Lord shone around them, and they were filled with fear. And the angel said to them, 'Be not afraid; for behold, I bring you good news of great joy which will come to all the people; for to you is born this day in the city of David, a Saviour, who is Christ the Lord

Orthodox religious people looked down on shepherds. Because of the way they looked after their flocks they couldn't keep the ceremonial law and keep up with all the ceremonial washings that the Pharisees demanded. But back in the Old Testament God didn't use a scribe or a Pharisee as an image of what he was like. He used a shepherd.

'I myself will be the shepherd of my sheep, and I will make them lie down, says the Lord God. I will seek the lost, and I will bring back the strayed, and I will bind up the crippled, and I will strengthen the weak, and the fat and the strong I will watch over; I will feed them in justice' (Ezekiel 34:15–16). The orthodox religious 'shepherds' had dismally failed to do their task, so God would do it himself. The birth of his Son was the beginning of the new way in which he would do it—so he sent the angels to the despised shepherds to tell them about it.

These were special shepherds. In the fields outside Bethlehem they looked after the flocks of sheep, with their lambs, from which the temple sacrifices were chosen. Now God had chosen them to go and see the one who would be both the perfect Shepherd of the sheep and the perfect sacrifice. 'Behold the Lamb of God, who takes away the sin of the world' (John 1:29).

To think about

Think of the shepherds who got dirty looking after their flocks . . . and think of the religious people looking down on them. Think of the stable in the inn at Bethlehem . . . with the smell and the dirt of the animals . . . Think of the baby who was going to be born . . . shepherd and sacrifice.

SB

Selfless service

God found in Mary a woman who was full of faith; someone who made herself instantly and utterly available to him. In Mary, he also found a person who put his Son and kingdom before herself. As one writer has put it: 'She is the selfless space where God became man.'

Or, as Jean Vanier, the founder of the L'Arche communities wrote:

*None like her
enveloped his body,
touched his body,
loved his body,
washed his body . . .
It was her body that nourished his body:
her breasts gave him
the energy and nourishment to grow;
her touch protected him
and revealed to him that he was loved . . .
For Mary, God was the one around whom her life revolved:*

Mary said, 'My heart is overflowing with praise for my Lord, my soul is full of joy in God my Saviour. For he has deigned to notice me, his humble servant and, after this, all the people who ever shall be will call me the happiest of women! The one who can do all things has done great things for me—oh, holy is his Name!'

God longs that our lives, too, should revolve around him—that we should touch, love, clothe, feed and protect him by pouring out such love to the poor and needy, the powerless and the helpless. As Jesus himself pointed out, when we feed the hungry, provide shelter for the homeless or clothe the naked, we feed, shelter or clothe him.

A self-offering

Lord Jesus, I give you my hands to do your work. I give you my feet to go your way. I give you my eyes to see as you do. I give you my tongue to speak your words. I give you my mind that you may think in me. I give you my spirit that you may pray in me. Above all, I give you my heart that you may love in me your Father and all mankind. I give you my whole self that you may grow in me so that it is you, Lord Jesus, who live and work and pray in me.

The Grail Prayer

JH

370

Pregnant with Christ

The person God chose to be the mother of his Son was someone who was full of faith, instantly available and a woman whose life revolved round God rather than round herself.

How did she feel when she knew that she was pregnant with Christ? Humbled? Awed? Overwhelmed? If her song is an accurate gauge, she felt all these emotions and many more. And how did she feel as she experienced the mysterious joy of motherhood: the seed gradually growing into a foetus with a life of its own? We are not told. In fact all we are told of the incarnation is:

The Word became flesh and made his dwelling among us.

NIV

The Word of God became a human being.

J.B. Phillips

What we are also told is that, before he made his dwelling among us, the Christ-child took up residence in Mary's womb. Quite literally her body became the temple of the Holy One; the sacred space where God hid himself. So wherever Mary went, the Christ-child in her womb went too.

It is easy to fall into the trap of so envying Mary for the unique privilege God gave her that we forget that there is a sense in which every believer is 'preg-

nant with Christ'. Paul hints at this when he speaks of a 'glorious mystery': namely, 'Christ [is] in you...' (Colossians 1:28).

The challenge which comes to every Christian is to follow the example of Mary. She allowed the Christ-child to form in her and then gave him to a needy world. We, too, need to recognize that our chief responsibility is to allow the indwelling Christ to pray, talk, work, heal, protect, support through us so that everyone we meet will encounter not us only but him.

For meditation

'The Eternal Birth must take place in you.' (Meister Eckhart) 'The birth of Christ in our souls is for a purpose beyond ourselves... His manifestation in the world must be through us.'

A project

Look back over the past year. Ask the Holy Spirit to show you some of the occasions when you have taken the Saviour into our need world.

JH

The light of the world

When Jesus spoke again to the people, he said, 'I am the light of the world. Whoever follows me will never walk in darkness, but will have the light of life.'

You are the light of the world. A city on a hill cannot be hidden. Neither do people light a lamp and put it under a bowl. Instead they put it on its stand, and it gives light to everyone in the house. In the same way, let your light shine before men, that they may see your good deeds and praise your Father in heaven.

'I am the light of the world,' Jesus said confidently of himself. His light pierced the darkness of the world—a world that God created good (as we are told many times in Genesis chapter 1), a world spoilt by the disobedience of human-kind who was put in charge of that world (Genesis 1:26). The darkness is still rampant in the world; take one glance at a newspaper to see that. When we follow him we are not taken away from the surrounding darkness, but we do not need to be absorbed by it. Instead, we let his light penetrate our own darkness and change us.

Then Jesus gives us an astonishing commission. As I look at my own imperfections I could not dare to claim to be light in the world. Yet that is just what he says that I am to be. 'YOU are the light of the world. Look at that town perched up on the brow of the hill, its lights visible all round! Think of the small oil lamps in your house; what fool would cover them with a bowl? I want you to shine with *my* light,' he says. Let your character and behaviour and words draw attention to our Father. What a privilege—and what a responsibility.

A way to pray

Imagine yourself in front of a huge, bright candle. Let its light shine on your blemishes. Then hold up a taper; light it, and walk off to take light to others. Then pray: Lord, please show me as I go through the day how I am to shine with your light.

RG

The light foretold

The people walking in darkness have seen a great light; on those living in the land of the shadow of death a light has dawned ... For to us a child is born, to us a son is given, and the government will be on his shoulders. And he will be called Wonderful Counsellor, Mighty God, Everlasting Father, Prince of Peace. Of the increase of his government there will be no end. He will reign on David's throne and over his kingdom, establishing and upholding it with justice and righteousness from that time on and for ever. The zeal of the Lord Almighty will accomplish this.

Yesterday's notes introduced us to the theme that takes us to the end of the year. Today we look at one of the Old Testament prophecies, often read at Christmas, that looked forward to the Light who would come. It must have been quite confusing for Isaiah's hearers, for he writes about a future event as if it had already happened. They could not see the Light; they had to believe a promise.

There are similar dark times in our lives. I remember periods of depression when I felt as if I was in a long, dark tunnel and wondered whether I would ever emerge. I would come out into the light temporarily and think the darkness was over. Then came the despair of plunging again into the gloom. Where was God? He was near, although I did not always know it. One day I was lying on the floor, crying in a sense of utter loneliness; then I realized that God was there. I could not feel him, but it was as if the floorboards were *him* supporting me. The peace of the Prince of Peace entered my aching heart.

A meditation

Choose one of the phrases Wonderful Counsellor, Mighty God, Everlasting Father, Prince of Peace. Spend two minutes thinking about those words and what they mean to you in your present circumstances.

A prayer

Father, thank you for the child born to us. I pray that this Christmas time I may see his light more clearly and that his government may increase in my life, and in the world.

RG

The light fulfilled

I, the Lord, have called you in righteousness; I will take hold of your hand. I will keep you and will make you to be a covenant for the people and a light for the Gentiles, to open eyes that are blind, to free captives from prison and to release from the dungeon those that sit in darkness.

Many Old Testament prophecies look forward to Jesus as Saviour. In some he is portrayed as a conquering king coming to rescue his people; these were easier for the Jews to accept than those that show him as a suffering servant. It is as if they were looking from a distance at two ranges of mountains, unable to see the valley between the two ranges. We live in the valley between his first coming in humility and his second coming in triumph. Today's passage speaks of his first coming.

Think of the ways Jesus lived out these verses. 'I, the Lord, have called you in righteousness.' Who else could possibly say, 'I always do what pleases Him' (John 8:29)? That summarizes Jesus' perfect righteousness. 'I will take hold of your hand.' He was always conscious of heavenly leading and protection, even when he was led into the wilderness to be tempted by Satan (Luke 4:1). 'I will make you ... a light for the Gentiles.' The Jews believed the Messiah was exclusively theirs and ignored his commission to the Gentiles; but when an old man in the temple, Simeon, held the eight-day-old Jesus he praised God for one who would be 'a light for revelation to the Gentiles' (Luke 2:32). And when John the Baptist, languishing in prison, doubted Jesus' identity he sent messengers who asked, 'Are you the one who was to come?' The reply was clear: 'The blind receive sight...'—yes, I am fulfilling the promise that the Messiah would open blind eyes (Matthew 11:3–5).

We can be excited afresh this Christmas that God's purposes, written down in 600BC, were fulfilled in Jesus' life. Now he wants us, his servants, to fulfil his commission in the world.

A prayer

We pray that our lives may reflect Jesus' righteousness; that we follow his example of dependence on his Father, that we shine with his light to others.

RG

The witness

There was a man who was sent from God; his name was John. He came as a witness to testify concerning that light, so that through him all men might believe. He himself was not of the light; he came only as a witness to the light of the world. He was in the world, and though the world was made by him, the world did not recognise him. He came to that which was his own, but his own did not receive him.

Presents, lights, turkey, sprouts . . . 'Have we got everything before the shops close?' Busyness and bustle are often the centre of Christmas Eve. We focus today on two men. First, *a man called John*. Unlike the other Gospel writers, John tells us none of the details of John the Baptist's early life; instead he sums up those miraculous events in *a man who was sent from God*. The writer does not want to draw attention to John, because John did not draw attention to himself. He came to be a witness to Jesus, the Light of the World.

Have you ever thought of yourself as being like John the Baptist? No desert life, no fiery preaching, no crowds round you . . . but a witness to God's light, sharing John's passion that *all men might believe*. Have you ever told another person the story of how God became real to you? Do you stand up for godly principles when a group of people are talking in an ungodly way? Those are both ways to be witnesses to Jesus.

One second focus is JESUS. He is *the true light that gives light to every man.*

Picture a blinding light in the sky above a black world. A dazzling star is detached from that light and enters a stable in Bethlehem. The star has all the characteristics of the incandescent light; but it is wrapped in swaddling cloths, and its splendour is hidden. Pause to meditate on the glory of that veiled light.

A prayer

Thank you for showing me your light. I confess that I am scared of speaking out, but I ask you for courage. May my lifestyle and my words help others to see your light.

RG

Life and light

In the beginning was the Word, and the Word was with God, and the Word was God. he was with God in the beginning. Through him all things were made; without him nothing was made that has been made. In him was life, and that life was the light of men. The light shines in the darkness, but the darkness has not understood it [OR the darkness has not overcome it].

'In the beginning God created the heavens and the earth' (Genesis 1:1). That is how the Bible starts. Before time, God was. He is the Creator, without him, there was nothing. 'In the beginning was the Word.' Jesus Christ, Son of God, did not merely have a share in creation. 'Without him nothing was made that has been made.' He is nothing less than the character and power of the eternal godhead. We must not allow the familiarity of the majestic words of this passage to mask their meaning. We use words as the embodiment of God himself. He is God's disclosure of himself to us. Our finite minds can never wholly grasp the infinity of God; nevertheless we contemplate the Infinite who entered the finite world.

God created life. God created light. So it is not surprising that John says that in Christ was both life and light. He was LIFE. Paul writes that 'we were dead in our trespasses and sins' (Ephesians 2:1). Jesus lived and died on earth to give us eternal life. He was LIGHT to shine in our darkness. The alternative translations of the last phrase brings notes both of

sadness and of hope. 'The darkness has not understood it.' Yesterday's reading showed him unrecognized and rejected; that is sad. But 'the darkness has not overcome it.' We see darkness all round us in today's world, many places where there seems to be only sadness and suffering. But it is unthinkable that the light of the eternal God could be quenched by the world's sin.

A Christmas thanksgiving

THE DARKNESS HAS NOT OVERCOME THE LIGHT! Rejoice in that assurance while you meditate on the humble circumstances of Jesus' birth and while you pray with compassion for people in deep need.

RG

A stark choice

This is the verdict: Light has come into the world, but men loved darkness instead of light because their deeds were evil. Everyone who does evil hates the light, and will not come into the light for fear that his deeds will be exposed. But whoever lives by the truth comes into the light, so that it may be seen plainly that what he has done has been done through God.

There is a powerful dramatic sketch entitled *The Light of the World.* Jesus moves forward into the centre of the stage—and people shrink back from him. 'Light has come into the world' but, says the script, 'the world's in a mess. So what's gone wrong?' Humorously, powerfully, the blame is put first on 'everyone else', next on the actors. The suddenly those in the audience are faced with their own responsibility in universal sin. Blows are heard. Jesus is seen to be crucified. Then the choice about him is clearly demonstrated. Some of the actors kneel in worship and adoration before the crucified Saviour; others turn defiantly away. Each person present is faced with the unspoken question: How do *you* choose?

I used to assume that because I was baptized, confirmed, a pretty regular churchgoer that I belonged to the light. In my eyes Jesus was a true, historical figure, and I was a reasonably good person. It was a shock to see that I had to make a definite choice; my passive faith was not vital enough to take me out of darkness into light. My 'churchianity' was good, but not enough. Holman Hunt's famous picture *The Light of the World* shows Jesus, holding a lantern, knocking at the door of a house covered in weeds. The door handle is on the inside; the occupant of the house must open the door to let Jesus come in with his light. I chose to let him into my life to take ownership of 'my' house.

A prayer

Lord Jesus, I do not want to be a person who loves the darkness of sin. I open the door of my life wide to you. Please come with your light to expose my darkness and to change me. Take control of all that I have and all that I am.

RG

Seeing the glory

The Word became flesh and made his dwelling among us. We have seen his glory, the glory of the one and Only, who came from the Father, full of grace and truth. John testifies concerning him. He cries out, saying, 'This was he of whom I said, "He who comes after me has surpassed me because he was before me." ' From the fullness of his grace we have all received one blessing after another. For the law was given through Moses: grace and truth came through Jesus Christ. No one has ever seen God, but God the One and Only Son, who is at the Father's side, has made him known.

'The Word'; 'the glory'; 'the One and Only'; 'the fullness of his grace'; 'no one has ever seen God'. First ponder each of these phrases that speak of the fullness of the deity, a God who is too big for us to grasp. Ask him to open your heart to worship the infinite, incomprehensible One. Pause in silent contemplation and worship before you read further.

But how amazing! That Word became flesh. He came and lived among us. He showed us his glory. He made known the invisible God. He pours his blessing on us. He actually wants us to know him and to keep receiving from him. Pause again to pray, to thank him, and to ask that you come to know him better.

One more thought for today. People sometimes think that there is opposition between the ways the Old and New Testament portray God. But Jesus told us, 'I have not come to abolish them [the Law or the Prophets] but to fulfil them' (Matthew 5:17). 'The law came through Moses.' The law is like a skeleton that gives the whole framework of a person. 'Grace and truth came through Jesus Christ.' He came to put flesh on the skeleton and to breathe life into the body, so that—wonder of wonders—we might truly know God and live more fully ourselves.

A question

What fresh understanding do you have this year about the meaning of Christmas?

RG

Living in light

This is the message we have heard from him and declare to you: God is light; in him there is no darkness at all. If we claim to have fellowship with him yet walk in the darkness, we lie and do not live by the truth. But if we walk in the light, as he is in the light, we have fellowship with one another, and the blood of Jesus, his Son, purifies us from all sin. If we claim to be without sin, we deceive ourselves and the truth is not in us. If we confess our sins, he is faithful and just and will forgive us our sins and purify us from all unrighteousness.

Last Christmas Day we visited a church which had printed on the front cover of the Communion service booklets 'Please do not remove from the church', followed by, 'If removed, please return.' I thought 'Isn't that like God!' he wants the ideal for us, but he recognizes our fallibility and tells us what to do about it.

God, in whom 'there is no darkness', wants us to have a relationship ('fellowship') with Him. Obviously that can only happen if we 'walk in the light'. But, to be honest, we know we are not perfect; our thoughts and speech and deeds do not meet our own standards for ourselves, let alone God's desire for us. 'Don't pretend!' says John. Admit you are wrong; then you can come to be forgiven. Even Christians make two big mistakes about sin. The first is to say 'That little sin; it doesn't really matter.' The second is to say, 'I'm guilty; I'm too bad for God to want me.' Read the verse again to see how both those attitudes are wrong.

I do a lot of pastoral counselling, and I often meet Christians who know the theory that God forgives them but who find it hard to grasp at gut-level. Reasons for these feelings can be deep-rooted but, if that describes you, start with this prayer.

A prayer

If I confess my sins, you are faithful and just and will forgive my sins and will purify me from all unrighteousness. Father God, please help me to know this truth deep in my heart.

RG

Light and love

Anyone who claims to be in the light but hates his brother is still in darkness. Whoever loves his brother lives in the light, and there is nothing in him to make him stumble. But whoever hates his brother is in the darkness and walks around in darkness; he does not know where he is going, because the darkness has blinded him.

My thoughts go back to 1973. My spiritual life had grown very barren, and I knew almost nothing about loving other people. So I read Paul's famous words about love in 1 Corinthians 13:4–8, and I prayed with one hand open, 'Lord, please give me that love.' But the other hand was firmly clenched, as my heart said, 'No thank you, it would cost too much. I would have to give of myself to others.' I stuck there for a year before a stressful situation melted my defences. As I received God's love through other people, it was planted in me, and I discovered that loving other people was not too hard after all. Instead of trying to live on a defunct battery I was connected to the mains of his love.

John's test for those who claim to be in fellowship with the God who is light is stringent; if you hate your 'brother' you are still in darkness. It is an uncomfortable truth, but perfectly logical, for we read in 1 John 4:8 that 'God is love'. We cannot choose to face his light without being willing to have any unlove in our hearts transformed by his love. Light and love are partners; so are darkness and hate.

But how should we interpret that word 'brother'? We can start with members of our natural families; then think of those who belong to the Christian family; finally think more widely of fellow humans, those we meet in our daily lives and those we watch on TV—politicians and terrorists alike!

A way to pray

Think about some of the people you do not love. Then choose whether you want to ask God to help you to love each one of those people. Our natural request is, 'Please change them.' The prayer must be, 'Lord, please change me.'

RG

A joyful responsibility

Even if our gospel is veiled, it is veiled to those who are perishing. The god of this age has blinded the minds of unbelievers, so that they cannot see the light of the gospel of glory of Christ, who is the image of God. For we do not preach ourselves, but Christ Jesus as Lord, and ourselves as your servants for Jesus' sake. For God, who said, 'Let light shine out of darkness,' made his light shine in our hearts to give us the light of the knowledge of the glory of God in the face of Christ.

Usually these notes focus on God or on his followers. But today we stop first to see what Paul says about those who are not Christians. He writes that they are unbelievers, that they are blinded, that they are perishing. These thoughts do not sit easily with us; certainly they are unfashionable in an age when we like to believe that all roads lead to God, and to discard any teaching about eternal damnation. We, too, can be blinded by 'the god of this age', Satan, who uses any means he can to distort the truth.

Belief in the 'lostness' of people without Christ does not lead us into hardness towards them. No, the love of which we thought yesterday brings compassion for their blindness. And the joy that we have in knowing the light of Christ in our own lives moves us to long that they should share that knowledge. Read the second half of the passage again to catch some of Paul's excitement and confidence in Christ. The passion of his life was to share 'the light of the gospel of the glory of Christ'. In my early days of vital Christian faith, I used to share his zeal to bring others to know that light. Then my youthful enthusiasm was tempered, and I found other—fruitful—ways, of serving Jesus. Now, in maturity, that longing is re-kindled; my prayer is that the light of Christ may shine so brightly in my own heart that it shines out to others, to give them 'the light of the knowledge of the glory of God in the face of Christ'.

A prayer

Will you pray with me?

RG

Corporate Light

But you are a chosen people, a royal priesthood, a holy nation, a people belonging to God, that you may declare the praise of him who called you out of darkness into his wonderful light.

During the last ten days we have concentrated on our individual response to Jesus, the light of the world, who calls us to live in the light with him and to shine as his lights in a dark world. Now we see that we are not separate dots of light but part of a whole. We, his Church, a people he has chosen to belong to him, have a mission 'to declare the praise of his wonderful light'. As we take that phrase apart, we notice: 1) we are in darkness 2) he has called us out of darkness 3) he has brought us into his wonderful light 4) we should praise him 5) not secretly, but as a declaration to others. It reminds me of the day of Pentecost, when the Spirit was poured out on the first Christians, and everyone in the huge cosmopolitan crowd heard the disciples praising God in their own languages.

Many churches in the world have earmarked the last ten years of this century as a Decade of Evangelism. As we pass into a new year we can make this a time of stocktaking, not only for our personal spiritual lives, but also for the life of the local church to which we belong. You could read Acts 2:42–47, which describes the vitality of the early Church and gives us a yardstick for our assessment. As you consider your own church write down one or two desires you have for it in the coming year. Then turn those desires into specific intercession.

None of us know what the coming year will bring, whatever particular expectations or fears we may have. So we finish our readings on the light of the world with these well-known words about trust, from Minnie Louise Haskins:

And I said to the man who stood at the gate of the year: 'Give me a light that I may tread safely into the unknown.' And he replied: 'Go out into the darkness and put your hand into the Hand of God. That shall be to you better than light and safer than a known way.'

RG

Notes from BRF

If you have enjoyed reading and using *Day by Day* you may wish to know that similar material is available from BRF in a regular series of Bible reading notes, *New Daylight*, which is published three times a year (in January, May and September) and contains printed Bible passages, brief comments, and prayers.

For further information, contact your local Christian bookshop or, in case of difficulty, The Bible Reading Fellowship, Peter's Way, Sandy Lane West, Oxford, OX4 5HG.

Anthologies from BRF

Two thoughtful and wide-ranging resource books of quotations, Biblical and other, which contain insights into 2000 years of Christian and religious experience, covering a broad range of subjects. For personal use, for sermons and talks, and for reflection groups, with advice about how to use the material with groups. An ideal gift for adult confirmation, ordination, birthdays or Christmas.

Visions of Hope
0 7459 2591 X

Visions of Love
0 7459 2522 7

Price: £9.99 each